The Big Walk

By

David Balph and Thom W. King

Castle Ring Books
New York – Chicago - Nashville

Vintage, historical, personal and promotional photographs, press clippings and media articles provided by David Balph from his archives.

Contemporary photographs provided by Thom W. King, commissioned for this copyrighted book.

Disclaimer about content: This book reflects the experiences of Roger and David Balph during their walk across America in the 1960s. While every effort has been made to verify facts, dates, locations, spellings, and the people mentioned, these are personal recollections, and may differ from other accounts of the same events. While based on fact, this is a recreation of passages made in road journals and diaries. Some names have been changed, and some events have been edited. A certain amount of artistic license has been utilized in writing this book. No misrepresentation was intentionally made.

Published by Castle Ring Books, a division of King Author Productions, P.O. Box 50214, Nashville, Tennessee 37205. Email: kingauthor@aol.com

Designed by Thom W. King

Press prep by Keith A. Gordon, Excitable Press, 35 Montclair Avenue, Batavia, New York 14020

For additional copies, bulk purchases, and related services contact: David Balph, Bal-Productions, 678 Harding Place, Nashville, Tennessee 37211. Email: Trumpet.Music@comcast.net

Website: www.DavidBalph.com

Printed in the United States of America.

ISBN 0-9720455-6-2

Table of Contents

Dedication

This book is dedicated to the Lord. Without the help of our Lord above, I am convinced we would never have made it across this country. So many difficult times, along with the good times, He was there to help us and to cheer us on. It was a risk walking all those miles in sometimes heavy traffic, dodging problem after problem. Being able to accept His grace in saving us so many times was reassuring, especially when it looked many times like it could or would be hopeless to continue. I thank Him for his blessed assurance and always being there for us. Praise the Lord!   - David Balph

Acknowledgements

To my brother Roger, his wife Mary, our loving mother Mary Jane Richards, and my wonderful wife, Trudy.

Brother Roger and I worked and performed together for many years before and during our long three-year trek across the United States. Roger is six years older than me, and unfortunately he became ill with Alzheimer's disease before this book could be written. My hope is he will still be able to comprehend some of its contents before it is too late. The Big Walk across America could not have been accomplished without his help, dedication, determination, and his attitude to "Find a Way" no matter what. The team of The Balph Brothers is what this book is all about, and it was a fifty-fifty effort to make it happen.

Mary Hinson was her maiden name. She was one very exceptional lady. Her constant, demanding, difficult work representing The Balph Brothers on The Big Walk was truly a study in persistence and dedication. Her tireless hours of stress-related situations and never giving up, were above and beyond the call of duty.

Our mother, Mary Jane Richards, came up with the original idea of The Big Walk. She gave her total support and help before and during our trek across America. Her ideas, dedication, persistence, contributions; and faith and prayers continued to build our confidence and determination. It was discovered 45 years after The Big Walk had concluded, and after she had passed away, that she had written us a wonderful prayer entitled "The Big Walk" exactly ten days after we walked out of Los Angeles. A dated copy of her prayer follows this acknowledgement.

And to my Trudy, who came on the scene during our side trip to Columbus, Ohio, for her constant letters of love and support during the good and difficult times of the remainder of The Big Walk. And for her devotion, dedication and everlasting love she has shown me during our long life together. –David Balph

Prayer written by David and Roger's mother, Mary Jane Richards, ten days after their departure on The Big Walk and discovered 45 years later

Over mountains and valleys – through
      desert terrain
Under hot sunshine and in the
      cool rain.
Keep their hearts ever beating with
      their greatest desire.
To become "name musicians", to set
      the world on fire!

Give them grace to be humble,
      patient and kind
To whomever they meet, & whomever
      they find.
Then when, at long last, they finally
      reach fame
May they ever be grateful for
      getting a NAME.
           CMB – 7/28/63

Introduction

The Big Walk is the story of David and Roger Balph's American journey across the country, starting in 1963.

Thousands of miles and years later, the journey ended with lives changed, viewpoints altered, and health issues compounded, with both brothers developing profoundly different outlooks about life in America.

They encountered everything nature could throw at them: heat, rain, snow, droughts, rabid animals, and poisonous snakes.

They met people from all backgrounds, religions, occupations, and mental attitudes.

From celebrities to politicians, from shysters to Good Samaritans, the brothers experienced the best and worst of humanity, up close and personally.

From the sweet lady by the side of the road who brought them ice cream delights to the drunken joy riders who thought it was funny to try to run over the guys and their cart; David and Roger experienced several lifetimes' worth of encounters on their Big Walk.

Through feast and famine, through good times and bad, the brothers faced unbelievable obstacles and survived to walk yet another day and blow their own horns.

They saw an America that is long gone, and never to be revisited. Walking towards the sun, before the nation became a network of interstates, before every town looked just like the next, before fast food franchises covered the highways and reduced each region's restaurants to a uniform set of yellow arches and oversized plastic big boys, The Balph Brothers took one step at a time and discovered a world of wonder.

Right in the middle of the Sixties, from the death of an American president to the British Invasion of The Beatles to the Civil Rights Movement to the War in Vietnam, the brothers lived through one of the nation's most turbulent times, taking each day step by step.

They experienced joy, sadness, fear, love, hunger, thirst, happiness, and total bliss along the way, with each step bringing them closer to their goal.

The lessons they learned changed their lives and those of the people around them. This is their story.

Chapter 1: The Beginning

David and Roger Balph, with their Mother,
July 18, 1963, the Day the Trek Began

"If you walk across the country, he'll have to put you on his show."

That simple statement would change lives in 1963.

It only took David Balph's mother a few seconds to say those words, but nothing would ever be the same after hearing them.

Thousands of miles and years later, everything in their lives would be changed by this American journey.

David was living in Los Angeles, playing the occasional musical gig with his older brother, Roger.

Both David and Roger had already served honorable stints in the nation's military. David had developed a reputation as one of the area's up-and-coming horn players, specializing in Dixieland Jazz. Roger, older by seven years, was the clarinet and sax virtuoso, and a natural showman. With his arsenal of instruments, ranging from a tiny chirping soprano sax down to the foghorn honk of his golden baritone, Roger was the master of the woodwind keys.

During his time in the military, Roger had experienced some national exposure and a modicum of fleeting fame when he was chosen to appear on The Ed Sullivan Show as one of the military's best musicians. This was back in a time when military bands were given spotlights on television as a matter of national pride. His spirited performance on the E flat clarinet, combined with his G.I.-issued crew cut, was so emotionally crowd-pleasing that Sullivan had him come over to the host microphone after his number, where he proceeded to literally run his fingers through Roger's hair in a rare moment of unbridled enthusiasm. Sullivan was truly giddy with excitement. This was a reaction that often followed Roger's performances.

The brothers played the occasional gigs with other bands in the area, but their main passion was performing classic ragtime tunes as a duo. Sharing the same bloodline, they intuitively knew when to soar and drive the melodies into a spirited frenzy. Sometimes all it took was a wink from Roger, and David would roar off into flights of fancy, propelled by the steady pushing of his brother's riffs. They had a comfort level that only comes from being siblings, and it made their music all the better for it.

Earlier, Roger had been very close to having a record deal with a regional record label based in Los Angeles. He had been wined and dined, and even signed a contract to produce an instrumental album of Dixieland classics. Studio musicians had been hired, arrangements had been made, and songs were actually recorded in the studio. They even made a sample cover of the album art, featuring a glorious vintage Mississippi riverboat at full steam. But somewhere between the sessions and the time when the album was released, Roger discovered that his passionate clarinet solos had been chopped out of the tapes with his name erased from the liner notes. There had been quiet whispers among the family about some fiasco on the casting couch of some unnamed producers. Too much wine, misguided signals, overblown expectations, and perhaps a twist on a Hollywood cliché. How could anybody not see that Roger was a ladies' man, through and through? Those testosterone-driven producers would have had to have been blind or simply in lust, to think otherwise.

Regardless, Roger's record deal had fallen through, and all he had to show for it was his demo copy of the professionally recorded instrumental tracks. It wasn't the same as having his own album out on the shelves of the nation's record shops, but at least it had the potential of being worth something.

David's mother repeated her statement, "I'm telling you, if you walk across the country, he will have to put you on his television show."

David wanted to laugh her suggestion off, but he knew it made sense. Or at least as much sense as anything else they had been trying to do.

So far every attempt had been met with total rejection. No. No thanks. Nope. Never. Stop calling us. Was it too much to ask?

The show was on the air every week. They had to have guests. They certainly gave enough time to other musicians. If Roger had been good enough for Ed Sullivan, in prime time on a Sunday night, surely the powers that be could see a way to find space for The Balph Brothers on Jack Paar's show. Why was this such a big deal?

For weeks they had been sending letters to Jack Paar, requesting an audition to be on his show. They knew if he would only listen to their music for a few minutes, he would see how great they were, how crowd-pleasing their songs could be, how their energy and passion would simply enchant his studio audience and the millions of viewers back home. If any duo was tailor-made for The Jack Paar Show, it was The Balph Brothers of Los Angeles.

So why were all of their efforts being met with a stone wall of silence and indifference?

Didn't they know what they were missing? Didn't they realize what a wonderful opportunity this was for Jack to showcase a clean-cut family act of hard-working, God-loving, American veterans, with a passion for that most American of all music forms, Dixieland Jazz?

A walk across America? The more times the idea bounced around in his head, the better David liked it.

He started getting that tingling in his leg, the one a person gets when he feels the electricity of an idea creeping up his spine.

This might be exactly what they needed to take their career to the next level, or for that matter, to any level.

Could it be done? Where would they start? How could they afford it?

How long would it take to walk from Los Angeles to New York?

To leave their home by the Pacific and march straight across to Jack Paar's studios in Manhattan, right through the heartland of America and into the hearts of the nation?

David could feel his own heart racing. His ears felt warm. The more he thought about the logic of the insanity, the more he liked the idea.

David had no doubts that he could handle the walk. He was 23, very athletic, and had never been sick a day in his life. He could literally have been the poster boy for your idealized vision of a California Surfer. He could have played volleyball with The Beach Boys or hung out with Jan and Dean in Surf City. Why, he was certain that he could walk 3,000 miles without breaking a sweat. With his eyes closed. With his hands behind his back. On one leg, if needed. No problee-mo.

With each passing minute, David's confidence grew and grew, bulging with the cocky confidence of youth and the innocence of the times. Ideas were spurting out of his head, aroused by the possibilities of such an epic journey.

It would be a piece of cake. A sweet, gooey, icing-filled big-time party cake.

Spend six months walking across the country, stopping and playing concerts for the legions of fans along the way, who would be following every step of the trip in the newspapers and lining the streets for autographs and a chance to touch the most famous walking musicians America has ever seen. Then, triumphantly walking across the Brooklyn Bridge with a police escort to the spotlights and red carpet, with Jack Paar himself waiting at the studio door to welcome them in.

David could see the crowds. He could hear the screams. He could even feel the glow of the spotlights. This was becoming so real in his mind, he could almost taste the Italian cannoli in the green room of Paar's studio.

Why hadn't they thought of this earlier? This makes so much sense on so many levels it would be a crime to let this opportunity pass them by. All David had to do was convince Roger to join him, and everything would fall into place. How hard could any of this be?

Six months of fresh air and sunshine, and then time on the couch sharing The Big Walk stories with Jack Paar.

It would be the stuff of legends. The Balph Brothers walk across America.

Chapter 2: Talkin' about Walkin'

Roger (on right) with Rock Band in Los Angeles

Roger didn't really enjoy being onstage with the rock band. He was doing the gig for the hundred bucks a week it paid. Though he had to admit that after all of his years performing Dixieland Jazz, it was kind of nice to take a break and just blow some new tunes that teens could dance to. Plus, he didn't have to sweat the details with this gang. It wasn't his band, his name wasn't on the marquee. All he had to do was show up at the bowling alley with his sax and do his thing. No headaches, nobody looking for him to save the day.

Roger was 29 years old and had been doing his thing with woodwind instruments since he was two years old when his dad taught him the keys. It had literally been his life ever since. All through high school, he had been in the orchestra, winning honors, touring the nation as an E flat clarinet soloist. He had been a staff musician for radio and television shows. He had even developed a one-man touring act that took him to college campuses in Ohio, Michigan, Indiana, and Pennsylvania.

He had followed that with stints in U.S. Army bands, forming a 13-piece band to entertain troops in Virginia, and then appearing multiple times on the Arlene Francis Army Recruiting Show on television.

And of course, he stole the show when he performed for Ed Sullivan.

But even though he was happy with his sextet of Dixieland Jazz musicians, he had to take sideline gigs, like the one with the rock band, just to pay the bills.

To be honest, he was somewhat dissatisfied with the way his career was going in California. He was playing steady gigs, making a name for himself, but he wasn't anywhere near as successful as he knew he could be.

He needed a break, and he knew it.

That is what it takes to make it in show business.

Sure, you have to have talent, but everybody has talent. The music business isn't lacking for people with talent. Never has been.

It takes something extra to claw your way to the top of the heap, and so far, Roger hadn't found that one thing that could change his life literally overnight.

He had a note waiting for him at the bowling alley when he arrived to play with the rockers.

His brother had called. Something important had come up that he needed to talk about.

Roger didn't have any idea what could be so important that would make Dave call him at work, but whatever it was, Dave was pretty insistent that they needed to talk tonight, not tomorrow, not next week.

Roger played his gig and enjoyed the energy of the crowd. He also enjoyed being able to pack his sax in his case and walk out the door, leaving the hassles to somebody else. They knew how to find him when they needed his services onstage. Have their people call his people. Roger was always ready, willing, and able to rock the house.

Dave was beside himself when Roger finally arrived.

He had been tossing the walking idea around in his head, over and over, and the more he thought about it, the more excitement it caused.

15

It was so real in his mind, he could almost feel the summer sun on his face, feel the asphalt highway under his feet, feel the satisfaction that comes with each step.

"Roger, Mom came up with an idea that is going to blow your mind. Are you ready?"

Roger had just spent the last 3 hours wailing onstage. He didn't need any teasing or riddles from his younger brother.

"Just say it. What is so important that you had to call me at work and demand that I come over here right now, tonight?"

"Ok. Try this on for size: we walk across America, right to Jack Paar's studio!"

David was absolutely beaming from ear to ear. He couldn't wipe the smile off of his face.

Roger just looked at his 23-year-old brother and waited for the punch line.

There wasn't one. David was dead serious. This apparently wasn't a joke.

Roger could tell that David was almost giddy with just the idea itself. He had obviously had a few hours to think about possibilities, so he was already racing ahead with specifics and details.

David started talking about how they could play at clubs and theaters along the way, making great money to pay for the trip.

He was going on and on about the press coverage they'd get from newspapers, radio stations, and television. It would be an event, a historical journey, a once-in-a-lifetime chance to get noticed and jumpstart their career.

Six months tops. Maybe seven. It was so simple.

See the country, generate fans, get rave reviews, make some decent money, and then build national publicity for The Walking Balph Brothers. And finally arrive in New York to the open arms of Jack Paar and his millions of loyal viewers.

Roger listened.

Sure it was crazy. Maybe just crazy enough to work.

16

Lord knows what they had been doing on their own wasn't setting the world on fire.

David was already mentally packing his bags and working out the details in his head. He would sell his car as soon as possible and take the money to build a cart to carry their instruments and sleeping bags.

They would sleep out under the stars, and see the country up close and down home.

Roger could tell this was going to be a long, long night.

Once David got something in his mind, he wouldn't stop until he made it happen.

David's 1957 Oldsmobile would soon be history.

The brothers didn't get any sleep that night.

By the time the sun came up, David had mapped out a design for the pushcart.

By the time the sun went down, Roger was making a list of corporate sponsors to approach for support and endorsements.

Their talkin' about walkin' was just beginning.

Chapter 3: Positive Thinking

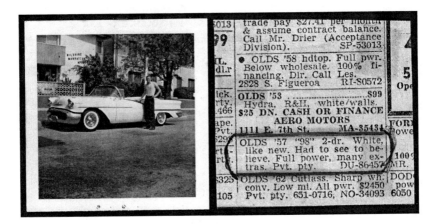

Dave Selling his Car to Fund The Big Walk

It had been a busy six weeks since that fateful night when the big idea first came up.

Two days after the all-nighter to consider the options, Dave and his mother had gone to the First Methodist Church of Los Angeles to listen to a lecture by Dr. Norman Vincent Peale on the power of positive thinking. It was almost like an omen. Just as the brothers were about to embark on the biggest journey of their lives, they had a chance to listen to one of the world's leading advocates of having a positive mental attitude. Surely this was a sign from above.

Dave was so positive of this that he bought a copy of Peale's book, along with Jack Paar's new book called *I Kid You Not*.

Armed with this vital set of information, Dave devoured the pages, soaking up the positive energy each book offered. Dave was doing his homework, developing questions, seeking answers.

His thirst for guidance even led him to contact the minister at the church where Dr. Peale had appeared. The day of the lecture, the minister's introduction of Dr. Peale had been heart-warming, emotional, and full of energy. Since Dr. Peale had already left town and moved on to the next stop on his book promotional tour, Dave figured the next best person to talk to about The Big Walk was the local minister, who had been such a strong advocate of positive thinking just days earlier.

Dave met with the minister, who listened to the details of the proposed journey. Dave was in his best form, explaining the benefits of the trip, the need for promotion, the current state of their musical careers. He was as full of passion and energy and yes, positive thinking, as he could possibly be. Surely the minister could recognize a kindred spirit and relate to the obvious wisdom of the journey.

Unfortunately, the dynamic, energized minister, who had captivated the audience with his spirited introduction of Dr. Peale only days earlier, had been replaced by a somber, dour, distracted lump of a man, totally lacking in anything related to positive thinking.

Dave felt betrayed.

The minister was not telling him what he needed to hear.

Where was his passion? Where was his rebel-rousing enthusiasm? What happened to his vision, his energy, his boundless spirit?

This man of the cloth was asking silly questions about money, weather, job security.

Dave was expecting a blessing, a most positive blessing, and this pretender to the cause was throwing a wet blanket on Dave's dreams.

Dave left his meeting with a deep mistrust of men who preach one thing from the pulpit, and then crush the hopes of their trusting followers when they get behind closed doors.

It had taken a few days for Dave to rebound from his meeting with the minister, a man of little faith when it came to the trip.

But he did recover, and with a vengeance.

Dave decided he had enough positive thinking to overcome any negative thoughts that might come his way, and it was as simple as that.

Several certified letters had been mailed to Jack Paar, requesting to be on his show.

The same day Dave started building the cart, the first letter to Paar was returned. The second one came back a few days later.

More negative energy.

But Dave was determined and focused. Each rejection just made him more determined and certain about the wisdom of the journey. He would show everybody. The six months spent walking to New York would be the best time he had ever spent. He knew this in the very soul of his heart.

Every rejection was just another step closer to a big enthusiastic yes.

By the time the last rejection letter from Paar's office arrived on May 29th, Dave was beyond stopping. It didn't even bother him that this one appeared to have been handwritten by Jack himself.

Dave had heard it all before, and he knew for a fact that, despite claims to the contrary, Paar did book live musical acts. If he wanted them to be on his show, no policies or network restrictions would prevent The Balph Brothers from having their moment of glory.

Each day found Dave more determined to make the journey, one step at a time, straight across the country, right into Jack Paar's NBC television studio at Rockefeller Plaza.

Besides, he had already sold his car, his pride and joy, his mint-condition, clean as a whistle 1957 "98" Oldsmobile convertible. He almost gave it away, selling it for $1,000 to the guy at the newspaper who had taken the order for his ad. You have never seen a guy smile as much as that buyer did when Dave gave him the keys to the Olds.

Dave was committed. There was no turning back.

Dave was positive that using his $1,000 for the trip was the best possible use of his hard-earned money.

Dr. Norman Vincent Peale would be positively proud.

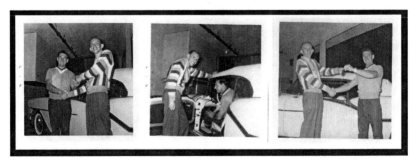

Happy Buyer Taking Delivery of Dave's Prized Convertible

Chapter 4: Preparations and Anticipation

*Trek Supplies, Left to Right: Camping Equipment, Sign Design,
Dehydrated Food, Ampex Tape Recorder*

This was really going to happen. If there had been any doubts before, they were long gone by now.

Dave, Roger, and their mother were all working on the to-do list every day.

It wasn't like they could simply follow an instruction manual and just start walking down the road.

There were so many aspects to consider, it was hard to know where to start.

Simple things, like which way to go, took days of studying and consideration.

Did they go along the southern part of Arizona, New Mexico, and Texas, walk through the South, over to the East Coast, and then stroll through Washington, D.C., into the welcoming arms of The Big Apple?

Maybe it made more sense to head north and cut over through the mountains, visit Denver, St. Louis, maybe even Chicago, and then cross over Ohio and visit their hometown of Mansfield.

All Dave had to go by was an educational map of the country posted on his bedroom wall, the kind you find in elementary classrooms to teach kids the difference between Florida and Michigan. Roger was working on getting better directional maps with detailed routes from the American Automobile Association, but right now, it was all just pretty colors on cardboard.

Sure, Dave could look at Los Angeles on the map and draw a line across the nation to New York City. It would take him all of a minute to accomplish that task.

When he stopped to think about what those pretty blocks meant, he was filled with a sense of anticipation. He had to stop his mind from flying off in a million directions every time he thought about the adventure ahead. The miles, the adventure, the places they'd see, the people they'd meet. Dave was positive that the next six, maybe seven, months were going to be life-changing.

They would show Jack Paar the stuff they were made of. Forget about Jack Paar. They would show the world.

But first things first. Dave had to build the cart or they weren't going anywhere.

This wasn't going to be a simple case of two guys walking down the road with backpacks and big smiles. Dave could only wish it was going to be that easy. They were going to pay their way across the country by performing as musicians at nightclubs and concert halls along the way, and that meant they had to bring their instruments, microphones, amplifiers, and their secret weapon with them every step of the journey.

Too bad they didn't just play blues harps that could fit in their back pockets.

Noooooooooo, that would be too easy.

The Walking Musical Balph Brothers were true musicians, with an arsenal of big, shiny, heavy instruments, each of which required a padded, bulky case to protect it from the elements.

Roger needed to have his collection of woodwind tools ready and waiting for him at each performance. Each instrument had a specific function and was vital for producing the big band sound of The Balph Brothers. That meant carrying his alto, tenor, and baritone saxophones every step of the thousands of miles. And don't forget his beloved E flat clarinet, the one that had won Ed Sullivan's enthusiastic applause on TV. And, of course, how could he be expected to perform without the companion B flat version? Those five instruments were essential and simply had to be present for every concert. Period.

Then Dave had to have something to perform with onstage. Though he only needed his trusty golden trumpet and slide trombone, they weren't things you could fold into a neat little package and carry in the knapsack.

And that was just the instruments and cases. Don't forget the usual support items like clothes, food, a tent to sleep in, sleeping bags for that tent, blankets, rain gear, even little things like a camping stove, canteens, and, of course, weapons for protection.

But those things were nothing compared to Roger's other secret weapon, the technological miracle that was going to make The Balph Brothers the talk of the nation.

While Dave had been busy working out a way to carry the orchestra across the country, one step at a time, Roger had been working his magic, wining and dining, talking and promoting, schmoozing and glad-handing his way to securing use of one of the most advanced recording systems in the world. This state-of-the-art tape machine would allow The Balph Brothers to give every audience along the journey the best concert experience of a lifetime.

While David was working on cases and the cart, Roger was devising a way to have a full big band orchestra accompany them with a mind-blowing world of sounds.

Roger still had his professionally recorded music tracks from his failed record label deal. Those tapes had top-notch performances by some of the best musicians in Los Angeles, or for that matter, the entire country.

Those tapes were going to provide the sonic wall of sound the brothers needed to put them at the top of the music business.

Roger had made the trip to the offices of The Ampex Corporation in Redwood City, near San Francisco. Ampex made the studio gear used by every record label and recording studio in the nation. Their machines were used to record everybody from Sinatra to Elvis to Johnny Cash.

Roger used his amazing powers of persuasion and salesmanship to secure the use of one of their top end portable tape recorders with powered stereo speakers. In fact, the engineers at Ampex were so impressed with the upcoming trip, they provided an even more expensive and rugged version of their recorder than the one Roger had originally asked for.

Roger had promised to display their logo at every concert and mention their name from stage as often as possible.

It would be great advertising for Ampex, and a secret weapon for The Balph Brothers.

It was also extremely heavy. The speakers alone weighed 40 pounds each, while the tape machine was another 80 pounds of dead weight. You have to remember that the invention of MP3 players, holding thousands of songs that you could stick in your pocket, was still decades away.

So Dave had his work cut out for him.

Then, Roger secured a 60-day supply of dehydrated food from the Bernard Food Company, in return for another mention on the journey and a sign with their logo on the stage.

At least they would have something to eat for the first two months, if everything else fell through.

If Roger kept this up, his gift for persuasion was going to produce a few tons of goodies to walk across America…one step at a time.

Chapter 5: Positively Heavy

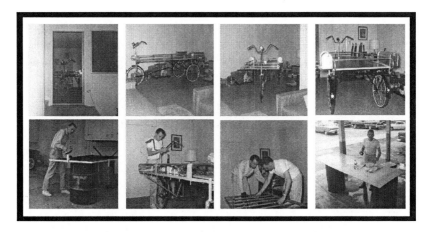

Building the Cart for The Big Walk Inside their Mother's Apartment

"Find a way!" That phrase summed up everything about The Balph Brothers, and always had. Whenever things in their lives took unexpected turns or situations threw new challenges in their path, they would simply find a way to overcome the obstacles.

Dave didn't realize it at the time, but he had been following the same principles detailed in Dr. Norman Vincent Peale's book *The Power of Positive Thinking* for most of his life.

His biggest battle now was building a cart that was strong enough to withstand the rigors of crossing the country.

They would be going through waterless deserts, rugged mountains, boiling heat, and freezing cold. Not only did he have to worry about getting their physical bodies across the thousands of miles, he had to make sure that the delicate recording equipment, the fragile precision musical instruments, and yes, even the 70 pounds of dehydrated food Roger had secured from Bernard Food Company survived the journey.

This simple task was turning into a logistical challenge worthy of Rube Goldberg. And unfortunately, Dave's efforts weren't for the amusement of readers of the comic pages. The very survival of the brothers was in his hands.

At least he had the $1,000 from the selling of his beloved convertible to help finance the expedition. How much could it cost to make a cart? Surely it couldn't be that expensive.

The basic problem was Dave didn't even know what it was he didn't know. He couldn't just go down to the local Acme Cross Country Carts to Go Store and walk out with a shiny red vehicle, complete with flags and a pretty little bell to ring.

No. The only way Dave was going to accomplish his very unique and totally specific goal was to build it with his own two hands.

While Roger and his mother continued to work on getting sponsors for the trip, Dave was literally knuckle deep in the nuts and bolts of the operation.

While his mother was busy convincing a local stationery store to pay for the large wooden signs that would go on both sides of the cart, Dave was trying to figure out how many wheels to put on the cart.

While the rest of the team was working on possible promotions and advertising angles, Dave was literally buying two automobile luggage racks from his local Sears & Roebuck to transform into their survival vehicle.

He spent two hours arranging all the parts on the floor of the store, trying to see what might work. He didn't have enough money to make many mistakes. David would have stayed longer if only this one obese customer, with a total lack of appreciation for the truly historic nature of The Big Walk, hadn't complained to the store manager that he couldn't get by the items on the floor. Didn't that guy realize this was a legend in the making?

He sometimes felt like he was chasing his own tail.

Without knowing how much weight they would need to carry with them, he couldn't decide on the kind of tires needed to support the cart. Every time Roger added another item to the must-have list, the pounds being pushed increased. Every microphone stand weighed something. The tent came in at 30 pounds. Vital items like a canvas bag and a metal can for water tipped the scales at 100 pounds.

Dave was pushing the scales every day. Those trusty bathroom scales had become his most important companion in the living room of his mom's apartment. Yes, her apartment. Not the garage. There wasn't any garage to assemble anything in, so David had taken over

26

his dear mother's living room, turning it into the international world assembly lab for The Big Walk cart.

Gravity was turning out to be one of his worst enemies. Why did everything have to be so heavy?

One of the main rules for most travelers is to pack light. Only take what is absolutely essential, eliminate all luxuries. Keep in mind that you can purchase items on the journey and cut down on the things you need to take with you.

Right. Dave could only wish it were that simple. Unlike most travelers, The Walking Balph Brothers had to take everything they needed with them. Department stores would be few and far between in the middle of the desert.

The pounds kept adding up and up and up. Dave was shocked when the first total came in at close to 1,000 pounds. Half a ton? How could that possibly be right? Had he added the numbers incorrectly? Did they really need to carry so many kinds of instruments? Couldn't they just play a kazoo or hum their way across the nation? And why did they need two heavy speakers? Was water really necessary? Who needs food?

Just when Dave thought he had a handle on the situation, the list of items would grow like a fungus, increasing, multiplying, and overloading his best-made plans.

Each day brought a new round of requirements.

Did they really need to take air mattresses in addition to their sleeping bags? How many winter coats do you need to bring with you when you are walking through the desert...in the summer?

The problem was that everybody had advice to give, opinions about the tiniest detail. Where did all of these so-called experts come from? They kept crawling out from under every rock and cranny. The collective bulk of their supposed wisdom was staggering.

Dave learned that he simply couldn't believe many of the things people were telling him. Simple things like how much weight a bicycle tire can handle before it explodes. The guys at the stores would look him straight in the eye and tell him that each bicycle wheel could support a 700-pound man. Using that vital bit of information, Dave figured a three-wheel vehicle would be able to easily support 2,100 pounds. A four-wheel cart should be able to support even more weight.

There wasn't enough time to test any of these theories. Dave had to rely on the wisdom of the experts, with the mental assurance that the wheels would support the load.

The truth was that nobody knew anything about anything. This was new territory. While snobby clerks and salesmen in clean white shirts might act like they knew what they were talking about, it would be Dave and Roger's lives on the line in the middle of the desert, with coyotes breathing down their necks, when things broke down and fell apart.

Dave couldn't even figure out how many wheels to put on the thing. He liked the idea of having one wheel on front of the cart, and two on the back. Seemed like it would be easier to handle and guide down the road. Three wheels would be less of a challenge to push and produce less friction. Or so he thought.

It turned out to be another thing that sounded great in theory.

Despite all odds, progress was being made. Things were coming together.

The cart was up and standing on its own.

Three wheels with a steering rudder in the back. Bicycle brakes on each wheel. Mom's cherished heavy wooden signs on each side, anchored to the Sears and Roebuck aluminum luggage racks.

The local newspapers were on hand to see the first steps of the first day of The Walking Balph Brothers' musical journey across America.

The air was electric with anticipation.

Roger's longtime girlfriend, Donna, stood by to give him good luck kisses, promising to pray for him every night of the six-month, maybe even seven-month, journey.

The cart was loaded with everything they had deemed absolutely essential, causing the trusty bathroom scales to gasp and groan in complete and total horror.

With the brothers dressed in their best military khakis, their boots shined and polished, the entire neighborhood cheered and waved for the journey to begin.

It was nine in the morning.

Taking a united push, Roger and Dave had found a way to start their Big Walk.

The months of planning, working, spending, and thinking positive thoughts had paid off.

There was no stopping them now. Good-bye, Los Angeles. Hello, America. The Walking Balph Brothers are coming your way. Tell The Big Apple we'll be there soon.

It was a day that would live in history. July 8th, 1963. The epic journey that would change the lives of so many people in so many ways was off, and while not running, at least walking, one step at a time.

Their first task was to push the cart from the alley behind their mother's apartment, go down the street in front of the building, and pass the waiting masses of cheering fans and supporters.

All they had to do was wave to the newspaper reporters, the crowd, their family, and other representatives of the glorious human race, eagerly attacking the pavement, each stride bringing them one step closer to their dream and Jack Paar's television studio.

It didn't happen.

They made it all of 396 inches...yes, inches. They had traveled less than 33 feet...yes, feet...less than 11 yards...yes, yards...when the darn front wheel crumpled and collapsed!!!

The entire cart collapsed right in the middle of the alley, just out of sight of their loving family, the waving crowds, the documenting lenses of the newspaper photographers.

The reporters came around to the scene of the crime, saw the collapsed heap of metal and dehydrated food packets, and promptly demanded that the brothers try to lift up the cart and fix the crumpled front wheel.

Always looking for a story angle, the reporters seized on the misery of the moment, forcing Roger and David to gamely struggle to lift the dead weight off the pavement. It was a losing proposition.

Despite their smiles and the encouraging clicks of the cameras' shutters, gravity had won the first round.

The launch had been crushed, and Dave realized there was only so much that positive thinking could accomplish when faced with half a ton of good intentions.

Where was Rube Goldberg when you needed him?

Cart Collapsed

Chapter 6: Encore, Encore

The cart was in pieces, crumpled and gasping in the alley after the infamous nose-dive into the pavement.

Most mortals would have taken this initial setback as a sign of divine intervention. If the cart couldn't even survive a journey of 11 yards, how would they ever be able to walk across the entire United States of America?

Most normal humans would have gone to Plan B, changed directions, and maybe tried to resume their thriving careers with the rock combo at the local bowling alley, but The Walking Musical Balph Brothers had never been considered "normal."

Normal people would never have been able to even dream up a trip of such majesty, such wonder, such all-encompassing grandeur.

They came from a long line of performers, achievers, and people who seized opportunities.

Their Grandfather Wilmer Balph was a self-made success who rose to the top ranks of The Westinghouse Corporation, spending 50 years in marketing, sales and advertising. He was one of the chief salesmen promoting the concept of circuit breakers, a then novel invention meant to replace electrical fuses. Never a man content to hide behind a desk in some office tower, Grandfather would go to construction sites and demonstrate the tangible benefits of this latest technology, usually in a flurry of electrical sparks and smoke. In his spare time, he was known for arranging his famous gambling nights of legal after-hours entertainment for the amusement of company employees and friends.

Their father, Dale Balph, was an acclaimed musician, who also served nearly 50 years with Westinghouse. With his background in big band performances, he had previously spent time on the Vaudeville circuit, earning a substantial reputation for his talent on the alto and tenor saxophones. During the day he worked in marketing the company's electrical products. In his spare time, he produced his own form of electricity as a prominent member of the company's top-notch house orchestra, known throughout Ohio for providing the best in music for dancing entertainment.

Everybody said the brothers came by their talents honestly. It simply ran in their blood.

In addition to their musical talents, the brothers also inherited Grandfather Balph's gift for smooth-talking, especially Roger. Though young Dave was no slouch when it came to using his silver-tongued assets, Roger had honed his talents to an even higher level of sheen.

That is how he was able to secure thousands of dollars' worth of brand-new recording equipment, pounds and pounds of dehydrated survival food, and who knows what else.

That is exactly why this stone-wall of rejection they had been receiving from Jack Paar was so vexing. It wasn't like The Balph Brothers were no-talent wannabes. They already had a proven track record of crowd-pleasing successes behind them. Everybody who saw them perform knew they had the goods, the stuff, the "it" factor.

Didn't entertainer Steve Allen tell them to their face that they were great? Didn't he invite them to audition for him after seeing them perform in California? Of course, he did.

Hadn't Roger already appeared on the Ted Mack Amateur Hour, and Ed Sullivan's Toast of the Town Show, not to mention several shows with Arlene Francis? The facts were as plain as day.

That is why it was so frustrating, irritating, and down-right almost insulting that Jack Paar was being so uncooperative.

Didn't he realize what an opportunity they were offering him?

They were giving him the inside track to showcase one of the best musical acts in the entire country, and he was being hesitant.

It was simply mind-boggling that a man of such supposed "taste," with an eye for talent, would be so oblivious about The Balph Brothers.

Why, having them on his show would help Jack Paar's reputation as much as it would help the brothers. This was his chance to go down in history as the man who brought The Balphs to America's living rooms.

Roger knew if he could only have the chance to speak man-to-man with Paar, he would recognize a kindred spirit and would extend an invitation with open arms.

While the brothers struggled with the damaged cart in the alley, the phone rang in their mother's apartment.

The phone had been ringing for weeks as family, friends, neighbors and the media found out about the epic journey. Most people thought they were crazy, but that just reinforced the brothers' willpower. The Big Walk was the talk of the town, and that is exactly what the brothers needed.

So, the phone ringing again wasn't anything that unusual.

The brothers continued to work on righting the cart, attempting to defy gravity and the sheer weight of the 1,000-pound payload.

Their mother came out back to tell them they had an important phone call. Roger left wondering if it was just another aunt telling them to drink lots of water.

How many times had well-meaning neighbors told them to take plenty of sweaters for those cold nights in the desert?

What could be so important about this one call?

Roger and David were more concerned about salvaging their aborted kick-off launch under the watchful eyes of the local newspapers and TV reporters than hearing yet another church lady beseech them to come to their senses and spare their dear mother months of worry and heartache.

Didn't they realize that the initial idea for the trip came from their dear sweet mother herself?

Roger reluctantly stopped working on the wounded vehicle and went inside to take the urgent call.

The call was from New York. Wow. It wasn't another aunt, neighbor, or friend.

A secretary from Jack Paar's office was on the phone, live and in person.

She was responding to the telegram the brothers had sent out early that same morning, before they took their first steps. They wanted Parr to know that The Big Walk was actually going to begin.

Roger felt his ears getting red, tingling with anticipation.

This was the moment he had been waiting for.

It was finally happening.

Roger was finally going to get the chance to talk with the man himself. The next few minutes would validate all those years of efforts and struggles.

Jack Paar would hear Roger's words of wisdom, admire his smooth delivery, and marvel at his measured thoughts.

They would form that instant bond that only fellow entertainers share with each other, recognizing the rare gifts of talent they both possessed.

Roger could almost hear the warm welcome that Paar was certain to extend their way, breaking down barriers, opening doors, making calls, introducing them to the homes and hearts of millions and millions of record-buying viewers.

Roger wanted to savor this moment forever.

He put the receiver to his ear, almost overcome with emotion.

All he had to do was make a little small talk chit-chat with the secretary and then wait while she put him through to Paar.

The rest would be history.

All of those certified letters they'd sent to Paar's studio had paid off. The morning telegram was just icing on the cake.

Maybe they wouldn't even have to make the walk. Maybe just the idea of the walk was enough to get them on the show.

Roger was certain that Paar hadn't yet heard about their disastrous first effort and crash in the alley. How could he? The dust was literally just settling down from the implosion.

Paar had to be responding to those initial letters, and it just took him a while to make the come-on-down-to-the-studio phone call. Everybody knew Paar was a busy man, so this was all just a quirky bit of coincidental timing.

Roger felt good about spending the money for the telegram. Maybe that was the little extra touch it took to show Paar they were serious musicians.

Maybe he was calling to wish them good luck. Bon voyage. God speed.

Roger answered the phone.

The voice on the other end was very businesslike, certainly not warm and friendly, as he had imagined.

In fact, her tone was downright abrupt.

What was she saying?

"We received your telegram this morning, and you're wasting your time and money."

Her words stung Roger's ears.

He couldn't be hearing what he thought she was saying.

Roger inquired if Mr. Paar had asked her to call them.

She confirmed his hunch.

Roger's mind was reeling. Was this a joke? A bad connection?

His thoughts were jumbled and whirling. He wanted to scream out, "No, wait, you don't understand... I'm sure if Jack would just get on the phone for a minute..."

He was tempted to smart off to her and say, "Do you think you can stop us?"

Time stopped for a moment as his mouth struggled to voice the thoughts tumbling around in his head. He wanted to tell her that this is a free country, and they didn't serve in the military so some pencil pusher in New York could tell them what they could and what they could not do.

Roger was hearing his thoughts as clear as day, thinking to himself, "Our cart is loaded, and we ARE coming to see you in New York."

Instead, he held his temper in check. His years of military training and good manners didn't fail him in this time of need.

He heard himself tell the voice on the other end of the line that he understood what she was saying, and that it was fine if Mr. Paar didn't want to see them. Roger was sure that other shows and talk show hosts would be interested in their story once they made it to The Big Apple.

He thanked her for her call as she hung up. He had been polite, controlled, and completely professional. All the rants and emotions had stayed safely bottled up inside of his head.

Her message was crystal clear. They did not have Jack Paar's approval. They did not have his support. He would not let them appear on his show.

Roger hung up the phone on his end, oblivious to the incessant dial-tone.

If there was ever a time when Roger was positive about the trip, this was it.

He'd show that silly secretary. He'd show the entire country before it was over.

Roger walked back to the alley. They had a cart to rebuild and places to go.

Time's a wastin'.

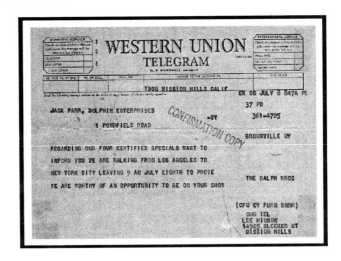

Telegram Sent to Jack Paar Announcing The Big Walk

Chapter 7: On the Road Again

On the Road Again

At least the paper spelled their names right.

Roger had always heard the saying that there is no such thing as bad publicity, but whatever wise guy came up with the silly thought didn't have to see his photo plastered all over the Los Angeles Herald Examiner.

There they were, right on the front page of the local news section, crouched on the ground, staring in unison at the bent and broken front wheel of the cart. To add insult to injury, the photographer chose a pose where they were grinning like big goof balls, and then had the nerve to say they were mourning in the caption.

Mourning?

That was not the feeling going through the brothers' minds. They were exasperated, plain and simple. Upset? Yes. Mad? Of course. Ticked off? No doubt. But "mourning"? The paper made it sound like they were crying in their boots, sobbing like little babies.

The Walking Musical Balph Brothers never mourned.

When life threw them lemons, they didn't just make lemonade, they produced a big sparkling pink pitcher of sugar and joy and sunshine, and then tossed in some juicy red cherries for good measure.

David spent the next week redesigning the cart to withstand the weight of the instruments and the jolts of the road. He was determined to make sure that the next version would be able to survive 10, 20, or even 50,000 miles of road abuse, bumps, rage, and turmoil.

The biggest design change was getting rid of the idea of three wheels. Tricycles might work for toddlers in Mommy's driveway, but David needed the security of four wheels touching pavement. The theory of less wheels being easier to push might sound nice in some science lab classroom, but David's short 396-inch virgin journey had proven that the concept was just nonsense in the real world. He now understood why his beloved little red wagon of childhood had a quartet of wheels.

The rebuilding of the cart had grown beyond the scope of their mother's apartment living room. They had been lucky that they were able to dismantle the first version and get the thing out the door the first time.

Rebuilding the Cart at Barbe's Machine and Repair Shop

The mammoth heavy-duty, reinforced, industrial- strength, new and improved Version Two of The Cart was assembled, fabricated, and forged in the macho facilities of Barbe's Machine and Repair Shop on El Dorado Avenue in San Fernando.

Version Two was strong and sturdy, a much more dependable and durable platform for the journey.

They had spent the ten days since the aborted first effort making sure that every item on the cart was essential to the journey. If they had learned anything from their first 11 yards of pushing dead weight, it was the need to only carry the most vital items needed to survive. Supplies and life support systems? Yes. Frivolous items that might be nice but were really non-essential had already been removed from the list.

One category of items that never even came up for possible elimination discussion was weapons.

The Balph Brothers were not going to cross the country without the means to protect themselves from the craziness of the road.

Even in those somewhat more innocent times, the brothers knew enough from their military backgrounds, and from just reading the local headlines in the newspapers, that the world was a wild and dangerous place.

That is why guns were right at the top of their list of essential road gear, just as important as food, water, musical instruments and the sacred Ampex tape machine.

If David and Roger were going to put themselves at the mercy of every car and truck going down the highway for 4,000 miles, they were certainly going to be able to defend themselves.

They had used part of David's sold Oldsmobile money to buy two shotguns, just in case they needed them.

Dave had designed spaces behind the wooden advertising signs on both sides of the cart to hold the guns and protect them from the elements. While they weren't being flashed around in plain sight, they were loaded and easy to grab if needed. Both brothers knew that trouble could arise any second, and when you need a gun, you NEED it immediately.

Feeling as secure as anybody can feel taking the second first steps of thousands and thousands of miles into the unknown vastness of America, The Big Walk of The Musical Balph Brothers began, again, on July 18th, 1963.

Unlike the first launch, the second departure didn't receive any newspaper coverage. The media had been invited, but the photographers must have found other mourning citizens to focus on. The fleeting spotlight of local fame and exposure had moved on to other dreamers and schemers.

The cart felt much improved over the first version. More importantly, the wheels didn't crumple and collapse. One initial trip of 396 inches was embarrassing enough, but the idea of a second failure was unimaginable. The welding job of the good men at Barbe's was up to the task. Gravity would be denied for yet another day.

The brothers felt good. Strong. Determined. Excited. The Big Walk was actually happening. No stopping them now. No looking backward. It was time to march forth. One step at a time. Multiply each step by a million and then repeat…repeat.

The brothers were glad they had spent the last three weeks playing basketball for hours and hours, building up their muscles and endurance.

This trip was going to be the marathon to end all marathons. The brothers chose to ignore the fact that the ancient runner of the very first marathon had collapsed and died when he reached his destination. Besides, that was ancient history. No time for mourning, and no photographer on hand to write a smart aleck caption.

Three blocks into their cross-country marathon, The Brothers made their first pit stop on Western Avenue at Sam Fain's Hall of Fame Stationers. Sam had generously donated the large wooden signs on each side of the cart as a favor to their mother.

Sam treated them to a bon voyage lunch at Blarney Castle, a steakhouse right across the street from his shop. Feasting on steaks and all the fixings, The Brothers stuffed themselves with celebratory nutrition. Filled to the gills with tasty beef, they resumed their walk with newly found purpose. If every part of the trip was going to be as enjoyable as the first three blocks, they had nothing to worry about.

They were somewhat concerned about being stopped in their tracks by Los Angeles' finest. They had originally written the Police Department, asking for permission to push the cart through town, but they had been denied. Maybe they were part of the conspiracy with Jack Paar to keep them out of the spotlight.

By the time they received notice of the city's denial, they were already in their own form of deep denial. They had spent too much time, too much money, too much effort to let a silly little thing like the law keep them from making their Big Walk.

They were too far to turn back, even if they had only walked 11 feet the first time.

So keeping with their philosophy of just making things happen, they had taken the precaution to contact an area lawyer to represent them, in the event that they were arrested before they left the city limits.

If they were successful in illegally pushing a 1,000-pound cart through the city streets of the second largest city in the United States, right under the noses of who knows how many cops, officers, patrolmen, and other law enforcers, they figured they could accomplish anything.

They had only walked a total of about six blocks when some jokers came up beside them and told them that they would never make it. Easy enough for bystanders to say. They weren't the ones pushing the cart, making the effort, taking the journey.

David was certain that deep inside, those guys were envious, or just plain jealous, of The Walking Balph Brothers.

This day would go down in history as the day that changed the lives of David and Roger. There was no stopping them now.

Let the small-minded people jeer and joke from the sidelines. That is exactly where they would remain, on the side, watching as life passed them by. Not The Balph Brothers. They weren't waiting for anybody or anything. They were seizing the day, making their own opportunities, and each step brought them closer and closer to their destinies.

David was somewhat surprised that after only six miles of pushing, he was starting to feel the weight of the cart.

They had been violently shaken when they crossed a set of railroad tracks, and David silently wondered if they would even make it out of Los Angeles without the cart falling to pieces.

A bystander came up and thrust two dollars in Roger's hand. A complete stranger. And only the first of many they'd encounter along the way. It was a welcomed sight having left home with only $100.

David saw this as a prime example of human nature. On one hand they had the jerks and jokesters who yelled and taunted them, throwing negative thoughts and actions at them with a vengeance. Then, on the other side of the coin, within the same 50 feet of walking, they would meet a Good Samaritan who wished them the best, kept them in his prayers, and provided hard cash money to help them on their journey.

David took each step with the renewed faith that this journey was one of the most positive things that would ever happen in his lifetime.

Now if only he could just make it through the first day, and the next, and the next, and the next... one step at a time.

Chapter 8: Steps of Reality

Their First Night's Lodging

They were doing it. Walking. Pushing. Straining. No more excuses.

The initial giddiness and euphoria of the first few hours had come and gone.

The reality of the task before them was starting to hit Roger and David in the gut like a sucker punch. Do you have any idea how far 4,000 miles actually is? Four thousand long, hard, relentless miles? Roger did the math in his head and realized they would be covering over 150 marathons before they made it to The Big Apple. And if that little fact wasn't mind-boggling enough on its own, they weren't just talking the distance. No, that would be too simple. To make the trip even more interesting, The Walking Musical Balph Brothers were going to push a 1,000-pound cart the entire way!

David realized that he would have plenty of time to ponder the wisdom of the entire effort. For that matter, he would have plenty of time to think about pretty much everything and anything that might cross his mind.

Step by step, nothing on this journey was going to happen rapidly. This was plain old hard work, back-breaking, brow-beating, leg-aching, mind-numbing physical labor. He thought about stories he read in school about slaves building the pyramids in ancient Egypt, the Chinese immigrant workers constructing railroad tracks in the 1800s, even chain gangs pounding rocks in the summer heat of the Mississippi delta. David felt a kindred spirit to those physical warriors.

What had they gotten themselves into? Surely there had to be a better way to get some attention for their musical careers.

They had survived the first day of Los Angeles city streets, arriving at Whittier, California, totally exhausted.

Their mother had arranged a promotional deal with Travelodge motels to provide free rooms for the brothers at the end of each day, in exchange for advertising on the cart and mentions in the hundreds of radio, television, and newspaper interviews that would be coming their way.

Thank God for mothers!

The idea of putting up their tent by the side of the road and trying to sleep with the noise of the highway after their first day of pushing was more than either brother could handle.

Their mother was waiting for them at the motel with freshly cooked chicken and all the goodies.

David had gobbled down half of the bird, according to his mother, but he didn't even remember it the next day.

The second day they made it to La Habra, but only after spending two hours at a gas station, fixing the first of many, many flat tires. It was very apparent that keeping the tires rotating was going to be a constant struggle. The combination of the heat from the summer sun and the weight of the cart were already taking a toll. There are reasons why the tires on cars and trucks aren't skinny little things like those on bicycles. David was experiencing those reasons firsthand. With the smog of Los Angeles still burning in his lungs, David realized a vital part of their plan was based on faulty logic, but what could he do about it? They simply had to keep on pushing ahead with the project, and, as always, find a way to make it work.

They had traveled about a hundred yards from the gas station when the same darn tire went flat again!

They pushed the cart, flat tire and all, to the next gas station, and repeated the entire process of taking everything off, removing the tire, fixing the problem, putting everything back on the cart, and then back to pushing and pushing some more.

At least this time they were able to fix the loose spoke that was poking the tire, causing it to go flat so rapidly and repeatedly.

Slowly, but surely, progress was being made, though the problems with the tires would prove to be an ongoing issue.

The routine of the days was starting to develop. They would wrestle with the cart, trying to keep it moving down the highways and out of the ditches. They would talk about the weather. Discuss their upcoming performances. Go over the musical arrangements and think about ways to improve the songs. They'd make jokes and comments for their own amusement, as the nonstop stream of vehicles flew past them, throwing pebbles and road trash in their faces.

The sun was blindingly bright. The heat was draining.

Even at this early stage of the journey, conversation between the brothers was lagging. The truth of the matter was there simply wasn't that much to talk about when you are pushing a cart down a highway. You weren't going fast enough for the scenery to change very often. You could see your next three hours' destination right before you off in the distance, so no surprises there. The only rapid changes happening around you were the trucks and cars whizzing past you, horns honking. Sometimes they came so close to the cart that the wind from the vehicles would shake the brothers and whip the tarp covering the instruments into a frenzy.

The biggest fear was that some distracted rubberneck driver would be so excited about seeing the cart on the road that he would forget what he was doing, lose control, drive right into them, crash his car, and kill the entire gang right there on the hot asphalt. The brothers could only hope that their little American flag waving on the antenna was enough to keep them safe and sound.

Their months of exercising and playing basketball had helped to build up their strength, but they were still adjusting to the road, and let's not kid anybody, this was hard work. Hard. Work.

By the time they had pushed the cart 40 miles to Pamona, they were worn out. Done. Despite their best intentions, their bodies needed rest.

They spent three days resting and healing. The sheer physical nature of the journey was not to be denied. This trip was not only a test of mind over matter, it was a quest of endurance and stamina.

Roger could tell that each day was getting a little bit easier as their bodies adjusted to the loads, but why did even the little hills of California have to be so hard to push over? He could only imagine how they'd be able to handle real hills or mountains.

They had been making their nightly calls to radio station KLAC back in Los Angeles. The disc jockeys had initially been extremely enthusiastic about keeping in touch with them as they made their way across California. The first few days of interviews had been energetic and entertaining, but David noticed that the last interview had seemed a little restricted, almost like the DJs were just going through the motions, and not really interested in the day's events. That was one of the problems with keeping the media focused on the story. All they cared about was murder, crime, fires, and accidents. They acted like the story was already old news, and The Balph Brothers hadn't even made it out of California. David could feel their support for the story getting weaker and weaker by the day. He realized that they would have to keep re-inventing themselves and find new ways to tell the same story over and over as they pushed their way across the country.

Maybe it would help them if they actually got shot on the trip. That would make headlines.

The Walking Balph Brothers robbed, shot, stabbed, abused, beat up, mugged on their trip to see Jack Paar! That would get them some press. The reporters would be lining up by the side of the road to get the juicy details.

The fact is, trouble wasn't that far away from them. David knew his imagined headlines weren't that far out of the realm of reality.

Outside of Pamona, some wise guys had pulled their car over to the side of the road in front of the cart, causing The Brothers to stop pushing. Four thugs had jumped out of the vehicle, looking for trouble

45

and possibly a fight. They were walking towards the valuable cargo of musical instruments, tape recorder, speakers, and all the survival gear of the Balphs, when David pulled his 12-gauge shotgun out from behind the sign and simply laid it on top of the tarp. He didn't even have to point it at the new arrivals to get their attention.

Evidently the mere presence of the $25 pawn shop purchase was enough to convince the would-be attackers to go on down the road.

They had roared off in a cloud of dust, leaving The Brothers to count their blessings, and check on their stock of ever ready shotgun shells.

This wouldn't be the last of the roadside welcoming committees they'd encounter along the highway.

Chapter 9: Illusions Can Be Deceiving

Waving to the Press

"One thousand, thirty-nine steps…one thousand, forty steps…wow, it sure is another hot day on the road…One thousand, thirty-seven steps…wait.. thirty-nine? Forty-two?"

David had lost count, again.

It is so easy to get distracted walking down the side of the road.

With Roger guiding the steering wheel, which came from an airplane, from the right side of the cart, it was David's job to push on the left side and then push some more.

There were only so many clouds that David could turn into buffalos and rabbits and train engines in his mind. Oh look, there's a big fluffy donut in the sky!

Small talk came to an end usually within the first hour of each day's journey, and unless some car tried to run them off the road or some jerks tossed cans of soda or something worse on them, there wasn't much to even think about other than pushing, and then pushing some more.

That is why David decided to keep count of his steps. How many steps does it take to walk a mile? Ten miles? Fifty? The quest for the answers to those questions helped him get through the hours, and the miles.

By the time this big walk was over, David would know exactly how many miles he could get out of a shoe heel plate, a shoe heel, even a shoe sole. And how many steps it took to walk a mile.

One step, two steps, three, four...

They arrived in Ontario with David wheezing and gasping for air. While Roger was having an occasional cough, David was obviously suffering at a much higher degree. A trip to the city's emergency room proved he was suffering the effects of breathing Los Angeles' smog. The doctors gave him oxygen to clear out his lungs, and it helped his condition considerably. They felt simply breathing the clean, fresh air of the countryside would soon restore his health. David was too choked up at the time to properly express his deep appreciation for their medical expertise, but he was relieved to know things would soon improve. He was afraid he had picked up some exotic disease from the road, and he was happy to discover it was just a normal reaction to inhaling his hometown's brown air.

Next stop was Riverside.

Reporters from The Daily Enterprise met the brothers outside of town for what would become a somewhat regular ritual. Earnest, probing small town news crews would venture to the edge of their respective city limits to greet the musical nomads preparing to enter their fair burgs. With movie news-film cameras rolling, still camera shutters clicking, and impressive broadcast-quality location microphones recording every utterance and word of wisdom, the esteemed press corps would ask a set list of questions, gather the who-what-when-where-and-whys, ask the brothers to smile, push, grunt, and then be on their way. Days or a week later, the resulting stories would appear and find their way to the brothers' eyes.

Dave and their mother were doing their best to keep track of the resulting press coverage, and so far there hadn't been much to worry about. As the trip progressed and the media exposure gathered momentum, getting copies of stories, articles and news clips would prove to be a constant challenge.

One of the reporters from the paper said he didn't think the cart looked like it was very hard to push. He implied it wasn't any big deal, a push over, a piece of cake. His smug tone was almost insulting.

Roger took him up on this challenge, right there on the side of the road in the middle of the blazing summer heat. It was a duel that Roger would issue many times before the journey ended.

The reporter gamely tackled the task, commenting how the first two, three, fours steps weren't so hard after all. He pushed and groaned a few more yards. Sweat beads lined his forehead. Large and growing wet spots developed under his arms while his crisp white dress-shirt decomposed under the heat. Then, reality hit him in the stomach. The cart was winning. He pushed the cart about a quarter of a mile before giving up, gasping his apologies. His departing words to the brothers rang true. "Boy, that thing IS heavy and hard to push!"

The next day, The Daily Herald featured a large photo of the brothers entering Riverside's city limits, accompanied by a lengthy article giving the details and quotes from the previous day's roadside interview.

This is exactly what the brothers had envisioned when they started the trip. Make some noise, bang their own drums, toot their own horns, and make the world take notice of The Walking Musical Balph Brothers.

Roger realized that they had a tiger by the tail. He also knew how inexperienced they were in matters of promotion and publicity. Sure, he had been able to get on Ed Sullivan's television show and perform before a national audience, but that had been nearly a decade earlier. And yes, there had been numerous press stories over the years about various performances and appearances, but nothing on the scale this journey offered.

If they played their cards right, with a little bit of luck and some smart planning, they had a very real chance of capturing the imagination of the nation. Getting on Jack Paar's show was just the beginning of a logical international marketing campaign. Being a guest on one show wouldn't make The Walking Balph Brothers into celebrities, but Roger realized that if they put as much effort into maximizing the publicity possibilities of the walk as the walk itself, by the time they crossed into Manhattan, being on Paar's show could be just a little side note to the much bigger picture.

Seven hundred twenty-five steps...seven hundred twenty-six steps...seven hundred twenty-seven steps...

David was determined to keep his count going this time.

Seven hundred twenty-eight steps...seven-hundred twenty-nine steps...

Roger had one of his eureka moments. Thinking about Mary, a lady friend he met back at the bowling alley while performing with the rock band, gave him a new idea. They needed a press agent, and Mary had everything it took to do the job. She had street smarts, was ambitious, easy on the eyes, and totally in love with the idea of the soon-to-happen trek across America.

Mary had been visiting the bowling alley lounge back in Los Angeles frequently, trying to get her mind off her personal problems.

During band breaks, Roger had noticed she was very attractive but seemed upset. Over several weeks, during their 20-minute breaks between sets, he was able to visit with her and get to know her. He learned about the serious marital problems she had been having for a long time. He also discovered her previous stint in Uncle Sam's Army. They were called WACS at the time. He realized she was very intelligent, having worked in the legal community, in addition to having some experience in promotion. As the weeks passed by, they got to know each other quite well. It began to bother Roger that he was growing very attracted to her.

He already had a faithful, devoted girlfriend named Donna, who had been his steady gal for many months. Roger knew he was preparing for the trek across the country and felt he would just walk out of Mary's life, and that would be that. Having been introduced to Mary earlier, Dave was aware of the situation and felt the same. The Brothers thought Mary would soon just be a pleasant memory in their minds within weeks of starting The Big Walk.

Things changed when Roger realized that Mary could be their secret weapon to making the trip a huge success.

With this new eureka moment on Roger's mind, knowing they needed a press agent, he also knew it was impossible for him to do the job. It was painfully obvious. He was stuck pushing the cart every day, every step of the way. He might as well have been handcuffed to Dave on the chain gang, doomed to spend every day, every step side by side, pushing and pushing some more.

The very gimmick that was going to turn them into celebrities was also keeping Roger from doing the job that really needed to be performed for the trip to mean anything.

Roger churned the logistics over and over in his mind. He couldn't take breaks from walking to chase down reporters and photographers. The cart had to keep moving. If they weren't actively making progress on the trip, nobody would ever take them seriously. It was bad enough that they could only walk ten to fifteen miles a day.

To take any time out of their main duty of walking down the highway, constantly marching forth, to schmooze the media, get court attention, and try to grab as much of the publicity spotlight as possible was a contradiction of purpose.

One thousand six hundred and one steps…one thousand six hundred and two steps…

David was keeping his eye on their trusty old bicycle odometer/speedometer anchored to the back of the cart. It was coming up on the next mile mark, and he was going to make the count this time. He was sure of it.

One thousand seven hundred and thirty steps…one thousand seven hundred and thirty-one steps…

Roger couldn't keep his thoughts to himself anymore. "We have to find a way to have Mary as our press agent," he barked.

"What did you say?" David asked.

"I said that we have to find a way to have Mary as our press agent. You saw the way the news crews met us at the edge of town and treated us like visiting royalty. We simply have to keep getting media coverage, and the only way to do that is to have somebody going ahead of us, making calls, developing contacts, shaking hands, drumming up interest in our story. I certainly can't do it while I'm pushing this cart all day," rationalized Roger.

David knew it made sense. He also knew it could make cents, and dollars, and more dollars. Having an attractive woman like Mary representing them could only help their cause.

David was positive she could get more television coverage, newspaper articles, and radio interviews just by tossing her hair, pursing her ruby red lips, and casting her spell with her glimmering eyes than the brothers could ever hope for on their own.

He also had no doubt that Mary's charming ways and flirtatious smile could melt the resistance of any male talent booker or night club owner she might approach about hiring the brothers for music gigs. Mary was a looker, and men certainly enjoyed looking at her.

And with their initial $100 almost spent, the need for paying gigs on the road could not have been more urgent.

Getting media coverage was fine and dandy. Great for the cause and nourishing for their egos, but the brutal facts of the matter were the brothers were going to be broke and stranded out in the middle of nowhere before they even left California if they didn't get some paying bookings. Soon.

David just had to get used to the idea of adding a third person to the team. He understood all of the advantages of having Mary on the job, but this trip was supposed to be the two brothers, united in their efforts, working towards the same goal. It was their dream, not Mary's. Would she be a blessing or a problem? Or maybe both? And what about the balance of power on the road?

David was already dealing with the pressure that came from being the little brother, walking in the shadow of his older and more experienced brother. Roger was already used to calling all of the shots. Would this new addition just make things worse? Would Mary and Roger gang up on him, and always get their way in any argument or discussions? Would Mary be fair and impartial? Would they even listen to his ideas?

The fact remained that money was running very short, and if they didn't do something about getting bookings, it wouldn't matter much about the power structure or personal politics. They needed a steady infusion of cash. While David was thankful for the 90 pounds of donated dehydrated emergency food rations they were carrying on the cart, he didn't want to have to dine on them every day for an extended period of time.

Roger was on a roll. The idea of having Mary on the job and with them on the trip made the blood rush to his head. She could follow along with them in her car, carrying support materials, and then drive ahead of them each morning, head to the next town, meet and greet, smile and flirt, and then get them paying jobs, while generating as much noise and attention as possible. Maybe she could work for them until they got to the state line. Surely by that time, she would be able to arrange enough work in advance to keep them going until they reached Texas.

And who knows. Maybe Mary would enjoy the job so much that she might just decide to join the brothers for the rest of the trip. Roger would love having her sweet companionship on the road, and it certainly had to be more exciting for her than her boring job and life back in Los Angeles. Sure, there would be a few minor obstacles to work out. Little things like the fact that Roger's other girlfriend, Donna, was waiting faithfully for him back home, praying for his well-being every night, and his safe return to her loving arms. And then there was that silly little legal detail about Mary that some small-minded people might consider an obstacle. It was more of a technicality in Roger's mind, certainly not a deal breaker, at least to him, but at that moment, Roger wasn't sure how that matter would be resolved. Every mile further they went from Los Angeles, the less that little issue would matter.

Roger was convinced. He had churned over the details and found no major obstacles to kill the idea. It all made sense in his head, and he didn't think it was entirely due to the exhausting, grueling, relentless, intense summer heat.

Now they just had to convince Mary to turn her back on her previous life and obligations and take on the task of providing media coverage for the journey, and booking enough paying gigs to pay for the expenses and survival of Roger, David, and, yes, even herself.

If she believed in The Big Walk, and the star-making, big money-earning potential of the brothers as much as Roger thought she did, this was already a done deal. She could bask in their reflected glory and share the spotlight, while taking the journey of a lifetime with a man she could grow to love.

Roger put a little extra pep in his stride, as they pushed the cart down the road towards Riverside.

David stumbled a little, trying to keep up with Roger's new urgency. That was one thing about pushing a cart as a duo. You had to keep up with whatever pace you and your partner decided on. If you didn't, you could literally find yourself gasping, confused, and out of step.

Roger was almost jogging into the city. He was focused. A man with a mission. He had to turn his illusions into reality, and having Mary on the team was the best way to do it.

As Dave worked to keep up, he realized he had lost count. Once again. Gosh darn, golly, gee-whiz.

One step, two steps, three, four, five...

Chapter 10: Working on
Their Mission at The Mission Inn

Could the name of the club of their first paying engagement since leaving Los Angeles have been more appropriate? The brothers finally earned some much-needed revenue with a two-day gig at Riverside's Mission Inn.

David took it as a sign from above and was truly thankful for whatever divine guidance came his way. It wouldn't be the last of his near religious experiences during the trip. He had a sense that angels were watching over them as they walked the miles. It wasn't anything as dynamic as visions of burning bushes in the desert or clouds over his head forming the words to prayers before his eyes. He just had this distinctive calm feeling of inner peace and focused purpose enter his mind at various times throughout the day's journey, letting him know that he wasn't alone. A man without faith might just blame it on the intense summer heat, but David knew otherwise.

Just being out in the open spaces was enough to humble him. The vast wonder of nature was overwhelming. David had no doubts that he was experiencing the glory of God, seeing his handiwork on a deeply personal level. The trees, the hills, the sky, the vast expanses. If anything ever brought humility to a person, walking across the nation was certainly having an effect on David. When he thought about the sheer magnitude of the journey before him, it was all he could do to keep putting one foot in front of the other. If he let his mind dwell on the lack of money, the hardship of the trip, even the sheer physical effort of pushing the cart, it would be all too easy to let his doubts and fears paralyze him.

This mission required a huge leap of faith, and God willing, The Walking Musical Balph Brothers were going to heed the call. Their faith, and hopefully their shoes, would see them through the desert, out of the wilderness, and into the golden gates, or at least into the concrete canyons of New York City.

Performing at The Mission Inn was just the replenishing nourishment their souls and wallets needed.

The audience had been receptive and enthusiastic. It felt good to be onstage, performing for a live audience.

The Ampex tape machine worked without incident, filling the room with the big band sound The Brothers had hoped for, allowing them to sonically appear to be a ten-piece orchestra. David had to admit this modern industrial-quality recording marvel was a vital component of their live show, even if it did add nearly two hundred pounds to the cart's weight. Seeing the joy and happiness on the faces of the audience helped David appreciate the blessing that came from having the machine. He kept reminding himself of those faces when the cart felt exceptionally heavy and backbreaking out on the road. He dreamed of a time in the distant future when some creative, apple-crunching technology nerd would invent a miniaturized pod-like device that could capture an entire library of music and sounds, while comfortably fitting into a shirt pocket. It was the stuff of dreams or heat-stroke hallucinations, but back in the reality of 1963, the shining hunk of heavy metal Ampex engineering was state-of-the-art.

Roger had enjoyed the way the shows came off. He always felt comfortable in front of a crowd, and this was no exception. Sure, the banter was a little stilted at first. And yes, it took a few moments to get used to working with the equipment and the tapes, but the concept was working. Performing live music is what Roger lived for, and all of this walking and pushing was just a sideline to his real passion and reason for being.

If The Big Walk worked out as they hoped it would, these five or six months spent pushing a cart would pay off in such a big way that The Brothers would never have to walk anywhere again. Actually, walking had never been the goal. If there had been an easier way to accomplish their quest, Roger would easily have given up the entire idea of walking thousands and thousands of miles, pushing a half-ton cart across the desert. Lest anybody be confused about the matter, the goal was not to see how totally impossible they could make things. They weren't out to torture themselves. The goal from day one was to spread the word about their music, build a national audience for their songs, and share their love for Dixieland tunes with brass and woodwind instruments with as many people as possible. It wasn't to see how much pain they could endure for an extended period of time. If all they had cared about was being noticed as a gimmick they could have chained themselves to the huge clock on the top of The Franklin Life Building on Wilshire Boulevard back in Los Angeles, and refused to have come down until they had a record deal. The press probably would have loved the idea of that just as much as them pushing an extraordinarily unique home-built cart across the nation.

Yes, the trip was a stunt, but it also made perfect sense from Roger's point of view. This was an act of faith on his part, just like it was for David.

The mission at the Mission Inn was to prove that the concept worked, and it did. David would continue to improve his speaking and playing skills with each performance, and Roger would keep working on his banter and ability to entertain live audiences. Since they were locked into a specific list of songs with the tape recorder, they would be able to develop and refine their act over the weeks and months, knowing that the recorded orchestra was never going to change tempo, miss a note, show up late, need a haircut, require shoes shined, or call in sick.

As long as Roger remembered to hit the start and stop buttons at the right times between songs, their band in a can, their combo on tape, their crew on the reels would deliver the musical goods, each and every time.

David loved seeing the reactions from the members of the audience. There was nothing like the thrill he got from being onstage, putting his heart and soul into his music. Those moments spent performing made everything else almost bearable.

He just had to make sure walking all day in the desert sun didn't ruin his lips. He could handle blisters on his feet, but if his lips gave out on him, that would be an entirely different matter. Unlike the always ready, always in tune, always energetic prerecorded backing tracks on the tape recorder, David had to be ready, willing, and able to hit the high notes live and in person at every performance.

They say the devil is in the details, and this certainly was the case with keeping The Brothers' bodies in shape on the road. There is a reason most people don't try to walk across the country. It is hard work. Hard. Work. You can only train so much. The reality of physics hits you when you actually stop talking, and start pushing.

Passing through Beaumont, California, they stopped at a local gun shop to stock up on shotgun shells. David spied a dusty old trumpet in the window, and asked the owner if he could blow a few notes on it. Replacing the discolored original mouthpiece with his own favorite, David soon had the walls shaking with a symphony of music. The owner dropped his jaws when he heard the sounds David was able to coach out of the old metal. He informed The Brothers he had never been able to get the trumpet to sound anything like that when he tried to play it. He was so appreciative of the in-store concert that he gave them free shoulder pads for their guns.

The first of many, many foot blisters hit The Brothers outside of Palm Springs. They limped over to the local Travelodge, counting their blessings for the comforts of modern motels.

The road was taking its toll.

They spent two days recovering and nursing their wounds.

The Desert Sun newspaper wrote a nice article about The Big Walk appearing on August 2nd.

Outside of Raleigh, California, the heat was winning the battle with The Brothers when they experienced a near religious moment. They were already running on empty after a day of intense heat and effort when they came upon a long hill. While it wasn't the steepest obstacle they would encounter, at the time, it seemed completely insurmountable. They were already totally shot, ready to give up and just surrender to the desert. The air was completely still, and they were feeling the weight of each and every one of the 1,000 pounds of payload on their cart.

Just as David was ready to crawl under the cart and pass out, an incredibly strong wind developed behind them, as if an answer to his prayer. The force was so strong it felt like another strong hand had joined their efforts. The wind was hitting at just the right angle on the wooden signs to function like sails. Had the Man Upstairs heard their pleas? David's faith told him it must have been true. Granted, there was a good chance that he was suffering the effects of a heat stroke, but even if he had been seeing things, the cart did go up the hill with The Brothers doing little more than steering their load.

When they reached the top of the hill, they discovered that the road beyond was relatively level. They also noticed that the blessed wind that had pushed them in their time of need had gone away, carrying away their dust of doubts and fears.

David accepted it as a true miracle, and found great comfort in knowing they weren't alone in the wilderness. The entire experience just added to his faith they were on the right path.

The more people heard about The Brothers along the way, the friendlier people seemed to be towards them, making their job a little easier.

When they had first left Los Angeles, the reaction they met on the road was more hostile. Drivers would honk their horns, yell insults, throw things at them, and generally act less than civilized. Slowly, but surely, things seemed to be improving as each mile passed by. David wasn't sure if the change in attitudes was due to increased news coverage about the journey, or if maybe people were just friendlier in smaller towns. All he knew for certain was he liked friendly supporters much more than their angry counterparts.

The Imperial Valley Press in Brawley did two articles on the trip. Reporter Dick Daniels was so supportive he took it on himself to make calls to various friends and contacts, working to get some additional promotions lined up in the next city down the road, El Centro.

It couldn't have come at a better time. Their original $100 had dwindled down to four big bucks by the time they left Brawley.

Once again, the powers that be intervened. Out of the blue, or more specifically, out of the desert, a truck passed them on the road and pulled over. Not knowing if their intentions were good or bad, the brothers braced themselves for whatever fate might come their way. While they didn't actually take their trusty shotguns out of their sheaths, it would have taken only seconds to arm themselves, if needed.

As it turned out, the occupants of the truck were friendly, supportive, and generous. They wanted to put the cart up in the back of their truck and drive the brothers on down the road to Yuma, Arizona. Like everybody else who saw the brothers, they were concerned about the heat. They didn't want The Walking Musical Balph Brothers to turn into a tasty meal for the scavenging vultures gliding overhead on the thermal breezes.

Once again, there are reasons why people don't walk through the desert. Locals who know the area and have personal experience with the heat and elements know better than to tempt the fates. So when compassionate, caring, and often times religious people encountered The Brothers walking in extreme heat out in the middle of nowhere, pushing a cart loaded with 1,000 pounds of expensive instruments and recording equipment, their hearts would go out to them. People wanted to help them, ease their burdens, and make their journey less painful.

Unfortunately, The Balph Brothers considered such aid to be cheating, breaking their self-imposed rules of the road. While they deeply appreciated each and every kind gesture, they couldn't accept the offer. Lord knows that while the idea of tossing the cart in the back of a truck and riding down the highway at 50 miles per hour was very, very appealing, The Brothers had to resist the temptation and stay focused on the goal. Get behind me, Satan.

Maybe it was just the heat talking, but The Brothers kept pushing, watching as their salvation truck drove on down the road without them, leaving them to cough and choke on the dust kicked up in their faces as the vehicle roared away.

But they did have ten extra dollars to show for their virtue. While they hadn't been able to take the Good Samaritans up on their offer to tote the cart, they did accept ten dollars thrust in Roger's hand by the driver, right before he roared off into the horizon. They had resisted temptation and instantly had been rewarded for their faith and virtues.

The lessons learned at the Mission Inn were paying off, step by step, almost as if it were all part of some big master plan.

David went to bed that night, counting his blessings and even more convinced that their mission was on the right path. He was sure his angels were watching over him every step of the journey. Was it wrong to wish that there weren't quite so many steps yet to be taken? David considered this thought for all of two seconds before falling off to sleep.

First TV Exposure

Chapter 11: Good Times at the Border

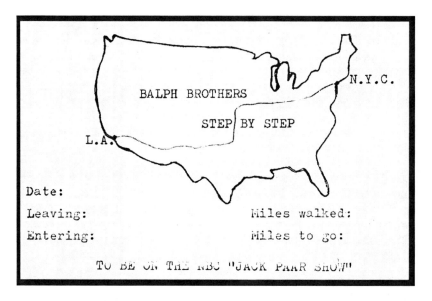

BALPH BROTHERS

STEP BY STEP

L.A.

N.Y.C.

Date:

Leaving: Miles walked:

Entering: Miles to go:

TO BE ON THE NBC "JACK PAAR SHOW"

Post Card Sent to Paar as they Entered each State

While you couldn't really say the grass was greener on the other side of the fence, or in this case, the borderline, things were looking up for The Brothers once they approached Arizona.

Sure, the desert was still hot and dry, and the road was just as rugged, but the promotions arranged by Mary in California were starting to pay off once they left the state.

Maybe they were just taking advantage of being the new out-of-towners passing through to greener pastures and the neon lights of The Big Apple, but there had been a positive change in attitudes and fortunes since they crossed the line and never looked back.

The trip potentially came to an early end right on the border. The newspaper coverage in El Centro had generated three days of work at the Barbara Worth Country Club. It brought them enthusiastic crowds, city-wide attention, and some much-needed revenues to replenish their empty wallets. They were paid $50 per show, earning enough cash to eat and enjoy some of the benefits of civilization.

They were almost too successful.

The manager of the Country Club extended their stay for three weeks. While they were determined to keep moving towards their goal of making it to New York City, it was impossible to turn down the chance at some steady money. Even though they knew that spending such a long time in one place would only make it that much longer before they shared the stage with Jack Paar, they didn't have any choice.

This was the first time they'd had to deal with what was going to be an ongoing conflict of interest.

The original plan was to push the cart as many miles as possible each and every day. Stay focused on getting to New York City, and then move on to the next phase of their careers and lives. They never planned on seeing how long they could stretch it out, or how many scenic side-trips they could venture down. In the best of all worlds, they would just walk night and day, making a beeline to the Big Apple.

But there was that pesky little reality of not having any money to survive on. They didn't have any big bucks from sponsors or an eccentric millionaire funding their epic journey. They had some boxes of dehydrated food pouches, a 200-pound tape recorder and speakers system, and a very loose arrangement for free rooms at Travelodge, if and when they could find one on the road.

So being offered a three-week paying engagement at the Country Club was very, very hard to turn down, even if it wasn't part of their master plan.

Roger knew how easy it would be to get stuck in a comfortable rut on the border, making ends meet but never really going anywhere with their career. It would have been safe and somewhat secure, but what would have been the point? If that was what he had been looking for, he could have just stayed at the bowling alley lounge in Los Angeles, and never pushed a cart anywhere, much less to the Arizona border.

While he reluctantly accepted the three-week extension offer, he made it clear that any offer to work beyond that period would have to be rejected.

One consolation of the extended stay was the opportunity to have a night out across an even bigger border. They found themselves with time to kill, seeing as how they were only hired to perform on weekends. That gave them a chance to get to relax and spend time with an assortment of local supporters during the rest of the week.

Dave had met a local girl who had enjoyed his talents with his horn, and had his first date of the trip in nearby Mexico. They went across the border, enjoyed a few hours of foreign delights together, and that was that.

It would be the first of many romantic opportunities that life on the road as a visiting celebrity would bring David's way. While Roger had Mary as his traveling companion, David would meet and greet his fair share of enthusiastic music fans and admirers along the journey. It would continue to amaze him how the spotlight of the stage increased his appeal with certain segments of the audience. He could see how a guy could get used to the idea of being treated like a celebrity. It sure beat living the life of an unknown back in Los Angeles.

David was young, energetic, and very single. Unlike his older sibling, David didn't see much benefit in being attached to one single person. He didn't have anybody faithfully waiting for him back in Los Angeles, other than his dear mother. He liked being able to enjoy the company of a wide assortment of appealing females knowing that he would soon be leaving for the next stop down the road. He enjoyed relaxing courtships at various times with no strings attached. He was always particular about who he would spend time with, and only if the business of performing and promotional activities such as radio and television interviews didn't interfere. A guy deserves to have some female company without fear of it getting too serious. Especially when each stay was usually limited, knowing the walk would be continued, no matter what. He made sure any girl he sparked a relationship with realized how serious the walk to New York City was. There was a certain convenience knowing he would be walking out of town. It always gave him the perfect vehicle to end relationships and not tick anybody off. On those rare occasions when the would-be fiancées wouldn't take the hint, they usually gave up on the idea of following their departing boyfriend within a few miles of leaving the city limits.

David had made friends with one of the local town cops who took an exceptional interest in their trek to New York. He was also a sportsman and a hunting enthusiast, and the idea of the adventures the brothers would experience along the way totally fascinated him. Taking David on a tour through the city hall, jail and several other points of interest in El Centro, they soon became pretty good friends.

It wasn't long before they decided to go out in the desert on one of their off days to do some target practice. They had driven the officer's Volkswagen Bug out into the boonies, and had gotten it stuck in the sand clear up to the axles. Despite their best efforts at pushing and pulling, with the officer trying to dig the car out with a shovel he had in the back seat, the car refused to budge. Alone and out in the middle of nowhere, David came to the rescue when he was able to start a nearby parked bulldozer, shift it into gear, lurch over to the stranded VW, and physically push the car to solid ground. The fact he was able to then return the massive specimen of heavy construction machinery back to its original location safe and sound was equally amazing.

While the policeman could have technically arrested David right then and there for everything from stealing government property to breaking and entering to reckless driving, he didn't. David's shooting buddy was too appreciative of David's on-the-spot ingenuity to even consider writing him up.

The brothers soon left town, confident that David's new comrade-in-arms would keep any pesky pursuing fans at bay. He knew the value of having the law on his side, pistols loaded and cocked. Their getaway from town was clean and painless.

The greeting into Yuma had been amazing. They were treated like visiting dignitaries. Members from the newspaper, radio stations, television crews, even the Chamber of Commerce welcomed them with open arms, flashing cameras, and hearty handshakes.

The plan was working. The world, or at least part of Arizona, was starting to take notice.

The manager of the Stardust Hotel offered them a two-week performance contract, putting their trusty cart in the middle of the hotel's lobby to advertise the shows in the lounge.

Their fan base was building each and every day.

Being off the road for two weeks gave them time to heal their road bruises, work on their music, and enjoy the comforts of being in a welcoming and civilized environment.

The timing couldn't have been better. Despite their best efforts, The Brothers were getting weaker and weaker each day. There had been times on the trip where Roger had looked over at David and had been truly shocked at how pale and ghost-like his brother appeared. They were losing the battle with the elements, and Roger was afraid something serious might happen out in the middle of nowhere. He knew people died from heat strokes, and he certainly understood how that could be a real possibility for either one of them.

A trip to the doctor in Yuma gave them new tools to fight the effects of the desert heat. Even though they had been drinking what they thought was plenty of water, they hadn't been replenishing their vitamins and nutrients. The entire concept of sports drinks and Gatorade was still years away. All the salt in their bodies would sweat out and wind up on their boots as white crusts by the end of each day's pushing. The doctor put them on a routine of high-potency vitamin supplements, and also told them to take at least six salt tablets each and every day.

Time spent off the road at the Stardust gave them time to build up their systems and get their body chemistries back in shape.

While they were working on their physical bodies, their band in the can on the tape machine continued to work flawlessly, providing a wall of sound to backup the live notes from Roger and David's instruments.

They had three prerecorded tapes to work with, providing a nice variety of songs and sets for an evening's entertainment. Audiences loved their version of "When the Saints Go Marching In," and Roger's frenzied solos on "Tiger Rag" always brought the audience to their feet. Each show had specific songs allowing The Brothers to display their talents, both as a duo and then as featured artists.

David enjoyed the power they had over a crowd. He loved seeing their reactions to his efforts. It was an energy that transferred from the audience back to him onstage, building and building into a crescendo that would sweep over the room like a tidal wave. He enjoyed seeing the joy and true pleasure the music created during those magical moments onstage. He savored watching the faces in the crowd when they realized these guys had real musical skills, and weren't just some cart-pushing no-talents looking for cheap attention and charity handouts from strangers.

While staying in Yuma, they sent a post card to Jack Paar, informing him they had left California, and were continuing on their journey to meet him in New York. The post card listed how many miles they had traveled and how many miles they had to go. This was a pattern they would follow every time they crossed into a new state. They wanted to prove that their efforts were legitimate, and focused. As time passed, they would also enlist the help of audiences, reporters, politicians, school classes, nightclub owners, radio announcers, and roadside supporters to send a constant barrage of letters to New York, asking Paar to please have The Musical Walking Balph Brothers perform on his show.

With so many people on their side, how could Paar possibly deny them their request?

The two weeks in Yuma flew by. There was only so long they could be "the new kids in town." Having been featured on every possible news outlet in town, and performing over a dozen nights at the Stardust Hotel, even The Brothers realized it was time to start pushing, and they meant that in the most literal sense, on down the road.

Time to take off the celebrity sunglasses, stop signing autographs, give up the free meals, temporarily cease flirting with the alluring ladies in the audience, and get back to the big walk, step by step.

Arriving in Arizona

Chapter 12: Beer and an Airplane

The Brothers Performed at The Stardust for Two Weeks

Leaving Yuma proved to be the kind of challenge that novelist Charles Dickens would have understood. It truly was the best of times, and the worst.

David had to wonder if maybe the concept of karma was hitting him upside the head. And the leg. And his neck.

If he had been raised Catholic, he might have thought it was penance for enjoying the wonderful hospitality of the kind people of Yuma maybe a little bit too much.

Maybe they were just getting soft. Taking two weeks off to immerse themselves in the pleasures of the Stardust Hotel had been extremely easy to get used to.

Now the reality of the trip was back on them, and the sun was blinding The Brothers as they struggled to get their road rhythms back.

Even on the best of days, it always took a few miles for their bodies to adjust to the rigors of the highway.

The Brothers were lost in their own thoughts.

Roger was thinking about how lucky they were Mary had agreed to continue working for them past the Arizona border, acting as their talent agent and promotions director and logistics coordinator and press agent and advance person and...and...everything else and more.

Mary had become such a vital part of their team since leaving Los Angeles that Roger couldn't imagine walking another step without her. Just knowing she was working her magic somewhere down the road a few miles ahead of them was enough to keep his energy levels high. They would start each morning with their respective duties, and then regroup at the end of the day to assess their progress.

In many ways, The Brothers had the easier job. All they had to do was keep pushing the cart down the road for as many miles as possible each day. While it was backbreaking work, it was very focused. As long as they kept the wheels out of the ditches, and followed the long black asphalt line into the horizon, they were doing their assigned duties.

Mary's job was much more challenging. She had to perform two main tasks: drum up as much publicity about the trip as possible and, most importantly, find paying opportunities for The Brothers wherever she could.

Approaching the local newspapers, radio stations, and television crews was getting easier each day they were on the road. The gimmick of pushing the cart was always good for at least an opening consideration by the editors and producers. As their press kit grew with each new story and article, Mary had more ammo to present to prospective media outlets. The Brothers were a happy story with great visuals. Who could resist two handsome, young, athletic, traveling musicians with their big smiles and boundless energy? Throw in the fact that they were pushing a half-ton cart across the country, and who wouldn't want to know more about them? This was the stuff of legends, and Mary had no problem selling that story to the press.

The constant problem was getting them paying gigs as musicians. While it was all well and good The Brothers were able to push a cart, it didn't mean a thing to the nightclub owners, talent bookers, and lounge managers who had to fill their establishments with eating, drinking, and, most importantly, spending customers every night.

The very gimmick that helped generate attention would sometimes backfire in her face. How talented could The Walking Musical Balph Brothers be if the only way they could get any jobs was by pushing a cart thousands of miles across the country? Did Sinatra or Elvis ever push anything anywhere? Could Roger and David entertain audiences? Did they have any talents? Could they even blow their own horns? And why did they have their band in a can?

Mary had to address every silly question, remain polite while they eyed her from head to toe, and then, once they showed any sign of acceptance, negotiate a legal contract that would pay The Brothers a decent amount of money for their performances.

Once the Doubting Thomases actually met and heard The Brothers perform, all doubts were left behind, but getting to that point would prove to be a constant challenge.

Meanwhile, The Brothers were back out on the road, grilling themselves under the intense desert sun. Step by step, pushing and pushing some more.

One aspect of the walk was different since leaving Yuma. Using their ice water container to chill down the bottles, The Brothers had decided to add liquid bread, better known as beer, to their diet. It was a tip they had picked up on the road from an enticing Budweiser billboard as a way to provide reliable food value. After much deliberation, they had agreed that having a nice cold brewski every five miles of pushing under the desert sun would keep them hydrated and happy. David was initially of the opinion he could easily handle more than one bottle, but the powers that be, meaning Roger, had decided one bottle was enough. They had been told drinking any more would make them useless and done for the day, but that scientific theory had yet to be proven in the field.

So, with their bodies healed and the reward of cold alcoholic nutritious beverages literally dangling right before their thirsty eyes, The Brothers hit the road.

No sooner had they consumed their first bubbly bottle than The Brothers thought they were seeing and hearing things in the desert heat. They heard the distant roar of a wasp or maybe a large

68

bumblebee. The sound grew louder and louder. Was it a train? Perhaps it was a horde of locust delivering their Biblical wrath?

A two-engine military airplane roared by, only feet from their heads. It was like a scene out of a Hitchcock movie. They were being attacked! From above! Had the Ruskies decided to attack Arizona? Was the Cold War over, and the hot one raging over their heads? Had they forgotten to pay their bar tab in Yuma? Did David's date tell some vicious lie to her father, her brothers, the entire Air Force? And why oh why did this have to be the day that they decided to start drinking beer on the road? The sins of the bottle were raining down on their heads.

The plane soared into the clouds, and then dove back towards the pavement.

To their total amazement, the airborne military vehicle of death did a touch-and-go landing on the highway directly in front of the cart.

Did they try to run for the hills, or pull out their trusty shotguns and defend Mom, apple pie, and the American Way right then and there in the middle of the barren desert?

The pilot was waving to them. Was this some Commie plot? Maybe they should just start firing and ask questions later. What would John Wayne do?

Before they had time to cock their shotguns, the plane was back in the air and circling.

It was one of their fans from the Stardust Hotel back in Yuma.

Now they remembered!!

He was a Marine pilot who had told them how much he enjoyed their music back in Yuma.

David vaguely remembered him saying something about taking his plane out to see them in the desert, but truth be told, there were so many people telling him so many stories during breaks in their performances that it was hard to keep them straight. Between signing autographs and accepting compliments, David didn't really pay much attention to the noise coming from the audiences.

The Brothers admired the government-issued machinery, and waved thanks for the aerial visit.

They braced the cart and themselves as the music-loving pilot circled overhead, tilting his wings to say goodbye.

Somewhat rested after the brief aerial assault, The Brothers chuckled about their recent invasion, and went on with the task at hand.

About an hour later, a policeman drove up, asking if The Brothers had seen an airplane land on the highway.

In unison, and almost a bit too well rehearsed, they replied, "What plane?"

While it was never their habit to knowingly tell falsehoods to authorities, there was a bond of honor between military men that held them to a higher standard.

The Walking Musical Balph Brothers were certainly men of honor.

Chapter 13: Bums, Sandstorms and Rattlesnakes

The road to Phoenix proved just as challenging as every other part of The Big Walk.

The novelty of being in a new state had worn off days earlier, and they realized that the western side of Arizona looked pretty much just like the eastern side of California.

While adhering to their strict rule of only allowing themselves one ice-cold bottle of beer every five miles of pushing, they encountered a fellow imbiber who obviously didn't have their level of self-control.

Plain and simple, the guy was drunk. There is no way to sugar-coat it. Out in the middle of the blazing desert sun, this fine fellow was already two, three, maybe four sheets to the wind. Snockered. Wobbly. Dazed and confused.

They met him on the side of the road while the man was trying to tie his shoestring. He might have had better results with his semi-skilled knot-making if he had taken the bottle of wine out of his back pocket, but even that is debatable.

Even in his drunken state, the man had enough wits about him to realize that his own version of a miracle in the desert had slowly, but surely, walked and pushed into his life.

Roger wasn't sure if the man thought The Brothers were angels marching towards the Pearly Gates, or if he was so accustomed to seeing things in his alcohol-altered blur that he simply accepted the vision of two guys pushing a 1,000-pound cart as just another day in the desert.

For all The Brothers knew, the man may have danced with 2,000 pound pink elephants just a few hours before, and that was why his shoestring was untied.

When The Brothers stopped to talk with their fellow roadside companion and help him to his feet, the man decided that the cart was his own personal taxi, literally his ticket out of the wilderness.

He told Roger what they needed to do was lift him up into the cart and continue pushing and pushing on down the road. Time was a wastin' and this fine traveler had a very important appointment with the local liquor store in the next town up ahead.

David was as kindhearted as the next guy, who in this case just happened to be his brother, Roger, but the very last thing he wanted to do at that particular moment in the middle of the desert in the blazing sun was to add another hundred or more pounds to his load, especially when the extra weight came in the form of a drunken bum who was leaking bodily fluids onto his untied shoes. David might have been stubborn as a mule at times, but he certainly wasn't anybody's jackass.

Roger told the man, while they wouldn't be able to grant his transportation wish, as tempting as it might have been, they were more than happy to have his company, walking along with them, helping to push the cart.

Even in his drunken state, the hopeful freeloader was sober enough to hear Roger's message loud and clear.

There would be no free rides on this day.

These walking angels had just passed judgment, and the bum was going nowhere fast.

His smiles and compliments immediately disappeared. All praises and appreciation evaporated in the desert sun.

He went from being their number one fan of all times to being an abusive, highly vocal, cussing loudspeaker. He insulted the brothers, their mother, their father, their ancestors, and several of their cats and dogs. His wrath was all-inclusive, and highly personal.

The Brothers were amazed at the variety and volume of salty cusswords that roared out of that man's vocal chords.

They could still hear his rants going at full steam as his image faded into the horizon in the cart's rear-view mirrors.

God bless his soul, and please cut off his bar tab.

The trip down Telegraph Pass had been just as difficult as everybody had warned them it would be. While performing in Yuma, dozens of people had made point of mentioning how backbreakingly difficult it would be to make it down the winding two-mile mountain pass twelve miles outside of town.

The Brothers were so concerned about the hazards of one stretch of road, they enlisted the help of Ron Hoffman, an Arizona State Patrolman. Officer Hoffman escorted the cart through the pass without incident.

The trip very nearly ended right at the Pass, had assistance not been forthcoming. The twisting road was so steep and narrow, Roger was certain the cart would have either been hit by traffic in the bends of the highway, or just out right smashed by the rocks when the brakes gave out. Having Officer Hoffman's patrol car leading the way down the Pass with flashing lights offered a much needed level of protection. The idea of an out-of-control runaway cart flying down the mountainside carrying 1,000 pounds of musical instruments was not a pretty image.

Once again, the kindness of strangers kept The Brothers marching forth.

At least for a little while.

Outside of Centennial, Arizona, a big sandstorm blew up out of nowhere. It was something that would happen to The Brothers several times during The Big Walk.

Anybody who has ever been in a sandstorm knows that it hurts and can be quite dangerous. Your face is literally being sand blasted. Just like industrial equipment that can remove paint from cars and decades of grime from the front of office buildings, the force of the flying sand can shred a person's face to a bloody pulp within minutes. Your vision is severely limited, even if you have goggles, and it can be impossible to breathe without choking. Wrapping material around your face helps somewhat, but grains of sand still manage to penetrate the cloth and lodge in your throat, each breath adding to the accumulation.

The Brothers stopped to change the batteries in the headlights on the cart and secure the tarp.

Once again, their angels were watching over them.

Had they walked another nine feet in the storm, they would have stepped on a very lethal rattlesnake in the middle of their path. While The Brothers had a first-aid kit with them, they hadn't wanted to put it to the test by dealing with poisonous venom snakebites in a desert sandstorm. Odds are they wouldn't have even noticed the fangs of the snake piercing their skin while the raging sandstorm was attacking every bit of exposed flesh. They would have just kept

73

pushing and pushing, pumping the toxic poison through their veins and into their hearts.

By the time they realized they had been bitten, it might have truly been their last thoughts... ever.

They spent the night camped out in a rest stop by the side of the road.

A traveler with a horse trailer pulled up to wait out the storm.

The Brothers were hungry, tired, and unable to sleep with the storm raging around them.

To add insult to injury, the horse in the trailer beside them spent the entire night kicking the bucket... no, not dying... but literally kicking the bucket in his trailer. You would have thought that the horse was trying out for the National Football League... maybe he was a fan of the Baltimore Colts.

The next morning, the sandstorm had roared through the desert, and The Brothers were greeted with sunny skies.

After enjoying a camp-side breakfast of cold spaghetti, David was rewarded with a bite on his neck from a blister bug.

These nasty little buggers are appropriately named. Their bites cause blisters, which soon turn into open wounds. This creates an ongoing process that produces even more blisters, and more open wounds. The juice from the blister ran down David's neck, leaving a stream of infections and irritations.

David wasn't in abject agony, and the blisters weren't very painful on their own. But added on top of the other ongoing health, physical, and weather issues, the open, oozing, dripping, running fleshy sores trailing down his neck weren't helping the situation in any shape or form.

Once again, the Lord provided roadside aid. Just when David needed it the most, a car of kind people stopped to see if The Brothers needed any assistance.

They gave him some healing powder to help keep his neck as dry as possible until The Brothers reached the next town.

David thought back to the cussing drunkard they'd met back in the desert, and counted his blessings as he counted his steps until the next town.

He recalled the sacred Biblical stories from his days in Sunday School. In particular, David recalled Moses and his 40 days in the wilderness. Who could have imagined back then in his innocent youth that he would ever experience his own personal version of that specific lesson?

Chapter 14: Barn Fire, Dead Lizard and Steaks

The Gila Bend Peace Officers'
Pistol Club
OF GILA BEND, ARIZONA

MEMBERSHIP CARD

Issued To ___Jack Parr___ Date 9-23-63

President _John E. Vike_ Sec.-Treas. S.W. Hanley

ORGANIZED IN JANUARY, 1962

Membership Card for Paar

The next stop was Gila Bend, Arizona, and they had already seen several days' worth of desert oddities.

They had watched a barn burn to the ground behind a small café in Welton. They kept thinking that the local fire department would soon arrive to douse the flames, but the entire time they were walking past the blaze, a period of well over 30 minutes, nobody came to the rescue. The building just burned and burned while a few citizens of the town stood off in the distance, watching the flames.

The Brothers had to assume that was just the way things were done out in the desert. No point in wasting precious water and energy for what was a doomed proposition.

Roger silently said a prayer to himself that their cart would never catch on fire so far away from a water hydrant.

After an arousing break for fire-watching, The Brothers were ready to resume their Big Walk when they spied an injured lizard, struggling to move in the middle of the road.

Having just witnessed the total destruction of some unknown person's property, assets, and very likely his livelihood, The Brothers decided it was time to put another creature out of its discomfort.

Whipping out his trusty pistol, David proceeded to send that wounded reptile to his favorite sunning spot in the sky.

The desert is a wild and dangerous place for creatures large and small, a fact The Walking Balph Brothers were all too aware of.

Outside of Gila Bend, The Brothers thought they were hearing things. For just the briefest moment, Roger and David both thought they were suffering yet another effect of a heatstroke.

David was the first one to perk up his ears.

Was it a trick of the wind?

Was Roger playing a joke on him?

He heard the sound again, and again.

He looked over at Roger, who seemed just as baffled as he was.

Moo.

Mooooooooooooooooooo.

Moo, moo, moo, mooooooooooooooooo.

The air was filled with the sounds of bovine vocalizing.

It sounded like they were in the middle of a cattle stampede, but where were the cows?

Was this some demented guilt manifesting itself as an auditory mental assault for killing that lizard back on the highway?

The wind shifted, and brought new evidence for yet another one of their senses.

Not only were their ears filled with the sounds of cows, but now their nostrils were overwhelmed by the pungent odor of soft, fresh, steaming, moist cowpies.

The smell was enough to, yes, kill a lizard. Maybe they had done the little green critter a favor up the road, sparing his delicate nose such a brutal assault of outright stink.

But where were all of these pie-making bovine factories?

As far as they could see to their left, it was flat and just as empty as the previous 40 miles. No grass-chewing, four-stomach methane producers to be seen.

The answer had to be on their side of the road up an elevated hill on their right, the one with a train track leading into Gila Bend.

The Brothers stopped pushing, unsuccessfully tried to find a patch of fresh air to inhale, and then scurried to the top of the embankment.

When they reached the top, the mystery was solved.

Separated by only the thin built-up mound of the train tracks, The Brothers literally stumbled into a vast holding corral filled with hundreds, maybe thousands, of living, breathing, mooing, snorting, and gas-emitting cows, steers, bulls, and all things bovine.

It appeared to be the stockyard of the Nation, right there in the middle of the Arizona desert.

It was a meat-producing assembly line for America's dinner tables, and The Brothers had unknowingly been walking right beside it for several miles.

It was overwhelming and almost enough to make them ignore the toxic smells bombarding their brains.

All of which made The Brothers hungry. Very hungry. Just seeing so many living, breathing, drooling T-bones, Porterhouses, Rib-eyes, Sirloins, not to mention thousands and thousands of ribs, prime and otherwise, right in front of their eyes was almost too much to endure.

They could taste the sweet juices, feel their teeth chewing the buttery morsels of prime beef. They were certain that several of those beasts had their names written on their backsides.

The thought occurred to them it would be much easier to hit one of those cows with a lethal blast from a pistol than it had been popping the injured lizard up the road. The heat and hunger were making their minds wander. While they had no intention of actually killing any of the cows before them, the thought did give him something to ponder. They were trying to figure out what the legalities of Western law were as they related to the shooting of food on the hoof. They remembered reading that they used to hang cattle rustlers and horse thieves back in the Good Ole Days, but maybe things had changed in the decades since Wyatt Earp ruled the West.

The Brothers hungry stomachs were overriding their rational thought processes. They saw dinner for 1,000 years standing, chewing, and releasing gas right before their disbelieving eyes, and they were hungry, extremely hungry. They could feel their trigger fingers twitching, as the temptation grew with each growl of their stomachs.

And once again, their Guardian Angels were paying attention.

They had no sooner walked back to their cart than they spied a car kicking up dust, heading their way.

In what can only be described as yet another miracle, the man in the car was a man by the name of John Hunt.

This man was no lizard wrangler. He wasn't even a member of the previously missing fire department that had let the barn up the road burn to the ground.

No.

Of all the millions of possible occupations that a person could have, John Hunt was the owner of...yes, you know this is just too good to be possible...The Hunt Steak House of Gila Bend!

This vision in the desert owned his very own restaurant, the success of which was built on serving some of the finest steaks in the entire state.

Hunt had heard about The Brothers and their big adventure on the local radio and had decided to drive out to meet them, rather than wait for them to struggle their way into town.

He came bearing hot lunches, cold beer, and assorted goodies.

It was truly manna from Heaven.

Hunt offered The Brothers a job playing four nights at his restaurant, paying $50 per gig, plus room and board.

David was beside himself with joy and gratitude.

It turned out that Mr. Hunt was also the Justice of the Peace in the town, and his enthusiastic support for their cause went a long way. With his seal of approval, they spent their weekend playing for at least 349 of Gila Bend's 350 residents.

They were able to shower, rest, regroup, relax, and still perform three shows to wildly enthusiastic audiences, while enjoying some of the biggest and juiciest steaks they had ever feasted on.

Families brought their children to hear the shows. Neighbors invited their neighbors to share the moments. Good times were had by all.

A mechanic at the local Chevrolet dealership helped replace some worn out ball-bearings, which certainly improved the ride of the cart.

Before they knew it, their weekend in Gila Bend was over, and they were back on the highway, pushing and pushing some more on their way to Phoenix.

A short distance out of town, Lucky Henley, the head policeman in Gila Bend, caught up with The Brothers pushing their cart. He brought them several boxes of shotgun shells to protect them from attacking lizards and cud-chewing cattle.

He also gave them a little card addressed to Mr. Jack Paar himself.

As it turned out, Lucky had served in the Navy with Jack, considered him a good friend, and was certain Mr. Paar would remember their times together and take that into consideration when it came time to book The Brothers on his television show.

With a great guy named Lucky on your side, how could they fail?

Chapter 15: Pot Holes,
Broken Metal And Hot Tempers

Whatever luck they had hoped would rub off on them due to their association with Lucky Henley outside of Gila Bend evaporated on September 28th.

They had been pushing the cart for about two miles when Roger accidentally drove off the road and hit a pothole. He hit it hard, and, unfortunately, it hit back even harder. Once again, the trusty cart proved to be no match for the physical challenges The Big Walk was throwing its way.

The force of the jolt broke the metal bolt holding the right front fork. Once again, the cart was crippled and bent.

It was also the straw that broke the camel's back, in this case, Roger's temper. He was furious with David over the fact that his younger brother hadn't had the foresight to bring along an extra back-up bolt to save the day. He yelled, stomped, and generally displayed his strong disfavor for his pushing companion. Roger's flair for biting words didn't fail him in the Arizona sun.

David was just as insulted his brother was blaming him for what had obviously been a simple accident on the road. How was he supposed to know that such an integral part of the cart would crack under such unexpected pressure? Was he expected to have brought an entire duplicate cart along with him in his back pocket?

It would have been just as easy for David to explode and yell at his older brother for not keeping the cart on the road and out of the pothole in the first place.

Hadn't Roger ever heard that an ounce of prevention is worth a pound of cure?

If truth be known, the strain of the journey and the heat from the desert sun were just as responsible for these roadside tensions.

David knew it was useless to get into a screaming match with Roger in the middle of the road. That wouldn't fix the cart any sooner, and it sure wouldn't help sibling relations any.

Needing some cooling off time from his brother, David hitched a ride into Phoenix, where he found a bike shop with the required parts.

81

Getting to and from the shop took most of the day, and by the time the cart was up and running again, they were only able to travel a total of six miles for the day.

They spent the night in Liberty, Arizona, sleeping in the yard of a local general store. It wasn't necessarily a night of peaceful slumber.

While David could only imagine what his brother was thinking, he knew he was still upset that Roger had blamed him personally for the delay.

If he had had any other place to go, David seriously would have considered leaving the entire mess right there in the desert, with his older sibling screaming and ranting at the tumbleweeds. Let the coyotes listen to his howling.

It would have been just as easy for him to have hitchhiked back towards California and never look back.

While Roger had Mary to give him support and comfort, David was all by himself, doing his best to keep the team moving, despite all odds.

There were certainly several decades' worth of sibling baggage at play in the desert. Roger was, and always would be, the older brother. He knew what buttons to push and wasn't hesitant to use them when it was to his advantage.

The journey was hard enough for David with Roger peacefully by his side, but when the brothers were fighting and squabbling, it just made things even more difficult.

David kept reminding himself he wasn't a quitter. Never had been. He knew this journey was going to be a challenge, and he accepted that. He just didn't think that Roger had to go out of his way to make everything personal.

Family matters. David knew this. He just had to wonder if Roger felt the same way.

Maybe the next day would bring about some new attitudes.

David drifted off to sleep, counting his blessings that the cart hadn't broken apart on them coming down Telegraph Hill. He could only imagine how Roger would have twisted that disaster into being his fault.

Chapter 16: By The Time They Got To Phoenix, They Were Waiting

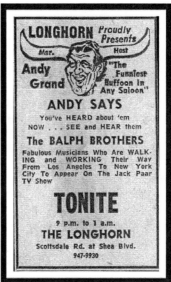

Featured on Cover of Hotel Guide in Phoenix and in Ad for Andy Grand and The Longhorn

Mary's advance promotional skills were continuing to pay off.

She had arranged news coverage from television station KTAR in Phoenix, which was a pretty big deal, by far the biggest media coverage since they left Los Angeles.

Unfortunately, they were on the outskirts of Phoenix on Friday, and the film crew couldn't interview them until Monday.

Once again, their Guardian Angels provided relief.

A fan at one of their shows at the Stardust Hotel back in Yuma had told them to give him a call when they neared Phoenix, and they did just that.

The fan was a gentleman by the name of Walter Ashbury of the Valley National Bank. He fixed them up with a guest apartment for their stay, solving one of their most pressing problems.

83

So they spent the weekend relaxing and regrouping.

They attended services on Sunday at the St. Augustine Church in Tempe and continued to count their blessings and ask for continued support along their journey.

Monday arrived with unseasonably cold weather for late September.

Among other things, the drop in temperature chilled the television station's interest in the cart and The Big Walk.

After walking 195 miles out of their way to Phoenix, waiting all weekend as requested by the news crew, they found out the station had moved on to other stories and had no intention of covering their story or interviewing The Brothers.

Roger had to wonder if their sudden lack of interest was motivated by powers that be in New York City.

To say that he was disappointed and discouraged is stating it mildly.

At least he couldn't blame this latest setback on David.

It was just another part of the process.

Roger had to keep reminding himself that nobody ever told them it would be easy.

Mary took each defeat very personally, and this time was no exception. She realized how important media coverage was to the success of the trip and the true survival of The Brothers, but there were so many things that were completely beyond her control.

She had to constantly fight to keep going, refusing to allow rejection or doubts get in her way. This wasn't some hobby she had taken up to pass the time away. She had left everything behind in California and was risking just as much or more than The Brothers. She was committed to doing her best until their triumphant stroll into Jack Paar's Big Apple studios.

She scrambled to get any coverage she could find in Phoenix.

She was able to arrange a ten-minute interview on KOR Radio.

She also got them on The Sherri Chessen television talk show, a fifteen-minute show in the afternoons. The interview was very entertaining and pleasant.

Sherri Chessen Interview

Tragically, Sherri had made national headlines due to her innocently taking prescribed Thalidomide while pregnant, which caused severe birth defects in her unborn baby. She went to Switzerland for a legalized abortion. She subsequently lost her main job at the television station, as the host of Romper Room.

Mary was also quite successful in generating newspaper coverage for The Brothers. All three of the major daily papers in Phoenix wrote features, devoting considerable space to the journey.

She also had decent luck with the local radio stations, so the loss of the television coverage was somewhat offset.

They still didn't have any paying gigs, which was somewhat unexpected, given their previous success at booking performances on the road.

Once again, their Angels came to the rescue, this time in the guise of another banker. Mr. Eberg offered them a paying concert at a party for The Phoenix Home Builders Association. The job paid $100 for a 20-minute performance.

As usual, the audience of 150 area builders loved The Brothers and demanded several encores before allowing them to leave the stage.

They had hoped the owner of the Smoke House Restaurant where they performed for the Builders would be so impressed by their musical talents that he would offer them additional work.

It didn't happen.

While the owner went out of his way to tell them how great they were and how much he had enjoyed their numbers, he didn't offer them anything other than good luck on the road.

The Brothers were starting to get the feeling the big city of Phoenix was more like cold-hearted big city Los Angeles than its friendly Arizona neighbors.

They found themselves in the classic impossible situation they had faced back home. In order to get jobs, they had to have a name, and, paradoxically, in order to get a name in the business, they had to get jobs.

The media exposure had been good for the scrapbooks, but it wasn't putting any food in their mouths.

Granted, they still had at least 70 pounds of their promotional dehydrated food packs, so they wouldn't starve...for a while, but it sure did make them fondly remember the genuine hospitality of the good folks back in Yuma.

Just when things were looking pretty bleak, they had another bit of bad news hit them right where it hurts.

Their deal for free rooms with Travelodge came to an end.

While their precious mother had arranged for the rooms in exchange for constant promotions at concerts, and mentions in every radio, television and newspaper interview, she hadn't gotten the commitment written down in the form of a legally binding contract.

Big mistake.

While their mother had operated on a basis of trust and goodwill, the longer they were on the road, and the further they ventured from Los Angeles, the less meaning the deal seemed to have with the corporation's executives.

In Phoenix, they discovered the deal was no longer worth the paper it wasn't written on, and there was nothing they could do.

Roger had felt this possibility coming for a while. It seemed the unwritten rules had been changing on them a few weeks earlier when one of the Travelodges was only willing to give them $50 worth of trade-out rooms for their stay. Instead of being supportive that their reception in the town had generated extended performing engagements, the motel management seemed to resent the fact that The Brothers were still in need of a roof over their heads.

So their association with Travelodge officially came to an end. While The Brothers were deeply appreciative of the kindness and lodging that the company had provided them, their traveling wasn't over by any means. They were still only one state over from California, and not even a fifth of the way to their final destination.

Remembering their constant motto of "find a way," Roger met with the promotion manager of Ramada Inns, a leading motel chain that just happened to be based in Phoenix.

Since most of their inns also had restaurants and lounges, Roger felt it would be a natural fit for The Brothers to perform at selected Ramada Inns along the route, in exchange for the modest promotional costs of a decent room at each stop. They could earn survival money by entertaining the guests of the restaurants, and then enjoy the sleeping comforts of the Inns each night.

Things had seemed to be working towards a signed contract. Then the executive asked if they had a firm commitment to appear on Jack Paar's Show when they arrived in New York City.

That's when things hit a rub. Roger couldn't lie to the man. While he didn't want to tell him that Jack Paar had been downright negative about the entire Big Walk from the very beginning, he couldn't alter the truth. All the motel executive would have had to do was pick up the phone and call Paar's office, and the truth would be known.

Then he asked Roger why they were even messing around with trying to be on Jack Paar's little television show.

The executive then stated he thought it made more sense to contact Ed Sullivan. Ed's show was much more popular by far, and he regularly booked musical performers on his telecasts. And hadn't Roger just told him about how he had performed on one of Ed's shows in the Fifties when he was in the military band?

At that moment Roger felt the sarcasm building in his voice.

He told Roger if he already had a commitment to be on Sullivan's show, Ramada Inn would be glad to sponsor The Big Walk all the way to New York City, and beyond. Roger knew this man would have a very hard time making his actions back up his big mouth.

Roger accepted the challenge and told him to call Ed Sullivan. If he would get him to guarantee The Brothers a shot on his show they would walk to his studio instead of Paar's.

Roger was surprised when the executive actually picked up his phone and told the company operator to get Ed Sullivan on the phone!

It ended up that he blew the operator's mind with his request, and together their call got about as far as the outside telephone pole.

They discovered what The Walking Musical Balph Brothers already knew all too well. It isn't so easy getting booked on national television shows, even if you do have your own executive operator place the call.

With the gauntlet thrown down, Roger had responded to the challenge as best he could, but once again, it was not to be.

Mary, hearing the news of facing yet another brick wall, turned her attentions to securing any kind of paying gig possible.

Phoenix was turning out to be a hard nut to crack.

Maybe there was a reason that town was named for the mythical bird rising out of the ashes.

Mary had certainly seen her share of burnt contracts in town, what with the failure of the promised television coverage and the aborted motel deals. Now she was waiting for the promised renewal from the ashes of defeat.

Salvation came in the form of a gentleman by the name of Andy Grand, owner of Andy Grand's Longhorn in Scottsdale.

Mr. Grand had patiently listened to Mary's pitch about The Brothers, and while he was somewhat skeptical about the musical talents of anybody pushing a cart across the desert, he was persuaded to take a chance and sign a contract. While there is no telling how much flirting Mary had to do to get the job, Roger was very thankful for her devotion and efforts.

Finally having a paying gig to perform, The Brothers left their guest apartment, generously provided by the kindly banker, and pushed the cart right through downtown Phoenix during the middle of the five o'clock rush hour.

The performances at the Longhorn were just as successful as all of the previous engagements.

Mr. Grand admitted that The Brothers were master musicians, able to please his customers, and worth every penny he paid them.

Mary was thankful to be able to add his name to the growing list of satisfied club owners. Every name on the chart helped to make her job just a little bit easier down the road. One thing she had learned about the entertainment business was that it was a small community of people who knew everybody and everything. A solid endorsement from a successful club owner like Andy Grand in Scottsdale or John Hunt back in Gila Bend went a long way with fellow owners. That is why every performance was always important. Good news travels, but bad news flies. That was one thing she never had to worry about with The Brothers. Regardless of the size of the audience, or the condition of the venue, once Roger and David hit the stage, they always gave each and every song their very best. Roger would dazzle the crowds with his flying fingers, and David would attack his golden trumpet until his lips bled.

Mary's constant challenge was getting The Brothers onstage so they could prove their worth and conquer all doubts.

The Brothers had their first encounter with a hoax while performing at the Longhorn. During their Thursday night concert, a call came in for them around 11:00 p.m.

A man by the name of Anderson was on the phone, claiming to be an attorney for Jack Paar. He wanted The Brothers to meet him the following morning at room 302 of the Safari Hotel.

On the way back to their guest lodging after the show, The Brothers stopped by the Safari and asked the desk clerk about the occupants of room 302.

At first the desk clerk wasn't very helpful. After Roger gave him the details of the mysterious phone call, the hotel employee finally revealed that two ladies had occupied room 302 for the last two years, and he was pretty certain that they didn't have anything to do with Jack Paar or show business.

The Brothers decided the entire deal was a hoax. What they couldn't decide was if it was a harmless prank or something more sinister. While they would never know what would have happened if they had gone to the room at the time requested, it did enter their mind that they might have been robbed, shot, or even worse.

The world is full of people up to no good, and Roger and David had certainly met their share of them over the years.

Giving it one more benefit of the doubt, they did call the hotel the next morning, paging the infamous Mr. Anderson.

Mr. Anderson never answered the phone, and was never heard from again.

On Friday, October 18th, The Brothers performed again at the Longhorn.

A fan by the name of Phil Stone was at the show, and after the performance, he had The Brothers over to his home near the restaurant. Over drinks, he made them a business offer, wanting to buy a sponsorship into the trip.

This was a new wrinkle on things.

While they had taken financial support in the form of the tape machine, the dehydrated food, the donated signs on the side of the cart, and even the occasional free night's sleep at a cooperating Travelodge, this was something new.

Mr. Stone was willing to partner up with The Brothers, provide them with a sum of spending money and support, in return for a piece of the entire endeavor. He fully understood the scope and national implications of The Big Walk, grasping how they had a tiger by the tail that could be ridden straight to the top of the entertainment world.

Once again, the famous Balph Pride entered the picture. Just like they had been forced to decline a free ride in the back of that truck in the middle of the desert a few weeks earlier, they had to turn down this offer from Mr. Stone.

They were determined to make it on their own, and that didn't include selling off part of their future glory and earnings at this point of the journey.

By Sunday, David had already forgotten Mr. Stone's offer and was enjoying his day off from performing at the Longhorn by having a date with yet another fan from the club.

There were certain continuing fringe benefits for being very famous in a very small area, and David deeply appreciated that aspect of the journey.

David had noticed how many of the fans in the area wore Western clothing, including elaborate bolo ties featuring turquoise stones and detailed silver work.

A lady at one of the shows owned the gift shop at the Westward Ho Hotel, and she invited The Brothers to visit her the next day.

Taking her up on her kind offer, The Brothers were told to pick out their favorite bolo tie clasp from the rack of merchandise on display.

David picked out one with the face of an Indian constructed out of polished woods, silver, and the ever-present turquoise.

Roger took a liking to a similarly constructed version of an eagle.

The shop owner told them the pieces were theirs, a gift from her to them for their fine musical performances.

David was deeply appreciative for this kind gesture, and told the lady that she was being much too generous.

She refused to take a penny for the ties, only asking that The Brothers wear them as often as possible when they were performing, and to think of her and their days in Arizona.

Proud of their New Bolo Ties

When they got back to their room, David took a closer look at the generous gifts. Thinking they had probably sold for five or six dollars each, you can imagine his total shock when he turned the pieces over and found the price tags still attached.

Roger's eagle was priced at $67.50, while his Indian was marked $89.50!

The generosity of the kindly shop owner was almost overwhelming.

David made a point of mentioning his benefactor at as many performances as possible the rest of the journey.

On Monday, October 28th, The Brothers stopped at the local post office to pick up their mail. General Delivery was the one and only reliable way for them to get letters and packages from their mother back home. David kept her informed by phone or post card of the towns and cities ahead where mail could be sent for them to pick up as they passed through. They always left a forwarding address so any missed mail would be sent to the various future locations.

While picking up another batch of mail, they bumped into a man named George Sarris, whom they had met back at the Travelodge in El Centro, California.

In the time they had been on the road, making their trip to New York, George had taken a job as manager at the Cornet Hotel in Phoenix.

When he found out The Brothers were playing at the Longhorn, he immediately booked them to perform at his hotel during their off-nights.

The night of their first performance at the Cornet had been very successful for The Brothers, and more importantly, for the hotel. The bar receipts for the lounge were up an amazing 60 percent, and George could not have been happier.

The next day the hotel had 22 phone calls from fans wanting to know when The Brothers were performing onstage.

That night the club was so packed with fans, The Brothers hardly had room to stand on the stage.

This was exactly the kind of promotional ammunition Mary needed for her press kits. Nothing makes a club owner happier than an act that can bring in drinking customers who are willing to spend money.

It had taken a while to find their moment in the Phoenix spotlight, but things were certainly looking more promising with each passing day.

Things were going just as well for them at The Longhorn. The owner, Andy Grand, kept extending their contract.

Just like their friend at the Cornet Hotel, Mr. Grand was able to see the tangible monetary proof of The Brothers' popularity when he added up each night's sales.

On October 29th, The Brothers had packed their bags, given up their guest lodging, and were officially on the road to Tucson, the next stop on their journey.

They were passing through Apache Junction when a police officer stopped them on the road and insisted that they push the cart backwards for safety reasons.

Apache Junction's major claim to fame was the fact every building had to be built out of redwood in the Western style. The entire town looked like a souped-up version of a Hollywood movie studio's Wild West back lot.

The misguided law official asserted it would be much safer if The Brothers turned their backs to the cart, put their hands behind them, and pushed so they could be facing the oncoming traffic behind them.

To put it quite bluntly, his concept was a stupid idea.

If anything, it would make the cart unable to control, and serve absolutely no purpose, other than to boost the ego of the misinformed policeman.

Roger politely informed the public official, while it was pretty hard to push a 1,000-pound cart forward, it would be next to impossible to do it backwards.

He then invited the uniformed enforcer of Arizona laws to show them how to do it.

Realizing it was easier said than done, the policeman rolled up the window of his patrol car, and drove away.

Having survived yet another encounter with the law, The Brothers buckled down to pushing and then pushing some more.

Soon the warm kindness of the fans of the Longhorn and the Cornet would be fading memories.

Or so they thought.

As it turned out, their popularity was too compelling.

Andy Grand had sent word to Mary that he wanted The Brothers back for another two weeks, and he wouldn't take no for an answer.

Once again, the lure of a steady paycheck proved too tempting to turn down.

Despite their best efforts to keep on pushing towards New York City, they kept getting delayed by the realities of the road.

While being offered more money for more performances was better than those times when the delay was caused because the cart was broken or the wheels were bent, the end result was just the same.

Their six-month journey was starting to look like a trip of several years, with too many side trip distractions to even calculate.

Towards the end of their return engagement at the Longhorn, their trusty Ampex tape machine stopped working in the middle of the show. Roger was able to coax it into working long enough for the final song, and then it died.

On Friday, November 1st, The Brothers almost met their first real celebrity since leaving Los Angeles. Frank Sinatra, Jr., came into the Longhorn to see his old friend, Andy Grand. He was performing at the nearby Arizona State Fair and dropped in to catch up on news and share a few drinks. Unfortunately, it happened to be The Brothers' day off.

When Andy told Frank, Jr., about The Big Walk, he was almost speechless. It seemed as if he couldn't fathom any musicians going to such lengths to be discovered or understand the dedication it took to make that first step so many miles back in California.

The Brothers didn't learn about Frank, Jr.'s reaction until the next day.

David later had plenty of time to think about what might have been if they had only been performing that night.

Could the son of Ole Blue Eyes, Mr. Sinatra, one of the world's most famous and successful performers, have helped their cause? Even on his own, Frank, Jr., was a pretty successful entertainer in his own right. Could he have aided their career? Maybe flown them directly to Jack Paar's studio on his private airliner? At the very least, he certainly could have picked up the phone and cut through layers and layers of red tape and roadblocks in New York City.

For that matter, forget about New York City. If Frank, Jr., had seen them perform, he could have hired them as his opening act at the Arizona State Fair. They could have joined him on his tours around the country. They could have warmed up those audiences just like they did at the Longhorn.

David could hear the applause in his mind. All he had to do was take the crowd reactions from the Longhorn and multiply it by a hundred times.

Frank, Jr., could have introduced them to the Rat Pack and let them entertain Sammy and Dino and, of course, Frankie. Once those guys had heard the Balphs' performance, there could have been no stopping them. Mary would have to fight off the offers with a stick. David could see their names in lights. If Frank, Jr., had only seen them perform at the Longhorn, they could soon have been headlining at casinos all over Las Vegas, America, Europe... for that matter, the entire world.

David could only imagine.

Chapter 17: Fast Cars, Shouting Preacher, Beer Bath, and Escaped Cons

Reluctantly accepting the fact that Frank Sinatra, Jr., had flown away without them, The Brothers went back to doing what they had to do...push and then push some more.

November 7th found them going past Florence, Arizona.

They were busy minding their own business, keeping the cart out of the ditches while continuing to push and strain and push some more.

Suddenly five cars traveling in a caravan flew by them at a high rate of speed.

Swoosh, and then they were gone.

The Brothers kept pushing and pushing some more.

A short time later, the same five cars came flying pass them, going the opposite direction.

The Brothers chalked it up to more desert weirdness, and kept on pushing the cart.

Then for yet a third time, the same thing happened. Same five cars. Same five guys driving. Same high rate of speed. Swoosh. Zoom. And poof, they were gone in a flash, leaving a trail of dust in the air for The Brothers to inhale.

Were they making illegal runs of unknown substances in the middle of the desert? Moonshine? Weapons? Forbidden fruits from across the border? Maybe it was part of some secret government intelligence operation that the general public wasn't supposed to know about.

Whatever they were doing and wherever they were going, it sure wasn't taking them very long to make their deliveries.

Roger had to believe that it would have made much more sense to just put whatever these five guys were hauling down the road into one big truck and be done with it. It would certainly have saved considerable time and large amounts of money. The illogical nature of their efforts convinced him even more that the government must have had something to do with it. How else could they justify such waste?

These men were burning rubber with a vengeance, and it was almost insulting to The Brothers how they continually flaunted their speed back and forth while Roger and David struggled to cover three miles an hour at best.

Roger was tired of eating their dust over and over and over.

When Roger spied the cars heading back towards them for yet a fourth time, it was more than he could handle.

He stood by the side of the road, waving his arms in an effort to get the mysterious vehicles to slow down long enough to provide some needed answers.

Evidently the driver of the lead car had some questions of his own in mind, because the cars pulled over, allowing The Brothers to approach them.

After the usual round of questions about the fact that they were pushing a 1,000-pound cart in the middle of the desert, The Brothers asked their own questions about the steady repeating stream of speeding cars.

As it turned out, the caravan belonged to Gates Tire Company, and the purpose of their short, high-speed, repetitive fly-bys was to test out new tires to see how they handled the intense road conditions of the Arizona desert.

Mystery solved.

It is amazing how logical things are when you know the reasons.

So much for top-secret missions or illegal transports.

Soon, The Brothers were back to being alone with their cart in the middle of nowhere, pushing and pushing some more.

Another car drove pass them and then pulled over to the side of the road.

A well-intentioned Evangelical preacher by the name of John Denmark introduced himself and wished The Brothers good luck.

He then bowed his head and started to pray for The Brothers. And boy, oh boy, did that preacherman pray. Right in the middle of the road. Oblivious to everything around him. He was shouting enough to knock down the walls of Jericho.

He prayed and he prayed and he prayed, each round of blessings a little louder and more energetic than the previous one.

He blessed the trees. He blessed the land they were standing on. He blessed the cows in the fields, the birds in the sky, the fish in the rivers. He blessed the rain, the rocks, the cactus.

Then he started blessing the cart, the tires, the wheels, the spokes, and every other part he could name.

David's leg was starting to fall asleep, and Roger was just praying that the praying would soon be over.

Yet the prayers continued. Prayers for the family back home. Prayers for the people they had met along the way. Prayers for the people they were going to meet on up the road.

He was very loud and very thorough. If he was leaving anybody out of his prayers, odds are they didn't matter, or exist.

While the preacherman was getting his second and third wind, Roger nudged David to start pushing the cart, signaling him to be as quiet as possible.

They left the man still shouting out prayers in the middle of the road, hoping they would be out of sight by the time he opened his eyes. They were betting that he would be too winded from all of that hollering to chase them down the road.

When he finally realized they were well out of range, he yelled after them, asking one simple question: "Have you been saved?"

They would have to save that answer for another time. The Brothers were off and running, or at least walking as fast as two people can while pushing a 1,000-pound cart.

They continued to push as hard and fast as possible to put as much distance between them and the preacherman as humanly possible.

They passed the imposing Arizona State Prison, wondering what the rifle-toting watchmen in the guard towers must have thought when they saw their cart slowly cross their lines of vision.

Ten miles down the road, an Arizona State Trooper stopped them to inform The Brothers that a desperate hard-core convict serving a lifetime sentence had broken out of the prison.

After inspecting every inch of the cart and their supplies, the Trooper was satisfied that the newly freed convict had evidently found a faster means of escape than by hitching a slow-moving ride with The Walking Musical Balph Brothers.

Roger thought about mentioning the fact they were carrying two loaded shotguns and a pistol for their own protection, but figured the Trooper had enough on his mind to bother him with more distractions.

The Trooper showed them a mugshot of the escaped felon, warned them to be on the lookout, and went on down the road in hot pursuit.

No sooner had the Trooper's dust settled than another car drove by.

At first, David thought it was another patrol car, looking for the escapee, but turns out it was a car filled with beer-drinking teenagers out joyriding and looking for trouble.

Just as they passed the cart, one of those fine, upstanding future leaders of America tossed a full opened can of beer out of the car window.

It soaked both of The Brothers.

Adding insult to injury, the wet beer mixed with the dust from the road, and turned their faces into dripping, muddy messes.

Fortunately for David, even in his moment of extreme disgust and humiliation, he had the presence of mind to memorize the license number of the drunken teenagers' hotrod.

Ten minutes later, another Arizona State Trooper passed by, in search of the missing inmate, giving David the opportunity to report the activities of the alcoholic can-throwing mob of teenagers that had just attacked them.

The Trooper radioed ahead to the roadblock hoping to capture the convict, and in an extremely satisfying moment of desert justice, the police were able to arrest the booze-bombing pack of juvenile delinquents for driving under the influence and disorderly conduct.

David would have loved to have been there to see their faces when they were arrested. In those decades prior to cellphones and instant communications, he was certain the teens had no idea how a pair of walkers pushing a cart in the middle of nowhere had been able to get word to the arresting officers in such a short amount of time.

Maybe it truly was a good thing they hadn't given in to their temptation back up the road at the cattle feedlot and actually shot one of those meals-on-the-hoof.

You just never know who might be watching you, whether you are throwing a beer can at a cart in the middle of the desert or mildly thinking about putting a few slugs in the hindquarters of some cows by the side of a railroad track.

Roger and David didn't need any more proof that it paid to follow The Golden Rule, even out in the middle of absolutely nowhere.

Arizona State Prison in Florence

Chapter 18: Putting Out and Smashing Pianos

Tidelands Motel in Tucson

While The Brothers were busy running from a shouting preacher and taking beer can showers near the Arizona State Prison, Mary had finished up her last details in Phoenix, and driven on to Tucson to work on securing more publicity and paying gigs.

She arranged for The Brothers to perform at the Tucson Elks Club the following Saturday.

Having that one solid booking confirmed, she then started working on filling up the rest of the days leading to the weekend.

She approached the manager of The Tidelands Motel.

This fine upstanding booker of promising talent listened to her pitch about the musical abilities of The Brothers. He seemed to be impressed with her expanding collection of glowing newspaper clippings. He read the letters of endorsement from previously satisfied club owners, and noticed their enthusiastic testimonials proclaiming how much their sales had picked up due to the Balphs' professional entertainment.

Sure, he would be glad to book The Musical Walking Balph Brothers, but only with one small addition to close the pitch.

Sex. Specifically, sex with Mary.

The man wanted Mary to join him on his casting couch in the adjoining motel. He wanted her to 'swing' in bed with him, to use his oh-so romantic come-on phrase.

Now Mary wasn't a prude, and this certainly wasn't her first time to the rodeo, to use some appropriate Western lingo; she just had to walk the fine line of flirting with the booker, holding out the promise of delivering on her part of the deal, without ultimately coming through with her feminine goodies compromised.

While she didn't kill the deal by giving the would-be Romeo a flat out humiliating rejection, she also didn't commit to anything beyond a very conditional and non-specific "maybe."

The sweaty-palmed lounge manager could enjoy his fantasies from a distance, while The Brothers proved their worth by performing three shows at his establishment.

When the crowds showed their approval by filling seats and buying drinks, the manager accepted reality and soothed his damaged libido with a cash register full of tens and twenties.

The following night was Tuesday, November 18th.

The Brothers had three more shows scheduled at The Tidelands.

While working on arranging their equipment on the crowded stage, they had to move the lounge's grand piano to the corner.

Just like gravity had attacked the front wheel on their cart back in Los Angeles, causing it to crash in a heap before their eyes, the wheel on the front of the huge wooden piano came off, sending the heavy musical instrument crashing off the stage. It missed Roger's fragile golden saxophones by mere inches before clanging to a sudden stop on the dance floor.

The resulting heavy metal noises caused such a commotion in the nearby coffee shop that customers jumped straight out of their chairs, spilling hot coffee on their business suits.

Had The Brothers' instruments been damaged, the trip would have ended right then and there.

While they were able to survive their bout with the crashing piano, Roger wasn't so lucky in his battle with food poisoning. It had hit him right in the gut during the middle of one of their performances. His fever hit, causing him to break out in such a sweat that it looked like somebody had thrown a bucket of water on him.

By the next day, waiting for Roger to recover, David decided he couldn't wait any longer to retrieve the cart from outside of Tucson, where they had stored it while performing at the Tidelands.

Mary drove him the eleven miles out to where the cart was stored. While they had removed the musical instruments from the cart in order to perform at the lounge, it was still loaded down with their tent, camping supplies, food, and other essentials.

It also didn't help that it was pouring down rain, literally attempting to drown David as he struggled down the road, pushing and then pushing some more.

It was hard enough doing the task as a duo, much less attacking the puddles and the miles in the middle of a thunderstorm.

If only they hadn't missed that meeting with Frank Sinatra, Jr....

David tried to look at the bright side of things as he sloshed and slipped his way to Tucson, but his eyes kept filling up with rainwater.

A lesser man might have been tempted to give up, stomping his way back to civilization, but once again, David had to find a way.

One step at a time.

They would need to have the cart in town with them in order to get their next round of publicity.

The clubs wanted the famous cart to be parked in front of their establishments, bringing in thirsty customers from near and far.

So David did his brotherly duty and pushed the cart to the edge of town, just as the sun was going down.
The rain had finally stopped.

Roger was able to get out of bed and meet David just in time to make the final push into the spotlights of Tucson, thereby sharing their moments of fame. The local NBC television station covered the event for the local newscast.

A radio station had them push the cart seventeen more blocks to the local record store. They followed behind The Brothers in a specially equipped automobile, doing a live broadcast, announcing their location with each step.

By the time they reached the store, a large and growing crowd had joined the journey, taking photos and asking questions.

While Roger was still suffering with a raging fever, and David was exhausted from his solo push across the desert, hundreds of adoring, screaming fans shared the excitement of being near such famous show business celebrities.

This was exactly what The Walking Musical Balph Brothers had been planning all those months ago in their mother's apartment back in Los Angeles.

It was so overwhelming that David didn't even give Frank Sinatra, Jr., a second thought.

Chapter 19: The President Dies and A Nation Mourns

Friday, November 22nd, started out like every other day in the desert. The sun came up, and Tucson stirred itself out of the previous night's slumber.

The business of daily living functioned as always, until around 11:30 a.m. Mountain time.

Everything changed once The Brothers went downstairs at the Tidelands Motor Inn for a noontime lunch. All of the customers in the coffee shop had their eyes glued to the television set, following every word of the reporters.

President John F. Kennedy had been shot while visiting Dallas, and in those first confusing minutes, people weren't sure of his condition.

Women, men, and children were openly sobbing, anxiously hanging on to every word, every update, praying for a miracle.

Less than an hour after the initial announcement of the shooting, White House officials announced that the 35th President of the United States of America had died.

It was a moment seared into the minds and hearts of every one of the nation's millions and millions of concerned citizens, regardless of political persuasion.

Roger and David were just as crushed and heart-broken as all the other customers in the coffee shop. An immense feeling of loss and despair engulfed the room, the motor inn, the nation.

The Brothers had been motivated by President Kennedy's renowned advocacy for physical fitness as part of their desire to make The Big Walk in the first place.

They had previously watched White House staffer Pierre Salinger on television, promoting the idea of walking to keep fit, and had decided if an office-bound civil servant could make the effort, two able-bodied, military-trained musical brothers could certainly attempt the same goals.

Even from their initial planning of The Big Walk, they had always planned on routing the journey through the nation's capital, making a triumphant pass in front of the White House on the way to the Big Apple.

In their most optimistic moments, they saw themselves meeting President Kennedy, and, in the best of all possible situations, having the leader of the Free World help them push their cart a few yards in testimony to the advantages of physical fitness.

That became another dream that would never be realized.

The night's performance was cancelled, along with all the rest of the events in the city.

People were too stunned to talk. The motor inn was filled with people watching the assorted television sets in total silence. They were just going through the motions of living, with their hearts and minds focused on the horror of the day's events.

People were starved for any information, trying to make rational sense of what was a totally senseless act.

President Kennedy was dead.

Vice-President Lyndon B. Johnson, who had been riding only two cars behind the nation's slain leader in the Dallas motorcade, was sworn in as the new leader of the nation at 1:38 p.m. Mountain time, while flying back to Washington D.C. aboard Air Force One.

Even though Lee Harvey Oswald had been arrested in Dallas an hour and 20 minutes after the shooting, he wasn't arrested for killing President Kennedy, but for shooting a police officer named J. D. Tippit, who had unfortunately bumped into Oswald on the street moments after the attack.

It wouldn't be until later in the evening that Oswald would be charged with the assassination of John F. Kennedy; so, in addition to coping with the stunning death of the nation's leader, people worried that the shooter was still on the loose, living as a free man.

The idea of playing their usual energetic concert of rousing Dixieland Jazz tunes didn't seem quite as appealing to The Brothers.

While the nation would gradually recover and heal, finding answers, making changes, and growing ever stronger, this night in Tucson was spent in tearful reflection, with heartfelt prayers going out to the Kennedy family specifically and the United States of America, in general.

Chapter 20: David's 24th Birthday

The day after the president's death just happened to be David's 24th birthday. Unfortunately, there wasn't much celebrating that day in Tucson or the rest of the nation.

While the enormity of the previous day's tragedy numbed millions around the globe, the manager of the Tidelands Motor Inn demanded that The Brothers perform their scheduled Saturday night show.

Evidently canceling Friday night's performance was the extent of the manager's consideration for the events in Dallas.

Most of the rest of the clubs in town followed a three-day moratorium policy, staying closed through Monday's funeral, a day of national mourning.

Not the Tidelands.

Following the traditional entertainment wisdom that the show must go on, Roger and David reluctantly took to the stage, and did their best to provide an evening of rousing musical entertainment.

Since they were performing with their backing prerecorded tapes on the Ampex player, they couldn't alter the order of their show. It was truly the first time in either brother's memory that their usual show stopper, "Tiger Rag" had ever seemed so totally inappropriate. Enough to make them feel the necessity to apologize to the audience for the style of music they had no control over, but were required under contract to perform. Visiting with the audience between selections to announce the upcoming song under the present circumstances, was the hardest thing they both had to do since leaving Los Angeles.

Roger and Mary tried their best to persuade the manager to call off the night's performance, but his logic fell on deaf ears.

Since all of the other clubs in town were still shut down out of respect for the nation's fallen president, the manager of the Tidelands saw the situation as a moment to be taken advantage of. He reasoned, or at least convinced himself, that the hordes of regular Saturday night music lovers and party-seekers would still be thirsty and hungry for a good time. And where would they go if all the other places were closed?

In his mind, it was his patriotic duty to be open on Saturday night, for the good of the city.

He was, first and foremost, a businessman.

All the manager truly seemed to be concerned about was hearing the sounds of his cash register ringing into the night.

While the lounge was filled with the usual assortment, the mood of the crowd could not have been more somber.

People were out in public, but lost in their inner thoughts. They drank their martinis and shots of whisky and just stared at the stage.

At the end of each song, there was an initial complete silence in a room full of customers, with one or two fans finally clapping half-heartedly, more out of habit than with any conviction.

More than a few were seen wiping tears from their eyes, still trying to make sense of the senseless violence.

It was simply not a night for spirited Dixieland music.

After what seemed like an eternity, the evening finally came to an end.

David went to sleep that night hoping he never had to perform in any similar circumstances the rest of his life.

While his 24th birthday had been one of the most memorable ones, it wasn't a night he ever wanted to repeat.

He would have to wait for another day in happier times for his birthday cake.

Chapter 21: Waiting for Wheels

Interview and Performance on KVOA's Dick Meyers Show

A week had passed since the death of the president.

Lee Harvey Oswald had been shot and killed two days after President Kennedy died. A Dallas nightclub owner named Jack Ruby fatally attacked him in the basement of the Dallas Police Headquarters while Oswald was being transported to The Dallas County Jail. The entire event was broadcast live on television, bringing another round of shock to a grieving nation.

Meanwhile, life continued, as people tried to get back to their normal daily duties and obligations.

The Brothers had appeared on KVOA television in Tucson, and finished up their contract with Tidelands Motor Inn.

They had ordered a set of heavy duty wheels for the cart, and spent the week waiting for their delivery.

While waiting, they heard about another family tragedy concerning one of their newly met friends back at John Hunt's Steakhouse.

The owner of the McCoy Chevrolet dealership in Gila Bend, his wife, and their two daughters were killed in a private plane crash.

The Brothers had proudly displayed the McCoy Chevrolet sticker on the side of their cart since leaving Gila Bend a hundred miles behind and were shocked to hear about yet another senseless loss.

Feeling that the shadow of death was perhaps too close, they moved out of town to a Texaco truck stop outside of Tucson, thinking their wheels would be delivered within a day or two.

The owner of the truck stop let Roger and David stay in the trucker bunk beds where the professional journeymen slept. They shared the large upstairs dormitory-style area with several dozen snoring, wheezing, and burping big-rig drivers. While it was certainly atmospheric, it made David and Roger long for the luxury of their private rooms back at the Travelodges.

As it turned out, the truck stop owner was a fan of music, and allowed The Brothers to turn one of his garages into a practice area.

Taking advantage of their unplanned wait for the new wheels, David struck up a friendship with one of the truck stop's secretaries.

Unlike his previous dates on The Big Walk, Lila hadn't heard a word about The Brothers or their cart or the fact that they were pushing their way to New York. She was not a fan. She didn't have any idea who David was.

David was surprised that she had been so out of touch with such vital news, especially since they had been performing in her own city. Even without being overwhelmed by his celebrity status, evidently she liked the way he looked in his walking garb.

In addition to being good company and a great date, she also had the distinct advantage of owning her own car, which she gladly provided as a taxi for David while waiting for the increasingly delayed wheels.

The weather had turned cold once December arrived, and The Brothers had encountered snow.

Having access to a car was a very attractive addition to the allure of Lila. The fact she made her car available when he needed it was a very nice aspect of their fleeting friendship.

The Brothers had come a long way from the heat and smog of Los Angeles in July, finding themselves approaching winter, freezing temperatures, sleet, snow storms, and possible blizzards in the desert.

As soon as the new wheels arrived, they would be back on the road, pushing and pushing some more.

David knew it would be hard to leave the comforts of the truck stop and the new friends they had made.

These were the times when the security of their known world made it just that much harder to load up the cart, say their goodbyes, and venture off into the unknown opportunities and possible dangers of The Big Walk.

In light of the recent random tragedies that had delivered such jolts of reality, Roger and David knew all too well how fragile life could be.

It was a time for renewed faith and focus, step by step.

But they weren't going anywhere until their new wheels arrived. It was another time for The Brothers to hurry up and wait.

Chapter 22: Best Shrimp Cocktail Ever

The new sturdier wheels, made for a sulky horse cart, were worth the wait. The Brothers had high hopes that the newest version would be able to handle the stress, bumps and jolts of the road much better than the original bicycle wheels that constantly broke spokes and bent rims.

Just as Roger and David were becoming more experienced and conditioned by their months on the journey, their cart was slowly, but surely, being improved and toughened up.

The Brothers had toughened up a bit by camping out in their tent for the first time. They found a spot behind a restaurant called The Stockyard, pitching their tent in the middle of the desert, surrounded by cacti as far as their eyes could see. They had slept in their clothes, inside their sleeping bags, and still almost froze. Knowing that there was a blazing fireplace only a few feet away inside the lobby of the restaurant certainly didn't offer Roger and David much comfort. Then there was the constant irritation of almost frozen rainwater dripping through a hole in the tent all night long. With winter approaching, they woke up to find snow covering their tent and cart.

The Brothers were certainly encountering everything Mother Nature had to throw at them on this Big Walk. From blazing oven-temperature heat and smog at the first of the journey, to rain, sandstorms, sleet, and now snow, Roger and David kept on pushing one step at a time.

The new wheels and tires promised to make the journey easier.

In the theory that the more air they put in the tires the better, they had forced 75 pounds of pressure into their new Goodyear white wall tires. These new slim lined marvels of rubber technology looked racy and classic, even when the cart wasn't moving. There had been some serious discussion about cramming 90 pounds of pressure in, but seeing as how the recommendation from the manufacture clearly stated that 20 pounds was enough, The Brothers had settled on being only four times over the limit.

It was a delicate balance. The higher the air pressure, the easier the job of pushing the cart became. They just had to live with the fact that the tires could blow out at any moment.

David just had to hope that the blow-outs happened on flat ground and not while they were coming down one of the high and long desert hills.

Mary secured a three-night gig at the Silver Spur Steak House in the next town up the road, Benson, Arizona.

The Brothers arrived to find thick, sizzling steaks waiting for them on the grill.

A local entertainer by the name of Blindman Pete was the regular performer at the restaurant. He played piano and flute, and was a legend in the area.

During their performances, Blindman Pete was led to the stage to introduce The Brothers. At the start of each show, Pete always said the same thing: that Roger and David had given Benson, Arizona, "a shot in the arm."

David had watched Pete while The Brothers were performing onstage, and he noticed how the blind musician smiled at the little riffs and musical moments that the normal drinking audience seemed to take for granted. It was obvious that Pete's lack of vision only increased his other senses, especially his ability to hear and decipher the various arrangements.

Pete had been amazed by the concept of using the backing tracks on the tape machine and took great delight in following the sophisticated orchestrations.

Blindman Pete's pure pleasure with the music had been an inspiration for David. Enough time had passed since the tragic events of November 22nd that the audience was starting to enjoy the music and clap along with the songs again.

Those sad, somber nights of tears in the audience and silence at the end of the songs were hopefully over and done with.

While Blindman Pete had certainly been one of their more positive memorable encounters, the one thing in Benson, Arizona, that made the biggest impression on David was the Silver Spur's wonderful shrimp cocktails. David simply could not get enough of them. They were the best things he had ever tasted in his entire life. David had gone so far as to beg the owner for the recipe for their amazing sauce. The secret ingredients were Mogen David wine and prepared mustard, and David thought that their sauce was the perfect combination, making their shrimp cocktails simply out of this world.

David would think about those wonderful morsels many, many times during the rest of The Big Walk.

In the middle of nowhere, completely out of the blue, right in the middle of yet another one of his millionth or so steps and pushes, David's mind would go back to those amazing shrimp cocktails, and he would relive the mental pleasure of those divine mouthfuls.

David made a promise to himself that once they made it to New York and national fame, he would find his way back to Benson, Arizona, and enjoy as many of those delightful culinary treats as his stomach could handle.

Until then, he would just have to savor the memories, lick his lips, and then push and push some more.

Chapter 23: Arizona Christmas High Balls

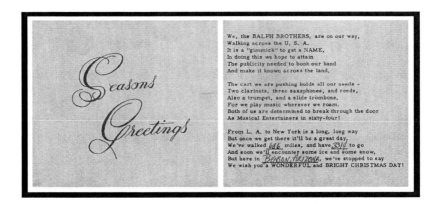

We, the BALPH BROTHERS, are on our way,
Walking across the U. S. A.
It is a "gimmick" to get a NAME,
In doing this we hope to attain
The publicity needed to book our band
And make it known across the land.

The cart we are pushing holds all our needs -
Two clarinets, three saxaphones, and reeds,
Also a trumpet, and a slide trombone,
For we play music wherever we roam.
Both of us are determined to break through the door
As Musical Entertainers in sixty-four!

From L. A. to New York is a long, long way
But once we get there it'll be a great day,
We've walked 686 miles, and have 2314 to go
And soon we'll encounter some ice and some snow,
But here in BENSON, ARIZONA, we've stopped to say
We wish you a WONDERFUL and BRIGHT CHRISTMAS DAY!

1963 Christmas Card

Their first Christmas on the road found The Brothers drinking high balls in Wilcox, Arizona, courtesy of a most unlikely source, the owners of the only motel in the town, a Travelodge.

Despite the fact that their promotional deal with the motel chain had fallen apart on them, the local owner, Mr. Williams, took matters into his own hands and almost adopted Roger and David as his own kin, insisting that they spend Christmas Day with his wife and family.

They were able to enjoy such luxuries as warm showers and clean beds for an entire week.

In return for the town's kindness, The Walking Musical Balph Brothers performed at The Women's Club for all of the school children in Wilcox. While drinking sodas and eating potato chips, the town's impressionable youth enjoyed what was most likely their first live concert of Dixieland Jazz.

A collection was taken up by the members of the Women's Club, raising $200 for The Brothers' survival fund.

Once again, the money couldn't have come at a better time.

After traveling about 80 miles on their pretty new white wall tires, the harsh Arizona road had ground the rubber down to the cords. The new sheen of their heavy-duty Sulky wheels was barely worn off, and now the tires were shredding like paper.

David had gone back to Tucson to the trustworthy Western Auto store to purchase some dependable Davis knobby tires. While they weren't as racy-looking as the glamorous white walls, they made up for their plain looks by lasting six times as long on the highway. Getting 500 miles out of a set, compared to only 80 miles with the white walls, made them almost worth their weight in gold to David.

The less time the tires were flat or needing to be changed, the better for The Balph Brothers.

The money from the Wilcox Women's Club also provided for the purchase of new zippers for the tent, allowing David and Roger to rapidly exit the tent from any side.

While using the tent in real world conditions, The Brothers had discovered a serious flaw in their sleeping arrangement. The way the tent was originally designed only allowed for them to go in and out of the tent on one end.

While trying to sleep in the desert cold in the middle of the true wilderness, it had occurred to The Brothers that the design put them at a serious disadvantage from potential threats or harassment.

All a potential attacker would have to do to completely overwhelm David and Roger in their slumber was pull out the stakes of the tent, allowing the entire structure to collapse on top of them. If that happened, The Brothers would have been trapped, unable to get to their shotguns or escape their canvas prison.

They would have truly been defenseless and at the total mercy of whoever or whatever was attacking them.

They had even toyed with the idea of sleeping in shifts, with one brother keeping watch while the other grabbed a few hours of shuteye, but all that accomplished was both of them having terrible nights of too little rest and too much stress.

Lord knows, there was already enough stress on the road as it was.

And while Roger and David wanted to see the best in everybody and had faith that their Guardian Angels would protect them in their times of need, they also didn't see any need in putting things to the test.

They had their shotguns, machetes, and pistol with them for good reason. Hadn't the nation's president, one of the most protected people on the entire planet, just been shot down and killed in cold blood?

116

It didn't seem too far-fetched to think that another mentally unbalanced person might find the idea of attacking such celebrities as The Walking Musical Balph Brothers as a ticket to spotlights and fame.

Hadn't Lee Harvey Oswald become known all over the planet for his sinister deeds?

They had already encountered more than their share of beer-throwing idiots and roadside harassing insulters before they even left California, so they knew all too well the dangers of the highway.

People went missing everyday, lost to the wilds of the desert, never to be seen again.

David was determined to provide as much security for The Brothers as possible. Buying those new zippers for the tent ranked right up there with buying new tires.

Being in Tucson also gave David the chance to provide Roger with another much-needed item of, if not survival, at least comfort.

With the money from the Woman's Club providing the means, David bought Roger a new air mattress.

His old mattress had a slow, but very steady leak in it. It would usually give out on Roger around 4 am, putting him on the hard frozen ground in zero degree weather. Sometimes Roger would try to just grin and bear it, literally taking his lumps as he found them. More often, he would locate the inflation nozzle near the pillow end and start blowing with all of his might until the sagging airbag responded.

The fact that Roger would inflate the mattress while still physically lying on top of it, only seemed to make the situation more difficult. Maybe it was his way of putting his years of musical training and excellent air control to good use. Or, possibly, he was just showing off. Or he might have simply been too tired and cold to bother getting out of his sleeping bag.

Regardless of the reason, it was as silly looking as it sounds.

If David gave in to his initial response of laughing at the insanity of the leaking desert moment, he risked making Roger even madder; so, he would usually just roll over on his firm, fully functioning, relatively comfortable mattress and stifle his chuckles.

Buying Roger a new air mattress improved the quality of living for both brothers, which was a very important aspect to be appreciated.

Anything that made life more tolerable on the road was worth consideration.

From sandstorms and insect bites to leg cramps and foot blisters, it was no wonder that simple things like zippers for the tent, an air mattress that didn't leak, and tires for the cart that lasted more than a few days of pushing would be considered the best Christmas presents possible.

Returned Christmas Card from Paar

The local radio station in Wilcox had The Brothers on the air two times in the week following Christmas, generating publicity for The Big Walk.

New Year's Eve found Roger, David, and Mary bringing in 1964 with the guests and owner of the Wilcox Travelodge. Long before the midnight hour, the local supply of hard liquor had been consumed. No bourbon, no vodka, not even a bottle of bubbly champagne was to be found. The crowd had to settle for bottles of beer as the final seconds of 1963 ticked away.

At midnight, everybody hollered, "Happy New Year!" Amid hugs, kisses, and rounds of cheers and toy-horn toots from their newly found hospitable Wilcox, Arizona, friends and supporters, The Brothers counted their blessings and reflected on their journey so far.

Roger, David, and Mary could only imagine what challenges and opportunities they would encounter during the next twelve months.

David prayed for good health and continued safe travels, and tires that didn't go flat every ten miles. He also prayed that his lips held up and that they never had to put the security of their new tent zippers to the test.

Mary prayed for decent club owners who offered real money-paying contracts and didn't expect any morally questionable fringe benefits from her. She also prayed that The Big Walk didn't kill all three of them before it was over.

Roger prayed that somebody with real clout in the music business would finally take notice of their talents and efforts on the road and make them a record deal they couldn't refuse. He also prayed that his new air mattress would be able to survive a night in the desert without springing a leak.

All three could only imagine what 1964 would throw at them, one step at a time.

Entertaining in Wilcox

Chapter 24: Train Keeps on Rolling

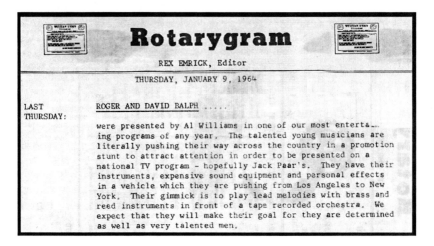

Rotarygram

REX EMRICK, Editor

THURSDAY, JANUARY 9, 1964

LAST THURSDAY:

ROGER AND DAVID BALPH .....

were presented by Al Williams in one of our most entert&...
ing programs of any year. The talented young musicians are
literally pushing their way across the country in a promotion
stunt to attract attention in order to be presented on a
national TV program - hopefully Jack Paar's. They have their
instruments, expensive sound equipment and personal effects
in a vehicle which they are pushing from Los Angeles to New
York. Their gimmick is to play lead melodies with brass and
reed instruments in front of a tape recorded orchestra. We
expect that they will make their goal for they are determined
as well as very talented men.

Rotary Club Publicity about Roger and David

Leaving Wilcox was the usual mixture of joy and sadness that occurred when it came time to hit the road. The Brothers were once again leaving the security and hospitality of their new friends, saying good-bye to decent people who had opened their hearts, homes, kitchens, and wallets to visiting musicians pushing a 1,000-pound cart through their town. Total strangers became lifelong friends within a matter of days, bonded together by their love of Dixieland music and support for The Big Walk.

Just when The Brothers started to feel at home in an area, the time would come for them to pull up stakes and face the vast unknowns before them.

It was always a challenge to leave the warm safety of their new adoptive homes, but the very nature of their trip constantly forced them to march forth.

There was always a fine line of overstaying their welcome and no longer being the new guys just passing through. They certainly didn't want to become the equivalent of the 30-year-old virgin at the senior dance, doing a cute little curtsy for fading audiences.

It was one thing to seek shelter and hospitality for a few days on their road to New York City and television stardom, but another situation all together when those days turned into weeks. People's enthusiasm for the visiting media celebrities tended to evaporate pretty rapidly if The Brothers stayed in any small town too long.

So, part of the challenge of staying in one location was always knowing when to leave, gracefully.

Roger knew that it was always better to leave on a high note, with the crowds begging for more.

Mr. Williams, the owner of the town's only motel, also happened to be the president of the local Rotary Club, and as a favor to him for his support, The Brothers had given a 20-minute concert for the members. Mr. Williams had smiled from ear to ear during the entire performance, beaming with pride.

David was thrilled that their gift of music had been so deeply appreciated. It was truly the kind of moments that he lived for and the main benefit of the entire trip.

The next day, this important civic leader of the community, and one of the town's leading businessmen, spent most of his valuable time helping David repair the bearings and broken spokes on the cart, preparing to resume their journey.

Such acts of kindness never failed to make a big impression on David. He made a vow to remember each and every generosity bestowed on him along the way, mentally promising to return the favors when he became a successful celebrity, living in his mansion lined with gold records on the walls. He took an oath to himself to never forget the humble everyday people he met on his way up to the top.

He would always remember the kind people and devoted fans of Wilcox, Arizona. He could only hope that he had made a positive influence on as many people as possible during his visit.

Maybe his visit had inspired some other talented boy or girl to take their musical lessons just a little bit more seriously, perhaps instilling a love for Dixieland Jazz. Maybe as a result of meeting The Walking Musical Balph Brothers, another generation of fans would find the courage to follow their own dreams.

David could only imagine what long-term effects their visit through Wilcox might produce down through the years. Just like meeting a movie star like Bob Hope or a famous athlete like Babe Ruth, David could only wonder what positive influences his presence might have on the impressionable minds of tomorrow's leaders. If he caused just one little boy to imagine a life outside of working in the day-to-day mind-numbing conformity of a so-called "normal" job like banking or selling insurance, he would consider his visit a success.

The two weeks spent celebrating in Wilcox had evidently made The Brothers a little soft. Being off the road for an extended period of time would do that to them.

Too many high balls, eggnogs, and home-cooked meals had taken their toll, and, despite their best efforts to hit the road with renewed determination and vigor, they only managed to push the cart a grand total of five miles that first day after leaving town.

They pitched their newly zippered tent at the only spot suitable within sight, a little patch of level ground about 25 yards from the ever-present train tracks.

Completely exhausted from their grueling five-mile march, they crashed for the night, dreaming of their next home-cooked meal.

With Roger safely supported by his non-leaking new air mattress, David was lost in dreamland, giving the performance of his life for presidents, royalty, and millions of screaming fans.

Their peaceful slumber was shattered at 4:30 a.m. by shaking ground, thunderous roars, flashing lights, and an overwhelming sense of total chaos and impending doom.

In the still of the night, five miles outside of Wilcox, Arizona, a racing diesel freight train came blasting down the tracks, blinding the darkness with its piercing spotlight.

In their confusion, The Brothers truly thought that the train was going to plow right through the middle of their tent. There wouldn't even be enough time to test out their new security zippers before being crushed to bits by the raging iron horse.

Now you may think that 25 yards is a sizable distance, if you are going strictly by a measuring tape.

Try being that distance from a deafening, smoking, belching, blinding, roaring snake of iron whizzing by your head in the middle of the desert in the middle of the winter in the middle of the night.

The airwave shock of the passing train was almost enough to rip the tent stakes completely out of the ground, sending the canvas flying off in the darkness, chasing the phantom engine as it huffed and puffed out of sight.

In the course of less than one day, they had gone from the civilized comforts of their beloved Travelodge room, with hot showers, warm beds, and working thermostats, to almost being smashed like wounded lizards by the side of the tracks by a long black train, roaring down the metal highway.

Making a mental note to always pitch their tent as far away from any railroad tracks as possible, David spent the next hour waiting for his heart to stop racing, while wondering if Frank Sinatra. Jr., or Sr. for that matter, had ever had to worry about getting hit by a train after a concert performance.

Chapter 25: Big Fun in Bowie

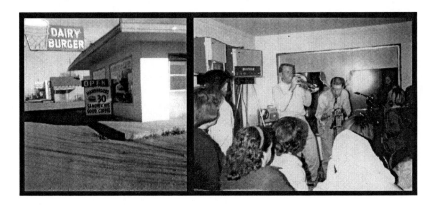

Jammin' at the Dairy Burger

The Walking Musical Balph Brothers' arrival in Bowie, Arizona, was a big deal in a very small venue.

Prior to their arrival, Mary had already been turned down by the high school principal when she asked about allowing Roger and David to perform. While the chief educational administrator said he would love to hear them play, he said that the school's coach would have a fit and never allow it to happen on school grounds. Mary wasn't sure if the principal was just trying to pass the buck, but his feeble explanation didn't seem to make much sense.

The Brothers had pushed ten miles to arrive in town, knowing they had already been turned down for very vague reasons.

Arriving in Bowie, they stopped at The Dairy Burger, in need of rest and a decent sandwich.

Their arrival created quite a stir among the local diners, bringing the usual round of questions about the cart, the journey, the details of their effort, and, basically, the sanity of The Brothers.

They wanted to know if Roger and David could put on a show for them in the diner.

The Bowie Dairy Burger was not a concert hall. It wasn't even a nightclub. It was a tiny little burger joint, maybe 40 by 20 feet at the most, filled with tables, chairs, ice cream machines, cigarette dispensers, and hungry teenagers.

The Brothers didn't see much room for a concert stage.

Thinking they might be able to avoid an awkward situation, Roger responded that they needed more space than was available to set up their speakers and instruments. He also mentioned that due to the tremendous effort required assembling their performance area, they couldn't just perform for free. They would need to be paid for any concert.

Instead of bringing the conversation to a screeching halt, the local teenage concert producers made a surprising counter-offer The Brothers couldn't refuse.

An offer of a free room at the motel behind the Dairy Burger was made. While this so-called "motel" would never be confused with a modern Travelodge, it did appear to be functioning and viable. David considered the rooms to be only slightly more than glorified shacks, but they did offer running water and beds.

The local event organizers told The Brothers to go over to the motel, take time to clean up and wash off the grime from the day's ten-mile walk, while efforts were made to secure suitable performance space and money to pay for the entertainment.

Mickey Rooney and Judy Garland would have been proud of these teenage producers. In the honored movie tradition of "let's put on a show," the music-loving, burger-munching citizens of Bowie came up with $30 for The Brothers, providing they would perform for at least an hour.

With the financial matters under control, the teens then attacked the contents of The Dairy Burger, creating a concert hall out of the dining area.

Kids carried all of the restaurant's tables and chairs, and pretty much everything else that wasn't bolted down, out into the street.

Word spread quickly throughout the town that big things were happening at The Dairy Burger. There is nothing more effective than a team of motivated high school kids intent on delivering the news that a concert was going to take place in their little burg.

In the two hours it took to clear the floor and set up the speakers and instruments, the place was filled to overflowing with anxious, attentive, enthusiastic music lovers.

It was as though this was the first time many of the kids had ever seen a live musician. Their support could not have been more rabid. Teens were jumping up and down, overcome with emotions and rhythms. It was a cultural happening of gigantic proportions.

The promised one-hour concert kept going and going. The Brothers were in their element, enjoying every second of every song. David was in rare form, hitting all of the high notes with ease. Roger was in his usual masterful showman mode, astounding the audience with his talents and energy.

The Brothers loved seeing the complete and total excitement their performance created in their audience.

Every time they tried to bring the concert to a close, the crowd clapped and screamed, demanding more.

They enjoyed seeing the crowd's standing ovation, which in hindsight was pretty much the audience's only option available at the time, seeing as how all of the tables and chairs had been taken outside.

Even so, David was pretty confident that the fans would have been on their feet even if they did have chairs to sit in. Their ear-to-ear smiles gave him all the proof he needed. Plus, they passed the hat and came up with an additional $25 for their efforts.

After the show finally ended, the now-seasoned teen concert producers asked The Brothers if they would attend the high school's basketball game Friday night, which was two days away.

The team hadn't won a game all season, and the local teenage concert producers hoped having Roger and David in the gym would bring good luck to the school and maybe result in a victory for their hapless athletes.

With little else to do in the way of performing options, The Brothers agreed to extend their stay in scenic Bowie, Arizona, and do their best to motivate the team, the teens, and the town with their inspirational music and their never-say-die attitude.

If anybody knew a thing about overcoming impossible obstacles with dedication and determination, it had to be The Walking Musical Balph Brothers.

Chapter 26: Good Luck and Bad Attitudes

While the teens of Bowie, Arizona, had taken Roger and David to their hearts, going so far as to christen them the high school basketball team's good luck charms, the high school's principal seemed to have a serious problem with all things related to The Walking Musical Balph Brothers.

It appeared that Mr. Stinson, the principal, was accustomed to running things his way, and his way only. When he originally turned down Mary's request a week earlier for a Balph Brothers concert at the school, he evidently assumed that was the end of the matter.

His word was the law in that school, and even though he had clumsily tried to pass the blame off on the boys' basketball coach, the fact remained that he was not very impressed with the plight of a pair of transient, jobless, smooth-talking, wannabe television stars from California, trying to take time, and more importantly, money out of the pockets of his students. He didn't care how great they could play "When the Saints Go Marching In" and he wasn't just whistling "Dixie."

What he hadn't counted on was the incredible thirst the students had for all things Dixieland, in general, and The Balph Brothers, specifically. The rising wave of teen affection and enthusiasm was sweeping over the town like an once-in-a-lifetime tidal surge.

The power of live music, coupled with raging hormones, supplemented by natural teenage rebellion, proved to be a force to be reckoned with.

The students weren't going to let a little thing like their clueless principal saying no to a concert in their school stop them in their pursuit for sonic delights.

If they couldn't put on the concert at the school, they would simply find another performance venue.

Hadn't these same motivated students just managed to turn a tiny, featureless, cement-block burger joint into a jumping concert emporium rivaling Carnegie Hall in spirit, if not acoustics?

When poor, misguided Principal Stinson laid down the law, a heretofore untapped rebel rouser by the innocent name of Shirley Davis rose to the challenge, convincing her parents to open their home to an after-the-game concert party featuring the legendary, soon-to-be world famous, Walking Musical Balph Brothers.

With the entire student body buzzing Thursday with news about the upcoming Friday night party, cold-hearted Principal Stinson refused to accept the reality of the situation, trying instead to prove his power and rule with a clunky iron fist.

He issued another pig-headed decree that any student foolish enough to attend any outlawed, unauthorized, non-sanctioned, off-campus gathering featuring live music would not be allowed to go on the traditional senior class trip in the Spring.

Feeling fairly certain that his threat would knock some much-needed sense into the rebelling student body, you can only imagine his rage and genuine disgust Friday, the day of the big basketball game, when he discovered that not only had his threat been laughed off, it had also provided fuel for the implausible musical fever that was sweeping the town.

Students, who had originally been rather lackadaisical towards the entire concept of two out-of-towners blowing wind through metal pipes, suddenly became rabid supporters when it became a game of tug-of-war between Ole Man Stinson and the town's teenagers.

Going to the after-game party concert at Shirley Davis' home was suddenly the patriotic civic duty of every single student of Bowie High School.

This had all the makings of a mid-60s Arizona version of some future Kevin Bacon movie, where music was outlawed by bone-headed adults in ill-fitting suits. Perhaps some budding film director was witness to the impromptu Dairy Burger concert and treasured that moment when his life was changed forever, all the way to theatrical glory in his adulthood.

So, even though all of the students tried their best to keep details of the party hush-hush, it was truly the worst kept secret in the school.

In a final desperate act of frustration, Principal Stinson let it be known that it was illegal to put on a party and hire musical performers without having a license from the city. If Shirley Davis charged anybody a penny to attend her illegal, highly immoral, late-night debacle of musical insanity, she would be nothing more than a common criminal, a low-life thug, a pathetic excuse for a law-abiding citizen of the community.

By this point, even the most casual of observers realized that the slightly esteemed and not-so-principled Mr. Stinson was blowing dubious hot air out of his pie hole, and making this entire matter much, much too personal.

From the mouths of their teenage fans, Roger and David were made aware of this man's pure and simple hatred for them, and were clearly puzzled by his reaction. David toyed with the idea of personally paying a one-on-one visit to the principal, but cooler heads, meaning, in this case, Roger and Mary, prevailed.

Roger argued that The Brothers had nothing in common with the man and very little to gain in a spitting match with one of Bowie's most powerful citizens. To confront the town bully in his own fortress, the center of his power, would serve no purpose, and would possibly put the students and yes, even The Brothers, in harm's way.

Besides, the students had been the ones to invite them to perform.

If they had learned anything in their months on the road, it was the simple fact that it was better to avoid trouble than go out looking for it.

So rather than confront their enemy in the private confines of his protected lair, The Brothers took their cause to the source of their power, in this case, the basketball court of Bowie High.

They arrived in their best on-stage performing uniforms. Shoes polished to a mirror shine, pants ironed and creased with perfection. Roger and David looked their best, and proudly took their place right in the middle of the student body's cheering section on the bleachers.

They were the epitome of clean-cut, God-fearing, polite, respectful, good-natured, awe-inspiring, visiting ambassadors of good will.

With The Walking Musical Balph Brothers on their side, Bowie High School's basketball team won their first game of the year, instantly becoming the source of legends for decades ahead.

When the final buzzer confirmed that Bowie's team had truly defeated their opponent, the gymnasium exploded with cheers and jubilation. The student body squarely gave Roger and David sole credit for the miraculous victory, somewhat embarrassingly overshadowing the efforts of the actual round ball athletes on the court.

Although only a few hundred spectators actually witnessed the miracle when it happened, David had no doubt that, in the years that followed, countless thousands would claim to have been in the gym

129

on that fateful night when the Lucky Balph Brothers delivered a much-needed victory.

The after-party at Shirley Davis' house was a genuine success on every level. While feasting on soda pop and more potato chips, the notorious civil protesters and would-be petty criminals enjoyed the fruits of their rebellious efforts.

They feasted on raw, living, breathing Dixieland Jazz, and it was good.

In a show of support for the students, and perhaps as a peace-offering concession for the obstacles misguided adults had thrown their way, the school's basketball coach even made an appearance at the party. The fact that his team finally won a game probably had something to do with his accommodating attitude. He also had the decency to make an early exit, allowing students to smoke without being watched by eagle-eyed, name-taking administrators.

Even Principal Stinson's edict that charging money at the party had turned out to be yet another advantage for The Brothers.

Since their esteemed adult role model had specifically informed the party organizers that selling tickets for a dollar would be illegal, these future leaders-of-the-world took Principal Stinson at his word, and decided to accept only donations at the door.

And, in a twist of fate that was simply too delicious to ignore, the party raised far more money from donations than they ever could have by charging a flat entry fee.

So, all in all, the concentrated efforts of the misguided chief school administrator only resulted in bringing more fans and more much-needed cash to The Walking Musical Balph Brothers.

It was an important real-life civic lesson that the students of Bowie High School could never have learned by simply reading a textbook in class.

Chapter 27: Horrible Meal,
But a Potentially Great Dog

Their New Watchdog "Steps"

While winning the basketball game and sticking it to The Man with their successful after-game party had been significant events to make their visit in Bowie, Arizona, memorable, the most tangible souvenir from the town came into their lives in the form of a dirty, flea-bitten, chain-gnawing, high-strung, three-month old, black female mongrel dog.

The Brothers had decided that they needed a good watchdog to help them along The Big Walk, one with a loud bark and a threatening growl. Their constant concern for security against the ravages and threats of the open highway had only increased with the passing miles. While shotguns, pistols, machetes, and their new quick-escape zippers for the tent offered a certain level of protection, the idea of adding a living, breathing alarm system to their arsenal was very attractive.

They simply needed to see a man, any man, about a dog.

This new canine came into the lives of The Walking Musical Balph Brothers courtesy of a casual conversation David had with the owner of the local grocery store.

The youngest Balph Brother asked if he knew anybody who might want to get rid of a dog, and ten minutes later, Mrs. Shirley Elkins was on the phone, offering a free dinner and, more importantly, a free puppy.

While the meal was extremely difficult to swallow, with rock-hard potatoes and deer meat too tough to chew, the puppy offered much more promise.

The Brothers were grateful for their meal. After so many months on the road, depending on their wits and the kindness of strangers, sharing any meal was a deeply appreciated act of generosity.

David could only hope that the new doggy would turn out to be as tough as the lady's serving of venison.

The owners claimed that the mutt was part Belgian German Shepard and showed so little concern about the creature that they hadn't even given it a name in its first 90 days of living.

The Brothers took this newest member of their defense team back to the motel for a much needed bath. While the owners had insisted that the puppy was the color of coal, until she actually emerged from the soapy water, David wasn't too sure what the true color of her fur might be under three-months of grime, mud, and filth.

Even at her tender age, the puppy was much too large for the bathroom sink, and, seeing as how the idea of personal cleanliness was totally alien to her, she decided to provide as little cooperation as possible.

She made it her goal to jump, yelp, wiggle, and splash as much as possible, drenching Roger, David, and a significant part of the motel room with large quantities of sudsy, dirty, wet, dog-smelling liquid.

Even though David was soaked to the bone from his bath-time canine wrestling match, he admired the spirit and determination the mongrel had shown during the cleansing ritual.

The last thing they needed on this trip was some sissy lapdog afraid of its own shadow. He was glad that their nameless pooch had put up a fight and shown a little backbone. Maybe she would turn out to be the perfect watchdog they needed.

The entire ordeal was so exhausting for the puppy that as soon as she was released from the slippery confines of the assaulted bathroom, she went to the bedroom, claimed her spot at the end of the bed, and proceeded to sleep for three hours, without so much as wagging her newly cleaned tail.

While doggy was sleeping, The Brothers went out and bought her a nice leash and collar. It was a thoughtful gesture, but in hindsight, they could have saved their time and money.

They took her outside and tied her to the cart. Bad idea.

Doggy proceeded to do her best impersonation of a raging bull, if not a wounded lizard. She simply had a downright fit, right there in the middle of the street. She cried and barked, twisted and pulled, flopped and flipped.

Just when Roger thought she had resigned herself to her fate, accepted her new reality, and decided to settle down, she bit her new leash into pieces and went flying off down the road to her hard-earned freedom.

David's recent enthusiasm for her bathroom spunk and never-say-die attitude faded almost as fast as the dog disappeared down the street.

The visual of The Walking Musical Balph Brothers chasing what appeared to be a scalded dog down the city streets was certainly the talk of Bowie, Arizona, for weeks to come.

When they finally had the puppy back in their control, they made yet another trip to the local grocery store, buying the thickest metal chain they could find.

It only took another two hours of mournful crying, futile gnawing, and pitiful whining by the side of the cart for the pooch to finally give up her struggle, and snuggle down for a much-needed nap by the wheel.

Seeing as how one of the main mottos of Roger and David on The Big Walk was to take each day step by step, they decided that the perfect name for their newest team member was a natural choice, painfully obvious when David thought about how far they had had to chase her just to bring her back to the cart.

Her name wouldn't be "Killer" or "Rage."

They didn't even name her after her supposed bloodline by calling her "Berlin" or "Hamburg" or even "Brussels."

That night, securely chained to the cart by the side of the motel in the middle of Bowie, Arizona, the previously unnamed doggy was given the perfect name for the rest of her life: "Steps."

Chapter 28: Liquid Revenge

Their new watchdog survived the night chained to the cart and spent the next day's journey of twelve miles of The Big Walk safely perched in a black box at the back of the vehicle, being pushed by The Brothers.

Listening to Roger and David repeat their mantra, "step by step," over and over like a military marching cadence, the puppy soon figured out that her name was not "Killer."

By the end of her first day on the road, "Steps" had learned her new name and responded with a slight bark when addressed accordingly.

David was positive that she was one of the fastest learning dogs ever known to man. Her amazing intelligence was a joy to behold. He wondered if there might be a way to take advantage of her superior brainpower, and perhaps work her into their stage show.

Unfortunately, any thoughts that adding the dog to their team would bring an immediate change in luck were put to rest the very next morning.

After packing up their tent, reloading all of their supplies, and carefully placing "Steps" in her spot of honor on the cart, they started their final march to the border of New Mexico, only to have the cross bolt on the front left fork break into pieces less than 50 feet from their campground.

At least Roger didn't explode in fits of anger this time around, unlike the last time when he seemed to blame David for everything under the sun, including the rising price of bread.

Roger hitched a ride into Lordsburg, New Mexico, and, after discovering that there weren't any bicycle dealers in town, finally found a local machine shop that was able to manufacture a new bolt on one of their metal lathes.

Another entire day's effort was shot for the lack of a dollar piece of metal.

It was 7:30 at night before they were able to get the cart back into running shape.

David had the dubious honor of unpacking the tent, taking off the supplies and equipment, and re-establishing camp in the very same spot they had tried unsuccessfully to leave twelve hours earlier.

Guess it was a good thing they didn't decide to name the new pooch "Lucky."

One advantage of being in such cold winter weather was the fact that their entire surroundings were nature's own freezers. The big outdoors was their refrigerator, allowing them to carry a pot of fully cooked chuck roast, potatoes, and carrots. Each pot would last four days when covered with a lid, and The Brothers simply heated up the contents each day on their trusty Coleman stove, eating right out of the same pan. Plates were for sissies, and why bother with napkins when they both had perfectly suitable pants legs? The Big Walk was certainly not a fashion show, and neither Roger nor David had time for wasted manners on the road.

They both agreed that eating their naturally refrigerated winter meals was much more satisfying than their normal summer menu of cold spaghetti and beer.

And now that "Steps" had joined the team, they didn't even have to worry about the leftovers going to waste.

After a few games of gin rummy, The Brothers decided to call it a night and hit the sack.

David invited "Steps" to come in out of the sub-freezing cold and share the inside of his sleeping bag.

Learning what Eskimos and fur-trappers have known for centuries, David soon felt the tangible benefits of sharing his bed with a living, breathing, warm-blooded mammal with a body temperature approaching 100 degrees. It was simply amazing how much heat came off of that one little doggy.

He had been soundly sleeping in heated bliss, dreaming of being onstage, blowing his golden horn for millions of admiring fans, when something seriously wrong woke him up at 2:30 a.m.

Was it a pack of wolves attacking the tent?

No.

Was it a band of drunken thugs looking for trouble?

No.

Was it a frigid ice storm blasting through the desert night?

No.

Had a deadly rattlesnake crawled into his sleeping bag, deeply biting its fangs into his tender flesh, sending poisonous venom racing through his veins?

No.

David felt something hot and wet running down his leg.

Had he been shot in his slumber, too numbed by the freezing cold to feel any pain, and was now bleeding to death in his sleeping bag?

David's mind raced with the possibilities. Anything was possible in the wilds of the desert. It could have been any of a hundred terrifying options, each one a little more horrible than the next.

David prayed to his Guardian Angels, asking for divine protection.

He carefully reached down to feel his lower limbs, hoping he would still have the ability to move his muscles, his legs, his toes, all of which he prayed still remained attached to his body.

He brought back his fingers, discovering they were covered with heated moisture. In the darkness of the tent, he could only imagine the dark crimson stains that must have been soaking the bottom of his sleeping bag.

He knew he should be feeling weak with the loss of so much blood and was still puzzled by the total lack of pain registering in his brain.

He had read about people being in shock after accidents, completely unaware of missing limbs, sheared arms, and mutilated legs and toes.

Maybe he was suffering from a similar level of total denial.

And if he denied his denial, then what?

It was a profoundly interesting philosophical exercise that would have to be considered at a later time, perhaps in a coffee shop filled with unemployed graduate students.

While his mind continued to race with similar unstructured gibberish, his hands fumbled for answers in the form of a flashlight.

Praying that the batteries hadn't died on him in the middle of the frigid cold, David pushed the switch in search of illumination.

The beaming ray of light revealed yet another mystery.

The tent was filled with steam.

Hot, sticky steam.

Then a very familiar scent hit David's flaring nostrils.

Who says that Guardian Angels lack a sense of humor? Didn't God create the entire concept of giggles?

David's prayers had been answered.

His limbs were intact. His blood was still contained within the confines of his body. He could even wiggle his toes and feel his legs.

It was a miracle.

The warm, radiating, life-affirming, dripping liquid soaking his legs in the middle of the western desert on a winter night with temperatures in the sub-teens wasn't blood.

"Steps" had peed on him.

Hovering beside the sleeping bag, peering out from the tinkle mist, the piddle fog, the ammonia-scented haze, David saw the truly smiling face of his newest bedmate. The dog had a look of complete and total satisfaction on her snout.

While David couldn't prove that the leaking incident had anything to do with the tortured previous days' treatment when "Steps" had spent hours and hours biting, twisting, barking, growling, and attacking her metal chain that kept her secured to the cart, it did give him reason to wonder.

Were dogs capable of holding grudges?

Maybe it was just a form of bonding in the animal world.

David could only hope that he had passed the test.

Chapter 29: An Understanding

Roughing It at the Border

Wednesday, January 15, 1964, found The Brothers camping outside of Lordsburg, still trying to push their cart into the town where Roger had so easily hitchhiked a ride two days earlier. Whereas he had been able to cover the miles within a few hours, grabbing rides with friendly strangers, it always took days to cover the same ground with the 1,000-pound cart, especially in the frigid winter weather.

David was still recovering from the previous night's moist encounter with Steps, and not looking forward to a repeat of the soaking experience.

By the time they established camp in a low flatland area known locally as "The Dry Lake," the temperature had fallen to ten below zero.

This is exactly the kind of weather that Eskimos called a three-dog night, meaning it would take the heat of not one, not two, but three Alaskan Huskies to keep toes warm on a night like that.

David didn't have three dogs. He was lucky to have the one "Steps," even if she was prone to leakage.

At least he'd know the cause of another hot, steamy fog attack this time around, and not think he was being attacked by some invisible fanged marauder.

Hoping man and beast had established a bonding understanding during the day's walk, David settled into his frozen sleeping bag. David's feet were beyond numb. He couldn't remember a time when he had been this cold.

The ground was rock hard, brutally frozen, and offered no comfort.

David seriously thought his toes might turn green and fall off in the bottom of his sleeping bag.

Just when he thought he wouldn't be able to take it any longer, "Steps" crawled into the tent, came up behind David's neck, and pushed her way all the way down to the bottom of the sleeping bag.

Reaching the end, she snuggled her back up against David's back, and didn't come back out.

At that moment, in that arctic cold, David wouldn't have cared if "Steps" had marked her turf with yet another round of liquid relief.

All he knew was the dog's body heat was real and warm, and before he realized it, he had the feeling come back into his toes. His living, breathing canine heater was working her magic, and David was deeply thankful for her company.

Maybe they had reached an unspoken, interspecies understanding. Did "Steps" understand the time-honored motto of the road stating that you don't mess where you sleep? Maybe her bladder was just plain frozen, and the waterworks would resume when the temperature rose.

It never even entered David's mind that good ole "Steps" might have been just as thankful for David's life-giving body heat as he had been for hers.

All David knew for certain was the fact that "Steps" was making his night bearable, and probably saving his long-suffering toes from gangrene.

Chapter 30: Speechless In Lordsburg, New Mexico

Mary had a gig lined up for The Brothers at the Lordsburg, New Mexico, Junior High School basketball gym, scheduled for Friday, January 17th.

They were going to be paid $35 for playing the assembly program.

They pushed the cart into town the day before and found Principal Stiles to be a very friendly and accommodating administrator, which was a welcome relief after their previous battles in Bowie with hardheaded educators.

Principal Stiles even allowed Roger and David to sleep on the stage for the rest of the week and use the locker room showers to clean off the road grime.

Once again, the kindness of big-hearted strangers came through for The Brothers.

They set up their equipment for the next morning's concert, and only had one minor setback when "Steps" reacted to hearing Roger play his baritone sax for the first time by running across the stage, peeing a steady stream with each and every step.

David wasn't sure how it seemed to always be his job to deal with every new canine urine issue, but he performed his duty with as much enthusiasm as he could muster, given the soggy circumstances.

With their actual road-tested cart right along side of them in the gym, they played their hearts out. They even introduced "Steps" to the one hundred or so Junior High fans in attendance. She joined Roger and David onstage, with appropriate crowd-pleasing tail wagging.

The principal of the town's high school heard about the success of their first gig, and offered them $25 to perform that same evening at the basketball game halftime show.

Even that offer expanded into playing for the reserve and then the varsity games, so they went from having one performance to three.

Although they were always thankful for good word of mouth and as many paying gigs as possible, all of this activity proved to be another round of mixed blessings.

While sleeping in the frigid winter freeze on the ground in the desert and dealing with one urinating dog and a leaking air mattress, Roger and David had managed to catch terrible colds. It was an occupational hazard.

Alhough they were still able to blow sufficient air into their instruments, and they certainly never had to worry about their prerecorded backup orchestra on the tapes, they both lost their voices.

David would try to introduce a song, and before completing the sentence, his vocal cords would completely fail him.

His lips would move but no sound came out.

Handing the microphone over to Roger would only repeat the painful process, resulting in more embarrassing moments onstage.

By constantly juicing their throats with medicinal spray provided by Mary, they were able to coax another three or four minutes worth of words out of their inflamed throats before sliding back into squawks and squeals, and then silence.

They were able to spend the rest of the weekend camping out on the stage and recovering from their colds.

And even though Principal Stiles didn't know it, he had also provided shelter for Mary, who brought in her own sleeping bag when the coast was clear.

The team's survival skills were certainly improving with each passing day.

Before leaving town, they discovered that several English classes at both the Junior High and High School wrote letters to Jack Paar, singing the praises of Roger and David, asking for them to be considered as guests on his show.

It is estimated that over 400 letters were sent to New York by the supporting students of Lordsburg, New Mexico. This was pretty amazing, seeing as how only 6,000 citizens called the place home.

This wasn't the first, and certainly not the last, time this would happen along the journey.

Surely the powers that be at Paar's production company had to take notice of the constant barrage of letters and postcards that kept

141

coming their way from concerned fans along the route of The Big Walk.

This genuine grassroots level of enthusiasm was exactly the kind of support that got the attention of advertisers, program producers, and the nation's media.

How could a reasonable man, who lived and thrived on providing crowd-pleasing family entertainment, ignore such an ever-growing wave of popular support?

Aren't you supposed to give the public what they want? Isn't that one of the main rules of show business?

How could anybody read those passionate letters and not be moved to take action?

Roger was positive that despite the hardships of the road, the huge personal sacrifices they faced every day, and even the wear and tear on their bodies, this epic journey was going to launch their musical career into the highest levels of the entertainment world.

Now all they had to do was convince a very, very small circle of people in The Big Apple.

Roger went to sleep that night, and so many, many more, dreaming of the day that the long-awaited and much-deserved call would finally come through.

Chapter 31: Kindred Spirits

In the middle of the desert, outside of Deming, New Mexico, The Brothers came face to face with a legend of the Wild West, a fellow traveler known as Old Joe.

They had heard so many stories about Old Joe along the way, they weren't sure if he was myth or reality.

Supposedly, he was this living relic out of the past, a man on a constant journey, crossing Texas, New Mexico, and Arizona in a covered wagon drawn by four donkeys, escorting a farmyard's worth of chickens and sheep.

He made his living selling postcards of his wagon to tourists and fellow travelers, and posing for snapshots when he was in the mood.

Looking like a central-casting extra from a classic Hollywood Western movie, Old Joe lived the part of a genuine cowboy wagonmaster from the previous century. With his long white beard flowing almost down to his waist, he could have just as easily been a citizen of the 1860s, or a century later.

They first saw him off in the distance, almost looking like a mirage in the desert sun.

As they pushed the cart closer and closer to the ever-growing approaching object, every story they had heard about Old Joe was validated.

They were able to see the team of donkeys leading the way, with Old Joe keeping secure reins on the progress. They could hear the sounds of the chickens and sheep, amid the clanging pots and pans, shaking in the back of the wagon.

When they were just about to pass each other from their respective sides of the highway, David waved and wished their fellow journeyman a good day.

Much to David's surprise, Old Joe ignored his heartfelt greeting and just proceeded down the road as if nothing had been spoken.

Had the old man seen him?

David didn't know if he had broken some unwritten code of the road, or if Old Joe considered such a gimmick as pushing a cart to be a foolish endeavor. Maybe the senior traveler was hard of hearing, or blind, or possibly both. Maybe he considered The Brothers to be competition for hard-earned tourist dollars and media attention.

All Roger and David knew for certain was that their very brief encounter with Old Joe had been decidedly one-sided and not very hospitable.

So much for any illusions to taking a roadside break, sharing a beer, and laughing over their similar circumstances.

Whatever hard-earned wisdom Old Joe had learned from his years on the road would stay safely tucked away beneath his magnificent flowing beard.

As these opposing caravans of seasoned desert travelers journeyed towards their respective destinies, David looked in his trusty rear-view mirror attached to the cart, hoping to catch a final glimpse of the receding legend.

Much to his surprise, he saw Old Joe hanging his beard over the side of his wagon, looking back towards The Brothers as they pushed the cart one step at a time.

So he had seen David's neighborly gesture!

Realizing that curiosity had gotten the better of Old Joe, David took this slight moment of human interest as an opening to send the elderly man another friendly wave. Again, it was unrequited.

Old Joe rebuffed yet this second attempt at roadside hospitality, ignoring the salutation, while promptly turning back in his seat, and going on down the road, never giving David so much as a second glance. In a few minutes, the wagon was a tiny fading spot in David's rearview mirror.

The Brothers could only imagine what amazing once-in-a-lifetime stories Old Joe could have shared with them if he had perhaps been in a more social mood.

David was lost in thought about what might have been had this kindred spirit been a little more receptive to fellow travelers passing like ships in the night.

Chapter 32: Close Call

Walking the final miles to Deming, New Mexico, could have possibly been the last miles traveled by The Brothers…ever, anywhere.

They were pushing the cart step by step, as usual, when an elderly driver flew over the crest of a slight hill, coming directly at them in his car. He looked to be at least in his seventies and must have been near-sighted, to boot. With only 20 yards, at most, to spare, he swerved to avoid hitting them, and his car turned completely sideways.

If he had hit the slightest bump in the narrow two-lane road, his car would have certainly been airborne, flipping over and over to certain disaster.

If another car had been coming in the opposite direction, there could very easily have been a multiple car crash right before Roger and David's eyes, or worse, involving the cart itself.

At the speed the man had been driving, there was little doubt that somebody would have died right there on the highway.

The Brothers were so shocked by the close encounter that they barely had time to think. Feeling the wind from the car hit their faces, they had both instinctively let go of the cart and jumped into the ditch on the side of the highway.

Alhough it only took a fraction of a second, it was one of those moments when everything seemed to move in slow motion. Once again their Guardian Angels were doing their duties.

Not only did Roger and David survive their jump, but the cart managed to coast to a stop straight in the middle of the highway. It could have just as easily veered off into the very same ditch, smashing wheels and destroying instruments.

The old man in the car didn't even get out to see what might have fallen off his vehicle. He just started his car back up, put it in gear, and drove off down the road, acting like nothing unusual had taken place.

David didn't even want to think about what might have happened to poor "Steps" if she had been walking in the road a few feet one way or the other.

So many things could have gone wrong so rapidly that it was almost mind-boggling to even consider.

They didn't even have time to catch their breath before it was all over.

The entire ordeal was just another little slice of life, and possibly death, in the desert.

They were constantly dancing on the razor's edge in so many ways along the journey, with so little margin for error.

They could have been killed. They could have been seriously maimed or injured.

At the very least, all of the tools of their profession, all of their recording equipment, all of their life-time possessions, and their means of transportation could have been ruined within seconds.

They didn't have any insurance. They didn't even have any money to call their own, being down to literally their last dollar.

There was absolutely no safety net for Roger and David, as they made their Big Walk across the country.

If David allowed himself to seriously stop and think about their dire straights, it was almost enough to paralyze him.

What in the world were they doing out in the middle of nowhere?

It was one thing to follow your dream. But what if the dream was actually a nightmare? A nightmare that might take years and years to unfold?

As Roger and David pushed nearer and nearer to Deming, New Mexico, both brothers were lost in their thoughts, considering what might have happened and wondering what fortunes waited for them up ahead.

Their faith was being tested in so many ways with each and every step.

Counting their blessings for being protected once again by their Guardian Angels, The Brothers said their silent prayers and kept their eyes on the never-ending road ahead of them.

Chapter 33: Flying Flutes

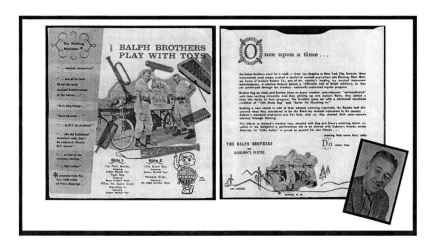

*The Balph Brothers Promo Record for Auburn Toy Company
and Photo of Company President, Dick Hodson*

The Brothers had arrived in Deming, New Mexico, with one dollar to their names, but their fortunes were about to change.

Mary had arranged a paying gig for the High School Band Boosters on Saturday, January 30th.

All Roger and David had to do was find a way to survive during the next six days before the concert.

While it was true that they did have their stand-by food rations, the idea of surviving on dehydrated meals was not very appetizing.

Once again the kindness of strangers came through at just the right time.

Fortunately the promise of money at the end of the week was enough for a local restaurant to come to their rescue and extend credit to the traveling musicians.

By the time their concert rolled around, they had run up a tab of $17.00, but at least they were able to keep their energy up and their lips in shape.

This was no small feat.

Although both brothers had to constantly struggle to stay in performance shape while out on the road, David had a tougher time dealing with the pressures of playing a brass instrument. Roger could rely on his woodwind reeds to provide the musical vibrations needed for his parts, but David only had his lips to coach notes from his trumpet. When his lips were chapped or cracked by the extreme conditions of the winter weather, it affected his ability to perform. He couldn't simply push the cart all day out in the cold, pull into a new town, bounce up onstage, and immediately start playing "Tiger Rag."

It was always his desire to give each and every audience the absolute best performance each and every time he hit the stage. As Roger always said, they played each concert like it might be their last, and even if they only had five people in the audience, somebody in the smallest crowd might have the potential to bring about the biggest changes, so they always gave their best every time.

That is exactly what happened at the Deming, New Mexico, performance.

While the show at the High School was a big success in its own right, the best part of the concert came after the show when they met Dick Hodson, the past president of the band boosters club.

More importantly for The Brothers, during the day Mr. Hodson was the president of The Auburn Rubber Company, one of Deming's leading manufacturers.

Contrary to what the company's name might lead you to believe, The Auburn Rubber Company manufactured a line of products that would immediately change the fortunes of David and Roger.

After having a late-night, after-concert meal with Mr. Hodson and his wife, The Brothers made arrangements to visit the factory the next day.

In addition to making a line of toys, the company also produced another hot-selling item, a plastic toy flute that sold for 49 cents.

The Brothers saw a big barrel of the instruments at the factory, and immediately discovered, even though they were low in cost, they were high in quality and were able to hold pitch as long as they played in the key of C.

Roger and David took the toy flutes with them that day, determined to see just how much music they could wrangle out of the plastic toys.

By this time, Mr. Hodson and his wife had already taken Roger and David under their wings, inviting them back to their home for another dinner.

After a wonderful home-cooked meal, Mr. Hodson even took it on himself to help David work on fixing a continuing problem with the cart. Despite their previous best efforts, the front forks were proving to be seriously flawed in design. They simply couldn't handle the weight of the cargo and the constant stress of the road.

Mr. Hodson arranged for some of his best engineers to design a new set of metal forks, and after determining that it would take three days to fabricate them, invited Roger and David to spend the days as their guests in his home.

With time to spare, they decided to work up some arrangements on the toy flutes.

All they originally hoped to be able to do was perhaps perform a few songs to show their appreciation for the kindness of Mr. Hodson and his family.

Working within the confines of the instrument's eight-note range, they were able to develop decent versions of "12th Street Rag," "The Old Gray Mare," and "When The Saints Go Marching In."

They were so pleased with the results that they decided to go visit Mr. Hodson at the factory, instead of just waiting for him to come home for dinner.

When they arrived at the plant, they found Mr. Hodson in the middle of a board meeting with his leading company executives.

Seeing Roger and David through the glass windows of the conference room, he motioned for them to come in and introduce themselves to the rest of the staff.

Roger was extremely relieved that they had decided to wear their clean clothes to the meeting, instead of just rushing out in their working outfits. Their mother would have been proud of their appearance.

They gave their impromptu toy flute concert their best efforts, and the reaction of the Auburn Rubber Company top executives could not have been more enthusiastic.

They told The Brothers they had never heard so much music come out of their humble 49-cent instruments.

Being businessmen, the Vice-President of Sales and the Director of Promotions immediately saw the marketing potential of having their toy flutes in the able hands of David and Roger Balph.

Seeing as how Mr. Hodson was closely associated with the Deming High School Band, a few calls were made, and before the sun went down, arrangements had been made for a local bass player and drummer to accompany The Brothers the next day on a demo recording session, using the trusty Ampex recorder to document their efforts.

The next day, Mr. Hodson saw so much potential in the resulting recordings that he immediately made arrangements with his advertising manager to set up a real recording session in El Paso, Texas, the home of his advertising agency.

While waiting for details to be made for the recording session, The Brothers worked on providing the Auburn Rubber Company with updated biographies, and helped the factory engineers place company emblems on both sides of the cart to promote their sponsorship of The Big Walk.

While working with the marketing department, The Brothers discovered that the Auburn Rubber Company had originally made automobile tires in Auburn, Indiana. When The Depression hit the nation in the 1930s, the company started making rubber replacement soles to glue onto the bottom of worn out shoes, a product that literally saved the company from bankruptcy.

When Mr. Hudson moved the company to New Mexico, they branched out into the toy business, selling popular lines of toy trucks, toy guns, and other children's toys, including the high-quality toy flute.

David found it somewhat ironic that their latest benefactor had a history of making two of the items most essential to the daily success of The Big Walk.

If anybody knew the value of having dependable tires and durable shoe soles, it was David Balph.

The day before their trip to El Paso, Mr. Hodson threw a good-luck party at his home, filling his living room with family, friends, and company employees.

Naturally, The Walking Musical Balph Brothers were the evening's entertainers, providing a lively performance featuring their tried-and-true horn arrangements with the added hometown bonus of their new toy flute songs.

With an open bar and plenty of free-flowing liquid refreshments, a grand time was had by all.

Even though the next morning, Wednesday, February 5th, found The Brothers slightly hung-over, they soothed their nerves and stomachs by riding to El Paso in Mr. Hodson's luxury Lincoln Continental.

The depth of his generosity was almost overwhelming.

Roger and David were so thankful for the kindness extended by Mr. Hodson and his entire circle of friends. The people of Deming, New Mexico, could not have been more accommodating or supportive.

They drove into El Paso fully expecting the recording session to be the answer to their dreams.

Unfortunately, things didn't go quite as smoothly as they had anticipated.

The plain truth of the matter was the musicians hired for the studio work weren't up to the task. Not only were they unable to play the arrangements in a professional manner, but also they had brought their girlfriends with them and arrived drunk or close to it.

They were too busy having a party with the women to focus on the detailed work of the recording, and it soon became very apparent to Roger and David that the entire session was a big waste of time.

Despite their best efforts, the tapes were simply not going to work.

They had spent almost $200 of The Auburn Rubber Company's hard-earned money, and David didn't think the results were worth fifteen cents.

Driving back to Deming at the end of the day in Mr. Hodson's Lincoln, The Brothers didn't have the heart to tell their benefactor that the studio sessions had been a big bust.

They quietly pulled into Mr. Hodson's driveway, parked the car, and silently called it a night in their guest quarters.

The bad news would have to wait until the next day.

Arriving at the factory the next morning, The Brothers delivered the sad verdict, and waited for Mr. Hodson's reaction.

While he was totally disappointed and disgusted with the behavior of the hired hacks in El Paso, he didn't take it out on Roger and David.

Proving he had what it takes to be a decisive businessman, he immediately told The Brothers to make arrangements for a professional recording session in their hometown, Los Angles.

He had had enough of dealing with small-town incompetence and people who talked a good game but couldn't deliver the goods.

He told The Brothers to call their favorite musicians back in Los Angeles, book studio time, and make flight arrangements as soon as possible.

Trying to save The Auburn Rubber Company whatever funds possible, Roger and David took a 2:00 a.m. flight out of El Paso that arrived in Los Angeles at 4:00 a.m. on Friday, February 6th. They made arrangements for their dear mother to meet them at the airport, covering in two hours the entire distance they had taken over half a year to push on foot.

In what can only be described as simpler times, The Brothers were able to entertain the flight stewardesses with stories about The Big Walk.

Before the flight ended, the flight crew had invited Roger and David to come up to the front of the plane and perform a few songs on their handy plastic flutes.

When their performance was over, the pilot came on the loudspeaker, telling everyone on the plane how much he enjoyed their version of "When The Saints Go Marching In."

He then proceeded to wish The Brothers the best of luck in their walk to Jack Paar's studio in New York.

Roger and David exited the plane in Los Angeles feeling like international celebrities. Fellow passengers were shaking their hands, expressing their appreciation for the in-air concert, and wishing them continued success and good health.

The entire ordeal seemed like a wonderful dream.

They awoke at 10:00 a.m. in their mother's apartment on February 8th.

It was almost too much to believe.

A few days earlier they had been eating dust in New Mexico, dealing with horrible musicians and their drunken girlfriends.

Now they were back in the comforts of their own apartment, sharing breakfast with their mother, and getting ready for a professional recording session at one of the best studios in Los Angles.

If that wasn't enough to make a person believe in miracles, what else would?

By 1:00 p.m., they were at United Recording Studio, working with three seasoned studio musicians they knew and trusted. Fred Potter played drums. Francis James was on bass. Al Hendrickson rounded out the band on guitar. These guys were real pros, two of them having worked with Roger back in the 1950s on an earlier album project.

It was like the difference between night and day, working with real musicians who knew their instruments and what it took to make recordings.

Roger and David were so thankful that Mr. Hodson had had the guts to scrap the El Paso efforts and put the time and money into making the recordings the best they could be.

Within three hours of studio effort, The Brothers had a top-notch, high-quality master recording to take back to Deming, New Mexico.

All too soon, it was time to say good-bye to their dear mother, and head back across the desert.

Adding to the dreamlike quality of the entire journey, the trip back was not taken by plane.

There were no attractive, uniformed, sexy stewardesses with cocktails in hand requesting in-flight concerts this time around.

Instead of flying back to Deming, Mary, "Steps," and their cart in a few hours, the return trip took considerably longer.

This time, they were driving back in Roger's station wagon, the same vehicle they had originally left behind at their mother's when The Big Walk began back in June.

They didn't have any choice.

Mary's car had finally given up, after half a year on the road. The dust, strain, wear and tear, and daily struggles of the desert had taken their toll on her trusty vehicle, and it was simply another bit of divine intervention, in the form of Mr. Hodson and the recording session in Los Angeles, that allowed Roger to journey back to his mother's apartment to retrieve his station wagon.

They left the comfort of their family at midnight on Sunday, February 9th, retracing their original path of The Big Walk.

They made it to El Centro, California, before pulling over to sleep in the car by the side of the road.

The next day they drove to Yuma, Arizona, stopping by The Stardust Hotel to say hello to friends they had made months earlier on their journey through town.

Two hours later they were in Gila Bend, where they dropped in on John Hunt, owner of the local steakhouse. After being hugged and kissed by Mrs. Hunt and their daughters, The Brothers spent the next three hours catching up on the latest news, while enjoying a fine meal, courtesy, as always, of Mr. Hunt.

People were amazed to see The Walking Musical Balph Brothers back among them.

They assumed the next time they would see Roger and David was when they appeared on Jack Paar's television show, and were truly shocked to see them alive and in person once again.

While driving to Tucson, they had problems with the car's generator and urgently needed a place to get it fixed. Once again, they were able to call on old friends to provide a rescue. A few months earlier, David had dated a girl by the name of Lila Sinclair, whose father operated a gas station in town.

They were able to get in touch with Lila, and even more fortunately, her father had the parts required to fix the faulty part and send them back down the road.

They were able to drive to Wilcox, Arizona, stopping in long enough to say hello to the Williams, owners of the local Travelodge motel, where they had spent their Christmas.

They finally pulled into Deming, New Mexico, at 3:00 a.m., safely returning to their accommodations at Mr. Hodson's home.

The next day they were able to debut the new tape recordings from their Los Angeles studio sessions.

All of the top executives at Auburn Rubber Company agreed the tapes were vastly superior to those made in El Paso with the drunken musicians, and well worth the time and expense it took to make them.

The advertising department decided to produce 15,000 copies of the songs to be used as promotional items at the upcoming New York Toy Fair. The executives were impressed with the high quality music The Brothers were able to coax out of their plastic toy flutes, and knew clients would be amazed with the professional results.

They were even designing new packaging for the flutes that would feature the likeness of Roger and David on the front and provide printed sheet music of the actual arrangements used by The Brothers at their recording session on the back.

Of course, the company was also going to provide Roger and David with several hundred copies of the record to give away at interviews and performances along the trip.

Roger was excited about having the ability to showcase their actual performances on record, instead of just relying on their backing tapes.

By Monday, February 17th, with promotional records in hand, the time had come for The Brothers to say good-bye to their circle of friends in Deming, and head off for Las Cruces, New Mexico.

Once again, Roger and Davis found themselves facing an unknown future, while leaving the kindness and safety of people who had opened their hearts and homes to them.

Making genuine promises to keep in touch with Mr. Hodson, his family, and the kind people of The Auburn Rubber Company, The Brothers left the warmth and comfort of Deming.

They would always remember the amazing generosity of these former strangers, who were now firmly entrenched in their hearts.

Chapter 34: Back to Reality

BALPH BROS.—They've got a long way to go with the only economic support coming from playing dates in whatever towns they push the 1000 pound cart through but morale is high. In the top picture Rog and Dave Balph are shown in a position that has become standard since last July. In the bottom pix, Dave (left) and Rog (right) eat out . . . way out. The boys camp with their rolling stock every night. They will be in Las Cruces at the Palms Motor Hotel for the grand opening of the Scotch and Sirloin room. The Bros. will also perform at Alameda Jr. High tomorrow afternoon at 4 p.m.

Cooking Out Near Las Cruces

It didn't take long for the dream-world kindness of the good people of Deming to be replaced with the harsh realities of pushing a 1,000-pound cart through the desert, step by step.

No more comfortable guest apartment accommodations. No more home-cooked meals and lively dinner conversations. No more all expenses paid airplane flights to Los Angeles. And certainly no more professional recording studio sessions with top-notch musicians in the City of Angels.

They were back to the nitty-gritty task of pushing their musical load step by step, and it just so happened that the 24-mile stretch of road between The Brothers and Las Cruces was extremely hazardous. The two-lane highway was curving and treacherous, and every bit as challenging as any part of their journey so far.

The original idea was to break the segment into two parts and take two days to cover the distance.

Mary had driven ahead to Las Cruces to pick up additional air mattresses to help Roger and David survive the cold night temperatures, or at least that was the plan.

The Brothers were able to push the cart eight miles before calling it a day. They set up the tent, and waited for Mary's arrival.

Unfortunately, she showed up, driving Roger's station wagon, empty-handed. She hadn't been able to find any air mattresses, despite her best efforts.

Realizing that any attempts to sleep on the frozen ground would be useless, The Brothers took the tent down, packing everything back on the cart, and kept on pushing through the night.

In an effort to make lemonade out of lemons, they convinced themselves that it was actually much safer to travel the dangerous road at night when there would be much less traffic and less chance of collisions.

They pushed the entire night, the rest of the next day, and kept going until they were at the point of total exhaustion.

Finally collapsing, they ate a rushed meal of chuck roast, putting up the tent as fast as possible.

They were running on empty, and the only thing they truly wanted to do was get some much-needed sleep.

Mary had finally been able to locate new air mattresses, so they wouldn't have to sleep on the frozen rock-hard ground, not that they would have even noticed, at that point.

By now it was almost midnight. The plan was to sleep as late as possible the next day, or even the one after that, if needed. It didn't happen.

Everything was fine and quiet until around 3:00 a.m. The Brothers were both in deep sleep mode when a car filled with several guys and a female pulled up near the tent.

"Steps" immediately started barking and doing her duty as designated guard dog.

Roger heard one of the men say something about making sure they grabbed the food.

Grabbed the food? Even in his sleepy confusion, Roger realized that didn't sound very comforting.

Despite the fact that "Steps" was growling and barking her head off, the intruders kept on marching towards the tent.

Roger opened the safety zipper at the end of the tent and fired his 12-gauge shotgun into the air.

The gang ran back to their car, and Roger thought that would end their aggression.

They could hear laughter coming from the occupants of the car, causing Roger and David to wonder if maybe the entire ordeal was just some good-natured, though misguided, prank. Maybe it was all a big joke being played out by some of their friends from Deming.

Evidently the combined courage or stupidity of the gang came back, because once again they got out of their car and started approaching the tents.

"Steps" continued to bark and bark.

Deciding that conditions might only get worse, David grabbed his 38 pistol and a flashlight from under his sleeping bag. He didn't have time to locate his pants.

Wearing his Army-issued long johns, a long sleeved shirt, wool socks, and a stocking cap, he ran out of the tent. Giving the intruders the slight benefit of doubt, he fired off three shots into the air.

He could just as easily have aimed directly in their midst, and who knows what the consequences might have been?

They were certainly close enough that somebody could have easily been killed. This wasn't a laughing matter. The Brothers were being attacked by unknown invaders, pure and simply.

Anybody bold enough to try to take away a person's food, in the middle of the night, in the middle of the desert, might have been capable of doing anything to Roger and David.

That is exactly why The Walking Musical Balph Brothers carried loaded firearms with them on The Big Walk. Their weapons were not just for show and tell, by any means.

Their tent was certainly their castle, and The Brothers had every intention of defending themselves.

Clouds covered the moon, and David couldn't even see his hand in front of his own face. In the darkness of the desert night, the powder flash from David's pistol illuminated the sky like a fireworks display.

Evidently, the would-be invaders took note of the armed intentions of Roger and David, and lost their appetites for The Brothers' food stock, and an out-numbered confrontation. They ran back to their car, and, this time, finally decided to drive away, cussing and hollering as they disappeared into the darkness.

"Steps" had certainly earned her keep that night. Without her alert barking, The Brothers might have easily been completely overwhelmed by the invaders, due to being totally exhausted by their night and day pushing efforts.

At the very least, they could have been robbed and left defenseless in the desert night. At the worst, they could have been killed; dead and gone, another tragic story for the local newspapers, with their bodies being picked over by vultures after being tossed by the roadside.

After determining that the threat was truly over for the night, David realized he had a severe pain in his left foot. Had he accidentally shot himself? Was he bleeding to death in the middle of nowhere?

He turned his trusty flashlight down towards his socks and saw that he was standing right smack dab on top of a crushed cactus.

It took him at least 20 minutes to pull all of the needles out of his toes with the tweezers in their first-aid kit. By the time he had removed all of the sharp stickers, his foot was a punctured bloody mess.

He went to sleep, once again, thanking his Guardian Angels for bringing "Steps" into their lives and protecting them in their slumber.

He also prayed that his foot would heal without infection, hoping that the morning wouldn't find his entire leg swollen to the size of a large oak tree.

And to think that only a few days earlier they had been flying on a jet airliner, drinking cocktails with sexy stewardesses, and entertaining a captive audience with their toy flutes!

Could anybody imagine that their lives could experience such extremes in such a short period of time?

Chapter 35: Old Friends, Hot Wax, and Cat Fights

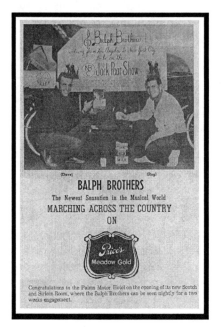

Promoting Meadow Gold

The Brothers arrived in Los Cruces, New Mexico, on February 20th, with David limping, but at least recovering from his late-night encounter with a cactus plant.

Mary had lined up a great job at The Palms Motor Motel for the grand opening of their renovated lounge. Unfortunately, the gig was scheduled for March 9th, a good two weeks away.

As usual, The Brothers were low on cash, getting down to their last five dollars.

They hadn't really made any decent money since they left Phoenix, and were surviving on the thinnest margin of cash and gifts from generous fans and supporters they met along the way.

It was a constant challenge that Roger and David faced every step of The Big Walk.

They had to enter towns, acting like celebrities, dressing as sharp as possible, and never letting anybody know how desperate things really were.

People just assumed that they had money in their pockets. How else would they have been able to survive on the road for such extended periods of time? Their fans must have thought that they had corporate sponsors footing the bills, or maybe that they had rich, silent investors, or money coming in from record sales.

The truth is that most of the people attending their shows only knew what they read about Roger and David in the newspapers and had no idea or concern about their financial situation.

The Brothers were doing good to keep gas in Roger's car, so Mary could continue to drive ahead and try to arrange bookings.

So having two weeks to kill before another paycheck came their way was not a good thing.

Mary knew this.

She always knew exactly how precarious the entire adventure was at any given time.

She usually knew right down to the penny exactly how much they had between the three of them, keeping the entire journey afloat.

While Roger and David had to deal with the daily grind of pushing the cart and staying in shape for upcoming performances, Mary had the constant stress and worry that everything would come crashing down around her if she wasn't successful in drumming up publicity and keeping those elusive paying gigs coming their way.

She was all too familiar with the gritty business side of the glamour world of entertainment.

She did her best to keep her frustrations about the constant rejections, the ludicrous demands, and the pitiful offerings to herself. It served no purpose to have The Brothers worrying over every detail, so she usually kept all negative news to herself, and went out of her way to play up any positive developments whenever possible.

She just wished that she had more good news more often.

When the news was good, Mary would be so excited that she would almost explode with joy.

Sometimes the payoffs were too few and far between.

For every bit of good news, there was just as much, and often times, even more, bad news.

She was able to convince the principal of the Alameda Junior High School to allow The Brothers to perform at an assembly.

That was the good news.

The bad news was that he refused to allow them to perform during the school day when it would be mandatory for all of the students to attend. If it had taken place during school hours, kids would have gladly paid 50 cents each to see anything, including a monkey jumping up and down, if it got them out of class.

Unfortunately, Roger and David could only perform after school hours, and they could only charge 25 cents per student.

So, instead of having a paying audience of 400 screaming students, they performed for 45 die-hard fans, earning a total of $11.25 for their efforts.

But even that minor financial victory was fleeting.

While helping them pack up their equipment after the show, one of the good-intentioned students sent by the principal to help clear the stage accidentally bumped into a footlight that then fell and knocked over Roger's baritone sax.

The fall damaged the keys on the sax, causing Roger to have to send it all the way back to Los Angeles for emergency repairs before the opening of The Palms in two weeks.

The money they made from the after-hours assembly performance didn't even cover a fourth of the cost of the repair.

They would have been better off if they had just kept their instruments in cases and whistled "Dixie" by the side of the road.

They could only hope that the 45 students who showed up for the concert came away with a deeper appreciation for live music.

Returning to the motel, they bumped into a man named Frank Logar, a drummer The Brothers had performed with years before back in Los Angeles.

He had been on the balcony when they were getting their clothes out of the cart and had spied his old friends in the parking lot.

Evidently he knew what to expect out of David and Roger after all this time. He didn't ask them what they were doing in the middle of nowhere or why they were pushing a cart across the desert. He seemed to think it was the most logical thing in the world to bump into the guys in the middle of nowhere. He simply asked them where they were performing.

It takes a musician to understand the lifestyle of a fellow musician, even when it comes to pushing a 1,000-pound cart to New York City.

The Brothers decided that rather than just kill the next two weeks waiting for the lounge to be opened, they would go on and start pushing the cart to El Paso.

Mary would be able to drive them back to The Palms in time for the grand opening, and they wouldn't go stir-crazy waiting around town with nothing to do.

Twelve miles out of town and 907 miles into The Big Walk, Roger and David were pushing the cart, step by step, when a car approached them and stopped.

Two people got out of the automobile and started running towards the cart, waving and hollering in broad daylight.

Was this a repeat visit from their recent night-time invaders?

Roger instinctively reached for his loaded shotgun.

As they ran closer, David realized that he recognized the man in the duo. He had certainly seen his face before, but with so many people entering and leaving their lives over the months, it was hard to keep up with everybody.

As luck would have it, they were Vine and Harry Suputsky, a nice couple they had met in Los Angeles the very first day of The Big Walk. They had invited The Brothers back to their motel room, insisting that they share a freshly cooked breakfast with the couple before they tackled the earliest miles of the journey.

They were school teachers who had gone back to New York City and taught almost an entire school year since leaving The Brothers behind in the California smog.

163

They were on their way back to Los Angeles for a vacation, and had spotted Roger and David pushing the cart down the road.

They told The Brothers they were living a few miles from the site of the ongoing New York World's Fair, a fact that made David's ears sting.

Roger and David's sister, Pat, had given The Brothers tickets to the event as a going away present when they started The Big Walk.

At the time, everybody assumed that The Brothers would rapidly make the trip across the country, appear on Jack Paar's television show, and then enjoy the exhibits and rides of the World's Fair, courtesy of the kindness of their sweet sister.

The reality of the situation hit David like a ton of bricks.

While his friends had gone back to New York, taught students for almost an entire school year, earned decent salaries, visited the World's Fair, and were now taking yet another vacation to California, David and Roger were still pushing a cart, struggling to survive on $11, and were not even in Texas, much less New York City.

A lesser man might have just tossed in the towel and given up, right then and there in the middle of nowhere.

The Suputskys gave them a big sack of fresh apples and bananas, and wished Roger and David the best of luck, urging them to be sure to look them up when they made it to The Big Apple.

David could only wonder when that day would come.

While The Brothers were running on empty, emotionally, financially, and physically, Mary decided that the time had come for some drastic measures.

She drove Roger's car back to Deming, New Mexico, and told their recent generous benefactor, Dick Hodson, president of The Auburn Rubber Company, the extent of their misery.

This wasn't a time for false pride.

The very survival of The Brothers was at stake.

Once again, Mr. Hodson came to the rescue.

He immediately opened his heart and his wallet, paying for a week's stay at The Palms Motor Motel, allowing The Brothers to get off the road, relax, regroup, and, just as importantly, rehearse for the grand opening concerts.

He also donated 300 of the famous 49-cent toy flutes to be used as giveaway promotions at the opening, and even provided a company truck to take the cart back to Los Cruces.

David and Roger remembered the words of their dear mother saying, "A friend in need is a friend indeed."

Mr. Hodson was certainly a friend of the highest order.

The rest of the week was spent recovering from the wear and tear of the road, while staying in the background of the construction crew at the motel.

Mary and the motel managers arranged for a parade on Saturday to go through town as a way of promoting the new restaurant opening.

In return for working on the details of the parade and arranging for Roger and David to return to town earlier than planned, the motel agreed to pay for room and board past the time covered by Mr. Hodson's generous donation. While it didn't cover any booze consumed, it did provide The Brothers with excellent steak dinners and the best the restaurant had to offer.

Cheerleaders from the local high school rode on top of the cart while The Brothers led the parade down Main Street. An ancient fire truck added noise to the festivities, while cars filled with students followed, honking horns.

The cheerleaders held up signs advertising the grand opening and Roger and David as the featured entertainers.

It was another one of those surreal times that pointed out the extremes of the entire trip.

One moment they were starving in the desert, down to their last few dollars, and the next they were surrounded by energetic cheerleaders, waving pom-poms and screaming with joy, while being the guests of honor in a parade down the center of town.

You simply can't make this stuff up.

The local news media covered the events, even featuring photos of Roger and David chugging down gallons of Price's Meadow Gold Milk, in an advertising promotion.

They did their best to drink as much of the free four gallons of milk they received as payment for their endorsements, but the fact is most of the precious liquid went to reward "Steps" for her faithful watchdog service, while the rest was put in the motel's refrigerator for safe keeping.

March 4th found Roger and David rehearsing and resting.

Things were building up to the grand opening on March 9th.

Everybody in the motel was friendly and supportive.

Relaxing at the Motel with "Steps"

This was despite the infamous napkin incident with "Steps."

As it turned out, their faithful watchdog had taken up a new hobby while enjoying the kindness of The Palms Motor Motel.

She had discovered that every day, just like clockwork, guests staying at the motel had this odd habit of placing trays full of leftover goodies right out in the walkway, just begging "Steps" to enjoy the tempting morsels, including a never-ending supply of cloth napkins.

Seems that "Steps" saw those linen towels as the perfect items to grab up and bury in the grass by the parking lot.

The motel staff couldn't understand why so many of their fine napkins suddenly were coming up missing.

It was only after the investigation of an attentive cleaning lady that the mystery was solved. Had "Steps" only been burying paper napkins, there wouldn't have been any problem, but the fact that she was putting a serious dent in the housekeeping budget simply couldn't be ignored.

After a serious discussion face to face with David and a firm swat on "Steps'" backside with a newspaper, the Great Missing Napkins Caper came to an end.

"Steps" had learned her lesson, and the motel's fine cloth napkins were no longer threatened or chewed up.

Opening night at the new lounge finally arrived with great fanfare.

Roger and David received standing ovations and did three encores for the wildly enthusiastic crowd.

The Brothers passed out all of the 300 toy flutes Mr. Hodson had provided, giving the atmosphere a New Year's Eve feeling.

The second night saw many of the same fans coming back for more live Dixieland Jazz, courtesy of The Walking Musical Balph Brothers.

Roger and David performed three full shows, and discovered that at the end of each show, the majority of the audience would get up and leave the lounge. Then, right before the next show, these same people would return and take their spots at the table.

While this was highly complimentary of the Balph's musical attraction, it wasn't what the lounge owners had hoped for.

Between The Balph Brothers' sets, the motel had arranged for another local band of young college musicians to perform. They had hoped to keep continuous music going for the audiences, encouraging them to drink, eat, and spend as much money as possible.

The only problem was that the other band wasn't very talented, and when compared to the professional performances of Roger and David, the second band looked and sounded horrible.

David thought the motel would have been better off just playing a jukebox between sets.

Being a fellow musician, David was somewhat embarrassed for the other guys, seeing the audience almost bolt from the room when The Balphs' performances ended.

At least he took pride in the fact that, as soon as David and Roger hit the stage, the crowds filed back in and resumed their drinking and clapping.

The third night at the Palms' newly opened lounge started off with much promise.

Little did Roger or David realize how quickly things would go downhill, with almost tragic results.

When they first arrived at the lounge, a young lady came up to them saying it was her birthday and requesting that they play a song for her during the show.

She had evidently been at the lounge quite a while, enjoying the liquid refreshments offered by the bar.

By the time the show actually started, this same young lady was extremely intoxicated. She was drunk. Plowed. Not two, but ten sheets to the wind.

While Roger and David tried to entertain the attentive audience, the birthday gal proceeded to yell and holler at the stage.

Things were somewhat under control during the musical segments, with the tunes drowning out any heckling from the woman. Between songs, when Roger tried to introduce the titles and make contact with the audience, the drunken woman would start making trouble again.

The lounge security staff was nowhere to be found.

David noticed that a couple at the woman's table seemed to be getting into fights during the music.

One guy pushed another guy, and once again, Roger and David expected the motel management to come to their rescue and handle the situation.

Things would calm down for a few minutes and then flare up again.

About 20 minutes into the second show, Roger had endured enough of the woman's insults and yelling.

He thought that maybe he would be able to embarrass her into calming down, or just outright leaving.

He had the spotlight put on her table and asked everybody in the audience to give her a big round of applause, which they did.

The drunken birthday girl stood up, accepted her moment in the spotlight, shaking her hands in the air and soaking up every bit of the attention she could muster.

Then Roger decided to take things one step too far. In hindsight, it probably wasn't the wisest thing to do, but by this point, Roger and David both had endured far more abuse than anybody could have expected.

Right when the applause ended, Roger said, "Ladies and Gentlemen, this is a perfect excuse for birth control."

Well, birthday girl might have been drunk, but she certainly wasn't deaf.

You could almost see the steam pouring out from under her pretty starched collar.

She stumbled to her feet, picked up one of the hot candles glowing on her table, and threw it at the stage with all of her intoxicated fury.

The molten, burning wax covered the stage, the instruments, and even a few members of the college band seated at the foot of the stage.

The burning wax hit one of the local trumpet players right in the middle of the crotch of his pants, and while it was comical to witness, you can imagine the personal pain it caused to the hapless bystander.

When David saw that some of the hot wax had splashed onto their backing tapes on the recorder, he realized things were getting completely out of hand.

He jumped off stage, went over to the bar, and asked the bartender to escort the birthday lady out of the lounge area.

The bartender had just turned 21, and this was his first job. He was completely frozen with fear and totally useless.

David started to walk back towards the stage, thinking that maybe he could talk on the microphone and get the manager's attention.

Walking past the candle-slinging woman, he saw that she had yet another glowing candle in her hand and was ready to throw it at Roger.

Roger was at the mike, trying to calm the audience down.

The club manager and his assistant were at the back of the lounge, a good 60 feet away from the stage.

David could see that they were holding drinks in their hands, and were evidently enjoying the grand opening as much as their customers, seemingly oblivious to the chaos happening onstage.

David saw the drunken woman preparing to throw the second candle, and all he could think about was how she could hit Roger in the side of his head, and possibly kill him right then and there.

Making a split-second decision to save his brother from potentially fatal injuries, David jumped across the table, bolting over the other couple sharing the birthday girl's party, hitting the candle-yielding woman directly in the face with the back of his hand.

She dropped the flaming candle and fell over into her seat.

Her female friend at the table immediately started whacking David over the head with her loaded purse.

All David knew for certain was that hands, fingers, purses, fists, and other assorted objects were hitting him repeatedly on his face, neck, chest, and shoulders.

Dazed and confused, it took a few moments for David to grab the second woman's wrists and settle her down.

Meanwhile, a tall, bearded man, who had overheard David ask the bartender to escort the candle-throwing floozy out of the club came over to the table and proceeded to jump right in the middle of things.

The bearded wonder was the birthday girl's friend and the husband of the purse-hitting lady. He was just as drunk as the two fighting women.

He also happened to be the sparing partner of the professional boxer Ezzard Charles. This was just David's typical luck. He couldn't bump into a meek, mild-mannered accountant. No. That would be too easy. He had to run right into a guy who makes his living beating full-grown men to bloody pieces.

Seeing his younger brother right in the middle of a growing riot of swinging bodies, Roger jumped off stage and ran right smack into the second woman who had flailed away at David's head with her purse.

She made the mistake of jumping up in Roger's face, swinging her hands and screaming.

Roger picked her up and tossed her across three tables, while rushing to David's rescue.

At least the fight was taking place on the club floor, and not up onstage where their instruments and sound equipment could have been destroyed.

Those fragile pieces of metal were the tools of trade for The Brothers, and losing them would literally keep them from earning a living, threatening their very survival.

With fists flying, people screaming, and general mayhem reigning supreme, the police finally arrived on the scene.

They arrested the birthday woman and the bearded man.

As it turned out, the bearded man used to work at The Palms as a bartender, until they discovered he was giving away booze to his friends and costing the club untold amounts of money.

Ever since they had fired him, he had been intent on causing as much trouble as possible.

To compound the issue even more, when his wife, the purse-toting lady in question, got too many drinks in her, she always caused trouble, picking fights and swinging her bag at whoever was close enough to hit.

The Balph Brothers had unknowingly wound up right in the middle of the cesspool, innocently trying to perform onstage while a festering fever had been growing and multiplying right before their eyes in the audience.

At least it wasn't anything personal. These people were just waiting for an excuse to fight, and Roger's little off-the-cuff on-stage comment about birth control was all it took to ignite the flames.

When the dust finally settled, the aggressive drunks had been hauled off to jail, and The Walking Musical Balph Brothers were left to pick up the pieces and call it a night.

David looked down at his tattered shirt and saw it was covered with dark red splotches of blood.

It was only then that he realized his lip was deeply cut open, with an open gash oozing crimson liquid down his chin, onto his chest.

Was his lip damaged beyond repair? Had a night of senseless violence robbed him of his ability to blow his horn and earn a living?

Was this the lasting souvenir of the opening of The Palms lounge that would follow him the rest of his life, taunting him every time he looked into a mirror and thought about what might have been?

All he knew at that moment was that his lip hurt like the dickens, and the sooner he was able to get some ice on it, the better.

He was thankful that Roger was still alive and breathing.

He was thankful that the flaming airborne candles hadn't caught the entire lounge on fire and killed everybody in the audience.

He was thankful that the police had finally arrived and taken the violent ill-tempered drunks off into the night.

But most of all, he was thankful that the birthday girl's big day had finally come to an end.

Tomorrow he would go to the doctor and see how badly his lip was damaged.

All he wanted to do at that precise moment was go back to his motel room and get as much healing sleep as humanly possible.

He could only hope that "Steps" hadn't gathered up another mountain of fine cloth napkins and left them by his door.

Chapter 36: Blood Brothers

David survived the night after the barroom brawl better than his lips did.

He woke up with swollen, bruised, and cut lips that were oozing blood. The simple act of eating was enough to open the wound even larger.

He had gone to a local doctor's office in search of some miracle cure but came away aching.

The doctor told him that the best thing he could do was just keep his mouth shut for at least the next two days.

That was all fine and dandy, and basically very sound advice, except for the minor detail that David was expected to blow his trumpet for three shows at the final opening engagements for the newly renovated Palms Motor Motel lounge that very night, then do it all over again the next night.

Roger performed the first two shows onstage by himself, accompanied by their ever-faithful backing tracks.

David stood on the sidelines, nursing his lips, while providing moral support for his brother.

It was the first time David had ever been on the outside looking in on his own stage performance. He didn't like the feeling.

The backing tracks, where he usually played his trumpet solos, seemed amazingly bare and empty.

Roger tried to fill the gaps in the show by covering David's parts on his saxophone, but it just wasn't the same.

On the songs that featured David exclusively, Roger had to turn his back to the audience and physically run the tapes ahead to the parts where he could join back in on the show.

While standing on the sidelines, David had been drinking more than his share of liquid encouragement, trying to numb the pain in his lips.

Finally, when the third and last show of the evening began, David couldn't hold back any longer. He simply had to get up on that stage and perform his parts for the audience.

Since the third show was the last show for the night, he hoped his lips would hold up long enough for the final encore. If he could just coax an hour or so of buzz out of his injured body parts, he would have another night to recoup and heal, out of the spotlight.

David bolted onstage, enjoying the hearty round of applause from the audience.

Roger was relieved to have his partner back onstage, sharing the duties and the various solos.

David made it halfway through the first song before his body surrendered. His lips gave out.

Blood ran down his face, over his chin, onto his chest, and proceeded to paint the front of his stage shirt a dark crimson.

To make matters even worse, his lips were still partially numb from the previous night's attack, making it next to impossible for David to control the sounds coming out of his instrument.

So not only did he look horrible, he didn't sound all that great either.

The audience was all too aware of the previous evening's chaos. News travels fast in a small town, so everybody in the lounge knew exactly what David had been through the night before.

They were all on his side, comrades-in-arms.

Perhaps that is why despite the missed notes, the awkward moments, and the steady steam of blood flowing down David's face, the crowd roared its approval for his efforts.

David could almost feel the healing energy and goodwill of the fans in the lounge as he did his best to follow The Walking Musical Balph Brothers constant motto, "Find a Way."

Roger was smiling from ear to ear, and couldn't think of a time when he had been more proud of his younger "blood" brother.

Chapter 37: Conga Coolers and Mystery Solved

Good news came to The Brothers on Friday, March 20th.

After finishing up their final week at The Palms, David's lip had finally healed.

Roger and Mary had been driving back and forth all week, traveling the 40 miles between Las Cruces, New Mexico, and El Paso, Texas, looking for musical gigs.

Their efforts paid off when they secured a three-week contract with The El Paso Manor Motel, paying the princely sum of $400 per week.

This was, by far, the highest paying job they had received since leaving Los Angeles. Maybe their luck was finally changing.

Saturday, The Brothers performed their last show at The Palms, giving four encores before leaving the stage for the final time.

Roger and Mary spent the rest of the evening and morning together, toasting their good fortunes and growing closer in their developing romantic relationship.

David was on his own, happy, single, and carefree.

He joined up with the assistant manager of The Palms and a new friend by the name of Gene Priestly, who was the editor of the newspaper in Las Cruces.

They decided to head across the border to Juarez, Mexico for a late, late night of drinks and relaxation.

Putting his trust in the hands of his local drinking buddies, they wound up at a joint called The Impala Inn.

Gene told David that he simply had to try the specialty of the house, a drink called The Conga Cooler. Everybody at the table raved on and on about how wonderful it was.

It wasn't hard to convince David, who just happened to be very thirsty and still glowing from the good news about the upcoming, high-paying gigs awaiting him in El Paso.

He eagerly consumed the pink icy beverage, noting that it tasted a little bit like a stick of licorice.

As soon as his first glass was empty, another one immediately appeared to take its place.

He was too happy to notice that he was the only one at the table actually drinking the legendary drink. All the rest of his drinking buddies seemed content to nurse beers.

When it came time to head back to Las Cruces, David discovered that the room was spinning when he headed towards the door.

While doing his best to sober up on the ride back to the United States of America, David tried to keep up with the conversations going on around him in the car.

He became vaguely aware of the fact that his fellow drinkers were talking about being shot at in the middle of the desert by two guys who were sleeping in a tent beside some cart filled with musical instruments.

Was David more intoxicated than he realized? Maybe he was dreaming.

He heard the guy from The Palms say something about how lucky they were that they hadn't been shot when that crazy guy ran out of the tent in his underwear and stepped on the cactus.

This had to be a dream. What in the world were these guys talking about?

Between the noise from the highway, the music from the Mexican radio station, and the alcoholic effects of the Conga Coolers, David was having a hard time keeping up with the conversation going on in the car, much less the one running around inside his head.

He heard somebody mention Mary's name and how much talking she had to do to keep them from canceling the entire contract when The Brothers had tried to literally kill their innocent welcoming committee out in the dark of the desert a few weeks ago.

By the time they made it across the border and back to Las Cruces, David had been able to fill in the details and realized that the mystery of the 3:00 am roadside invaders who came in the night, trying to steal their food, had been solved.

176

It was the guys from The Palms Motor Motel, coming out to find the The Walking Musical Balph Brothers and welcome them to the town. They had read about Roger and David's impending arrival in the local newspaper, which Gene happened to edit, and had decided to form a greetings party to extend hospitality to the traveling musicians.

Instead they had been met with blasting shotguns and flaming pistols.

David said a silent prayer of thanks that he hadn't aimed his shots directly into the car when he thought he was being attacked.

If it wasn't for his Guardian Angels, there was no telling what might have happened.

Fortunately, his riding companions had a good sense of humor about the ordeal and didn't hold any grudges.

They stopped at Gene's apartment for a final nightcap.

By now it was 5:30 in the morning, and David was ready to head back to the motel for some dream-time sleep.

He was still feeling the remnants of The Conga Coolers and knew he had consumed enough alcohol for one night, or two.

The other guys were still in a party mood, seeing as how they hadn't consumed any of the infamous Coolers.

They wanted to have another round of drinks while watching the sun come up.

David asked them to give him a ride back to the motel, and they just laughed at him.

Seeing as how it was only a mile and half to the motel, he decided to take matters into his own hands, or feet, and run back to his clean bed.

The guys didn't want to hear anything about one of the gang calling it a night. They were still having too much fun to end things.

David ran down the stairs, and discovered that Gene, the newspaper editor, was chasing him, laughing and yelling all the way.

It was one of those moments that only make sense when a person is buzzed from a night of heavy drinking and partying.

David easily climbed the brick wall at the bottom of the stairs, landing on the other side and staring at the growling teeth of a Chow watchdog.

David, in his still-buzzed stupor, looked at the dog, said "hello" and went on about his way.

Following right behind him, Editor Gene landed on his feet, saw the drooling living alarm system, and immediately was attacked by the dog.

The Chow evidently sensed the fear in Editor Gene, who was slightly more sober than David.

While David rapidly walked out of the doggy's enclosed gated backyard, Editor Gene turned around and scrambled back up and over the brick wall, trying to protect the seat of his pants from canine tooth marks.

Feeling that immediate danger was now over, David proceeded to jog on towards the motel.

By now it was 6:30 in the morning, and David was running down the main drag of town, wearing his tuxedo, laughing all the way.

Casually looking over his shoulder, David saw his drinking buddy, Editor Gene, back in hot pursuit, rapidly gaining on him.

David picked up his pace, bolting down the sidewalk. Just as he passed a little Catholic chapel, one of his shoes came off.

As David turned back to retrieve his foot protector, Editor Gene caught up with him, grabbing him by the shoulder and demanding that he go back to the apartment for a few more friendly drinks.

Before David could come up with an answer, the local priest of the chapel came out and took Editor Gene by the lapel, telling him that he needed to come to morning prayer service.

Seizing this moment of divine intervention, David counted his blessings once again, and ran all the way to the motel, never looking back.

He hit his bed without even bothering to take off his tuxedo, dreaming of Conga Coolers and tasting licorice.

Chapter 38: Conga Revenge and the Bull Wins

David, Mary, Roger and Friends Enjoying Music in Juarez

David woke up after a few hours of sleep, realizing he had lost his battle with the infamous Mexican Conga Coolers.

Although he did his best to help Roger pack up all of the instruments and deliver them in two carloads to their next gig in El Paso, he felt sick and cold, and just this side of completely horrible.

Maybe there had been something besides alcohol in his drinks. Seeing how powerful they were, he didn't see how any germs and trot-inspiring bugs could have survived being in the tasty, but evidently toxic, beverages.

He stayed in bed most of Monday, hoping he would recover in time for the paying gig on Wednesday at Gadsen High in El Paso.

Roger and Mary tried their best to find a few ounces of sympathy for the younger Balph Brother, but it was hard to muster much compassion for David's late-night shenanigans across the border.

Mary was secretly thankful that Roger had spent his time with her at the hotel, instead of following his brother to Mexico; who knew what trouble might have been waiting for him.

She had enough on her hands just keeping the journey moving forward, without worrying about what David was getting into when he wasn't around them.

Besides, Roger had promised to take her to see a genuine bullfight in the upcoming week, while taking care of some personal business Mary needed to deal with as soon as possible.

The less time Roger spent with David offstage, the better things seemed to be for everybody.

Between pushing the cart and performing together, The Balph Brothers had more than enough time to get on each other's nerves; so, any time apart was usually healthy.

There was very little nurturing for David and his monster Mexican hangover.

Mary just hoped he got over his so-called "illness" in time to perform with his usual energy and enthusiasm.

Fortunately, Wednesday morning found David alive and kicking off the last of the cobwebs from his alcohol-induced malaise.

The Walking Musical Balph Brothers performed for 1,400 screaming students, who acted like they had never seen any live musicians before.

Those high schoolers screamed and clapped with such rabid appreciation that the school's principal decided to extend the assembly program for the entire morning, allowing The Brothers to perform all the way until lunchtime.

David was amazed that none of the students requested any rock and roll music. They seemed to enjoy hearing all of the Dixieland Jazz arrangements, without even considering that they could perform different kinds of music, if requested.

The Brothers left Gadsen High feeling like celebrities, having signed hundreds of autographs.

If even half of the students who promised to write Jack Paar actually came through on their promises, his office should have been flooded with fan letters.

Mary was just glad that David wasn't still green around the gills, wobbling from the effects of his Conga Coolers.

Their first performance at The El Paso Manor lounge was successful, despite having to deal with an odd liquor law.

The town had a very curious attitude toward the demon known as liquor.

Hotels and nightclubs were not allowed to advertise any entertainment in newspaper ads or television commercials.

It was strictly word of mouth, with almost a wink and a secret handshake.

In order to get a drink in the club, a potential alcoholic sinner had to secure a special pass from the front desk of the hotel. This card made the holder an official member of the club, allowing for the purchase of demon rum or whiskey or vodka.

But that was just the first step in the charade, a drinking game that Roger assumed had evolved as a convoluted method to appease the city's God-fearing church ladies and their genteel sensibilities.

Once the card holder made his way into the club and took a seat, the rules of the game became even more surreal.

The waitress was not allowed to ask customers what they would like to drink. That simple act would be a criminal offense, punishable by fines, loss of job, and possible jail time.

All the waitress was allowed to ask was "How can I be of service to you?"

Woe be the thirsty outsider who didn't know the secret phrases, unwritten laws, elaborate handshakes, and the correct combination of winks.

This strange combination of rules even extended to the check-in desk at the hotel.

The desk clerks were not allowed, by law, to tell arriving guests that The Balph Brothers, or anybody else, for that matter, were performing in the lounge.

That hideous act would have been considered promoting the sale of liquor in the city of El Paso, and that was absolutely, positively forbidden.

So, with most of their usual advertising vehicles illegal, Roger and David did the best they could, while trying to work around the arcane laws and regulations.

They arranged to play a benefit concert for a local crippled children's clinic and were able to advertise the performance in the newspaper, adding the curious detail that they were visiting the city and staying at The El Paso Manor while in town.

They could only hope that people would read the ad, drop by the hotel, see the cart in front of the lounge, and figure out that perhaps The Brothers were performing at the fine establishment when they weren't doing free concert for kids who couldn't walk.

It was a very, very indirect way to advertise a concert.

The good drinking people of El Paso, Texas, evidently knew how to make their curious system work because both Friday and Saturday night shows were filled with customers who knew the right passwords and handshakes.

The club manager paid Roger and David the promised $400 for the first weekend of shows, and The Brothers felt like they were truly the wealthiest guys in the world. Frank Sinatra, Jr., had nothing on them, by golly.

After being so consistently broke along the trip, having money burning holes in their pockets was a completely sublime experience.

They decided to take their Sunday afternoon off to give Mary her promised trip to a genuine Mexican bullfight in nearby Juarez.

While David had seen a bullfight or two during previous trips to Tijuana when he was in the military, Roger and Mary were true virgins when it came to witnessing the ancient blood-sport battle between man and beast.

Even though some people objected to the violence and gore of the traditional matches, David found the battles exciting.

It didn't bother him to see blood gushing from the wounds in the side of the animals, as the human attackers danced and pranced through century-old pageantries.

The fact that some gringo spectators would actually pass out in the bleachers only added to the experience.

David appreciated the skill and energy it took to perform in the arena. He knew how long and hard the matador and his support team had to work to become professional bullfighters.

The spectators came to the fight expecting to see blood.

What they hadn't counted on was the fact that sometimes the bull wins.

And of course, it had to happen at the very first bullfight Roger and Mary ever attended.

Right at the peak of the excitement, in the midst of all the costumed glory, the esteemed matador misjudged his raging, snorting, horned bovine opponent, and was gored by the bull.

The human target was thrown 15 feet in the air and landed with a sickening thud on the blood-stained ground.

Putting all pomp and rituals aside, the medical crew ran out into the middle of the arena, taking the damaged, limp, crumpled warrior away on a stretcher.

The tourists in the crowd didn't realize how unusual it was for this event to happen.

Even in a slightly seedy, border town bullfighting arena, the odds were heavily stacked in favor of the humans winning the fight.

When you consider that the bull had already been stabbed and punctured by an entire supporting cast of costumed picadores to weaken the neck and lower the bulls head, long before the star matador even entered the ring, the fact that the roaring beast won the conquest was even more amazing. Perhaps because he did fight so valiantly, his life was spared for breeding, and he lived to fight another day.

The fate of the matador remains unknown.

Entertaining at the Children's Clinic

Chapter 39: Bouncing Checks
and Falling Bullets

The Old Amador Hotel in Las Cruces

The next two weeks at The El Paso Manor passed without incident. While the club didn't have enough business during the week to justify three shows per night, the crowds had been decent, and just as importantly, thirsty, even if they did have to navigate the curious drinking rules of the city.

On Sunday, April 5th, The Brothers performed at the grand opening of a new neighborhood subdivision for The Mock Home Development Company in Las Cruces, New Mexico.

They had met the developer a few weeks earlier, where he promised to call them when he was ready for his ribbon-cutting, and, unlike so many big-talking people The Brothers had met along the journey, this fellow actually came through with his offer.

The developer had arranged for local radio stations to broadcast the event live over the air to listeners in two states, covering all of Las Cruces and most of El Paso.

He gladly paid The Brothers with a company check, and couldn't have been more supportive of their efforts.

Having The Famous Walking Musical Balph Brothers appear live and in person at his opening had added an element of show business to the event that was hard to come by in that part of New Mexico. The developer was so impressed with The Brothers that he invited them back the following Sunday for an encore performance.

It turns out that live Dixieland music was just the right background soundtrack for selling houses.

Roger and David spent the next week continuing their successful engagements at The El Paso Manor.

David had a nice date with a local girl named Amy, while Roger and Mary continued to find their own private times to be alone between shows, promotions, and the usual obligations.

They were even able to sell Mary's old car before it totally and completely fell apart.

The local Ford dealership interviewed The Brothers live on television, while showcasing the new models. Since it wasn't a form of paid advertising, they were able to mention the fact that they were appearing at The El Paso Manor lounge without breaking any of the city's odd laws concerning alcohol.

Try as he might, David couldn't understand the logic of the assorted rules and regulations, but was happy whenever they were able to work around them and accomplish their goals of getting seats filled at the nightclub.

They played yet another weekend at The Manor, and did their repeat performance for the housing development in Las Cruces.

Once again, the developer gratefully presented The Brothers with a company check for a job well done.

Friday, as they were preparing for what they thought was their last weekend in El Paso, they discovered that both of the checks from the real estate developer had bounced.

To make matters even worse, they had cashed the checks at the Manor, and now the manager of the hotel was threatening to withhold their other payments to cover the bad ones.

Just as Roger and David were finally getting to the point of having a little bit of financial security as reward for their weeks of hard work in El Paso, everything was suddenly in jeopardy.

They drove back to Las Cruces, determined to solve the dilemma.

Everything else would just have to wait until this matter was resolved.

The developer was apologetic and told them to simply run the checks back through the bank. He was certain that they would clear without any additional problems.

Sergeant Stroud

While back in Las Cruces, they met up with a friend from The Palms Motor Motel who had previously offered to sell Roger a used 45 pistol for $30. Sergeant Stroud was a good-natured fellow who enjoyed live music and making a few extra dollars moonlighting as a bouncer at local bars.

While David had use of his 38 pistol and a shotgun on the trip, Roger had only been able to use his shotgun for armed protection.

With the purchase of the well-used sidearm, Roger would be more comfortable facing the dangers of the road.

The thought did occur to him that perhaps it might come in handy if certain pieces of financial paper kept on bouncing from New Mexico to Texas and back again.

David arranged to meet their gun-selling friend at an old hotel in Las Cruces, while Roger ran some errands for Mary, picking up hair tonic and other mysterious beauty supplies that were deemed absolutely essential to her feminine needs.

David couldn't help but smile when he saw his big, jovial, bald-headed friend at the hotel. Even then the hotel looked more like a museum or a relic from the distant past than an operating business.

David had wondered if the old wooden stairs would support his weight long enough for him to make it to the upper floor where Sergeant Stroud lived.

They talked a while, with David telling him the latest stories from the road, while catching up on assorted gossip.

Eventually, the gun and money changed hands, and David was getting ready to say his goodbyes when he noticed a pair of handcuffs over on the nightstand.

For reasons that only David could possibly understand, the youngest Balph Brother decided he just simply had to inspect those shiny chrome manacles, and before he realized it, Sergeant Stroud was offering to give them to him, saying that they might come in handy out on the road.

Being his typical inquisitive self, David simply couldn't resist putting the handcuffs on and, what else, locking them securely around his own wrists.

While Sergeant Stroud had assured him that the key was safely tucked away in the pocket of his pants, when it came time to actually use the key and unlock the cuffs, the key couldn't be found.

Bad timing.

Not the best situation to find a person in.

Visualize the scene.

Sleepy old-time hotel in a rundown part of an even sleepier small town in New Mexico.

We have young, out-of-town, energetic, athletic, semi-famous David Balph of the famous Walking Musical Balph Brothers alone in a private room with a much older bald-headed, laughing guy named Sergeant.

Semi-famous celebrity David is handcuffed while cash money and a 45 pistol are lying on the bed.

And the promised key to unlock the shiny chrome restraint device is nowhere to be found.

If it had happened to anybody other than himself, David would have been rolling on the floor with laughter, choking on his spittle, gasping for air.

To semi-quote legendary film comedians Laurel and Hardy, "This was another fine mess David found himself in."

While David was squirming and counting the seconds until his release, Sergeant Stroud continued to rummage through his pockets, searching for the elusive key.

After much too long a time, he decided the key must be down in his car, parked outside the hotel.

Seeing as how Roger had had plenty of time to finish running his errands for Mary, David was even more anxious to be freed from his self-imposed bondage.

It was one thing to be embarrassed in front of Sergeant Stroud, but an entirely different level of humiliation to have to face his older brother while handcuffed in a seedy hotel in the middle of nowhere.

Time was a wastin'.

David picked up the newly purchased pistol with one of his cuffed hands, grabbing a box of bullets with the other shackled one.

Right when he reached the wooden stairway going down to the parking lot, Sergeant Stroud innocently placed the gun's leather holster over David's shoulder, as it was included in the gun's purchase price.

The added weight caused David to wobble, dropping the box of bullets in the process.

They made a tremendous noise in the hallway, bouncing and rolling down the stairs, each cascading step creating another round of clangs and bangs.

One of the potentially lethal bullets rolled over the side of the banister and dropped directly on the head of a little old bald-headed man who was reading a newspaper in a chair 15 feet below. The impact caused him to let out a yelp.

As it turned out, the man was completely deaf.

But he wasn't blind.

And he certainly had feelings in his head.

He looked up to see a handcuffed David stumbling down the wooden stairs, heading in his direction with a pistol waving in the air, while local resident by the name of Sergeant was escorting him down from his room.

Of course, all of the noise from the bouncing bullets attracted everybody's attention, and the hotel parking lot filled up with curious spectators.

One of the wise guys in the crowd just had to recognize that David was the same guy who had been in the paper a few weeks earlier, and then another guy said he had seen the very same handcuffed kid playing trumpet at The Palms the month before.

If there had ever been a time that David had wished he hadn't been so gosh-darned famous, this was one of those moments. His ears were burning crimson red with embarrassment.

After what seemed like an eternity of stares and good-natured kidding, the crowd finally let David and Sergeant through to his car, where the long-missing key was retrieved.

While David endured the jabs of the other longtime residents of the hotel, Sergeant removed the chrome shackles and made sure the bald-headed, newspaper-reading man on the stairs was still alive and uninjured.

It had been another close call that could have ended in disaster. Once again, David's Guardian Angels had been on duty, even if they did allow a little bit of humiliation to come his way.

By the time Roger made it back from his errands, David's ears had returned to their normal color.

When Roger asked David if anything had happened while he was gone, David calmly told him that everything had been fine, just another typical day on The Big Walk.

On Saturday, April 18th, The Brothers gave their final contracted performance at The Manor.

All joy and enthusiasm for the performance evaporated when the club manager told them he was holding back $300 from their payment to cover the still-bouncing checks from the dead beat home developer in New Mexico.

Despite the developer's repeated assurances, the checks still weren't worth the paper they were written on.

Roger felt his trigger finger itching.

They had all of Sunday to fuss and fume over the matter.

They spent the day packing the car, washing the car, inspecting the car, and then cleaning their guns.

By Monday, Roger was tired of lame excuses. He took matters into his own hands, not by using his newly purchased $30 pistol, but by calling the District Attorney in Las Cruces.

The D.A. told the home developer that he had 15 days to make the checks good or face going to jail.

The Big Walk was on a big hold until those worthless pieces of paper turned into cold, hard, green cash.

David was determined to make the home developer pay for the extra hotel costs and whatever additional expenses were caused by his bad checks.

On Tuesday, the home developer called and said that the money would be wired to the hotel by the end of the day.

Big surprise. It didn't happen.

On Wednesday, April 22nd, the home developer finally showed up in El Paso with the long-promised cash to cover the bad checks that had been bouncing in two states.

Evidently, the call to the District Attorney got through to him.

Evidently it is hard to be a big-shot real estate developer when you get tossed in jail.

Amazingly, Mr. Big Shot Developer was mad and disgusted by Roger's actions, conveniently ignoring the fact he had kept The Brothers waiting six days, listening to his empty promises.

He acted like he was the one who had been wronged, injured, and delayed.

If Roger hadn't taken matters into his own hands, they might well have been waiting another month, and then never even seen a penny of their hard-earned cash.

The developer's parting words to The Brothers was to tell them to go to hell.

The guy was a real class act to the bitter end.

Roger calmly replied that he would go gladly to hell, and on the way he would make sure to give Mr. Hot Shot Developer some publicity about his shady little housing development.

David was just thankful that they finally had their money in hand, and that Roger's 45 pistol had remained in its holster.

Chapter 40: Dramatic Exit

The El Paso Times

Leased Wires of The Associated Press (AP) and New York Times Service—Member of Audit Bureau of Circulation.

EL PASO, TEXAS, FRIDAY, MARCH 27, 1964

Pushing Their Way To Top!

While many musicians eventually make a pilgrimage to the nation's music mecca, New York City, few choose the mode of transportation used by Rog and Dave Balph.

Like earlier pilgrims, they are walking. The brothers disbanded a six-man combo in Los Angeles last July and hiked some 900 footweary miles to arrive in El Paso Tuesday, March 24. Engagements at clubs and hotels along the way gave blisters and a chance to heal temporarily.

Rest stops included the Mission Inn, Riverside, Calif.; Stardust Hotel, Yuma, Ariz; Coronet Hotel, Phoenix; Tidelands, Tucson; and The Palms in Las Cruces. They are currently playing at the Mardi Gras Club in El Paso Manor on North Mesa.

The decision to make the long hike was made during the period of early enthusiasm for the late president's national health program. Dave Balph points out that while they have actually gained a few pounds on the trip, they are enjoying a healthier distribution of pounds overall.

An important element in their exercise stint is the homemade luggage rack they are pushing from Los Angeles to New York. Mounted on bicycle wheels, the loaded carriage weighs 1,000 pounds.

Roy Balph suggests that few musicians have chosen this method of "pushing" their way to

the top of their profession. Interest in the unique hike has brought them many engagements along their route, ranging from club performances to concerts at high school assemblies.

Primarily, the brothers are musicians, not stunt men. Rog began playing the saxophone at the age of 2, with his father fingering the keys. Dave delayed starting his career until he was 6. Rog, a graduate of Westlake College of Modern Music in Los Angeles, plays baritone, tenor and alto saxophones, and B flat and E flat clarinets.

Dave attended the Naval School of Music, Washington, D.C. and doubles on trumpet and trombone. They play all seven instruments during their performances at the Mardi Gras Club.

Before forming the Roger Balph sextet in Los Angeles, Rog had been featured soloist with the Pee Wee Hunt, Les Brown and Woody Herman bands. Earlier, he was a six-time winner on Horace Heidt's Youth Opportunity

Show. He has also appeared on Ed Sullivan's "Town of the Town."

Since starting their odyssey, they have cut a disc titled "Balph's Play with Toys." It resulted from an entertainment stint in which the brothers played such numbers as "13th Street Rag," "Saints Go Marching In" and "Toy Flute Medley" on children's toy flutes. The record was used at the national Toy Fair in New York and is now receiving nationwide distribution.

HIKERS PARK PUSHMOBILE—Dave, left, and Rog Balph park their 1,000 pound luggage rack in El Paso, completing the first leg of their push toward the top of the musical entertainment world. The brothers left Los Angeles in July and have been walking and pushing their way to New York between engagements along the way. Following a two-week engagement in El Paso Manor's Mardi Gras Room, the two musicians will pack their seven instruments, load their homemade pushmobile and push along on their trek. They make no forecast for their arrival in New York.
—Times Staff Photo

El Paso Publicity

A week later than expected, The Brothers were finally leaving scenic El Paso.

The long promised cash to cover the bounced checks allowed them to settle up their outstanding bills in town, and make things right with The Manor office that had been holding their last performance check due to the insufficient funds fiasco.

They made it a grand total of two and a half miles before the right rear tire blew out.

The tires had to be kept at such high levels of air pressure just to be able to push the cart down the road that they were like overfilled balloons just waiting to explode at any moment.

Every time a tire blew out, The Brothers had to take everything off of the cart, the entire 1,000 pounds of instruments, supplies, and support materials. Then they had to take the wheel off, remove the tire from the rim, patch the tire or totally replace it, put the tire back on the wheel, put the wheel back on the axle, secured the axle to the fork, and then push the cart on down the road until the next blowout.

It could take anywhere from an hour to an entire day to replace a simple thing like a flat tire, depending on how far they had to walk or hitch a ride to find a replacement. So, naturally, it was a big relief when the mission was accomplished, and the tire was holding air again.

They resumed their walk, coming down a long sloping hill on the edge of El Paso's city limits.

They were going through a streetlight, passing by a policeman who was directing traffic on a busy intersection when a sharp bang echoed off the buildings.

It sounded like a shotgun shell going off, and The Brothers instinctively flinched, ducking for cover while looking for the source of the loud noise.

The policeman just about swallowed his whistle, reaching for his service revolver. Was his city under attack?

Like The Brothers, he scanned the nearby buildings, looking for the profile of a sniper or perhaps a bank robber.

There was that split second where time seemed to stop, and everything moved in slow motion like a Steve McQueen action movie.

The cop noticed that the cart was wobbling on the left side, limping to a stop in the middle of the street.

Had some disgruntled fan, jealous of The Walking Musical Balph Brothers growing fame, gone berserk, lost his grip on reality and taken a crack shot at Roger and David, right in the middle of daylight on the dusty streets of El Paso?

No. As it turned out, it was not an attack by would-be assassins who failed to appreciate good Dixieland Jazz.

It was not the bullets from a bank robbery gone bad.

It was not even a carefully planned revenge ambush by Mr. Hot Shot Real Estate Developer, who wrote the bad checks, trying to send Roger to Hades ahead of schedule.

194

No. The reason for this latest round of near heart attacks was another case of too much air pressure in yet another tire on the cart.

Within sight of where the right rear tire blew out, the left rear counterpart followed suit and gave in to the high-pressured demands of over-inflation.

David was totally disgusted and ready to kick the other tires into submission, and he probably would have if Roger hadn't calmed him down.

Two hours later, all four wheels were rotating once again, but by then the day was shot.

They had traveled a total of three miles before checking into a seedy little motel on the outskirts of El Paso.

Some towns were much harder to leave than anybody could ever have expected them to be.

They collapsed in their motel room, worn out, fed-up, and massively frustrated. They had been off the road for three weeks, and it was always a challenge getting back into the pushing routine after so many days.

The fact that not one, but two tires had blown out in one day only made things that much more irritating.

Fortunately, Mary's day had been more productive.

Mary came back to the motel with a paid contract in hand for the very next day, Friday night, in Fabens, Texas.

It was always easier to push the cart when they knew they had a performance waiting for them. Just knowing that fans were anxiously anticipating their arrival was enough to put a little extra pep in their steps as they pushed and then pushed some more.

This was good news.

The Brothers' joy at having another paying gig was immediately dashed when Mary informed them that Fabens, Texas, was 23 long, tedious, tiring miles down the road.

It was going to be another extremely long day on The Big Walk.

Chapter 41: Best Efforts for a Huge Crowd

Roger and David were up and out the door of their no-name motel by 5:00 a.m.

They managed to cover 18 of the 23 miles to Fabens, Texas, by 2:30 in the afternoon before admitting defeat, storing the cart at a local residence, putting their equipment and horns in Mary's car, and allowing Mary to drive them the five miles into town.

Along the way, Roger had been able to take some practice shots with his newly purchased 45 pistol, popping cans on the side of the road. If any lizards happened to be sunning themselves in the desert heat, they had the good sense to stay out of sight.

Roger enjoyed the kick that each pull of the trigger produced. There was no denying the fact that this $30 pistol was one powerful weapon.

While it is possible that they probably could have kept on pushing the remaining distance, by the time they traveled the miles they would have been completely useless onstage for the evening's performance at 9:00.

Unlike some big time performers, who had crews to set up equipment while the headliners enjoyed champagne and chocolates in luxurious dressing rooms, The Brothers not only had to push a 1,000-pound cart down the road, they also had to unload the heavy equipment, drag it onstage, make sure everything was in working order, and then give the performance of their lives, each and every time they hit a stage.

Maybe Frank Sinatra, Jr., did have something on them after all.

According to Mary, the owner of Chino's Lounge was expecting a huge crowd to show up for the concert.

The term "huge" is very subjective.

Having recently performed in front of 1,400 students at Gadsen High, David had his own idea of what a decent turnout should look like.

Maybe the entire town would show up for the gig.

Would they be packed to the rafters, swinging from the lights?

David let his mind daydream as the five miles into town slipped by him in the car.

He was still limp and drained from having just walked 18 miles, and the simple act of being able to rest his legs was a big relief.

You never know how wonderful the entire concept of gasoline-powered vehicles really is until you try to push a 1,000-pound cart across a desert, step by step.

While watching the fluffy clouds float by outside his window, he made a solemn vow to never take combustion engines for granted.

David awoke from his semi-conscious state of slumber just as Mary pulled into the parking lot of the legendary, world-famous Chino's Lounge of Fabens, Texas.

It was somewhat less than expected.

So much for any fantasies about thousands of screaming fans, demanding a dozen encores.

David figured the place would be doing good to hold 30 people, maybe 50 at best.

At least it was a paying gig, and would certainly be more fun than changing tires on an overloaded cart in the middle of a traffic intersection.

The show went off without a hitch.

Roger and David had the three dozen or so paying customers jumping with enthusiasm. They stomped and clapped, shaking the floor of the lounge.

They couldn't get enough of the big sounds coming out of those shiny instruments.

It was nice to see smiling faces wall-to-wall. When it came right down to it, David and Roger enjoyed performing for small crowds almost as much as they did playing for the larger ones.

With smaller crowds, they could see the reactions on people's faces, and perform for specific members of the audience. They could make eye contact, flirt, show off, and truly entertain the crowd without feeling like they were neglecting other parts of the audience.

They loved the intimacy of smaller gatherings, thriving on the energy given back to the stage by their fans.

As long as living, breathing people appreciated their efforts, Roger and David were happy to give each and every concert their all.

Maybe those people were bouncing around with such enthusiasm because they knew how many miles they had walked just to be able to be with them.

Or maybe they were just happy to hear live music, drink cold beer, and enjoy being off from their daytime jobs, sharing good times with their neighbors and friends.

While the huge crowd at Chino's Lounge was only huge by local standards, they certainly made a big impression on the hearts of Roger, David, and Mary.

Having never even heard of Fabens, Texas, a week earlier, the town would remain in their memories for years and years down the road.

Chapter 42: Free Bullets
and Passing the Hat

Sunday, April 24th, found The Brothers packed up and ready to head on down the road.

They stopped at the restaurant in the motel they were leaving and struck up a conversation with a group of police officers having dinner.

Coming from a military background, Roger and David had many friends in law enforcement, and, for the most part, felt comfortable being around men in uniforms, carrying weapons.

Except for the few instances when they found themselves on the wrong side of local traffic laws or guilty of unknowingly breaking the unwritten rules of the land, they enjoyed hanging out with the men in blue, sharing stories about the road, talking about guns, and, of course, drinking beer.

Roger and David usually found local law enforcement officials to be among some of the friendliest people they met along the way. Perhaps it was simply a case of male bonding, or maybe the policemen envied The Brothers for being able to follow their dreams, despite all odds.

Just like previous times, the generosity of the policemen was overwhelming. When they found out that The Brothers had pistols for protection, they gave David a box of 38 shells and presented Roger with a box of 45 bullets. It was the neighborly thing to do, perhaps a bit of time-honored Southern hospitality.

After sharing dinner with the officers, everybody went outside, relaxing in the patrol cars while keeping an ear on the police radio.

A call came out that there was trouble at a local bar, and the police officers asked Roger and David if they'd like to ride along with them for a little Sunday excitement in a small Texas town.

It turned out to be just a catfight between two women. The cops arrived to see one somewhat elegant, but obviously intoxicated female taking a swing at her equally buzzed lady drinking companion, who was in the process of pulling her friend's hair out by the roots.

No big deal, at least not in that part of Texas, evidently.

The cops sent the women to opposite corners and told them to calm down.

These fine Texan ladies either got the message, or forgot what they were fighting about. Regardless, within a few minutes they were back to being best friends and crying in their beers. The potentially dangerous threat to society had been resolved.

Back at the restaurant, the now thirsty gang of law enforcers ordered another round of drinks and continued telling stories.

In appreciation for the policemen allowing The Brothers to go along for the ride to the catfight, Roger and David decided to unpack their instruments from the cart and share a little Dixieland Jazz with their new friends.

The original idea was to just grab their horn and sax out of the cases and play a few tunes before hitting the road.

Before it was over, they had unpacked all of their equipment, set up the speakers, assembled the tape recorder, and were giving a full-blown concert for the entire restaurant.

By this point, Roger and David were no longer playing for strangers. They were entertaining friends, kindred spirits, and comrades-in-arms.

The fact that yet another day had passed without them even making it a single mile down the road to New York City and Jack Paar was simply not important.

As it was becoming more apparent each and every day of The Big Walk, this epic adventure they were on was more about the journey than the destination.

Jack Paar and The Big Apple would always be waiting at the end of the line.

Sometimes it was more important to share a meal with new friends, break up a catfight on a lazy Sunday evening, and share their music with appreciative fans. The Brothers had been totally content to perform for a few free beers.

The fact that the policemen passed a hat around and collected $35 for the impromptu performance was simply an unexpected blessing that was deeply appreciated by The Walking Musical Balph Brothers.

Chapter 43: Sharing Time
with Fellow Travelers

Four miles outside of Fabens, Texas, The Brothers called it a day, and pulled the cart over to the side of the road.

Since it was almost the end of April, they were able to sleep under the stars, putting up their cots to keep them from being directly on the ground. Their sleeping bags provided enough warmth, and as long as rain wasn't in the forecast, they didn't even have to bother putting the tent up.

After a full day of walking and pushing the cart, anything that saved them time getting the camp ready was a welcomed blessing.

Mary had joined them after a futile day of trying to find work for The Brothers down the road.

Around 3:30 a.m., "Steps" started growling, while holding ground in her favorite spot under David's cot.

She didn't bark or move around, but she certainly sensed something or somebody moving around the area.

David poked his head out of his sleeping bag, rubbed his eyes, and tried to see what was causing "Steps" to growl.

He didn't see any cars' headlights. Didn't even hear anything out of the ordinary. As far as he could tell, it was just another typical night in the Texas desert.

He promptly rolled back into his sleeping bag and was soon dreaming about performing in front of millions of adoring fans.

"Steps" growled again. Then again. Then again and again and again.

The last time she growled, David could hear the steps of somebody walking nearby on the road.

Carefully taking his pistol in hand, David rose up from his cot just in time to see a wooly looking man walking down the road. The man didn't have a coat on, and his white shirt gleamed like a lantern under the moonlight.

David could see that the man had long unruly hair, a scruffy beard, and was wearing tattered blue jeans.

He walked within a few feet of the three cots and could have easily tripped over the cart, but instead he didn't seem to even notice Roger, David, Mary, "Steps," or the cart itself.

He never broke stride, never paused, never even acknowledged that he had any companions around him in the middle of the night in the middle of the desert.

He just kept on walking down the road, mumbling to himself, talking to the voices he evidently heard in his head, while ignoring the real, living, breathing people he had almost physically bumped into by the roadside.

David was amazed and thankful that "Steps" had been able to sense the man's impending arrival at least 20 minutes before he crossed their paths.

It was nice to have some advance warning in the wild, wild West.

The next morning, April 28th, Mary was up at the crack of dawn, in search of those elusive paying gigs.

The Brothers pushed on to Van Horn, Texas, bumping into an even smaller town called Tornalia.

Even in the smallest of small towns, people would stop and talk with Roger and David, asking the usual assortment of questions, and wishing them the best of luck with The Big Walk.

Every other person they met would promise to send Jack Paar a letter, even if they hadn't heard a single note from The Brothers' instruments. Maybe it was just more southern hospitality, or maybe they assumed that anybody willing to push a 1,000-pound cart across the country had to have some talent.

Another six miles down the road, they stopped at a small beer joint named The Border Bar, had a few beers and then, with the permission of the bartender, walked out back and did a little target practice, shooting at rusty beer cans and sending all the local lizards scrambling under rocks.

After their early morning encounter with the silent walking man, The Brothers felt the need to sharpen their shooting skills, just in case their next nighttime visitor proved to be a little more interested in their belongings.

They had plenty of free bullets at their disposal, thanks to the continuing kindness of various policemen, military officers, and fellow gun-shooting enthusiasts who kept giving them cases of ammo along the way.

It was the only way Roger and David could afford the luxury, seeing as how 50 shots for David's pistol cost $5.95, and a dollar more for Roger's 45.

Being able to fire off a few rounds every now and then helped break up the sheer boredom they faced every day on the road.

After pushing their cart all day, they certainly appreciated the combination of cold beers and free bullets, rejoicing in the relaxation and pleasure those distractions provided.

Revitalized by their cold brewskis and the smell of spent gunpowder, they pushed another mile and a half down the road before pulling over at a roadside park.

They met a man named Ed Williams there, with his camp already put up. He was on his way to Big Bend National Park and seemed to be a veteran camper.

It started raining just as The Brothers were claiming their spots, so they just moved over to the covered picnic tables, grateful for the government-provided shelter.

Mr. Williams was friendly and generous with his advice for successful camping and hiking.

After sharing a few road stories and some cold beers, David provided some after-drinks entertainment on his trumpet, working to keep his lips in shape between performances.

Everybody settled in for a night's rest, with "Steps" claiming her normal spot under David's cot, where she slept for four hours, then spent the rest of the night guarding The Brothers.

This was her normal routine. Sleep. Guard. Walk beside cart. And occasionally jump into a nearby river or creek or pond along the road. The Brothers had trained her to plunge into any fresh bodies of water they stumbled over, hoping that the outdoor baths would help rid her of fleas, ticks, and assorted bugs.

There were certainly days when "Steps" took more baths than Roger and David did.

203

Wednesday, April 29th, found Mr. Williams packed and ready to head down the road on his journey.

Before leaving, he continued giving The Brothers advice about how to cook on the road, how to shave, how to clean clothes, how to find water, how to avoid stepping on rattlesnakes, and on and on and on.

David assumed that it was Mr. Williams' effort to prove how much of an outdoorsman he was, and since his advice was sound, even if they already knew most of it first-hand, The Brothers appreciated the well-meaning advice freely given by their fellow journeyman.

They wished Mr. Williams the best of luck along his trip and waved as he drove off in the distance.

While packing up the last of their own gear, they realized that Mr. Williams had been so busy giving out free advice that he had forgotten to gather up his own sleeping bag, leaving it on a picnic table.

Since he was already miles and miles down the road by the time The Brothers found his gear, they didn't have any choice other than to take it with them.

They figured they would eventually find somebody going in the opposite direction that could deliver it to Mr. Williams.

It made more sense than just leaving his equipment on the ground.

A few miles from the picnic area, a highway patrolman stopped The Brothers, asking if they happened to see any missing sleeping bags on the roadside.

Unfortunately the Texan law officer was a little bit late in reaching Roger and David, because less than 15 minutes earlier, an Air Force Captain named Fred Potts had met the cart, heard the story about the abandoned camping equipment, and had promised to take Mr. Williams' items to the next town's police station, in hopes that they could catch up with him and return the items to their rightful owner.

The Air Force officer had been extremely friendly, and seeing as how he had his family in the car with him, The Brothers felt he was a trustworthy deliverer.

They found out that he was based at Andrews Air Force Base and was a member of the elite Air Force Pistol Team.

That fact naturally started a round of conversation about guns, pistols, and bullets, and before five minutes had passed, the Air Force Captain was giving Roger and David more free bullets for their sidearms, while leaving them his address, in case all efforts to return the sleeping bag failed.

It is amazing how much effort went into getting a simple sleeping bag back to its forgetful owner.

David was certain that such efforts would not have been made had the equipment been left in Los Angeles or another big city, instead of out in the middle of the desert.

It was times like these that restored The Brothers' faith in humanity.

The Brothers walked another three miles, relieved that Mr. Williams' camping gear was out of their hands and safely on the way back to him.

They stopped at a little store called The Riverside Grocery, hoping to buy a few soft drinks to quench their thirst.

Even though the store was small, it seemed to carry everything from soup to nuts. A group of elderly men held court on the front steps, shooting the breeze and waving to each and every customer entering the store.

There was so much dust covering the cans of food on the shelves that David figured customers were accustomed to giving their groceries baths before opening the containers.

In addition to buying some cold drinks, The Brothers also purchased a second used car jack to help them lift both sides of the cart when they had tire trouble. This unexpected find would save hours of effort on the road, allowing them to take the strain off the wheels, without having to remove every single item from the cart.

They walked on to Ft. Hancock, looking for shelter for the night.

They discovered that the lady who owned the local drug store also had some old apartments for rent behind the retail establishment.

While they were pretty broken down, the price of $3 per night was very attractive to Roger and David.

Plaster was falling off the walls of the room. A single bare lightbulb was hanging down a long cord in the middle of the ceiling, with a coat hanger attached to turn it off and on.

The furniture was mismatched, with one of the chairs having a broken leg. Every single window had broken panes of glass, but, fortunately, cold air wasn't blowing in.

At least the sheets were clean, and the hot shower worked.

Those were the most important things to consider.

The Brothers discovered that the rooms were less than a mile from the Mexican border and evidently were considered prime targets by nearby thieves, who seemed to consider anybody staying in the rooms an easy target.

There wasn't even a fence protecting the border, so the entire town of Ft. Hancock was at the mercy of thieves, thugs, and petty criminals.

Roger and David were so concerned about losing their instruments and tape recorder that they kept "Steps" on the cart the entire night, and slept with the windows open, pistols at hand.

Roger slept with one eye opened, watching the shadows in the tall, uncut grass outside his window, waiting for the tell-tale growls of "Steps" to warn him about any nighttime visitors coming their way.

He awoke at 10:00 a.m., finding his loaded pistol still in his hand, and fortunately, the cart and its contents safe and sound outside the window.

Their Guardian Angels and "Steps" had once again provided protection through the night.

After a hearty breakfast of cold beer and just as cold canned spaghetti, they left their luxurious accommodations and pushed the cart down the highway to the next spot in the road, curiously named Tommy's Town.

Chapter 44: Terrific Times in Tommy's Town

It was already dark by the time Roger and David were within a few miles of Tommy's Town.

Just when they were almost ready to call it a night and pitch camp by the side of the road, the owner of the town, a man by the name of Tommy, naturally enough, drove up in his car, with his headlights blazing, providing a guiding beacon the rest of the way to the city limits.

They arrived at their destination to find Mary already there and waiting for them.

Tommy, his wife Marie, and their jackass were the entire population of Tommy's Town, 1,400 acres of Texan farmland surrounding the little restaurant where the entire gang enjoyed a wonderful steak dinner.

Tommy was building a replica of the 1846 fort that stood on the land a century earlier, Fort Quitman, seeing it developing into a major tourist attraction for the area, bringing in millions of dollars.

He saw it as a Texan version of California's Disneyland, with the emphasis on history and heritage, a tribute to the pioneers and founders of The Lone Star State.

Meanwhile, the area offered more promise than reality, surviving on the proceeds from the sole restaurant, one small gas station owned by another gentleman who didn't actually live in the town, and a tiny liquor store tucked away in the corner of the steak house.

It took a man willing to put his efforts, money, time, and even his name into a project the size of Tommy's Town, someone who could see the potential of the plan, while facing the current modesty of the operations.

Tommy seemed to be just the man for the job.

After enjoying one of the best meals they had eaten on the entire Big Walk, everybody enjoyed drinking whisky and sodas, sharing stories about the road, and hearing Tommy talk about his big plans for his tiny town.

Every once in a while, the town's solitary jackass could be heard voicing his approval outside in the darkness.

David made another one of his solemn vows to return to Tommy's Town someday after they had conquered New York City, and catch up on their respective success stories.

With their stomachs filled, their legs rested, and their minds slightly glowing from an evening of spirited liquors, they called it a night, retiring to the comfortable hospitality of their host and hostess.

Compared to their morning breakfast of cold beers and canned pasta a few miles up the road, they had enjoyed a truly terrific time in Tommy's Town.

Chapter 45: One Thousand Miles Down, Two Thousand More to Go

David and Mary were up at 9:30 the next morning, getting ready to resume The Big Walk.

Roger took another hour to get up and stirring around.

Maybe he had enjoyed the evening's whiskey a little more than the rest of the crew.

While waiting for the elder Balph Brother to join them, David and Mary enjoyed two complete roast beef dinners, courtesy of Tommy's Town's only citizens.

By the time Roger joined them at 12:30, Tommy, his wife, Mary, and David were making promises to keep in touch with each other for the rest of their lives.

David promised them front row seat tickets to any and every concert The Walking Musical Balph Brothers gave anywhere in the world.

Tommy assured his new best friends that they would always have golden ticket passes to his fort and entertainment empire.

By 2:00 p.m., with their bellies full and the day half over, Mary drove ahead in the car to try to find yet another paying gig, while David and Roger reluctantly left the comfort and pleasures of Tommy's Town behind them.

As if to keep them humble after being so richly entertained by Tommy and his wife, the next ten miles were straight up a long, tiring Texas hill.

Step by step, pushing and then pushing some more.

Same as it ever was. No steak dinners. No free beers.

Just ten miles of hard road with the constant battle with gravity made even worse by the incline of the hill.

Even in the best of times, pushing the cart was hard enough.

Trying to get the cart up a ten-mile hill was particularly cruel.

Four miles up, the trusty odometer reached the 1,000-mile mark, a long awaited milestone.

One thousand long, hard, relentless, trying, tiring, impossible miles had passed by since they left Los Angeles and the comfort of their mother's loving arms.

Roger and David pulled the cart to the side of the road, took two stools off, sat down, and enjoyed two cold beers.

It would have been nice if the milestone had taken place in the middle of a crowd of thousands of adoring fans, with television cameras recording the popping of champagne corks while newspaper photographers captured the historic moment with the flash of a hundred bulbs.

It would have been wonderful if Jack Paar had flown in to share the moment and present them with an engraved invitation to join him in his television studio.

It would have been joyous if the event had taken place in a real city with traffic lights and busy sidewalks, instead of out in the middle of the Texas scrubland, halfway up a torturous hill that sapped their spirits and their energy.

So, with only "Steps" and whatever lizards were lurking behind nearby rocks witnessing the event, Roger and David took the final chugs of their refreshing malty beverages and went about their task of pushing and then pushing some more.

With 1,000 miles under their belts, The Brothers now knew that they could expect to get 500 miles wear out of a shoe sole.

A shoe heel would last 300 miles before giving up.

They could count on walking 150 miles on a shoe heel plate.

They had learned that they could have one beer for every five miles of walking in the desert. Anymore than that, and they would be done for the day.

They had discovered that when people told them that a place was "only a mile up the road," 99 percent of the time they were flat out wrong, with the true distance usually being three to four miles.

They also discovered that advice was almost as cheap as small talk, and worth even less.

They even discovered that you should never take camping advice from a man who can't remember to pack his own sleeping bag before leaving it on a picnic table.

But the main thing they had discovered over the past 1,000 miles was no matter how hard things were on the road, The Walking Musical Balph Brothers were always going to find a way to keep pushing and then pushing some more.

They had 1,000 miles under their belts.

Roger and David had no doubts that the next 2,000 miles would be over before they knew it.

Or maybe that was just the beer talking.

Chapter 46: The Smart Bird and the Musician Who Couldn't Shoot Straight

In what can only be considered yet another act of divine intervention, David had his faith rewarded shortly after celebrating the completion of their 1,000[th] mile on the road since leaving Los Angeles back in July of 1963.

He discovered that the barrel on his 38 pistol was damaged and wasn't shooting straight.

This was a serious matter to resolve. David wasn't just using his gun to pop holes in beer cans by the side of the road. He counted on his firearm to provide protection in times that truly could mean the difference between life and death.

There was nothing to do other than send his treasured pistol back to the Colt Firearms factory in Connecticut for much-needed repairs.

How could he expect to function in the wild and wooly West if his aim wasn't true?

Reconciling himself to his fate, he accepted the fact that he would be without his trusted Widow Maker for who knows how long. It could take months for the repairs to be made, and then he could only hope that the mailman would be able to find his location on the road.

This was a very disturbing predicament for the younger Balph Brother.

He wasn't even shooting blanks. This was far worse. He was, once again, reduced to whistling "Dixie."

Granted, he still had his faithful shotgun, but over the miles, he had come to trust the flexibility and ease with which he could draw his pistol and rapidly face any threats.

Just as David's mood was turning extremely sour, they bumped into a Texas miner by the name of Sam Harper.

While the sharply dressed cowboy geologist didn't look like an angel at first glance, that is exactly what he turned out to be.

Dressed in light tan slacks, wearing a large belt buckle with a brightly colored western shirt, he was the very opposite of the stereotypical grizzled miner, panning for gold in a mud puddle.

Even his cowboy boots looked expensive.

He was well spoken, obviously very intelligent, and a quick decision maker.

After meeting Roger and David, and spending a little over an hour and a half talking with them, Sam offered to loan David one of his extra pistols until the damaged one was returned from Connecticut.

David was completely overwhelmed by this generous gesture.

Sam told The Brothers that he could tell they had honest faces. He had no doubt that David would take care of his loaned firearm and would promptly mail it back to him as soon as possible.

David was absolutely positive that such a kind gesture would never have happened on the mean streets of Los Angeles.

So within the course of a couple of hours, David had experienced a roller coaster of doubts, fears, relief, and pure joy.

It was enough to make a believer out of the most cynical journeyman.

David almost thought he saw an angelic dove flying off in the distance, but it was probably just a bit of dried-up tumbleweed taking flight in the Texas desert winds.

Pushing on to the next wide spot in the road, The Brothers came upon a Gulf gas station, run by a lady named Kathy.

While Kathy wasn't much of a talker, her very vocal mynah bird was talking up a storm.

When David and Roger entered the gas station, a loud voice greeted them by saying, "Hello there, Cowboy."

When The Brothers were too dumbfounded to respond in a prompt manner, the clever bird retorted with, "Can't you talk?"

Was the bird a heckler? A disgruntled music fan?

Perhaps the Don Rickles of the bird kingdom?

Maybe the bird had somehow witnessed David's previous nighttime romp to Mexico and back with the Conga Coolers when he jumped over a fence, faced down a watchdog, almost tripped a Catholic priest walking on the sidewalk, and then ran a mile to his motel room while wearing his tuxedo.

Or maybe the bird was just an astute judge of character.

David finally stuttered out the fact that yes, he could talk.

The bird then responded, "Don't you know that birds can't talk?"

And went silent.

David was just glad that he hadn't bumped into this highly expressive and slightly belligerent feathered animal after a night of Conga Coolers.

Pushing on to the very top of the ten-mile hill that had been in their face for far too long a time, they pulled the cart over into a roadside park at the summit.

Roger had picked up a couple of blisters and was in agony. His trusty Dr. Shoals footpad that was supposed to provide cushioning for the soles of his feet had managed to slip to one side while climbing up the torturous incline.

He was literally walking wounded.

They decided to call it a day and put up camp for the evening, enjoying the scenic view from the top of their Texan hillside.

Mary arrived after a day of futile efforts to find work for The Brothers. She was tired, discouraged, and not in the best of moods.

The next two days were spent stuck in the same spot at the top of the hill.

Roger's blisters were still causing him fits, refusing to heal after 48 hours of rest.

The stress of pushing the cart up ten miles of Texas inclines proved to be too much for Roger's feet.

There was nothing to do but wait and hope for healing to take place.

They spent Sunday, May 3rd, enjoying the beautiful weather, relaxing, and trying to keep their minds off their aches and pains.

David took advantage of the time off to shave off his three-day growth of whiskers. It was so easy to just let his stubble grow when they were walking on the road, and this simple act of personal grooming always made him feel better on so many levels.

He didn't want to ever be mistaken for that crazy bearded man with the unruly hair who walked by them in the middle of the night, mumbling and talking to the voices in his head.

Mary brought some fresh eggs from the car, and with the aid of their trusty Coleman stove, the trio was soon enjoying a hearty breakfast of fried eggs.

By 2:00 p.m. Roger was getting a little stir-crazy.

He simply didn't have the patience to just sit on the ground, watching and waiting for his oozing blisters to heal up.

It was worse than waiting for water to boil, and just as exciting.

He talked the trio into getting out the shotguns and taking a slow walk up into one of the nearby mountains.

Making it very clear that this was not going to be a foot race with David or "Steps," they cautiously set out for the nearby mountaintop.

From their roadside park viewpoint, it looked like climbing the nearby summit would be a simple effort of following a straight line right to the top.

Looks can be deceiving.

They soon determined that the so-called straight path was filled with obstacles, trees, rocks, and countless diversions.

"Steps" even stumbled over a living breathing danger when she inadvertently found herself nose to nose with a territorial and somewhat stubborn porcupine.

She barked and ran in circles around the curious animal, trying to decide if the prickly creature was a plaything, food, or a potential threat.

The porcupine had the advantage of its natural armor and was content to let the clueless dog waste precious energy yelping and barking in a futile effort to prove superiority.

This was the porcupine's home turf, and he wasn't going anywhere.

When the barbed tail of the desert critter came just a little bit too close to "Steps'" tender nose, the faithful watchdog decided to trot on down the mountain trail and let the porcupine claim victory on the hillside.

By the time the trio made it to the top of the other mountain, they were limping, exhausted, and doubting the wisdom of their spontaneous jaunt.

Roger made an offhand comment that struck a deep chord within David.

As they struggled to overcome the unseen obstacles facing them, Roger quipped, "If you try to walk a straight line to the top of the mountain, it is impossible. But if you try different paths, going back and forth around the curves and bends, you will eventually make it to the top."

Savoring his sage moment of profound thoughts, Roger had a genuine "eureka" moment.

He continued his line of reasoning by adding, "That is exactly what the music business is like. If one way doesn't work in a straight line, you have to try many different avenues that may take you to the desired goal of success."

"That is what we are doing with The Big Walk, making our own path to the top of show biz."

With slightly over 1,000 miles under their belts after nine months of effort, David could only hope that Roger's words of wisdom proved to be true.

He was truly betting his life and future on it, each and every step of the way.

Chapter 47: Sand Storms and Convoys

Tuesday, May 5th, found The Brothers caught in the middle of the worst sandstorm they had seen on the entire trip.

They could hardly see in front of their noses, and to make matters even worse, they were sharing the crowded two-lane highway to Van Horn, Texas, with hundreds and hundreds of military trucks, flying by their cart, missing them by only a few inches at most.

Even on the best of days with sunny skies and wonderfully refreshing breezes, David hated pushing the cart down two-lane roads. There was never enough room for their cart and the traffic at the same time.

Cops would stop and force them to push the cart on the side shoulder of the highway, which made their task even more difficult. Pushing their 1,000-pound load through hard gravel was next to impossible.

Regardless of the state they were traveling through, the conditions on the shoulders of the road were always deplorable. From California to Arizona to New Mexico, and now Texas, the sides of the highways were always pitted, neglected, rough, and dangerous.

Dealing with the dreaded combination of being on yet another two-lane road in the middle of a sandstorm only increased their strain and anxiety.

A man in a camper had come so close to hitting the cart in the desert blindness that Roger and David had to jump into a ditch to avoid being struck by his vehicle. They were just lucky that the cart got stuck in a pothole on the shoulder and didn't take off down the road on its own, to certain tragedy.

On top of the destructive force of the raging tides of abrasive sand, they had also suffered the usual fate of broken spokes and flat tires.

It had taken over two hours of struggle by the roadside to replace one of the tires, and in another test of faith, the replacement tire only lasted another mile before going flat itself.

They had been forced to use their last backup spare, and if this one blew out, they would simply be stuck, without the ability to move.

While it is true that the entire Big Walk had been taken without much in the way of any safety nets, it always made David anxious when their margin for survival was so razor thin.

They were always one sprained ankle, a couple of tick bites, or a few oozing blisters away from complete and total disaster, much less dealing with the prospects of being crushed by some of the U.S. Army's finest transport vehicles in the middle of a blinding sandstorm. Toss in flat tires, broken forks, damaged pistols, roadside attacks, plus a constant lack of money, and the odds were certainly against The Brothers.

David couldn't help but wonder where Frank Sinatra, Jr., was right at that moment. Maybe he was sharing a big steak dinner with Jack Paar. And Johnny Carson. And Ed Sullivan. And Lyndon Baines Johnson.

The storm was making his mind play tricks on him.

Even with his goggles firmly clamped on his face, sand was stinging his eyes, causing them to burn and tear up.

Despite the fierce sandstorm raging all around them, The Brothers were able to push another 12 miles to another road side park.

They had to cook their evening meal inside the tent in order to keep sand out of the food. The heat from their Coleman stove made the atmosphere inside the tent almost unbearable.

They went to sleep that night, covered with sweat and sand, as miserable as they had been on any single day of the journey so far.

This night was about as far from being show-biz glamorous as was humanly possible. No free steak dinners. No shining spotlights. No applause from adoring fans. No nice paychecks waiting for them at the end of the show.

They were still 22 miles from Van Horn, and the best they could hope for was that the sandstorm would blow over by the time morning arrived.

David also prayed that a blinded military truck driver didn't swerve off the highway and run over them in the middle of the night as they lay helpless in their overheated tent, smelling like dogs and picking sand out of their body parts.

Chapter 48: Low-Flying Rockets

The next day started with The Brothers discovering that they had a visitor, watching them from the rocks, hiding in the grass.

As usual, "Steps" was the first one to detect their silent observer. Her growls alerted David, causing him to investigate the immediate area around the tent.

A few yards from where the trio had just been sleeping, David spied a baby deer with adorable white spots on its back. David knew that the cute little creature's mother had to be nearby, and had this been normal times in deer hunting season, he would have been reaching for his pistol.

These weren't normal times.

Besides, they already had enough baggage to push without having to tote several hundred more pounds of highly perishable venison.

He was jarred out of his mercy rationalization by the sight of the fawn scampering up the hill, bouncing out of range, with its furry tail-waving goodbye.

For some odd reason, seeing that innocent little animal dashing out among the rocks of the desert gave David a renewed sense of optimism.

He packed the cart with a renewed vigor, anxious to see what the day would bring him.

By the time they made it to Van Horn, one of the front forks on the cart was wobbling so badly that it was almost impossible to steer.

They found a man named Lyle Johnson, who owned a welding shop. He said he could solve their problems for $25, and, even though that was almost all the money they had left, The Brothers didn't really have any choice. Keeping the cart in running condition was even more important than buying food.

It took most of the day and a good part of the evening for Mr. Johnson to finish the repairs, so it was highly unlikely that he actually made any money on the job.

Like so many people they had met on The Big Walk, Mr. Johnson turned out to be a decent person who felt the need to take Roger and David under his wing.

There was something about the sheer insanity of the entire effort to push a cart to New York City that seemed to bring out the generosity in perfect strangers.

Or maybe it was the fact that Roger and David were just so All-American likeable, with their crew cuts, shiny instruments, and winning smiles.

After spending the day watching him work, David went to dinner at Mr. Johnson's home, meeting his wife and family.

During dinner conversation, David discovered that his dinner host was quite an enterprising welder and master tinkerer. He paid his bills by welding broken farm equipment and industrial machinery, but he also used his mechanical skills to produce racing go-carts, capable of reaching speeds as high as 90 miles per hour.

He was also a bit of an eccentric inventor with a sense of humor. After retiring to the living room, Mr. Johnson was proud to show off one of his creations.

He had rigged up an old player piano with a vacuum cleaner, creating a very noisy version of an electronic organ right in the middle of his parlor.

It was almost as much fun to watch it in action as it was to listen to the contraption.

Mr. Johnson was as proud of his roaring instrument as David was of his treasured trumpet.

While Roger and Mary found time to be alone, David spent the next few days enjoying the hospitality of Mr. Johnson and his family.

On Friday, May 8th, David and Mr. Johnson took one of the custom, hand-built, hot-rod go-carts out to the local runway at the town's small airport, and gave it a spin.

The cart had a motor for each of the back wheels, and was the closest thing to a land-running rocket that David had ever experienced.

Roaring down the smooth landing strip, with his tail end literally inches from the asphalt, David felt like he was strapped to a missile. It was all he could do to keep the cart from literally flying off into the desert hills.

He wondered what The Big Walk would be like if Mr. Johnson put his creative crafting skills to work on The Brothers' heavy non-motorized cart, welding some of his high-powered lawn-mower engines to their tired old vehicle.

Maybe this could be a new angle for Mary to promote.

Instead of being The Walking Musical Balph Brothers, grunting and grinding each and every torturous mile between Van Horn and New York City, maybe they could change their routine and become Roger and David Balph, The Rocking Rocketeers.

David could certainly get used to the idea of zipping down the highway at 90 miles an hour, flying up and over ten-mile hills without even breaking a sweat, waving at the poor saps stuck plodding along at normal speed limits.

It would be sweet justice for all of the hassles they had already endured along the way. The more he thought about the possibilities, the better he liked the idea.

Why make the trip as hard as possible, when the same results, the same promotions, the same attention for their musical career could be achieved with so much less effort?

All too quickly, David noticed that Mr. Johnson was flagging him down from the side of the tarmac, ending his flight of fancy.

Mr. Johnson informed David that he was probably zipping around the runway at no less than 60 miles per hour.

David felt like he had been flying by at least four times that fast.

Zooming four inches off the ground with the likelihood of complete and total disaster being just one bump in the road away was absolutely the best possible medicine for David.

He reluctantly relinquished control of the go-cart back to Mr. Johnson, feeling every nerve in his body pinging with explosive energy.

David didn't even notice the squished bugs in his teeth.

Chapter 49: Remains of a Classic Texan Con Job

Mr. Johnson took it upon himself to be David's tour guide during the rest of his stay in scenic Van Horn, Texas.

He gave him the insider's tour of the local courthouse and the old jail.

They took a trip outside of the city limits to visit the site of Old Van Horn, an abandoned ghost town, which was reduced to a few crumbling wooden buildings and a long-forgotten graveyard.

David could feel the spirits of the town's ancient miners, gunslingers, saloon gals, and cattle rustlers looking down on them as they walked through the decaying relics of the former wild and wooly Western boomtown.

Before heading back to the comforts of modern civilization, they made a detour to a place that held special interest to Mr. Johnson.

All David initially saw was an old gravel bed where long gone railroad tracks used to be.

Seeing that his cart-pushing guest was thoroughly, though politely, unimpressed with the scene before his eyes, Mr. Johnson decided it was time to educate his trumpet-playing greenhorn about the historical significance on one of the greatest con jobs ever conceived in the Lone Star State.

He proceeded to tell David the legendary story of the Gooch Railroad, built in 1860 at huge expense, while based on a complete and total deception.

According to Mr. Johnson, modern con men could certainly learn a few things from the enterprising Mr. Gooch.

The infamous saga began with Mr. Gooch buying several mule-drawn wagonloads of Mexican coal from across the border.

He delivered the coal to an abandoned and virtually worthless mine to which he had recently bought rights.

He had specific instructions for his laborers as to how he wanted the black rocks placed inside the caverns of his mine.

He didn't want the combustible stones placed in neat convenient piles.

No.

He didn't want them arranged near the front of the mine's entrance where they could easily be retrieved.

No.

He wanted the energy-providing rocks taken inside the worn-out mine and scattered about like they had just been picked out of the cavern's walls, freshly mined and only recently freed from the bowels of the earth.

Once this mission was accomplished, the Not-So-Honorable Gooch put his ingenious plan into action.

He contacted the owners of the leading Texas railroad company, proposing that they build a 35-mile long train track to his mine, connecting his enterprise to the railway network of the state.

The titans of the railroad saw the wisdom of tapping into this motherlode of hard black gold, and sent a crew of engineers and appraisers out to the site to see if Mr. Gooch's story was true or not.

According to Mr. Johnson, David's generous tour guide, the railway officials liked what they saw, or at least what they thought they saw, and within a few weeks, Mr. Gooch had a signed contract worth $100,000 of 1860s money to build the train track for the company.

In a delicious bit of Western irony, the much-too-busy railroad executives gave Mr. Gooch the right to hire and pay any and all workers needed to construct the 35 miles of steel tracks.

Naturally, the always industrious Mr. Gooch hired the cheapest labor he could recruit from nearby Mexico, using many of the same workers who had carefully placed the deceptive coal in the mine in the first place.

That old circus showman P.T. Barnum would have been proud of Mr. Gooch's bold audacity, not to mention providing possible inspiration for even modern day government contractors.

But of course, it didn't stop there.

After hiring the cheapest labor possible, Mr. Gooch also controlled issuing payrolls. This allowed him to take half of the money owed to his laborers, and simply keep it for himself, calling it a "processing fee."

Was this guy ahead of his time or what?

According to Mr. Johnson, it took 15 years to build the railroad, and by the time it was finished Mr. Gooch was one of the richest men in the Lone Star State.

And all the while, his original wagonloads of Mexican coal were still gathering moss in the depths of his synthetically enriched mine.

It is estimated that Mr. Gooch was able to put at least $50,000 of the 1860s railroad company's hard cash in his pockets before conveniently disappearing, just as the mine was scheduled to deliver the long-promised trainloads of valuable coal.

It was a con of classic proportions.

David wasn't sure if the story was fact, or just a local legend told for the amusement of naïve gullible tourists, but it was obvious that somebody's dreams had been smashed to pieces along the way.

As David and Mr. Johnson walked through the hand-chiseled egg-shaped railroad tunnels, carved out of immense Texas hills, following the route built to carry the phantom tons of Van Horn coal, David couldn't help but wonder how many men had broken their backs, lost their lives, and been cheated out of their hard-earned wages by the smooth-talking, sharply dressed, wheeler and dealer from out-of-town, spinning tales of glory, while stealing the food out of the mouths of the people who actually did the work.

David didn't see how a person could be so deceitful and still have any self-respect.

He would never look at another piece of coal without thinking about Mr. Gooch and his railroad to empty promises.

Chapter 50: Flaming Waste and Smoke Signals

After leaving the hospitality of Van Horn, The Brothers pushed the cart seven and a half miles before pitching camp at the first roadside park they found.

Mary joined them after a day of searching for work in Pecos, Texas, 58 miles down the road.

She came back with a paying contract for a gig the upcoming Saturday night at the opening of the town's new Ramada Inn.

While David set up the tent, Roger and Mary drove back to Van Horn to pick up supplies for the road trip.

Enjoying his time alone, David felt the call of nature and walked over to a nearby bridge to relieve himself, carrying his priceless roll of toilet paper with him, safely clutched in his fists. A person never realizes how important a simple convenience like toilet paper can be until he has to go without it. The very idea of being forced to use a cactus leaf was enough to bring whimpers out of the best of men.

Rounding the curve of the pathway, David was ready to take care of business when he stumbled over the bleeding, decomposing bodies of two freshly killed goats. Their entire chest areas were gone, probably devoured by the hungry mountain lion that made the kills. The rest of the carcasses were intact and undisturbed. The mountain lion must have been a picky eater.

Walking a little further down the pathway, David found a nice squatting area and proceeded to let nature take its course.

Just when he was in his most exposed position, a big, bright green snake, about eight feet long, slithered out of nowhere and stared at David directly in his face.

If David hadn't already been in the middle of doing exactly what you think he was doing, he would have certainly started doing it when he saw the snake eye-to-eye.

It was a muscle-moving moment, affecting numerous parts of David's body all at the same time.

Thankful that gravity worked, and his stance was wide, David avoided a potentially embarrassing moment.

The resulting noise, or maybe the fact that snakes have amazing senses of smell, caused the huge reptile to disappear down a nearby hole, possibly heading for China.

David struggled to his feet, catching his breath and staggering back to the pathway.

The combination of the dead goats and the slithering snake had sent his mind reeling.

He finished his personal hygiene duties and found he had a mess, literally, on his hands.

Trying to be a good citizen, he didn't want to leave the area soiled with used toilet paper, so he decided to burn the crumpled pile of tissues and spread the ashes.

Big mistake.

In his heightened sense of reality from such a close encounter with so many forms of nature, David hadn't noticed that desert winds were kicking up the sand around his knees.

He had no sooner fired up the odorous pile of stained paper than a rolling tumbleweed flopped on top of the blaze and exploded into flames, bouncing down the path, sparking more fires with every roll.

As David watched in stunned amazement, the resulting wildfire immediately consumed the bushes around him and leaped into the nearby brush, instantly igniting the branches and limbs like an abandoned dried-up Christmas tree.

It seemed like the entire world was ablaze, and there was nothing David could do to stop the destruction.

And what was even worse, this was all David's fault. Or maybe the green snake's. Could he possibly put the blame for the flames on that hungry mountain lion?

David panicked.

He was alone.

The desert was on fire.

And with the winds blowing all around him, it was easy to think that miles and miles of Texas might simply go up in ashes, all for lack of a flushing toilet with running water.

With the smoke billowing and flames racing around and down the hillside, David ran back to the highway, waving his hands, trying to get anyone to stop and help.

He grabbed the five-gallon olive green Marine canvas bag they used to carry "Steps'" drinking water, and lugged the 50-pound container back to the raging fires.

His well-intentioned efforts were much too little too late. The water immediately vaporized and disappeared in a sooty mist as soon as he tried to douse the sparks.

In desperation, he took the now empty canvas sack and started beating the burning bushes in a futile attempt to kill the flames.

While actually just helping to fan the flames, all he accomplished was to cover himself with more soot and ashes.

With his world burning to pieces in front of his eyes, David ran back to the highway, looking for help of any kind.

Miraculously, a few moments later an ancient fire truck with a hand-cranked siren came to David's rescue.

Throwing himself on the mercy of the law, David anxiously explained how he had seen the bleeding goats, met the green snake eye-to-eye, and in his shaken state, had accidentally started the fire while trying to be a good citizen and not leave behind a messy pile of smelly litter.

He certainly didn't mean to burn down half of Texas.

He was talking so fast that he wasn't sure the fireman understood what he told him, but he felt better for having his roadside confession.

The fireman turned out to be the area's fire chief, the head man in the area when it came to fighting and controlling blazes in that part of Texas.

Reports of the blaze had come in from the nearby watchtower, so help had been on the way before David even made it back to the highway.

He just didn't know it at the time.

Instead of throwing David in jail, or fining him thousands and thousands of dollars he didn't have, the fire chief told David that he had done the state a favor.

A favor?

Were David's ears playing tricks on him?

Had a spark flown into one of his ears and burned out his mind?

He had almost burned down the entire Lone Star State, and this government official was thanking him for setting the place on fire.

If this was the punch line, David sure didn't understand the joke.

Turns out the fireman had been planning on burning off the tumbleweeds and brush in the area to prevent major fires later on.

It was a regular ritual in this part of Texas.

He was actually thanking David for saving him a day's worth of hard work.

David looked around and realized that the flames had died out as soon as the weeds and low-lying plant materials had been consumed.

Texas was not on fire anymore.

He hadn't burned down the entire Lone Star State after all.

He looked towards the sky and was absolutely certain beyond a shadow of a doubt that his ever-faithful, always-present Guardian Angels were smiling down on him from above.

David was sure that he made a pretty sight for his angelic protectors, seeing as how he was covered head to toe with soot and ashes.

Thanking the fire chief for his help and understanding, David walked back to the tent and tried to collect his thoughts.

It was amazing how much had happened in such a short period of time.

It just made David realize how fragile life really was.

He decided to take "Steps" down to the nearby creek and join her in a refreshing and reinvigorating bath in the cool Texas water.

That is where Roger and Mary found him when they returned from their trip into Van Horn for supplies.

He was butt-naked, floating up and down on the refreshing mountain stream waters, letting his cares and worries drift away with the current.

Roger smelled the burnt tumbleweeds and the pungent aroma of decomposing goats. He had passed the returning ancient fire truck heading back to Van Horn, and now that he could see the blackened hillsides, his mind raced with a dozen questions.

What did any of this have to do with his younger brother, now aimlessly bobbing up and down in the Texas stream?

David was too busy smiling from ear to ear to even try to explain the situation.

With "Steps" keeping careful watch for slithering green snakes and hungry heart-eating mountain lions, David was content to play hide the submarine in the cool waters, gleefully splashing away in the Texas stream.

He was counting his blessings and only vaguely concerned about where he had left his precious roll of toilet paper when all of Texas caught on fire right in front of his eyes.

Chapter 51: Twelve and Twelve on the Twelfth

Tuesday night, May 12th, found The Brothers still 50 miles away from Pecos and their scheduled performance at the Ramada Inn grand opening on Saturday.

There had been the usual problems with the cart, the usual struggles to push the weight. Some days it felt like the cart was stuck in molasses, going nowhere fast.

They had now gone through a total of 12 tires since leaving Los Angeles, and it always seemed to be a losing battle between rubber and the road.

By the time they called it a day, David was beyond ready to collapse under the Texas skies and take his mind out of gear.

There was nothing like stargazing to put things into perspective.

They had also seen a total of twelve satellites in the nighttime skies in the last four days.

David liked to watch them pass over his head, as he lay on his cot, trying to make sense of The Big Walk, his musical career, and life in general.

It was so easy to let his mind wander as he stared at the big sky cosmos twinkling and drifting millions and millions of light years off in the distance, occasionally intersecting with the man-made blinking beacons passing through his line of sight.

He stared at the almost blinding light of the silvery moon and wondered when men would actually walk on that cratered surface, so tantalizingly close, yet out of reach for all of mankind's history.

He remembered reading textbooks in elementary school saying that the gravity on the moon was a mere fraction of the earth's, allowing future astronauts to literally bounce around the moonscape with the greatest of ease.

After spending the last ten months pushing a 1,000-pound cart across the American West, David was all for anything that helped him win the never-ending battle with gravity.

The last thing he remembered thinking before surrendering to the night's moon dust was the fact that, in such a vast universe, his struggles seemed very small.

Sometime in the early morning hours, David's peaceful slumber was interrupted by the headlights of a large tanker truck pulling into the other end of the roadside park where they were camping.

The Brothers were far enough away from the nighttime activities to stay out of the spotlight of attention, safely cloaked in the desert blackness.

Four cars pulled in beside the tanker, forming a line.

As soon as one automobile was filled with what was obviously heavily discounted fuel, the next one took its place in line.

From the way all of the participants were hurrying around, it was obvious that this covert encounter was strictly off the books.

Within ten minutes, the now lighter tanker roared off into the distance, with the four cars and their now filled gas tanks scattering like roaches in the night.

David rolled over on his cot and promptly went back to dreamland, thankful that "Steps" had chosen to remain silent during this unique desert moment.

"Steps" rubbed her nose, somewhat overwhelmed by the pungent drifting gasoline fumes invading her sensitive nostrils.

Chapter 52: Hotel Hassles

Pecos Ramada Inn Grand Opening

The Brothers limped into Pecos just in time for their Saturday night gig at the Ramada Inn.

Roger had picked up a terrible rash on his leg and was hobbled by the constant pain.

They arrived with the idea that they would be able to check into a courtesy room at the newly opened lodging facility, take showers and clean off the road grime they'd accumulated over the past few days.

It was a nice idea. Too bad it didn't happen.

As it turned out, the Ramada Inn didn't want hired employees, even including semi-famous traveling celebrity musicians, staying in their new rooms.

Reverting to Plan B, The Brothers went to the local Travelodge, hoping to utilize whatever remnants they could salvage from their previous sponsorship with the motel chain.

Though the deal for free lodging along the route their mother had verbally put together for them before leaving Los Angeles had fallen apart before they even left Arizona, The Brothers had continued to promote Travelodge in interviews and appearances on the road.

Seeing as how they hadn't even tried to get any free lodging for several months, they were hopeful that in their time of need, their previous good intentions would pay off for them.

When they arrived at the Pecos Travelodge they were surprised to find a letter waiting for them from the chain's promotions director.

Maybe it was a golden pass, providing rooms and meals for the rest of their journey. Perhaps their efforts to remain positive and always say good things about the chain had paid off.

Maybe the powers that be in the corporation had seen the numerous newspaper articles spotlighting The Walking Musical Balph Brothers, and realized the error of their ways.

No. The letter professionally and soundly stated that there would be no more free accommodations for Roger and David anytime, anywhere within the entire motel chain.

No extended stays. Not even the minimum two days in one city that had sometimes been extended when The Brothers pressed the issue.

All of The Brothers' good-intentioned public praises for the chain were for naught. There was truly and literally no room for them in The Inn, or The Lodge in scenic Pecos, Texas.

Facing the grime and grimy reality of their homeless situation, The Brothers took what little remaining money they had and secured a paid-for room for the night.

They barely had time to clean up and change into their stage outfits for the evening's concerts. As always, the three concerts were warmly received, with the audiences demanding encores at each show.

The Brothers were also able to meet yet another noted celebrity, movie and television star Peter Graves, who was the guest of honor at the motel's grand opening.

This was actually the second time that Roger had performed for the man who would later go on to star in the television series "Mission Impossible."

Back in 1957, in Los Angeles, Roger had performed for Mr. Graves, who also happened to be the brother of James Arness, the star of "Gunsmoke," one of the most popular shows in the history of television.

Arriving at Pecos Ramada Inn

David wasn't sure where Peter Graves ranked in the entertainment world status at that precise moment in time, but he figured he had to be right up there with Frank Sinatra, Jr., their previous encounter with a genuine celebrity.

When the excitement of the grand opening wore off, Roger realized the rash on his leg had grown much worse during the activities, and required some professional medical attention.

It was hard to feel like a celebrity when his lower body was so inflamed with pain.

He suffered through Sunday, hoping his rash would miraculously disappear if he just stayed off his feet.

This was one miracle that didn't materialize.

Monday morning found Roger at the local clinic, where the inspecting doctor voiced his amazement that he had been able to walk two feet, much less the almost 60 miles from Van Horn to Pecos.

He prescribed an ointment, promising things would clear up within a few days. That was easy for the non-walking, non-cart- pushing man of medicine to proclaim.

Roger could only wonder if his body would heal in time for their next 60-mile walk through the desert.

They wound up spending yet one more day at The Travelodge, paying out another chunk of their limited funds for the convenience of having flushing toilets, running water, hot showers and clean beds.

Roger's rash seemed to be healing, but his legs were still extremely sore. David, meanwhile, was suffering his constant battle with blisters, limping around the motel room.

The simple fact remained that human bodies are not machines, and the constant strains of The Big Walk had tangible effects on The Brothers' bodies.

They were putting decades of wear and tear on their systems, despite the fact that they were young, athletic, and in decent physical shape.

David could only hope that the success of their trip didn't kill them in the process of building their musical careers.

On Wednesday, May 20th, they packed their bags, loaded the cart, and left scenic Pecos, limping down the highway. They had pushed and pushed some more before coming upon a bridge outside of town.

Stopping to take a break and drink a nice refreshing chilled beer, they leaned against the bridge's guardrail and discovered that it was covered with wet paint. The Brothers both had fresh paint all over their backsides, and noticed that even "Steps" had managed to get her nose covered by moist pigment.

Stung by the added humiliation of being marked like chain-gang prisoners, David couldn't help but feel shackled to the 1,000-pound cart and his grumbling, complaining, limping older brother.

Where was Peter Graves when you needed him?

Chapter 53: More Texas Adventures

Performing at the Midland Ramada Inn

The Brothers realized how big the Lone Star State actually was.

They were walking across the entire state from the most western tip to the Arkansas border.

Even though it was only May, their days were filled with grueling desert heat, with temperatures exceeding 100 degrees.

They prayed for days when occasional rainstorms would blow across the prairie and provide a few moments of moist relief.

Roger continued to struggle with the rashes on his legs that were made raw by the constant friction from rubbing his pants with each aching step.

David's battle with blisters was constantly painful and always a losing proposition. To make matters even worse, he had picked up the same rash that was tormenting Roger.

Doctors kept giving them various salves and lotions to dry out the infected areas. The brown paste burned like fire and didn't seem to provide much healing.

The major problem with the rashes was the fact that they needed to keep their legs and thighs dry so the medicine could have time to work.

There was no way in the world to accomplish this goal when they were faced with pushing a 1,000-pound cart in 100 degree weather.

The mere act of breathing was enough to make them break out in a dripping sweat; so, they were fighting a losing battle with each and every step.

They kept imagining how much easier life would be if they had only been able to rig up some high-powered go-cart engines to turn the cart into a low-flying rocket.

"Steps" continued to provide protection and companionship, occasionally running out into the desert to chase and battle the taunting prairie dogs that seemed to take devilish delight in barking and challenging "Step'" mere presence on the Texas roadways.

Towns with the names of Pyote, Monahans, and Wickett came and went, one step at a time.

They continued to receive acts of kindness from complete strangers.

Outside of Penwell, they met a man riding a motorcycle from Los Angeles to Wisconsin. He had just finished serving his country as a U.S. Marine and was on his way home to friends and family.

He offered to ride ahead on his cycle and bring back some food and cold drinks. While it seemed doubtful that his broken down motorbike would make it another mile down the road, much less all the way to the scenic lakes of Wisconsin, The Brothers decided to trust this stranger with three dollars of their hard-earned money. Proving that their instincts hadn't been misguided, their roadside friend returned 90 minutes later with nourishment and refreshing beverages.

With their faith in humanity and nutritional energy restored, The Brothers went back to pushing the cart, watching the friendly biker sputter off into the distance.

On Tuesday, May 26, 1964, The Brothers spent the night at The Phillips 66 Truck Stop in Penwell. The owner put them up for the night and even allowed them to bring the cart inside, so The Brothers didn't have to worry about vandals tearing things up.

The next morning, after walking 20 miles the day before, it took them 45 minutes to push the cart up one very steep hill just outside of town. The good news was they only had 13 miles to go to reach Odessa.

Odessa and Midland were close enough to each other that Mary and The Brothers were able to pursue jobs in both towns at the same time.

Mary had leads for work at The Midland Club located in Odessa and was looking into possible engagements at private dinner clubs in both cities.

The Brothers found a roadside park five miles outside of Odessa and planned to spend the weekend there camping out. They wanted to be in Midland on Tuesday of the following week so they could get maximum television exposure, having learned that arriving in an area during the middle of the week seemed to generate the most attention.

A man named Bob Bourn saw the cart and stopped to chat for a while. After determining The Brothers were sincere in their efforts, he offered to let David, Roger, and Mary stay with him in his nearby home. With this sincere generosity, Roger and David, after giving careful consideration, decided to push on to his house where they found he had plenty of rooms to spare.

Mary Serving Dinner to David at Bob Bourn's House

The man was going through a divorce and was living in a small, unfurnished house. There was a simple bed and dresser in his sleeping area, and the rest of the house was basically empty.

The Brothers and Mary brought in their cots and sleeping bags, going so far as to use their blankets as makeshift curtains for the bare windows.

Using a small ice chest as the house refrigerator and a tiny gas stove like The Brothers had as kids in their basement back in Ohio, Mary was able to create home-cooked meals for the guys and provide some level of domestic comfort.

With Roger and David still suffering from their various rashes that refused to go away, they passed their time playing cards with their new roommate.

Mary desperately kept pursuing any possible gigs. As always, money was tight. They had to make every penny last.

They had confirmed gigs at places like The Midland Club, only to have them fall through at the last moment. In this particular case, while the manager of the establishment wanted The Brothers to perform, the owner killed the idea before a contract could be signed. No explanations. No reasons. Just a big resounding "No."

Mary lost count of how many times she was rejected.

The stress and anxiety of the job were certainly affecting Mary's health.

While she didn't have to deal with the blisters and rashes that constantly attacked Roger and David, she had developed recurring stomach pains. They got so bad in Midland that she had to go to a doctor for tests to see if she had cancer, ulcers, or maybe gallstones.

One unexpected benefit of Mary's visit to the doctor was the fact that it gave Roger a chance to get a second opinion about his endless rash.

That was the only way he discovered that he actually had a severe case of ringworm, and the burning medicine that Roger and David had been painfully applying to their tender parts was not solving the problem at all.

Meanwhile, Mary, regardless of her cramps and pains, had to keep hitting the clubs, bars, and motel lounges, trying to keep The Brothers employed and performing.

Jobs would evaporate and disappear right before their eyes, sometimes right in the middle of a meal with the managers, bookers, owners, and decision makers. A meal that The Brothers usually couldn't even pay for.

Meanwhile, The Brothers had to look successful and professional, never letting prospective customers know that they were often running on vapors and good intentions.

Mary was finally able to secure a booking at the Midland Ramada Inn.

She got the contract while David and Bob Bourn were passing time by riding around town in Bob's truck. Roger had slept in that day.

With a contract in hand, some of the pressure was off.

Mary drove back to Bob's house, picked up Roger, and left a note for David, giving him the good news.

The good news was they had a paying gig.

The bad news was the gig was that very night.

David and Bob scrambled to get the instruments off of the cart, into his truck, and delivered to the Ramada Inn in time for that night's performance.

After days of waiting and spinning their wheels, things had to happen fast when contracts were signed.

They previously had done as many local television and radio shows as they were offered, and readily posed for the local newspapers that continued to run stories about the visiting musicians.

Billy Miller, the female host of "High Noon," a show on the NBC station in Odessa, interviewed Roger and David, going so far as to shoot film of The Brothers with their cart.

They had been able to push the cart inside the actual television studio, located less than 200 feet off Route 80.

Viewers seemed to be more interested in the condition of "Steps" than they were about the welfare of The Brothers. One caller was almost beside herself with worry as to if the dog was getting enough water to drink.

Billy Miller was certainly one of the best interviewers they had encountered on the trip so far.

She asked intelligent questions, treated Roger and David with respect, and seemed to be genuinely interested in The Big Walk.

Miller promised to send copies of the interview directly to Jack Paar's New York studio.

She wound up doing follow-up interviews and even brought her daughter to one of their shows at the Midland Ramada Inn.

The crowds at the Ramada Inn were wildly enthusiastic about the music, and couldn't get enough of the good Dixieland Jazz being served up by Roger and David.

The local radio station did a live broadcast from the Ramada, and you would have thought that little motel lounge was the center of live entertainment for the entire Lone Star State.

By the time The Brothers ended their run in town, it seemed as if every citizen of legal age had been in the audience.

When the time came to leave the area, their new best friend, Bob Bourn, even drove them back to his home-away-from-home and helped them load up the cart for the big push to Midland and beyond.

The level of deep friendship that consistently developed between The Brothers and complete strangers in the matter of a few days along The Big Walk always restored their faith in humanity.

It was always difficult to break their newly formed ties and march forth to the next destination, and the next, and the next.

Some towns were friendlier than others, and there was no way to gauge which opportunity would be more rewarding than the next.

In Midland, due to the extensive press coverage they received, they had been treated like visiting stars.

Pushing the cart through town, they passed the very same Ramada Inn where they had performed the previous week. The manager, Ben Grigg, graciously put The Brothers up for a night, so they could be rested for the next part of their journey.

As so often happened on The Big Walk, even this blessing had a bad side-effect.

While The Brothers were enjoying a restful night, a nighttime vandalism attack occurred on the cart, in which unknown punks had torn the promotional photos off, stolen the three attached bicycle horns, and bent the headlight in an attempt to steal it.

It was truly the best and worst of times, often during the same single day.

One newspaper in Big Springs went so far as to write up a feature story on The Brothers, taking dozens of photos, only to kill the story when they found out Roger and David were performing at a local bar.

The newspaper was owned by conservative religious church people that didn't condone drinking. Even though they loved the story about The Big Walk, there would never be any coverage promoting an establishment serving demon rum.

End of story. Literally.

In Big Springs, they played two sold-out nights at a club called El Triango. The owner collected a hefty cover charge from each customer and was thrilled with his revenues.

Due to the success of the first two nights, he didn't feel the need to advertise the following days' performances, thinking the crowds would faithfully show up for more live Dixieland Jazz.

Instead, customers assumed that The Walking Musical Balph Brothers had left town, and they wound up playing to nearly empty rooms. The club owner had figuratively killed his golden goose.

To make matters worse, when it came time for the owner to pay The Brothers, he was nowhere to be found.

They wasted an entire Sunday and most of the following Monday trying to get paid the money that was rightfully owed to them.

After giving them a bad check and causing them to stay an extra night in a local motel, the club owner finally came through with the cash due for the performances.

But, he refused to pay for the additional charges incurred by spending an extra night at the motel while waiting for payment.

Roger and David told the motel manager that the money owed them was the responsibility of the nightclub owner and proceeded to pack up and leave.

They had borrowed a microphone stand from one of the local radio stations prior to their performances, and they made a point of dropping it back off at the radio station before leaving town.

The disgruntled nightclub owner proceeded to call the local police and report that Roger and David had stolen an expensive microphone stand from him, and he was pressing charges.

Fortunately, the radio station confirmed that the microphone stand in question had always belonged to them and not the conniving, lying nightclub owner, and it had been safely and legally returned to the station.

The police realized that this was all just an attempt to cause trouble for The Brothers, when in fact, the nightclub owner was the one on the wrong side of the law.

They were living in a world built on very shaky cards and illusions, and many times were only one wrong move away from complete and total disaster.

Had the radio station not come to their defense, Roger and David could literally have been thrown in jail, unable to post bail, and left to rot.

Fortunately, their dealings with shady characters like the nightclub owner were the exception and not the rule.

They continued to meet generous, considerate people, who took them under their care and treated Roger, David, and Mary like members of their own families.

Days turned into weeks, which then turned into months, as their trek across Texas continued.

They enjoyed wonderful meals, received free bullets, admired fellow sportsmen's gun collections, and shared the lives of complete strangers for as many days as they remained in the towns of their hosts.

Then the time would always arrive when they would have to hit the road once again, pushing the cart one step at a time, and then pushing some more.

Chapter 54: Massive Indifference

Colorado City Performance

The Brothers arrived in scenic Colorado City, Texas, at high noon, June 24th, with much fanfare.

Mary had arranged for the Jaycees to sponsor a series of concerts at the town's Civic House, and the entire promotions network was already on the job, spreading word about the visiting musical celebrities.

They had a police escort down the center of Main Street, pushing the cart, with Mary following behind in Roger's car. With sirens blasting and their Auburn toy flute record playing at high volume from a speaker on top of Roger's car, they were certainly the town's center of attention.

The parade ended right in front of the Civic House, where The Brothers parked the cart on display to advertise the following night's performances.

Having pushed the cart 30 miles in 36 hours with less than three hours of sleep, The Brothers were thankful that one of the civil-minded Jaycees had made arrangements for two nights of free lodging at the local Western Motel.

The Brothers were once again running on empty, and all they wanted to do was take hot showers and grab a few hours of much-needed shuteye.

As was often the case, even that minor luxury was interrupted when Roger was bitten on his little toe by a wooly tarantula spider that crawled out of the drain.

David truly thought the shower had somehow fallen down on his older brother, based on his screams.

Roger had smashed his hungry four-inch long attacker into a gooey blob by the time David made it to the bathroom.

They flushed the hairy remains down the toilet and hoped Roger didn't get some exotic spider fever.

When they returned to the bedroom area, they discovered that "Steps" had gotten sick and had made a big mess all over the floor. It was always something. Always.

Evidently the heat from the strenuous walk had taken its toil on their faithful canine companion, and she was also suffering the ongoing effects of The Big Walk.

David gave her half an aspirin and a little bit of a salt tablet, and in a little while "Steps" was drinking water and wagging her tail again.

Due to all of the unforeseen activities, The Brothers didn't have any time to take naps. They went to their 7:00 p.m. rehearsal at the Civic House, working with the local Jaycees on lighting cues and staging issues.

Finally satisfied with the rehearsal, they went back to their motel rooms and collapsed, keeping a close eye out for spiders, snakes, scorpions, and any other attacking desert creatures.

Friday morning, Roger and David performed for the local Lions Club luncheon, promoting the evening concert at the Civic House.

Dozens and dozens of civic-minded citizens came up and shook their hands, promising to bring their friends and families to the upcoming shows.

News about the Jaycees' concerts had been on the town's radio stations for a full three days. The local paper showcased a highly flattering story on the front page of Friday's edition. And don't forget the traffic-stopping parade they had, right down the middle of Main Street.

Mary's excellent promotional efforts had certainly been utilized in scenic Colorado City.

A person would have to have been living under a rock to not know about the night's Walking Musical Balph Brothers upcoming performances.

Roger and David arrived at the celebrated concert hall, expecting to see a full house of excited music fans waiting for the music to begin.

Where were the adoring masses? Had they gone to the wrong address? Maybe there was another Civic House in Colorado City.

A grand total of 28 people showed up for the gala performance.

Always the show-biz troopers they were, Roger and David gave the meager audience the best shows possible, performing two entire sets of spirited Dixieland classics.

The sponsoring Jaycees felt so bad about the pathetic response to their fund-raising efforts that they decided to set up a dance for Saturday night.

They would play popular records, get the crowds dancing, and allow The Brothers to perform between dance sets.

The industrious Jaycees called their friends and associates, beating the bushes to make sure Saturday night's sock hop was a smashing success.

They received solemn promises from dozens and dozens of the town's leading movers and shakers that they would be front and center at the dance, swelling with civic pride and tapping toes.

According to the oral commitments they produced with their networks of phone calls, the organizers were confident that their second try at putting on a show for the town would produce a massive crowd of happy, dancing music lovers.

Colorado City, Texas, was going to have itself a big time party, a night to remember for years to come.

Roger and David spent their afternoon before the show putting on a small surprise birthday party for Mary, having bought her a cake, a watch, and a pen and pencil set. While it wasn't very extravagant, Mary seemed to be warmly touched by their thoughtfulness.

They arrived back at the Civic House, ready to do their part to make the record hop a memorable success.

Surely the grand performance facility would be filled with enthusiastic fans this time around.

Promises had been made by trustworthy citizens.

No. It was another night of massive indifference.

It was even worse than the night before, as if that were possible.

A total of eight, yes, eight paying customers decided to spend the night of Saturday, June 27th, 1964, at the legendary Colorado City Civic House, dancing to the latest records and enjoying the live efforts of Roger and David Balph.

The Jaycees had talked about how the city's residents were always complaining about the lack of entertainment in the area, and yet when they had a chance to actually come out and support the community, they stayed away in droves.

David and Roger were truly disheartened by the lack of response to their monumental efforts.

It certainly hadn't been for lack of promotions.

They wondered if anybody could produce a crowd in this entertainment-starved town.

The Brothers had their doubts that even the newest musical sensation to hit American shores in decades, those long-haired British guys named after insects...what were they called...oh yes, The Beetles...or was it The Beatles...David and Roger both felt certain that if John, Paul, George, and Ringo had been booked to perform at The Colorado City Civic House, even they would have been lucky to bring out a dozen or so paying audience members.

At least David and Roger were able to find comfort with those thoughts.

They turned their minds to wondering if any of Mary's birthday cake was left waiting for them back at the motel room.

Roger could only hope that tarantulas hadn't already carried every single crumb back down the shower's drainpipe.

Chapter 55: Drive-Ins and Recycled Beer

Camping at the Drive-In

The Brothers left Colorado City with much less fanfare than when they entered the town.

No police escort with sirens blasting.

No parade down the middle of Main Street.

It was back to the usual routine of the road: broken tire spokes, aching body parts, and long hot days of relentless pushing, and then pushing some more.

They had spent one night camped out at an empty drive-in theater, parking the cart next to the metal speakers used to hear the movies.

After almost a year on the road since leaving Los Angeles, The Brothers had become masterful at finding places to store the cart, pitch a tent, and set up camp.

Drive-in theaters offered secluded flat areas to park the cart on level ground and were always empty in the morning hours when The Brothers were trying to pack and get back out on the road.

They also discovered that they could usually find safe sanctuaries behind gas stations and small restaurants along the route.

While some people could never imagine the idea of spending one night, much less months and months, camped out under the stars, Roger and David had no fears that they could survive on their own with the bare minimum of life's basic necessities.

In many ways, it was very liberating to realize they were very self-sufficient when it came to dealing with the realities of the world.

They had proven that, despite impossible odds, they could and were surviving in the wild, wild West, on their own terms.

They had learned to reach out to people, embrace new experiences, open themselves to any opportunities that came their way, and through sheer willpower find a way to keep The Big Walk moving.

Unlike so many of their friends who only talked about their dreams, Roger and David were actively taking control of their own destinies, each and every day.

They were willing to take risks that most of their peers could never even imagine, and David had to believe that somehow, someway all of their sacrifices would pay off in the end.

Roger couldn't even imagine what it would be like to have a so-called "normal" nine-to-five office job, carrying a briefcase and commuting to work in his beige sedan Monday through Friday.

These were the kinds of thoughts that crossed their minds as they pushed the cart on to the next Texas town, and the next, and the next.

A car filled with guys passed them on the highway, slowing down to stare at the cart and read the posters.

They roared off down the road, only to stop about a quarter of a mile away from The Brothers.

Two of the passengers got out of the car and carefully placed two shiny objects by the side of the road before jumping back in the vehicle and driving off into the distance.

With little else to do while pushing the cart, The Brothers naturally anticipated what gifts these fellow travelers might have left by the roadside.

It wasn't unusual for people to leave donations of a dollar or two under a rock when they passed the cart making its way to The Big Apple.

Sometimes Good Samaritans would leave an apple or orange, or a loaf of bread, or just some small gesture of kindness to show support for The Big Walk.

Perhaps they had seen one of the numerous newspaper clippings or heard one of the radio interviews, and just wanted to do their part without any big fuss or attention drawn to their generosity.

Maybe they were just too shy to actually stop and meet such esteemed celebrities as The Walking Musical Balph Brothers face to face.

As they approached the deposited presents, David could see that the shiny items were two gleaming beer cans.

What a pleasant surprise!

The idea of stopping for some cold refreshing complimentary suds was enough to make David and Roger pick up the pace and push the cart a little faster.

They could almost taste the frothy goodness, the nourishing liquid, the bubbling brew.

David picked up one of the cans, ready to savor the icy roadside pleasure when he realized the can was warm to the touch.

This was not a good sign.

He then noticed that the can top had been opened, right about the same moment as the distinctive aroma of fresh urine assaulted his dry nostrils.

Big joke.

The can was frothy for all the wrong reasons.

He could just visualize the car's occupants laughing their heads off, thinking that The Brothers had been stupid enough to choke down questionable cans of hot liquid left by giggling strangers.

Some people have absolutely no sense of honor.

Chapter 56: Working with The Pros

*Marquee at Hiway House in Abilene, and Cart at
Entrance with Rear Wheels being Repaired*

The Brothers were walking towards Abilene, surviving on the one candy that could handle the scorching Texas heat of July: M&Ms.

David could certainly testify that it was the delicious candy that melted in his mouth and not in his hands.

He wondered if maybe they should contact the candy company about sponsoring the rest of The Big Walk.

He certainly could handle the idea of munching colorful pieces of candy-coated chocolate across the country.

It beat dealing with recycled, human-filtered frothy beer any day of the week.

Seven miles outside of Trent, Texas, a man drove by in a truck, saw The Brothers suffering in the sizzling heat, and stopped to share a juicy ripe watermelon with them.

It was the most delicious fruit The Brothers had ever tasted in their entire lives, easily worth its weight in pure gold.

This simple act of kindness was exactly the kind of thing that gave Roger and David the willpower to keep on pushing, step by step.

Mary arrived with news of an offer to perform at The Hiway House in Abilene, and after leaving the cart behind yet another cooperative gas station, they were soon riding down the road to another lucrative series of performances.

Only it wasn't that lucrative.

While they had been able to command such hefty fees of as much as $400 a week in previous engagements, this time Mary had a tough time getting the manager of The Hiway House to even agree to pay them $125.

It was the same old argument she had heard time after time before. How good could The Walking Musical Balph Brothers be if they had to push a cart across the country to get any attention?

Did Frank Sinatra, Jr., ever walk anywhere to get a job?

At least the offer included free room and board; so, Roger and David would have a roof over their heads for the Fourth of July, 1964.

Roger sincerely wished that they didn't have to deal with such arrogant people in order to get such low-paying jobs.

David just wanted to tell the pompous guy to go jump into a creek.

But as always, they desperately needed the money and had to bite their tongues and smile for the fancy gentlemen controlling the money.

Mary had arranged for the usual barrage of newspaper and television interviews, including a spot on Channel 12's evening news programs.

The manager of The Hiway House was also a local singer of some acclaim. He was a semi-big fish in a pretty small pond and evidently believed that he was able to walk on water.

This was the same guy who had given Mary such a hard time about hiring The Brothers in the first place.

David heard him perform with the local house band and was not impressed. He had no doubts that the guy would have been laughed out of Los Angeles and told to hit the road.

The Brothers had to set up their equipment around the existing house band instruments.

The stage was extremely small, with barely enough room for one band, much less two.

David made a point of telling the pompous manager to be careful around the wires running to their Ampex recorder and speakers, specifically instructing him to not move the piano unless he wanted all of the equipment to topple to the ground.

Evidently this crooning bag of air was too busy admiring himself in the mirror, because as soon as he jumped up onstage between the first and second shows of the night, he did exactly what they had asked him not to do.

He moved the piano.

And David's warning proved valid.

One of The Brothers' rugged heavy-duty performance speakers immediately fell six feet to the hardwood floor, crashing with a resounding thud.

The by-now intoxicated singer/club manager was more concerned that his precious dance floor had been damaged than he was about The Brothers' expensive and vital speaker.

Against all odds, the speaker was still in working condition when David wrestled it up off the floor.

The next week was spent waiting for that weekend's shows at The Hiway House.

As usual, The Brothers found themselves with plenty of time to kill while waiting for their four or five hours of magic time on the stage.

It was a constant battle of hurry up and wait.

And wait.

They appeared on a game show on KPAR television, hosted by Pat Hutcheson.

A panel of local Abilene residents had to guess what Roger and David were doing in town.

Needless to say, there was no way in the world they could figure out the answer to that particular question, so Roger and David won the grand prize of new leather billfolds and tickets to the local movie theater.

Too bad they weren't on "The $64,000 Question" television show.

They could have certainly used the money.

After winning their elaborate prizes, The Brothers performed a song for the viewing audience.

Or tried to.

They were supposed to play along with their toy flute record, with the sound of the recording taking the place of live music in the studio. In other words, they were supposed to pretend.

So Roger and David had their trusty plastic flutes in hand, waiting to hear the music and play along.

They kept on waiting.

There was complete silence in the television studio, but evidently the record was audible to the viewers at home.

The station's engineer had neglected to push the button that allowed the studio audience to hear the music. For what seemed like an eternity, but was actually only a few seconds, the camera was frozen with Roger and David standing motionless with their toy flutes, waiting for the cue to begin that never came.

Trying to overcome the awkwardness of the moment, Pat Hutcheson came on camera and announced that The Brothers would now perform "The Wabash Blues" on clarinet and trombone.

The studio audience politely clapped their approval.

When the music began, it was the wrong song.

They were playing the previous tune featuring the toy flutes, while David and Roger were standing on camera holding their big shiny professional instruments.

The Brothers scrambled to grab their toy flutes, futilely trying to salvage the last of their musical reputation on live television.

By now the show had run out of time, so the station cut the performance, as it was, and went to a commercial.

Everybody at the television station was laughing, everybody except David, who was upset almost to the boiling point.

He didn't care if others were seen as dumbbells, running around like a bunch of monkeys. If they were content being fools, so be it. He just didn't like it one bit that the station's mistakes made him look like an idiot on live television.

He wanted the chance to go back on the air and redeem himself, and was willing to fight for the right, but once again, calmer heads prevailed.

They left the studio with Roger chuckling and David's ears still burning in rage.

In a world filled with so many incompetent people, David faced a constant battle.

Mary arranged for a follow-up interview the next day, securing six minutes of airtime for a proper interview with Roger and David.

They arrived at the station to discover that the young girl receptionist at the front desk was going to do the interview.

Her name was Sherry Fowler, and even though David was positive that she couldn't be much older than 22 years old, she insisted on referring to The Brothers as "boys."

Her big plan for the interview was to simply introduce David and Roger, then let them talk about themselves for six minutes.

She didn't have any questions lined up and didn't seem to have much curiosity about anything related to The Big Walk.

Where were the station's more experienced reporters?

Was this interview with The Balphs her reward or her punishment?

Was this her ticket to a better job in a bigger city or another thankless task dumped on the person on the lowest rung of the reporting ladder?

The Brothers proceeded to do her homework for her by providing her with their biography, a copy of their toy flute record, and a promotional photo of them pushing the cart. Then they came up with a list of extremely interesting questions any reporter would be glad to ask.

Their efforts paid off.

Sherry performed like a seasoned professional interviewer on air, and The Brothers didn't have to stand around looking like idiots.

It felt good taking matters into their own hands, and for once, David's ears weren't burning when he left the building.

The payoffs from the positive exposure paid off almost immediately.

The owner of the local Oldsmobile dealership allowed them to use a brand new Olds for the next two weeks in exchange for promotions and playing a party at his home. He even threw in a set of new brakes for Roger's old car that Mary depended on for her daily efforts to find work. If that wasn't already enough, he agreed to fix a broken motor mount that had needed repair for quite some time.

It was amazing how fast good things could come together when there was a little motivation.

So, instead of walking from interview to interview, The Brothers were able to arrive in style, enjoying the wonderful air-conditioning of one of the latest Detroit luxury vehicles on the highway.

Life was good.

David spent his day off, swimming and relaxing with a local girl at their motel.

Roger was able to get some needed repairs made on his alto sax.

With the deluxe Olds at their disposal, they were able to attend a party that night, enjoying the hospitality of the good people of Abilene, Texas.

As always, when things were just starting to run smoothly, and life was somewhat easier, David returned to his motel room to discover that "Steps" had spent the evening chewing three holes in the left pant leg of his stage costume.

There was no way he would be able to wear them at the next night's performance, and he couldn't simply replace them with a quick run to the local clothing store.

The pants were part of his Army uniform, and even though an Air Force base was nearby, those uniforms were blue, not brown.

The desk clerk at the motel knew a lady seamstress who was supposedly able to work miracles with her scissors and thread.

The fate of David's pants was now out of his hands, and "Steps'" teeth.

He spent Sunday, July 12th, enjoying yet another party on the outskirts of town. A successful businessman named Jack McQueen invited David to a cookout on the lake, which turned into another big time of water-skiing and all-day partying.

Roger had been invited, but didn't want to go.

David had enough on his mind without worrying about the ever-changing mood of his older brother, and didn't see any reason to miss the party.

If truth be told, David sometimes enjoyed being out of Roger's large shadow and his controlling ways.

While he loved his brother, he didn't enjoy the power plays and mind games Roger liked to pull on him.

Regardless of what David was able to accomplish in his life, he would always be the younger Balph sibling.

He had no doubts that even when Roger was 70 years old, he would still be treating David like a kid.

So, David went to the party and had a great time, never giving his brother a second thought.

When he arrived back at the motel, he discovered that "Steps" had been at it again.

No, she didn't chew up yet another pair of David's pants. That would have been too easy. This time she had managed to get sick and go to the bathroom all over David's motel room.

The operative phrase here is "all over."

David was amazed by how many places she had found to mess up and soil. It took him almost three hours to clean up her juicy deposits, while holding back his gag reflexes.

The cashier at the motel's lounge offered to take "Steps" home with her for a week or so where the dog would have the chance to run around in the fenced-in backyard and enjoy being back out in the fresh air.

Roger and Mary returned with news that the manager of the club at The Hiway House Motel, the very same pompous singer who knocked over their speaker and who had also given Mary such a hard time, had decided to exercise the two-week option in his contract.

Giving club managers the option of extending their contract was one of the ways Mary tried to sweeten the deal for reluctant buyers along the trip, and most of the time it worked to The Brothers' advantage.

Unfortunately, this time the clause wound up taking money out of their mouths.

Despite repeatedly filling the club with thirsty, paying customers during their previous engagements, the manager was only willing to pay $75 a week for the extended performances.

The Brothers had been insulted by the previous payment of $125 per week, and after doing good work and producing tangible results for the club, this was how he treated them?

As usual, they were short on cash and weren't in a position to turn down any paying offers.

David felt like they were constantly trying to squeeze blood out of a turnip.

Arrival in Abilene

Chapter 57: Happy Anniversary

First Anniversary Celebration of The Big Walk
(Note that the photographer cut off the faces of Roger and David)

On July 16th, 1964, Barry Goldwater became the Republican candidate for U.S. President.

On July 17th, 1964, The Brothers gave a two-hour performance at nearby Dyess Air Force base. It was always a pleasure to entertain the military. Roger and David supported the efforts and missions of the troops, and were proud to do their part to boost morale.

July 8th, 1964, marked the one-year anniversary since The Big Walk began, even if it was only their first initial 33-foot journey down their mother's alley before the cart crumpled under the weight of their load.

The fact remains that they really had been on the road for a year, and while things hadn't gone exactly as planned, at least The Brothers were still alive, performing and pushing their way to New York City and Jack Paar.

It had been a real education for The Brothers and Mary.

David could only laugh when he remembered how they initially thought the entire cross-country trip would take five or six months, at the most.

What were they thinking? Or not?

He remembered using a wooden ruler in his mother's apartment, placing it on a map of the country, carefully calculating how many miles they could easily walk per day until they reached The Big Apple.

How could they have been so totally and completely clueless?

He remembered following the tiny line on the map, casually racing through California, Arizona, New Mexico, Texas, and beyond without realizing how monumental the task before them really was going to be.

It was so easy to talk about pushing a cart across America while posing for photographs and being interviewed by Los Angeles television stations.

Talk was cheap.

If he had possibly had any idea of what The Brothers were getting themselves into with The Big Walk, odds were he would never have taken that momentous first step.

There had to be easier ways to build a musical career.

Twelve months later, David found himself getting ready for yet another performance at The Hiway House lounge in scenic Abilene, Texas.

The waitresses at the lounge gave Roger and David an anniversary cake featuring a map outline of the United States, showing the progress of The Big Walk to date, ending with their present location in Abilene.

They had 12 flickering candles on the cake, each one representing a month of memories, efforts, and struggles on the highway.

David could only wonder how many more candles would be burned before they reached the end of the road.

Chapter 58: Crazy Women and Mugs Shots in Abilene

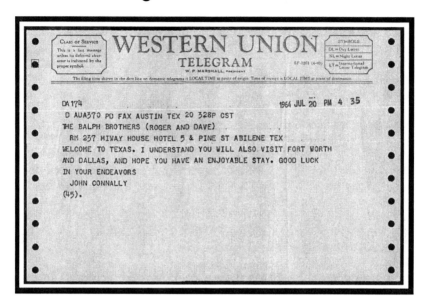

Texas Governor Connelly's Welcome to Texas Telegram

Their time in Abilene was coming to an end, or so they thought.

Mary had already been working on lining up gigs in Fort Worth, and The Brothers were looking forward to moving on to new opportunities.

On Monday, July 20th, they were surprised to receive a telegram from Texas Governor John Connelly, welcoming them to The Lone Star State, and wishing them good luck with The Big Walk.

Connelly had been in the national spotlight when he was wounded, riding in the same motor caravan that killed President John F. Kennedy in Dallas the previous year.

The Brothers assumed that some connection with one of the local newspapers or perhaps a television station had brought about the telegram.

Maybe the esteemed politician just wanted to share a little of the spotlight with The Walking Musical Balph Brothers?

David was also relieved to discover that his grandfather's 38 pistol, which was being repaired at the Colt Firearms factory in Connecticut, had been delivered by railway express.

The trusty old family heirloom looked like a brand new weapon. David was certain that his ancestor would have been proud of the way it had been restored to perfection.

Mary's son, Dennis, arrived by bus from Los Angeles, having not seen his mother in over a year.

He was interested in pursuing a career in the military, and seemed to have a good head on his shoulders.

David felt this trio of good news called for a bit of celebration, and decided to make a run to nearby Impact, Texas, a curious benefactor of local laws concerning alcohol.

Abilene was officially a dry town, meaning a person couldn't buy liquor anywhere within the city limits.

To get around this bit of legal obstacles, you had to bring your own bottles of alcoholic beverages.

And those bottles of booze had to come from somewhere.

Seeing a golden opportunity of supply and demand, four local citizens of Abilene bought some property three miles outside of town, incorporated it as the new city of Impact, elected a mayor, and immediately passed a law allowing the purchase of all things alcoholic.

They then proceeded to build a huge supermarket to sell, what else, alcoholic beverages of all shapes, colors, origins, and tastes.

While the good churchgoing, tea-sipping citizens of Abilene had fits, there was nothing they could do about it.

The crafty owners of Impact, Texas, laughed all the way to the bank.

There were definite advantages to owning the only liquor store within a hundred miles of town.

On Sunday, July 26th, David, Roger, Mary, and her son, Denny, spent the day at Jack McQueen's lakeside cottage, swimming, boating, and water-skiing.

Nobody broke a leg or drowned, and a good time was had by all.

David enjoyed listening to Denny talk about his plans to attend the Naval Academy and build a life for himself in service to the country.

Back at the motel, they all hit the sack after a wonderful day of watery relaxation.

Around 3:15 in the morning, the phone rang.

A woman by the name of Robbie was on the line, asking to speak with Roger.

David told her that Roger was sleeping, and she'd have to call back at a more decent hour.

A few moments later the phone rang again.

This time Roger grabbed the phone, told this same Robbie that it was too late to be calling anybody, and promptly slammed the phone back down on the receiver.

On Friday, July 31st, much sooner than Mary had imagined, it was time for her son to take his 30-hour return bus trip back to Los Angeles.

David had spent the week dating a girl named Kathy, and had made plans to see her Monday night after he finished the second show at a place called The Westward Club.

Kathy must have been the impatient type, because she called the club, leaving a message that she needed to know what time David was going to pick her up.

David immediately called her when he took a break, and told her he expected to be at her apartment around 11:30 p.m.

As a courtesy to his lady in waiting, David called her number right before leaving the club.

Kathy's roommate answered the phone, and was quite upset that she had been disturbed at such a late hour.

David apologized and explained he was on his way, at that very moment, to pick up Kathy and take her out for the promised evening date.

The roommate told David that Kathy wasn't there, but just as she started to hang up, Kathy grabbed the phone and assured him that she was, in fact, ready and anxiously waiting for their date to begin.

Forty minutes later David arrived at the home Kathy shared with her roommate, finding the windows dark.

In hindsight, it probably would have made more sense for the younger Balph brother to have just called it a night and let sleeping dogs lie, so to speak.

But, by this time, David had put considerable effort into keeping his promise with Kathy, and he had already passed the point of no return.

He stood on the doorstep, ringing the doorbell over and over, until the lights came on in the apartment.

Looks like somebody was finally awake.

Unfortunately, the person answering the door was the ill-tempered roommate, a woman by the name of Robbie England.

She was livid with rage, screaming about the time, and insisting that Kathy wasn't going anywhere with David or anybody else at that time of night.

Looking past this screeching banshee, David could see Kathy, his date, sitting on the couch.

Walking past the angry roommate, David discovered that Kathy was obviously seriously intoxicated, a state he hadn't seen her in on any of their previous dates.

It was evident that Kathy was not going to be sharing dinner, coffee, or anything else with David.

By now, the crazed roommate was beside herself with outright rage, demanding that David leave the apartment immediately.

David politely walked to his car and drove back to his motel.

On the way back to his night's lodging, three police cars flew by him with lights flashing and sirens blasting.

David assumed that there must have been a car wreck somewhere down the road, and he immediately slowed down his own car as a precaution.

Safely back in his motel room, he was getting ready to jump under the sheets, when his phone rang.

It was Kathy, still intoxicated, but slightly more sober, calling.

David told her that he wasn't interested in talking with her when she was so inebriated, adding that he was disappointed that they hadn't been able to spend any time together.

Kathy told him that Robbie, her roommate, had called the police, telling them that David had thrown her against a wall, breaking her arm and smashing the apartment to pieces.

Robbie was also claiming that David had also kicked in the door, threatened the entire household, and, last of all, used foul language.

Those passing police cars that David had met on the road were looking for him!

David didn't know whether to believe her or not.

She was obviously drunk, and David knew he hadn't laid a finger on the raging roommate.

And what was the point about supposedly using foul language?

It had struck David as an odd phrase to use on top of all the other allegations.

He decided that the whole ordeal was just a horrible joke, and he decided to grab some much-needed sleep after a long day.

He didn't even bother taking off his clothes, just collapsed face down in his pillow.

An hour after calling it a night, David was rudely awakened by the sound of heavy banging on his motel door.

It hadn't been a joke, or a bad dream.

The cops had a warrant for his arrest, and took him to the police station, booking him on charges of assault and battery and of using foul language.

There was that odd phrase again.

Why was everybody making such a big deal about foul language in this Texas town?

Bail was set at $40, which David didn't have.

Roger took charge of matters and was able to reach the pompous club manager, sometimes singer, of The Hiway House, where The Brothers had just spent the last month performing.

Thankfully, the manager took pity on the sad plight of the younger Balph Brother, making a call to the motel's attorney.

The club manager also placed a call to the notorious roommate pressing charges, Robbie England, a woman known in the community for being a troublemaker.

This wasn't the first time there had been a run-in with this person.

His efforts to get Robbie to calm down were futile. She was sticking by her story and refused to drop any of the charges.

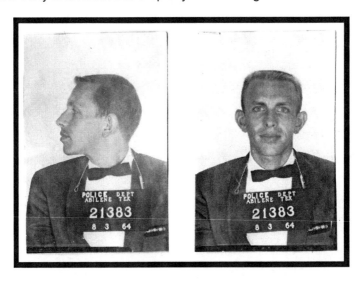

David Reluctantly Poses for Photos in his Tux

Meanwhile, David was fingerprinted. Mug shots were taken with David still wearing the tuxedo he had performed in at The Westward Club.

A call came in to the police station.

Robbie England called to drop charges.

The nightmare was over.

And, then, it wasn't.

Unfortunately for David, once he had been fingerprinted, it was too late to drop anything.

David was released on bail, provided by the nightclub manager, and told to return to the police station at 7:45 am.

By this time it was already 4:15 in the morning.

When David arrived back at the motel, the nightclub manager met him in the lobby and proceeded to lecture the younger Balph Brother about the errors of his ways.

While David was deeply appreciative of the man providing bail, did he really need to preach at that precise moment?

At 7:45, David joined his fellow accused criminals and faced the judge.

He told the honorable man of law that he was decidedly not guilty.

The trial was initially set for August 19th, a full two weeks away.

Pleading his unusual circumstances, David asked if the trial could take place any earlier.

The judge set the trial for 3:30 p.m. the very next day.

As soon as he returned to the motel, they called Jack Bryant, one of Abilene's most highly regarded attorneys.

Jack told them to come on over to his office. When he heard the details of the case and, more importantly, the name of the accuser, Robbie England, he laughed and told David not to worry about a thing.

The rumors about Robbie England were true. She evidently made a career out of pressing charges against anybody possible, hoping for a pretrial financial settlement.

They also learned that the enterprising Robbie had faced previous charges for sharing her dubious feminine charms with numerous lonely gentlemen in exchange for cold hard cash.

Turns out this woman was a pro on many levels, and David had innocently played right into her hands by repeatedly ringing her doorbell in the middle of the night.

Efforts to have the case thrown out of court failed.

The city attorney that Jack Bryant normally counted on to help out with favors was out of town, and the remaining city official went strictly by the book, much to David's disappointment.

David arrived at court for his trial, with several local friends on hand to testify about his good character.

The lady from the motel, who was keeping "Steps" in her backyard was firmly on David's side.

Jack McQueen, the man who owned the party cabin by the lake was good to his word, testifying that the younger Balph was a decent, law-abiding, former military man.

David was disappointed that Kathy, his date who had been the initial source of all this trouble, was nowhere to be seen.

She could have cleared up the entire matter in a matter of moments.

Maybe he did deserve that nightclub manager's stern lecture after all.

The money-seeking accuser, Robbie England, got on the stand, and under sworn oath, proceeded to lie, lie, lie.

David couldn't understand why lightning didn't come out of the sky and just strike the lying banshee right there in the courtroom.

She told the judge that young David had broken into her quiet home in a drunken rage in the middle of the night. She testified that he then hit her in the face and broke her arm.

Broke her arm?

When David's attorney pointed out that neither of her arms were in casts or even wrapped with bandages, Robbie suddenly seemed to remember that she was supposed to be in severe pain, grabbing her arm theatrically.

She then stated that even if her arm wasn't technically broken, it was extremely sore.

David was surprised that she wasn't wearing a nun's habit with a heavenly halo floating around her head.

She then had her 12-year-old son testify on the stand and verify her story.

The little accomplice in crime swore that he saw The Musical Balph Brother throw his dear mother against the wall of their apartment and threaten her very life.

David listened to the false accusations in complete disbelief.

Of course the boy would say what his mother had taught him to recite, but surely the judge had to realize the insanity of the statements.

The prosecuting attorney asked David to please explain to the court exactly why he was in Abilene, and David truly thought the man was joking for a moment.

Hadn't the city's attorney done his homework? Didn't he know whom he was talking to? Hadn't he read a newspaper in the last month, listened to any local radio stations, or watched any television news broadcasts?

Despite the seriousness of the situation, David couldn't help but politely ask the attorney if he had paid any attention to local news recently.

David calmly told the man who could literally help send him to jail that perhaps he should read the front page of Abilene's newspaper if he didn't believe that The Balphs were indeed walking across the country, pushing a 1,000-pound cart.

The esteemed judge, in all of his wisdom, decided that he had heard enough. After three hours in the courtroom, he decided to drop the battery and assault charges. Those were the biggest threats to David's freedom.

Then he addressed the charges of that odd phrase, the one accusing him of "foul language."

As it turned out, it is against the law to call anybody a "whore" in Abilene, Texas, even if it is technically true.

David was found guilty of that charge and promptly fined $25.

You'd think that would be the end of this particularly sordid mess, that David would realize how lucky he was, pay his civil fee, and leave the courtroom a happy man.

You would be wrong. Instead of counting his blessings and gleefully dancing out into the street, the younger Balph Brother immediately told his attorney that he was appealing the decision, taking it to a higher court.

Meanwhile, David's attorney notified Robbie England that he was pressing charges against her for perjury.

She had testified under oath that she had no prior knowledge of David or Roger Balph, and had never met them, talked to them, or had any dealings with them in any manner.

She was asked this question two times on the stand, and both times had sworn that she had never, ever had any contact with The Walking Musical Balph Brothers.

David's lawyer then notified Robbie England that Roger Balph had indeed met her at a previous performance at The Hiway House Motel, and had turned down her request to have drinks with her at the nightclub.

He was also ready and willing to testify, under oath, that this very same Robbie had been the one who called his motel room at 3:30 in the morning, not once, but two times, demanding that he get out of bed and come meet her for a round of early morning drinks and partying.

Yes. The woman causing all the trouble for David, literally trying to take away his freedom, was the very same woman who had called their room a week earlier.

This whole ordeal had been her revenge for David and Roger hanging up on her in those twilight hours.

That old saying that "Hell hath no fury like a woman scorned" was true in August 1964, in scenic Abilene, Texas.

David Balph of The Famous Walking Musical Balph Brothers could certainly testify, under oath if necessary, to the truth of those words.

Chapter 59: Slim Pickings

Returning the Olds

Finally leaving Abilene behind, with the lingering issue of appealing David's court ruling for "foul language" hanging over their heads, The Brothers were determined to march forth and not look back.

It served no purpose to second guess what might have been or dwell on how the situation could have been avoided.

David's lawyer told them to check back every week or so and see how the appeals process was proceeding, but not to let this legal dark cloud control their lives.

It could have been much, much worse. David could easily have been sharing a cold jail cell, and maybe a bunk, with a toothless criminal named Bubba or Tiny.

Since leaving Abilene, several of their friends had driven out for final visits along the roadside before The Brothers pushed out of close reach.

They found out that the notorious Robbie woman had called two of the people who had testified on David's behalf, saying she was going to sue them for defamation of her stellar reputation.

David's attorney also informed them that if he decided to follow through with his intentions to charge Robbie with perjury, she would be facing a felony rap, and David would be required to return to Abilene to testify.

Those issues would have to be decided at a future date. Meanwhile, The Brothers were back to their normal routine of pushing the cart and then pushing some more.

They had sadly returned the new, loaned, courtesy Oldsmobile that had been their luxurious means of transportation for two glorious weeks, and were back to facing the grim reality of hard, physical legwork as their primary means of locomotion.

Mary had spent four entire days in Fort Worth, scrambling to find any kind of paying jobs for The Brothers, but had returned empty-handed.

At first she thought that maybe it was the result of bad publicity from David's arrest and subsequent court trial, but it turned out to be just more cases of massive indifference.

The happenings in a small town like Abilene were of no interest to nightclub owners in a major city like Fort Worth.

They didn't know, and they didn't care.

Mary's struggle to book engagements was always like starting over from zero.

Despite her ever-growing book of newspaper articles and letter after letter of glowing testimonials from satisfied nightclub managers, it was always a major hurdle overcoming the perception that two musicians pushing a cart across the country were capable of being professional entertainers.

It most definitely did not earn The Brothers' respect for talent bookers.

It was almost like the very gimmick that brought The Brothers attention in the first place was the same obstacle that held them back from decent jobs.

Meanwhile, their limited resources were continuously being spent for gasoline to keep Mary knocking on doors, motel rooms to keep a roof over her head while she was out prospecting, and little things like drycleaning, lipstick, and fresh stockings to keep her looking like a professional businesswoman while trying to secure contracts.

In very real and tangible ways, Roger, David, and Mary were all facing daily trials and tribulations.

272

Just like clockwork, Roger's rash had flared up again, making each step pure torture.

David's battle with blisters was constant and unrelenting.

On August 15th, it was 101 degrees in the shade, until the skies opened up, raining cats and dogs down on The Brothers, turning the desert into a sea of mud.

The cart sank in the muck so badly that they had to flag down a passing truck to pull them out with a metal chain.

Soon they hit the part of Texas where the hills seemed to go straight up and never end.

Roger and David were doing well to push 50 feet without having to stop and rest. It was all they could do to travel seven miles a day.

It was enough to make Roger long for the flat highways of Arizona, where they could push 20 or 30 miles a day on a regular basis.

The fact that Mary kept coming back with bad news certainly didn't help their mental attitudes.

They reached Cisco, Texas, with 1,415 miles on the odometer.

They had been too tired to put up the tent, choosing just to sleep on the cots under the stars. It didn't seem like much of a gamble. The stars were shining, the moon was glowing, and there wasn't a cloud to be seen in the sky. It was a good night to get some fresh air and dream sweet thoughts.

As usual, their luck took a turn for the worse. At 4:00 a.m., the skies opened up, and a flood worthy of Noah descended from the dark thunderclouds that had blown in from nowhere.

There weren't even any nearby trees to run to for shelter. It took them at least 15 minutes to get the tent up, and, by that time, everything they had was soaked to the core.

So much for the continued glamour of show business.

Chapter 60: Welcome to Eastland, Arrested...Again

Eastland Jail

Monday, August 17th, turned out to be another milestone day on The Big Walk.

David was arrested. Again.

To make matters even worse, Roger was his cellmate, along with an alleged speeder named Fred, and an accused thief named Johnny.

It all happened because Mary had booked The Brothers for an interview on a radio station in Eastland, Texas.

They were pushing the cart right across the city limits when two law officers drove up and pulled them over to the side of the road.

They identified themselves as Officer Rogers and Sergeant Sozabe.

It was obvious these fine civil servants were not fans of Dixieland Jazz, looking for autographs from The Walking Musical Balph Brothers.

David tried to politely explain they were late for a live interview on one of the city's leading radio stations, and they would appreciate any consideration possible.

David thought there might be a chance the kind policemen would give them a ride to the studio, in the interest of community service.

He was wrong.

The police officers were not interested in anything to do with radio stations or interviews.

Sergeant Sozabe walked up to David and removed his grandfather's recently restored pistol from the side holster.

It was painfully obvious that this was no friendly greeting to the city.

The officers informed The Brothers that they were under arrest for carrying pistols and walking on the wrong side of the road.

In disbelief, David asked them what he was supposed to do with the cart, and Officer Rogers said that it wasn't any of his concern.

Any kindness David might have expected from these uniformed community protectors was evidently in short supply.

These two officers were hostile and humorless.

It was almost as if they had been waiting for The Brothers to cross the line and enter their kingdom.

Roger was able to convince these paid city employees that their entire lives were invested in that cart, that it contained irreplaceable, expensive musical equipment, and that there would serious repercussions for the city of Eastland if it was just left by the side of the road.

The arresting officers begrudgingly allowed Roger and David to push the cart a fifth of a mile down the road to the next gas station, where it would at least be off of the road.

They left "Steps" in charge of keeping all of their worldly possessions safe and sound, as The Brothers dealt with this latest crisis.

In the patrol car, Sergeant Sozabe told David he just might have to make him eat his grandfather's pretty pistol.

Roger, in a moment of elementally bone-headed vocal diarrhea, retorted that he had never seen a man eat a gun before, immediately realizing that this wasn't a time for joking around with strangers in uniforms.

For once, David kept his mouth shut.

They hauled The Walking Musical Balph Brothers down to the courthouse, and brought them in front of the Justice of the Peace.

Headlines in Eastland

The charges against David for carrying a firearm on his side had to be dismissed when they discovered that it wasn't against the law to do that in Texas.

While this news was evidently surprising, they were able to locate the specific law stating which side of the road people were allowed to walk on, and there was no doubt that The Brothers were, literally, on the wrong side of this very specific law.

While The Brothers were being arrested, transported, and booked, Mary had stumbled over the cart parked at the gas station.

When Roger and David failed to show up for their scheduled radio interview, she knew something had gone wrong and was beside herself with worry when she found "Steps" guarding the cart.

A mechanic at the gas station told her about their arrest, and Mary immediately drove back to the radio station to pick up support in the form of the two reporters who were supposed to interview Roger and David on the air.

The Justice of the Peace asked The Brothers if they wanted to plead innocent or guilty.

David told the Justice they had pushed their cart 1,500 miles on the right side of the road, including 500 miles in Texas, and had never had any problems.

He also told the Justice they had been advised in California that it was safer to walk on the right side of the road when pushing a cart since going with the traffic allowed cars to see them from a distance, which would avoid collisions on the highway.

The Justice didn't care one bit what people thought was safe in California. He was in Texas, and he enforced the laws of The Lone Star State. Period.

David couldn't remember a time when a public official had been so rude to him.

It was obvious to everybody that this particular Justice of the Peace was used to running things his way, and he didn't have any respect for two unemployed brothers from Los Angeles coming into his fair city, breaking laws, and smarting off to him in his own courtroom.

He placed a $200 property bond on Roger and David before having them hauled off to their jail cell.

The key words in that particular phrase are "property bonds." As they were being escorted to their metal cage, they were informed that a property bond meant that The Brothers couldn't just post $200 and be released.

No. Their money was no good in this fine court of law.

By making their bond a property bond, the esteemed Justice of the Peace thought that he had assured The Musical Walking Balph

277

Brothers would spend their time in jail, with no chance of freedom before their trial.

The only way they could have posted a property bond was if they owned property in Eastland, Texas, and were able to post with that real estate securing the bail.

It was a racket designed to keep out-of-towners accused of breaking local laws under lock and key for as long as possible.

The Balph Brothers weren't going anywhere, fast.

David and Roger were completely searched from head to toe before being thrown into the cold metal slammer. They even confiscated David's shoe rag that he used to polish the toes of his boots when people would stop them on the road and take photos.

Roger and David were locked up for six hours before Mary was finally able to free them. Through contacts with the local radio reporters, she had been able to reach a local attorney named Mr. Russell.

In what can only be described as another act of divine intervention, Mr. Russell had seen one of The Brothers' recent performances back in Abilene, and was a big fan of Roger and David's musical talents.

After meeting Mary and hearing about the rude reception The Brothers had received in his hometown, he took it on himself to get personally involved, calling the police and volunteering to put up the elusive property bond.

Evidently Attorney Russell was a man of considerable means and influence in Eastland, because the Justice of the Peace allowed Roger and David to be released on their word, requiring them to be in court at 9:00 a.m. the next morning.

It was now 12:15 a.m., and The Brothers had spent the last six hours getting to know their fellow cellmates and the scoop on the town.

As it turned out, they weren't the only ones treated poorly by Eastland's fine law enforcers.

Fred was a college student with very little money. He had been found guilty of speeding and reckless driving. He couldn't afford his $275 fine, so he was serving a 90-day jail term. He had been locked up for 11 days.

Johnny had been arrested for theft, but according to him, there was no evidence or proof in any shape or form. He had been locked up for 3 days, and didn't know when he would be released.

To their amazement, they also discovered that the Justice of the Peace was paid a commission from the fines he collected. The more fines he ordered, the more money that went directly into his pocket.

This was not a good place to be poor, or friendless. The town also had a reputation for being a speed trap and for passing odd laws on a whim.

The city had recently made international headlines when they passed a law banning smoking anywhere within city limits. The fine was $1,000, plus ten days in lock-up. Though the law only lasted a few weeks before being repealed, it served to put Eastland in the center of the world's media spotlight.

Roger and David had stumbled into a private kingdom ruled with an iron fist by a bunch of good old boys that handled matters pretty much any way they saw fit, all under the questionable guise of enforcing Texas law.

They also discovered that meals were served three times a day, and cigarettes were worth their weight in gold behind the bars.

Breakfast consisted of two pieces of toast and a cup of coffee. Lunch and dinner were beans.

Fred had been living on beans and toast for 11 days.

Dinner had already been served by the time The Brothers were locked up, so they didn't even get any beans of their own.

When Mary secured The Brothers' freedom at 12:15 a.m., the first place they went was an all-night diner, starving for nourishment.

Being a prisoner made David extremely hungry. He also picked up a carton of cigarettes, taking them back to the jail for Johnny and Fred, trusting that the jailers would actually give them to their luckless cellmates.

Attorney Russell had a small guest cottage on his property, and he graciously let Roger, David, and Mary spend the night there.

Even at that late hour, Mary was on the phone to her list of contacts, trying to prepare for the next day's court case.

She was able to reach Jim Glass, the Vice-President of Auburn Rubber Company, back in Deming, New Mexico, the company that made toy flutes and had produced the record of David and Roger performing songs using their products.

Mr. Glass was also the head of the town's newspaper, and Mary wanted to see if he could use his connections to get the arrest story on the wire news services, which would generate some national publicity for Roger and David.

Since Eastland, Texas, seemed to like being in the news, Mary was determined to make as much noise about this latest injustice as possible.

The town's honorable Justice of the Peace truly might have met his match.

Mary was not going to allow The Walking Musical Balph Brothers to be abused, mistreated, or harmed by anybody without putting up a good fight.

By 6:30 a.m., the local radio station was reporting the details of the arrest all over the county. They also criticized the police for their actions, and the Justice of the Peace for his misuse of power.

This was not something the powers that be were accustomed to.

The last thing they wanted was to be the focus of any broadcasted criticisms, local or otherwise.

Their strong-armed methods worked better in silence, without the nation's reporters and news crews breathing down their necks.

Evidently, people were calling people who were calling people.

Attorney Russell told them he would pay the silly fine if they would just plead guilty and go on about their business.

Mary placed another call to Mr. Glass in Deming, New Mexico, telling him the issue would be resolved if The Brothers followed Attorney Russell's advice and let him pay their fine.

Mr. Glass told them that if they admitted guilt, they would have to walk on the other, more dangerous, side of the road the rest of their time in Texas, or they would face even harsher fines each and every time they were arrested.

It was a dangerous no-win situation.

Meanwhile, The Justice of the Peace got wind of the radio station's coverage of the arrests.

He was not happy.

This was not how things were supposed to go in his town.

The Justice offered to dismiss all of the charges, providing The Brothers would walk on the left hand side of the road while they were in Eastland.

Did that end the dilemma?

What do you think?

By now Mr. Glass in New Mexico had brought his boss, Dick Hodson, president of the Auburn Rubber Company into the picture, and Mr. Hodson knew people who knew people.

Mr. Hodson was the man who had treated Roger and David like his own family, giving them support above and beyond the call of duty, all along the way.

He put calls into the office of the Governor of New Mexico, requesting help in reaching Governor Connelly of Texas.

This was the very same Governor Connelly who had recently sent Roger and David a personal telegram welcoming them to The Lone Star State and wishing them a safe journey.

Mr. Hodson was pretty confident that having The Brothers arrested in Eastland was not Governor Connelly's idea of a decent "welcoming."

Mr. Hodson also wired some much-needed money to The Brothers, knowing all too well their fragile financial condition.

Once again, Mr. Hodson proved to be a trusted friend when they were indeed in need.

With Mary, the local radio station reporters, Dick Hodson, Attorney Russell, and Mr. Glass back in New Mexico, all making phone calls, The Brothers realized that it pays to have friends in high places.

Though Governor Connelly happened to be out of the country on official business, word evidently made it to his ears, or at least to those of his staff in Austin, the State's capitol.

The Justice of the Peace delayed the trial until the next day.

They were at a standstill. The law was the law, pure and simple.

That afternoon, calls came in from Washington, D.C.

Another call came in from the chief law officer for the state of Texas.

Somebody somewhere noticed the law specifically mentioned walking.

Was that the key word? What did the law say about pushing? Was there any mention of pushing a cart down the road?

In a place so strictly run by laws, did the fact that carts were decidedly not mentioned in writing mean anything? Was this the face-saving out that all parties so desperately needed? Had they fallen down the mythical rabbit hole made famous by Alice in Wonderland?

Efforts were being made to issue a one-time-only permit, exclusively for use by The Walking Musical Balph Brothers.

Things were completely out of control by the time Roger and David appeared on the local radio station, pleading their case to the listening public.

By this time, everybody from the highest levels on down wanted the matter resolved and over with.

The local law enforcers needed to get back to the normal routine of arresting anonymous out-of-towners and collecting hefty fines without the blinding glare of the nation's media spotlights.

While politicians were irritated by the situation, The Balphs were literally fighting for their survival.

They truly believed walking on the so-called "legal" side of the road would be an act of suicide, putting them directly in the path of danger.

This wasn't some amusing little story for public giggles.

They knew from 1,500 miles of real world cart-pushing, road-walking experience that following the Texas law would put their lives and countless others in jeopardy.

It was easy for the uninformed to pass laws that sounded good on paper.

This was not a case of The Balphs being stubborn and hung up on principles.

Their stakes in the outcome went far beyond those of the pompous paper-pushers levying fines and barking out orders.

Word came down from nameless sources that nobody would say or do anything if The Balph Brothers just took their cart and pushed their way straight out of Eastland, Texas.

They could push on the left side, the right side, or, for that matter, right down the center of the main highway, and nobody would give a flying hoot.

The only time the local police would do anything was if they were hit by a car or fell over dead in the middle of the street.

While no one was officially telling them to break the law, the message was plenty clear to anybody with half a mind.

Don't ask. Don't tell. Wink. Wink.

Roger and David pushed their famous cart down the right side of the road, exactly like they had done every single step of the previous 1,500 miles, going directly past the Eastland Courthouse.

David made a point of watching it fade from view in his rearview mirror as he pushed and then pushed some more.

Goodbye, Eastland, Texas. Goodbye, small town politics.

David couldn't wait to get to Jack Paar's studio couch and tell the nation's television viewers exactly what happened to them in America's Heartland, the Land of the Free, the Home of the Brave.

Chapter 61: Birthday Rip-off

The Brothers celebrated Roger's birthday, August 22nd, on the road, pushing the cart, trying to get as far away from Eastland, Texas, as possible.

It rained most of the morning, so they were only able to push 12 miles through the Texas hills.

They promised each other they would properly celebrate all birthdays, Christmases, Easters, and all of the other holidays they had endured on The Big Walk when they made it to New York City.

Until their moment of glory, they would just have to make do with whatever they could find to celebrate along the highway.

They walked through a Texas ghost town named Thurber. Once it had been a thriving community with over 10,000 citizens, mostly working in The Lone Star State's only coal mining district. All that was left was a gas station and a small café.

David and Roger shared some sodas on the front steps of the gas station with two elderly gentlemen who hadn't seen each other since 1938, listening to stories about Thurber's good ole days.

They told a story about a miner who had been killed on the job, and all the mining company offered his grieving widow was $25. They said the union kicked in another $50, and that was the end of the story.

Roger could only wonder what kinds of human sacrifices had been made over the decades in those rolling Texas hills.

They continued to struggle with flat tires, having gone through 18 since leaving Los Angeles. There didn't seem to be much logic to the wear and tear on the rubber. Some tires would last 400 miles, while others gave out after as few as 60 miles.

They always dreaded when the right rear tire went flat, since that was the one connected to the speedometer cable and always took twice as long to repair as the other three.

Another few miles down the road, they stopped at a small Texaco gas station for some cold liquid refreshment.

David purchased 60 cents' worth of orange drinks, handing the clerk his last remaining five dollar bill.

Placing the six sodas in a brown paper bag, the clerk tossed the change in the sack, since David had his hands full.

Roger and David walked another three miles up and down the hilly road, finally coming to a decent-looking place to eat.

When David went to pay for his meal, he discovered he was four dollars short. This was reason for alarm. Those missing four dollars were truly the last of his money. After frantically digging through all of his pockets, emptying the contents on the truck stop counter, he realized he must have only been given change for a dollar three miles back up the road at the Texaco gas station. There was nothing to do but walk back to the station and try to reclaim his four dollars.

Leaving Roger to finish putting up camp behind the truck stop, David ran most of the way back to the Texaco.

The same clerk was still behind the counter when he arrived, so David thought he would be able to calmly explain the honest error and be on his way, with his missing four dollars safely clutched in his tight fist. As usual, he once again overestimated the honesty of yet another person. The clerk all but called David a flat-out liar, almost chuckling with spite.

Unable to prove the error, David could only hope the man's sense of decency would somehow kick in and allow him to admit his mistake. So much for wishful thinking.

Having just survived two recent encounters with Texas justice, David wasn't willing to get into a shouting match with yet another local citizen, where it would be his word against the other person's.

The three miles back to Roger and their camp gave David plenty of time to inspect the path in front of him on the outside chance that maybe he had just dropped the money out of his pocket while pushing the cart down the highway.

More wishful thinking, and eye strain. While he dutifully noted every abandoned candy wrapper, tossed napkin, and even a copy of the previous day's newspaper, his money was not to be found.

He returned to find Roger valiantly trying to muster up some birthday joy in the Texas countryside.

Chapter 62: Possible Change of Route

David Keeping Up his Trumpet Chops in Roadside Park

The endless Texas hills were taking their toll on The Brothers, causing them to reconsider their original route, so carefully plotted out in their mother's apartment, back in Los Angeles, over a year earlier.

The original plan was to coast across Texas; glide through Mississippi, Alabama, and Georgia until they hit the East Coast; and then follow Route 1 all the way to New York City and Jack Paar's welcoming arms.

They had also originally planned to push their way across the country in five, six, or at the most seven months.

Their plans were obviously built on shifting sands, seeing as how they weren't even halfway to The Big Apple, after over a year of pushing and pushing some more.

Studying alternative routes on their trusty Automobile Club maps, they decided it made more sense taking a northern route through Arkansas and Tennessee.

That path had the benefit of bringing The Brothers to the doorsteps of nine more television stations than the southern route offered.

It would also take The Big Walk through more small towns where it seemed to be easier to find paying jobs. For some reason, Mary seemed to have a harder time booking The Balph Brothers in the larger cities.

Even if the money offered in small town clubs was less than it should have been, at least they were able to actually get some offers.

While it was a nice idea to hold out for gigs paying thousands of dollars in big metropolitan areas, if they never developed, they were nothing more than pipe dreams.

The Brothers needed to play more often, keeping their lips in shape and keeping at least a few dollars in their wallets.

Whenever they were on the road too long between gigs, their musical performances suffered when they finally were able to play for live audiences.

David was still optimistic enough to worry if somebody like Jack Paar or Johnny Carson did suddenly sweep down from the heavens and offer them a spot on national television, their lips would be so out of shape that they wouldn't be able to perform.

Meanwhile, they had to keep pushing the cart through those endless Texas hills and hope that Mary found them some work very, very, very soon.

Chapter 63: Everything but Money

The Auburn 49 Cents Toy Flute Featuring
The Balph Brothers on the Packaging

Sunday, August 30th, found The Brothers six miles outside of Fort Worth, waiting at a roadside park.

They had an entire day to kill on Monday since Mary had arranged for newspaper and television coverage of The Brothers posing by the City Limits sign.

It was all about timing and appearances.

If the local media wanted happy images of Roger and David joyfully pushing the cart past a certain road sign at a specific time, they were only too pleased to cooperate.

Even if it meant hiding out in a roadside park for a day, cooling their heels.

Seeing as how it had been a few weeks since The Brothers had been able to take a decent bath, they decided to borrow Mary's car, which in actuality belonged to Roger, and drive three and a half miles to scenic Weatherford Lake.

They weren't being tourists.

They were seizing the opportunity to grab a bar of soap, jump in the water, and scrub weeks of grime and grit off of their road-weary bodies.

Roger was thankful that the television cameras weren't around to capture that moment.

When they returned to camp, cleaned and closer to being human, Mary took the car into Fort Worth to follow up on a lead she was working on for a possible job.

She returned later that evening with good news, and more good news.

The local Holiday Inn had agreed to provide rooms and free meals for a week if The Brothers would perform one night in their lounge.

She had also made a deal with the local Oldsmobile dealer for free use of a flashy new car during their stay in town.

Because they had a total of $11 between the three of them, this was wonderful news.

It would have been better if they were actually getting paid for their performances, but at least they would be able to eat, have a room with hot showers, and be able to drive around in a brand new Olds.

They basically had everything but money.

The following morning, television crews from KTT-TV and WBAP-TV came out, shot film of The Brothers pushing the cart past the city limits sign, and conducted their roadside interviews.

Roger and David shared some cold beers with the big city news guys and laughed when the city slickers became slightly tipsy in the desert heat. David could tell they had been spending too much time in their comfy air-conditioned automobiles, cruising down the highways.

The Brothers were featured on that day's 6:00 p.m. and 10:00 p.m. broadcasts, then once again at noon the following day.

Hundreds of thousands of viewers saw film of them pushing the cart, heard The Balph Brothers talk, and learned about the details of The Big Walk.

Roger and David couldn't help but believe they were building a name for themselves.

September 1st began with a 15-minute interview on The Bobbi Wygant Show on WBAP-TV.

The show was in living color, and Roger thought it was the best interview on the trip so far. Bobbi seemed genuinely interested in The Big Walk, and there weren't any technical problems like the ones that had made Roger and David look silly in previous appearances.

The local Oldsmobile promotions man was on hand and was so thrilled with the interview that there was talk of sending a tape of the show to General Motors headquarters in Michigan to try to arrange a national sponsorship for The Big Walk.

As usual, when good things started happening, they tended to just take off like a rocket.

On Thursday, September 3rd, The Brothers performed on a children's show called The Icky Twerp Show on KTT-TV. Roger and David passed out boxes and boxes of plastic toy flutes, provided by their loyal sponsors, The Auburn Rubber Company, and the kids seemed to really enjoy their presents.

On Friday, September 4th, they appeared on WBAP radio, one of the nation's most powerful stations with 50,000 watts of clear channel power. Nick Ramsey, the talk show host, told them he had listeners all the way to Canada.

That afternoon they had an interview with Jack Gordon of The Fort Worth Press, one of The Lone Star State's leading newspapers. Gordon covered the entertainment beat, and was blown away when Roger and David played a few songs for him in one of the side rooms at The Holiday Inn.

He had been in the newspaper game for a long time, with friends in every level of show business. He casually mentioned he had Jack Paar's personal address, having interviewed him for the newspaper. After hearing The Brothers perform, he offered to send a copy of his story about The Big Walk to his good friend Jack.

David smiled from ear to ear, thinking how only days before he had been sharing a jail cell with his brother in scenic Eastland.

Just as Mr. Gordon was finishing up his interview for the paper, Bobbi Wygant called, saying she had some extra time on her show, and if The Brothers could make it to the television studio by showtime, she would give them another spot on-air.

Jumping in their spanking brand-new courtesy Oldsmobile, they arrived at the studio, and gave a live concert on air featuring their toy flutes.

Mary's hard work was paying off.

Roger and David were the latest media darlings of Forth Worth, Texas, and they were enjoying every single minute of it.

As long as their luck held out, they could live like millionaires for at least a few weeks.

Chapter 64: Gas Cards, Chicken Bones, Fan Clubs, and Union Problems

Holiday Inn's Venetian Club

The Holiday Inn in Forth Worth extended their agreement with The Brothers for an additional week, continuing to give them free food and free rooms.

The arrangement was literally keeping The Brothers alive.

While the local media kept showcasing Roger and David's efforts, they hadn't been able to turn their widespread publicity into any paying contracts.

Roger and David were doing their best to look the part of successful, prosperous performers, but the fact was they couldn't even afford to buy dog food for "Steps."

David had spent an hour in the motel's kitchen, pulling leftover meat off of chicken bones remaining on diners' plates, just so he would have some food for his faithful canine companion.

The best financial news happened when they unexpectedly received two long-requested gasoline credit cards. They had filled out application forms way back in New Mexico, using their mother's apartment in Los Angeles as their address, and it had taken a while for the mail to catch up with them in Texas.

At least the plastic wonders allowed them to keep gas in Mary's car. They would worry about paying the bills later.

They were even having problems with The Musicians Union.

A Union representative had paid a visit to their performance at The Holiday Inn, thinking they were getting paid for their performance. While they were receiving room and board for their musical efforts, such compensation was technically against union rules. It was hard for the union to collect a percentage of a night's sleep.

The Union enforcer also had an issue with the fact that Roger and David used a tape recorder in their shows, instead of having a live band of union dues-paying band members.

If it hadn't been for the fact there was another house band performing dance music most of the week, the Union representative might have tried to shut down their performances.

Unions enforced their rules pretty seriously, especially when it came to taking jobs away from their own people.

It didn't matter how many glowing newspaper articles or colorful television reports touted The Walking Musical Balph Brothers. If the Union decided to make life tough for Roger and David, they could certainly accomplish their goal.

If the Union decided to blackball The Brothers, Mary's job would be made even more impossible.

To keep The Holiday Inn from getting in trouble with the Union, Roger was instructed to fill out a contract saying they had been paid $585 for their performance in the lounge.

Roger could only wish it had been true. The Brothers couldn't even afford a tube of toothpaste. Meanwhile, they had to continue to keep up the illusion of success and hope that the motel's supply of slightly used chicken meat didn't run out.

While they didn't have any money in their pockets, they did have a new fan club devoted to their cause.

A tenth grader named Kathy Hall had read about The Walking Musical Balph Brothers in the newspaper, and she wanted to start a fan club for them. She had called The Holiday Inn, leaving a message about her plans.

David called her back and invited her to bring her family to their Sunday night concert, promising to give her one of their records featuring The Auburn Rubber Company toy flutes.

A short while later, another classmate of Kathy's called, asking if she could also bring her family to the show.

This was the first time since they had left Los Angeles that any mention had been made of a fan club. David thought it was a wonderful idea.

Meanwhile, Mary's efforts to secure a paying gig with a nearby Air Force base came up empty, after a week of waiting and hoping.

David was down to having eight cents in his pocket.

They went to the Continental Bus Station to pick up another batch of trusty Auburn Rubber Company toy flutes and were pleasantly surprised to discover that their loyal benefactor, Dick Hodson, had enclosed an extra $150 to keep their heads above water.

Roger and David felt like they had just won the lottery.

Their Guardian Angels were continuing to come through for them at their crucial moments of need, and The Brothers were thankful beyond words.

If anybody had seen the extremes of human nature, from great kindness to extreme negativity, it was Roger, David, and Mary.

The Brothers played for the last time Sunday night at The Holiday Inn lounge.

Mary was expecting the talent booker from The 21 Club, a large nightclub in Dallas, to show up and bring her a contract for paying gigs the next week.

Big surprise. He didn't make it.

David had scanned the audience for any signs of the new president of the one and only Balph Brothers International Fan Club and was disappointed that even she hadn't made it to the show. While he knew that fame was fleeting, this was ridiculous.

Chapter 65: Avoiding The Beatles and A Midnight Visit to an Assassin's Grave

Waiting for The Beatles to Leave Town

On September 18th, 1964, The Brothers discovered that The British Invasion had arrived in Dallas, the next town on their Big Walk.

The Beatles had come in the previous evening, and the local television stations were already covering every bit of Mop Top Mania.

Three teenage girls had been rushed to the hospital after breaking through a glass door at the hotel where The Fab Four were staying, determined to touch or grab or kiss either John, Paul, George, or Ringo.

That was just the tip of the iceberg.

All of the news broadcasts featured hysterical girls of all shapes and sizes, screaming and sobbing at the idea of actually meeting their teen idols.

David watched the broadcasts in wonder, halfway thinking it was all some crafty act devised by some promotion-seeking manager behind the scenes.

Could there really be that much mass excitement for a band? These guys certainly weren't Elvis. It had to have been manufactured by the record label to create a buzz.

While The Balph Brothers had certainly seen their share of enthusiastic fans since leaving Los Angeles, they had never imagined that such rabid hero worship was possible.

Meanwhile Roger and David continued to deal with the reality of their far more humble situation.

They had already wasted most of a perfectly good afternoon trying to put a deal together with a man with whom they had already had a previous run-in.

The man was the manager of The Western Hills Hotel, only a few miles down the road from The Holiday Inn in Fort Worth, where they had successfully performed for room and board for two weeks.

This same manager had already led Mary on for almost a week, prior to The Brothers' arrival in town.

First, he acted like he wanted to hire Roger and David, and then he would change his mind, always coming up with some silly excuse.

He went so far as to claim that Mary had sassed him during the final of a long chain of useless phone calls.

Roger knew that wasn't possible. If anything, he believed Mary was far too polite to these rude characters they kept being forced to work with along the road.

David felt the man just liked to talk with pretty women and act like a big shot.

When they were finally pushing the cart out of Forth Worth, they passed in front of The Western Hills Hotel and were surprised when the rude club manager walked out in the street to make The Brothers an offer.

This was taking place right on the side of the busy city street.

He asked them if they would be interested in performing in his lounge for four consecutive days, and despite their better instincts, The Brothers quoted him a price.

He immediately agreed to their fees and told them he would draw up the contract right then and there.

The single demand he made was that he would only deal with Roger and David, not Mary.

While The Brothers' ears sizzled with thinly veiled rage, they realized they weren't in a position to turn down any paying jobs, even from a pompous jerk.

While talking with the shady club manager, another restaurant owner came by and invited the entire gang, including his competitor, to get out of the hot sun and take a meal break at his place.

As Roger and David enjoyed a complimentary departure meal, the manager of The Western Hills Key Club got on the phone, calling his contacts at the local paper, arranging for ads and media coverage.

He was also going to sign The Brothers to perform at The Ridglea Country Club, of which he said he also owned a percentage.

Just as Roger and David were ready to put their signatures on the dotted line, a person who worked on advertising for The Western Hills Key Club joined them at the dining table, whispering something in the manager's ear.

The deal was off.

Just like that, it was over.

The Brothers were completely dumbfounded.

Roger asked the man what could possibly have happened in such a short time to kill not one, but two, paying engagements at once.

The manager mumbled that he didn't think he could get enough publicity for the performances in such a short time.

Always being creative thinkers, The Brothers said they could delay their performances long enough for the local media machines to kick in gear and make some noise in town.

They had effectively called the man's bluff.

He was all talk and no substance.

Maybe this was just the way he got his kicks, dangling bogus contracts in front of starving musicians and then laughing himself silly when they took the bait.

Roger wanted to pick up a chair and smash the smiling buffoon over his pointy head.

David just wanted to get out of Fort Worth as soon as possible, and never look back.

Even as they were leaving, the slimy manager told them to look him up on their way back from New York, as if they were ever going to have to push a cart anywhere once again after they proved their worth in The Big Apple.

They were on the outskirts of Dallas, only to discover that every single second of news time devoted to visiting musicians was going to promote four funny-looking, funny-talking, long-haired English fellows who sang simplistic songs about holding hands and girls who were seventeen, just standing there.

The fact that The Beatles' concerts had long been sold out, and the promoters had already made their buckets of cold-hard cash, only served to irritate matters even more.

The Walking Musical Balph Brothers desperately needed the media coverage.

The Fab Four didn't.

While passing a place that advertised alterations on the front window, The Brothers stopped to see if they could get some holes in their khaki pants mended.

The generous staff immediately stopped what they were doing and patched up four pairs of The Balphs' hole-ridden uniforms.

When they discovered the details of The Big Walk, the seamstresses refused to even accept any payment for their kind deeds.

While it didn't rank with the wild enthusiasm The Beatles were receiving, a few miles up the road, The Brothers were deeply appreciative for these random acts of kindness.

They even picked up an unexpected $1.75 in change from customers who wanted to do their part.

As they were leaving the alterations shop, a high school freshman named Nancy Masters approached Roger and David, asking if she could interview them for her speech class at school.

While she wasn't screaming her head off like those hysterical Beatles' fans, it did make David feel a little bit better to know that somebody in her teens was interested in their story.

Maybe she could be the one to actually start The International Balph Brothers Fan Club, instead of just talking about it, like that other girl in Fort Worth had.

David gave her one of their biography sheets, a toy flute, and a copy of their 45-rpm record. He also gave her 30 of The Balphs' business cards, asking her to pass them out to her classmates and perhaps get them to send some letters to Jack Paar.

A few miles down the road, they met yet another fellow traveler, walking across the nation's highways.

This guy was walking from the state of Washington, heading to Florida, with his living, breathing jack-ass carrying his worldly possessions behind him.

His body odor was so bad, The Brothers could only get within six feet of him as they all paused by the side of the road.

The pungent smell was enough to bring tears to David's eyes. Even "Steps" had problems dealing with the aroma, whining and rubbing her nostrils against Roger's leg, in effort to kill the sweaty assault on her sensitive snoot.

David would never complain again about how raunchy he felt going without a shower for a few days.

On even his worst day of days, he knew he looked like Clark Gable compared to this poor soul.

Trying to make up for lost time with all of the distractions, The Brothers kept pushing through the evening darkness. At least it was somewhat cooler than trying to deal with the fierce daytime heat.

They found themselves passing right by the gates of Rose Hill Cemetery, where John F. Kennedy's assassin, Lee Harvey Oswald, was buried.

Despite the fact that it was now one in the morning, The Brothers knew they wouldn't be passing this close again.

They parked the cart across from the entrance, leaving "Steps" in charge of protecting their means of survival.

They took their lantern, and pistols, and went looking for the grave of one of the most hated men in the history of civilization.

It didn't take long to find a sole police car parked in the middle of the cemetery.

Even after almost a year since the senseless killing of the nation's president, there was a fear that some misguided people or ghoulish souvenir seekers would try to steal Oswald's body.

The fact they had buried the cold-blooded killer in 13 tons of cement wasn't even enough to calm the fears of government officials, who were afraid that various radical groups might try to take the decomposing earthly remains and turn his bones into a martyr's shrine.

All Roger and David wanted to do was to be able to say they had seen his headstone.

There really wasn't any more thought given to the entire ordeal beyond that simple gesture.

It certainly wasn't some big master plan they had developed months ago while pushing the cart.

They didn't have a political agenda.

Trying to make as much advance noise as possible while walking up behind the parked, occupied patrol car, The Brothers had the good sense to remove their gun holsters and place them over their shoulders.

This time, they wanted to be noticed.

They loudly announced their friendly intentions as the government official bolted out of their police car, shaken by the pre-dawn arrival of two unknown visitors.

After Roger and David's previous dealings with various men in uniform, the very last thing they needed was another misunderstanding, or worse, a graveyard confrontation.

Fortunately, these late-night guardians were much friendlier than some of their fellow Texan law officers.

They were able to see that Roger and David were kindred spirits and didn't offer any threats.

While having a friendly chat with one of the armed officers, the other one got back in the car and resumed reading his Donald Duck comic book.

Yes. A Donald Duck comic book.

Here these fine government officials were pulling the third shift, dutifully guarding the remains of Lee Harvey Oswald, a name that would forever be vilified in the nation's history, and one of the policemen passed his time on the clock by reading a Walt Disney cartoon book.

While The Beatles were, no doubt, partying with screaming, attractive hordes of female fans back at their luxury hotel suites, Roger and David were hanging out in an empty graveyard, looking at an assassin's tombstone, while uniformed law officers read the comics.

David could only assume that it made just as much sense as anything else that had happened on The Big Walk.

He just wondered if anybody would ever believe him.

Mary, David and Roger at Oswald's Grave

Chapter 66: Skunk Juice, Priceless Quarter, and A Thousand Dollars of Nothing

While The Beatles were collecting tens of thousands of dollars for their hour or so onstage, The Balph Brothers had found yet another drive-in theater to hide the cart in so they could grab some rest for the night.

Mary rejoined them after her day's efforts to find work in Dallas. It was quite a visual sight.

There were the three Army surplus sleeping cots, the ever-present cart, "Steps," and a brand-new 1964 Starfire Oldsmobile, still on loan from the dealership.

They were careful to park the car out of sight, not wanting anybody to know they were in such desperate straits that Mary, their promotional manager, was reduced to sleeping under the stars with The Brothers.

To add insult to injury, in the middle of the night, "Steps" took out after a visiting skunk and lost the battle. She was hit front on by the full force of the wild animal's most effective defenses.

The entire camp area smelled like burnt rubber, sulfur, and wet stink. It was enough to make the humans gag and the dog yelp in horror.

David grabbed his pistol, in case the furry creature decided to attack their sleeping area, but by that time, the skunk had moved on to other vistas. Maybe he had already seen the movie playing at the drive-in.

David tried to ease "Steps'" obvious pain by pouring the entire contents of their canvas water bag over the odorous canine. Eventually their noses simply surrendered to the attacks, and the entire crew tried to salvage a few hours of much needed sleep.

In the morning, they decided to go back to nearby Rose Hill Cemetery to show Mary the site of Lee Harvey Oswald's grave and to take some photos by the tombstone. The photos would become somewhat somber souvenirs of The Big Walk, long after the various nightclubs and lounges had been forgotten.

The cemetery felt like a completely different place in the light of day.

Outside of Arlington, Texas, they stopped at The Forest Park Motel, where Mary had secured a complimentary room for one night while the owner considered hiring them for a four-week stay at The Round Table, their lounge.

When The Brothers pulled the cart into the motel's parking lot, they noticed an old broken-down car parked by the office.

The owner of the ratty automobile looked just as bad as his banged up vehicle. His clothes were tattered, and David had serious doubts that he had the money or the means to make it to nearby Fort Worth, his stated destination.

While David took the instruments and performance gear off of the cart and into the motel, Roger continued to politely answer the man's questions about The Big Walk. He was totally fascinated The Brothers were trying to push a cart to New York City, and seemed genuinely thrilled to meet them.

When Roger finally came inside the motel to join David, he casually mentioned that, the man in the tattered clothes with the barely running jalopy, had insisted on thrusting a quarter in Roger's hand before leaving the parking lot.

The stranger's generosity touched The Brothers' hearts, knowing his sincere gift of 25¢ was probably the equal of another man's $100.

This was the kind of simple gesture that always restored Roger and David's faith in humanity.

Unlike the man they met later that week, who heard The Brothers perform at The Round Table and made a big deal about how much he wanted to help them make it to New York City.

He gave Mary a check for $1,000, which The Brothers naturally took down to the closest bank at the earliest possible moment.

Big surprise. The check wasn't any good. It was totally worthless. There wasn't enough in the account to even cover a ten-dollar check, much less anything as grand as a grand.

David could just imagine the big-talking big shot having a good laugh over his funny joke at the expense of two traveling musicians.

At least the man in the shabby clothes with the broken-down car had given them a real quarter.

303

Chapter 67: Crazy Times, Lawsuits, and A Breach of Contract

Arrival in Arlington

The signed contract with the owners of The Forest Park Motel seemed to offer The Balph Brothers a certain degree of security.

Like so many other things on The Big Walk, the only thing certain was the fact that everything was uncertain.

It clearly stated that the contract was good for four weeks, paying $200 per week, while also providing room and board, bringing the total value to around $1,500. Signed, sealed, and delivered.

As long as Roger and David showed up for the performances, they would get paid. Or so it seemed. After a promising start, relations with The Round Table lounge couldn't have been any worse.

The first week of shows had been successful by most standards, just not wall-to-wall, standing-room only crowds. The club manager seemed to think that, with all of the publicity The Brothers received, the crowds should have been five times larger.

Maybe all of the news about those screaming Beatles' fans had raised everyone's expectations, but the fact is the crowds for The Balph Brothers were decent and growing.

Just not fast enough. By the second week, there was big time rumbling from the club manager.

There had been issues with a bossy bartender, who seemed to enjoy giving Roger and David marching orders, which The Brothers certainly didn't appreciate.

David had a feeling the bartender had perhaps been instructed to make life a little harder for The Brothers, in an attempt to stir up trouble or provoke a reaction.

It certainly wouldn't have been the first time there had been a personality clash between club staff and The Walking Musical Balph Brothers.

By the end of the second week, the lounge management just wanted to end the contract and send Roger and David on down the road.

By this point, The Brothers had already endured too much abuse over the previous 15 months from shady club owners, con men, rude staff, drunk patrons, and cat-fighting women; and were in no mood to tuck their tails and run away in the darkness.

They had a legally binding contract and stood willing and able to perform their part of the deal. They refused to leave.

Roger contacted a local attorney, paying him a $100 retainer.

Meanwhile, other aspects of their lives were taking a decidedly downward spiral, as well.

Their local deal with Oldsmobile came to an end, and efforts to arrange for use of a new car through the national marketing offices in Michigan also fell apart.

The official excuse was they weren't able to arrange for loaner cars that crossed from state to state. If they were only going to stay in Texas, they might have been able to work something out, but seeing as how the plan was to go all the way to New York, that option was impossible.

Roger thought it all sounded like a bunch of mumbo jumbo, not a valid excuse.

The fact the national promotions person from Michigan never showed up to see any of their performances, after assuring The Brothers that he would, was more revealing than any technical excuses.

They also discovered a big feature story in one of the largest newspapers in Dallas was not going to happen.

As it turned out, the reporter was more interested in Mary and dating her on a very intimate level than he was in covering The Walking Musical Balph Brothers. When it became apparent that Mary was not included on the menu, the big time, big city reporter lost all interest in the cart, the dog, the instruments, and everything related to Roger and David. It was the end of that story before it was even written.

Then, there was the problem with David's back, which was thrown out of whack. In fact, it felt cracked and attacked, more pain than he could hack or comfort with an ice pack, causing him to black out.

He had tried to lift "Steps" into the cart, when he felt his back pop out of joint. His legs felt numb just walking back to the motel room, and while climbing the stairs, he passed out and fell backwards, hitting his head on the railing.

Fortunately, Roger had heard the commotion and was able to get him to the room.

David was just this side of being crippled and was in immense pain, aching to the very core of his body.

By the time things fell completely to pieces with The Round Table lounge, The Brothers had been kicked just one too many times.

The lounge manager had called the Musicians' Union, unsuccessfully trying to get the contract terminated. The Union representative then called The Brothers and told them to continue honoring their end of the contract.

That meant showing up at the appointed times, ready to perform, even if the club refused to let them go onstage.

The lounge also took The Brothers' name down from the marquee, replacing it with a bogus name for a made-up band, The Secret Boiler Boys.

The club offered Roger and David $300 to just walk away.

Realizing their lawyer, and even the musicians' union representative told them they had a legally binding contract worth $1,500, they politely but firmly refused the offer.

The lounge then told them to evacuate their motel room. The Walking Musical Balph Brothers were being kicked out of their living quarters.

By now, I'm sure you've realized that Roger and David refused to budge.

They had a contract. They were doing their job. The audiences that had showed up for the performances had loved them, demanding the usual encores at every show.

By The Brothers' logic, they had done absolutely nothing wrong, and they refused to be kicked to the curb like an unwanted dog.

The motel responded by turning off the electricity to the room, cutting off the phone, and refusing to provide room service.

The Brothers responded by bringing in their trusty Coleman stove from the cart, cooking meals in their room.

Meanwhile, Roger worked on getting his faithful 1955 Chevy wagon back in shape for regular road duty. The odometer had 101,990 miles on it, up from 30,000 when they picked it up in Los Angeles.

It was certainly a big change from riding around in the brand new Oldsmobile that had been at their disposal for the previous month.

Just as worrisome was the fact that Mary was complaining of body pains that seemed to indicate she might be suffering from gallstones.

Some days the pain was enough to keep her bedridden, which only compounded issues financially since Mary was the very fragile engine keeping The Big Walk train on track. Without her marketing and promotional efforts, everything would truly run out of steam.

The lounge upped their go-away offer to $600, but it was too little, too late. Roger had already passed his point of no return, and he went ahead and filed lawsuit papers in court.

By this point, the only thing left for the motel to do was to bring guns to their room and shoot Roger and David.

Once again, in what can only be seen as another act of divine intervention, right in the middle of one of The Brothers' darkest hours, when they were literally being tossed out into the mean streets, another unexpected friend from the past came to their rescue.

During one of their first shows at The Round Table, they had been surprised to see a fellow musician named Bill Swift walk into the club.

Bill was a friend of theirs from Abilene, Texas, where he played organ for the house band at The Hiway House lounge.

He saw Roger and David perform at The Round Table when things were still civilized and cordial, all of two weeks earlier, and had even volunteered to run their spotlight during the show.

That act of kindness had only generated a negative response from the club manager, who stated that maybe The Brothers should take some of their earnings and hire a professional lightman for the subsequent shows.

In hindsight, that snotty comment was certainly a harbinger of things to come. The club management was just looking for excuses, any excuse, to charge The Brothers with breach of contract.

Bill had been aware of the steadily declining relationship between the club management and The Brothers, so when push truly came to shove, in the most literal sense, he stepped in and offered to share his small apartment in Fort Worth.

The Brothers were facing being homeless for an extended period of time until they either won their lawsuit or found more work.

Once again they found themselves broke, drained, waiting, and spending their extremely limited resources on more legal battles and lawyers.

It was hard enough taking care of the musical part of their careers without trying to deal with the relentless emotional, physical, mental, and now legal hassles that kept assaulting them each and every day.

Why did every single step of the way have to be such a major challenge? What was the point of the never-ending torture?

Roger, David, and Mary were risking their health and well-being each day of The Big Walk.

Just when it seemed like things would get a little easier, some other big time disaster would pop up out of nowhere, tilting the cart and everything else in the process.

Why hadn't Jack Paar just called them that very first day of The Big Walk, back at their mother's apartment in Los Angeles, and told them to catch a plane to The Big Apple?

Paar's audience would have been richly entertained.

It would only have taken Paar a few minutes of kind consideration and saved Roger and David years of struggles.

The Brothers' career would have been well on-track.

They wouldn't have had to push a homemade bucket of bolts through thousands of miles of deserts, hills, storms, and blizzards just to get some attention.

David would have been just as content to fly over Texas, while sipping a martini, and sharing humorous stories about the biz with his traveling companion, Frank Sinatra, Jr.

And everybody's sanity would have remained intact.

Instead, Roger, Mary, and David's bodies were being maimed. They were struggling to keep their broken-down car running, their 1,000-pound cart moving, and thankful to even have a roof over their heads.

Chapter 68: Golden Boys at The Golden Ball

Forth Worth Newspaper Coverage

While The Brothers were being evicted from their motel room, continuing their lawsuit battle with The Round Table, and being portrayed as the worst possible characters in the music business by certain slimy lounge managers, they were doing their best to give back to a community that hadn't been all that hospitable to them in the first place.

As a favor to newspaper reporter Jack Gordon, who had been one of their most steady supporters, they took a break from all of the hostilities to donate their musical talents to The Fort Worth Golden Ball, an annual dinner for all couples who had celebrated their 50th wedding anniversaries or more.

While it would have been easy to mope and drown in self-pity, cursing their streak of bad luck, that simply wasn't The Walking Musical Balph Brothers' style.

Their parents had always taught them to rise above their difficulties and be proud ambassadors of the Balph name.

When Mr. Gordon asked them to join the festivities, they didn't hesitate.

Since the gala event featured a full live house band, Roger and David didn't even have to bring their tape recorder support system.

It was such a treat to work with living, breathing musicians who could change tempos, follow leads, and play for as long as the audience demanded.

It was such a big difference from their own stage shows.

While Roger and David were extremely grateful for the professional support of their donated Ampex recording equipment, it was a constant constraint trying to perform in front of live audiences and meet their demands, while working with the mechanics of a machine, albeit a very good machine.

Their performances of "Tin Roof Blues," "Wabash Blues," and "When the Saints Go Marching In," were true showstoppers at the grand old Texas Hotel ballroom.

With David and Roger actually leaping off the stage and marching among the 250 or so honored guests, the entire room was clapping and buzzing with excitement.

This was entertainment, pure and simple.

No politics. No hidden agendas.

This crowd of happily married Texan couples couldn't get enough of The Balphs and their energetic music.

Let The Beatles have their screaming fans.

Roger and David would take their appreciative audiences any day of the week.

When Mr. Gordon took the microphone and told the crowd the details of The Big Walk, you would have thought that major movie stars along the lines of Bob Hope or even Clark Gable were in the ballroom.

The room was electric with positive enthusiasm.

The line of people wanting autographs stretched the entire length of the stage, with one woman even thrusting a five-dollar bill into Roger's hand.

While Roger and David were sharing some of the events from their 15 months on the road with the audience, Roger mentioned that it felt like they had been pushing their cart for at least 50 years.

That comment brought the house down with laughter, seeing as how every couple in the room had truly survived at least 50 years of marital bliss. It wasn't just a figure of speech for this crowd.

The guests of honor were Mr. And Mrs. Goddard, who had celebrated their 69th wedding anniversary.

He was an energetic 91, and she was the still blushing bride at 84.

Mr. Goddard's parting words to The Brothers were that he was going to come back to The Golden Ball when he could play like The Balphs.

Seeing how much their music meant to the hundreds of chosen guests was exactly what Roger and David needed to help them ignore their own woes and troubles.

With so many distractions and annoyances, it was easy to forget the entire point of everything they did on The Big Walk was to showcase their instrumental talents and the music they loved.

Mr. Gordon could not have been more appreciative of Roger and David's support.

He assured The Brothers he would do anything possible within his power to help them find more work in the area.

Chapter 69: A Change of Fortunes

A Welcomed Gig at the Colonial Country Club

As so often happened on The Big Walk, one single phone call once again changed everything in an instant.

A simple "yes" from The Colonial Country Club in Fort Worth made life bearable.

Their musician friend and temporary roommate, Bill Swift, had put in a good word for The Brothers, resulting in a $500 contract for three Saturday night engagements, starting Oct. 24th.

What was even better about this particular series of performances was the fact it gave Roger and David plenty of time between gigs to work on finding fill-in jobs.

This, being one of the nation's premier golf courses and country clubs, was the perfect venue for their music. Their members were much more likely to appreciate quality jazz music than the typical honky-tonk lounge The Brothers often found themselves dealing with.

While their particular brand of music was energetic and easily enjoyed by audiences of all ages and backgrounds, there was no doubt it worked especially well for society crowds with a taste for refined arrangements.

They shared a congratulations and thank-you dinner with Bill and his steady girlfriend, an attractive woman who just so happened to be Miss Texas, making a point of letting him know how vital his personal recommendation had been to securing the contract.

While toasting their recent change of fortune, David was tickled to watch the last night of Steve Allen's television talk show.

He found it particularly ironic that Mr. Allen was telling his audience how sorry he was his show was going off the air because he wouldn't be able to provide exposure for young talent looking for their big break.

David laughed out loud when he heard those insincere words come out of his television set. He felt like he was listening to a politician, who had just been caught with his hands in the till, crying about how he wouldn't be able to help the little people anymore.

The Walking Musical Balph Brothers had certainly witnessed firsthand how hollow Mr. Allen's words had been back in Los Angeles.

Mr. Allen had seen them perform at two separate shows, and each time he had made a big point of telling them how great he thought they were and how he wanted to have them appear on his show.

Roger and David had innocently taken the man at his word.

Little good it did.

It was a good thing they hadn't been holding their breath all this time, waiting for Steve Allen to come through on his promises.

The fact Mr. Allen was now going off the air did not cause Roger or David to lose any sleep.

Their friend, reporter Jack Gordon was good to his word, continuing to mention The Brothers in print, putting in recommendations to friends and associates.

Even his write-up about the newspaper's recent Golden Ball read more like a review of Roger and David than coverage of an event.

It was nice having positive press.

The Brothers had been a little disappointed that their efforts to get coverage about their lawsuit with The Round Table lounge hadn't produced any results, but they could certainly understand the reluctance to cover bad news.

It wasn't any fun living through the bad news either.

That's why the moments of good fortunes were so deeply appreciated.

The Big Walk was certainly filled with roller coaster moments of extremes.

With the security of The Colonial Country Club contract in hand, The Brothers could focus on getting their lips back in shape for the upcoming performances.

The wasted time spent dealing with the mind games of their lawsuit hassles had affected their musical chops.

Roger arranged to use some spare studio space at WBAP-TV for rehearsals. The Brothers were able to get their lips back in shape, and not have to worry about disturbing Bill Swift's sleeping neighbors.

It was great while it lasted. The studio was a perfect practice hall.

They were able to come and go as they pleased, until one night when they lost track of time and suddenly found themselves locked up in the television station at 1:45 a.m.

Evidently everybody just assumed somebody else would stay around until The Brothers were ready to leave.

After walking up and down the empty halls of one of the largest television studios in Texas for almost an hour, trying to find an unlocked door, they had finally been forced to open a window in the ladies' restroom, climb out, and go back to Bill Swift's apartment.

It is a wonder they hadn't set off alarms all over Fort Worth, seeing as how the television station was filled with millions of dollars of broadcast equipment.

The next morning, their friendly contact at the television station called with news that his bosses were not amused by their late-night exit, and they needed to come and get their instruments out of the building as soon as possible.

Their contact at the television station evidently hadn't asked for specific permission from his superiors, and now his act of kindness had bitten him in the backside.

So another fine opportunity came to a somewhat premature end.

Mary came back with rather amazing news.

She had managed to finally get a contract with The Western Hills Hotel from the man who had led them on and on for weeks, going so far as pulling Roger and David aside on the road as they were leaving town to dangle a job offer in front of them.

Having long given up on the man and his flimsy offers that never came through, this one did.

When it was least expected, they suddenly had a contract to play two nights a week for three weeks, while also working at The Colonial Country Club.

In the feast or famine cycles, they had evidently entered a rare feasting stage.

November 1964 was finally turning out to be a decent month for The Brothers.

As usual, even in the best of times, they still had their share of sleazy proposals and half-baked deals come their way.

Mary had encountered yet another man dangling the supposed offer of a contract to perform at a large convention on the 26th of the month. It turned out he was much more interested in knowing Mary on an intimate level than he was in booking The Brothers.

Mary often wished she could just wear a sign stating she was not available for sex, instead of having to play silly games with would-be Casanovas.

The delicate balance between innocent flirting and outright indecent proposals was often razor thin.

She was constantly trying to be professional in a world of slimy sleazeballs with over-inflated egos and highly dubious character.

She kept these depressing details from The Brothers.

The Brothers only had very vague ideas of the kind of constant harassments Mary faced on a daily basis. Mary had no doubt that Roger would have tried to knock some sense into any number of her pursuers; so, she did her best to shield The Brothers from her sordid assaults.

It was better that Roger didn't know the details, for the safety of all parties concerned. Let the reptilian club owners hiss all they wanted.

Mary wanted to keep Roger and David focused on their music, and out of any more cold jail cells.

The crowds at The Colonial Country Club and The Western Hills Key Club were appreciative, civilized, and enthusiastic.

The Brothers were thrilled to learn their father, an accomplished musician in his own right, would be able to see them perform in decent surroundings when he came to visit them on the 19th of November.

David had been worried their dad would hit town when they weren't working and were completely broke.

It had literally made his stomach churn to think he would be such a disappointment to his father after so many months of the road.

He could only imagine how his dad would have felt being with them as they were barred from performing and evicted from their hotel room.

David was so thankful their recent change in fortunes had come at such a fortuitous moment, a fact that was duly noted in his nightly prayers.

Chapter 70: Like Sons, Like Father

Their Dad, Dale, Shares the Stage with David and Roger

November 22nd, 1964, found The Brothers observing the first anniversary of the death of President Kennedy on the outskirts of Dallas, the site of the assassination.

Their father, Dale, arrived in town with his new wife, Betty, and the rest of the day was spent catching up with family news.

It had been two long years since they had seen their father, and the fact that he had made the long trip from Mansfield, Ohio, to celebrate David's 25th birthday on the 23rd made things even more significant.

They enjoyed a wonderful celebratory meal at The Western Hills Hotel restaurant where The Brothers were performing, and were pleasantly surprised when management picked up the entire tab for the steak dinners, even the drinks.

For the first time in recent memory, two generations of Musical Balphs were able to perform onstage together Wednesday night, November 25th, at the lounge.

They worked up arrangements of "Tin Roof Blues," "South Rampart Street Parade," and "When the Saints Go Marching In," featuring the three Balph gentlemen onstage.

The senior Balph brought the house down. The audience kept clapping and begging for more. Proving talent and showmanship certainly ran in the family, the newly reunited Balph Trio closed the show with "When The Saints Go Marching In," as all three of the natural-born hams marched and mingled throughout the audience, instruments roaring.

This wasn't their father's first time onstage, by any means.

Dale Balph had been a professional sax player since the 1920s, working in show and society bands in vaudeville and on The Keith Circuit, a chain of theaters stretching from the east coast to Ohio.

He once took a job performing in the band on an ocean liner offering free passage to and from England in exchange for his musical talents. During the trip, some of the other musicians tried to stage a mutiny at sea by refusing to perform without getting paid. Dale Balph assumed the role of negotiator between the ship's captain and the protesting performers, eventually restoring musical harmony for the duration of the voyage.

That experience taught the senior Balph some working musicians could not be trusted. He did his best to instill honor and respect for binding contracts into the hearts and minds of his two musical off-spring, Roger and David. That is part of the reason The Brothers always did their best to meet and exceed every part of their contractual obligations, going above and beyond their written minimums.

Dale Balph used to tell stories about his days working in the dance halls of Mansfield, Ohio, during the Depression, when people paid ten cents a song. Those meager coins went to pay the musicians to keep their families fed. When times got tough, people kept coming out to hear the free music, but they stopped spending money for dances.

The money to pay the bands dried up and disappeared.

Roger and David weren't the first Balph musicians to be vastly underpaid for their musical skills.

On his last job at the dance hall, Dale Balph came home with 28 cents, the total payment he received for four hours of energetic, professional-quality, big-band performances.

Even in The Depression, 28 cents was pitiful compensation.

The need to support his growing family forced the senior Balph to take a factory job with The Westinghouse Manufacturing Company. Even then he still managed to keep his hand in the music world by becoming a vital member of The Westinghouse Orchestra, an acclaimed company performance band that had a stellar reputation and professional ethics standard.

Roger and David had grown up seeing their father perform at company functions, sharply dressed in tuxedos, playing the big band music he loved.

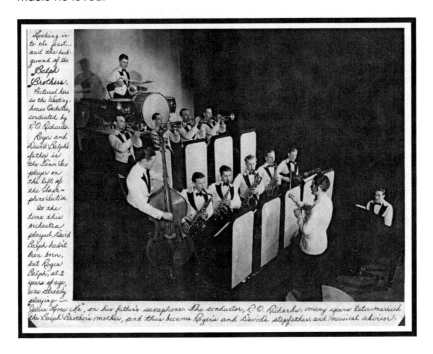

Their Dad Performs with Westinghouse Orchestra
(front row, seated at far left)

Dale passed his love for the music on to his children. He taught his sons how to play their instruments, starting with Roger on sax and clarinet, then bringing the younger David into the ranks on trumpet.

Their father would spend countless hours coaching The Brothers to stay in pitch, and just as importantly, to keep the rhythm correct and steady, even if the notes were wrong. That way, The Brothers could always end up together at the end of the song, even if the notes were off a few times.

David could remember his dad patiently pounding out the beats for him on the edge of the piano for hours, with the youngest Balph just this side of tears from trying so hard and just not quite getting it right.

Roger remembered his dad never encouraged them to get into the music business, always telling them what a tough way it was to make a living, and how there was only one Benny Goodman.

Even then, Roger was fast to remark that at least Benny Goodman got to the top somehow, and that meant there had to be room for The Balphs, too.

Seeing his father perform with them in The Western Hills Hotel nightclub brought back a long forgotten memory David had from when he was eight years old.

His mother had taken him to see a live musical performance at a theater, and David had been truly impressed by one musician who was performing black faced in a minstrel show, which was still accepted back in the 1940s on the fading vaudeville circuits.

Little David had been so overwhelmed by this one particular performer's riveting solos that he had asked his mother who the man was, certain he must be some visiting celebrity.

His mother replied, "That's your father."

Decades later, on this November night in that Texas nightclub, that same immense feeling of pride swept over David Balph like a rushing river of emotional joy.

Chapter 71: Buckeye Sidetrip, Christmas, and New Year's in Ohio

Jazzin' It Up with their Dad at Olentangy Inn

The Brothers and Mary celebrated Thanksgiving 1964, with their father, Dale, his new wife, Betty; their musician friend, Bill Swift, and his beauty pageant girlfriend, Miss Texas.

They performed to a somewhat smaller crowd at The Western Hills Hotel lounge than the previous show, but it was just as enthusiastic for the musical musings of The Three Musical Balphs.

After the show, with the afterglow of the night's performance only enhanced by sharing a fifth of bourbon, their father casually asked them if they would like to take a break from The Big Walk, and spend Christmas with him back home in Mansfield, Ohio.

The more they talked about the idea, the better it sounded.

Their father was pretty confident he had enough contacts to get The Brothers several booking engagements in the area, so the trip could be a working vacation.

Roger and David were adamant they could only leave the trail of The Big Walk if they were able to earn some much-needed cash, and keep their lips in shape by performing.

They didn't want their father to think the past year and a half's efforts were just some gimmick to get attention.

They were just as serious about accomplishing their goal of pushing the cart from Los Angeles to New York and Jack Paar's studio as they were on the very first day when they left their mother's apartment.

Their father said he understood the seriousness of their mission and only wanted to help their cause, not hinder it.

He asked them to give him a few days making calls to his nightclub contacts when he got back to Ohio, and they would take it from there.

Dale Balph was a man of his word.

On Tuesday, December 7th, a gentleman named George York called from Columbus, Ohio. He represented The Olentangy Inn, and wanted to hire The Walking Musical Balph Brothers for two weeks' worth of performances.

Ohio Hotel Promotion

Their father had come through for them.

Thursday evening, Roger, Mary, David, and yes, even "Steps," had their 1955 Chevy packed to the hilt, and hit the road at 9:00 p.m.

They had arranged to leave the cart parked at the home of Barbara Wilkerson, a nice young lady who David had been dating for a few weeks.

She assured them everything would be safe and sound at her parents' house for the two or three weeks The Balphs were going to be in Ohio.

That was a big relief.

Figuring out what to do with the cart was always an issue of worry and discussion.

It wasn't like they could just fold it down like a tent and stuff it in a closet.

Knowing the cart was secure solved one of their major issues.

They drove straight through to Mansfield, Ohio, with each brother taking 100-mile shifts at the wheel.

This was a true homecoming in every sense of the word.

Not only were they able to visit their father and his new wife, but in the time since they had left their mother in Los Angeles in July 1963, she had remarried and moved to Columbus, Ohio, with her new husband, Bob Richards.

During The Big Walk, Roger and David's family ties to Los Angeles had literally disappeared; so they couldn't go back there, even if they wanted to.

The life they had known there was gone forever.

Time waits for no one.

Roger was able to introduce Mary to childhood friends and family, and David was able to reconnect with running buddies he hadn't seen since high school.

There was the usual assortment of holiday parties, dinners, and reunions with relatives and buddies.

It was exactly what The Brothers needed to take their minds off the strains and hassles of The Big Walk and recharge their mental and physical batteries.

Of course, it gave them the opportunity to tell everybody near and far all about their unbelievable experiences on The Big Walk.

How many people can say they've pushed a 1,000-pound cart 1,500 miles through the American West, and lived to talk about it?

One night at their mother's new home, they spent the evening watching old home movies, laughing and sharing memories of everything from childhood to Roger's 1955 appearance on The Ed Sullivan Show, performing with The All Army Talent Show.

When David stopped and realized, only a few weeks earlier, they had been sleeping in the desert, fighting off skunks and late-night attackers, it was almost more than he could comprehend.

The previous months' experiences seemed to take on a dreamlike, or maybe nightmarish, quality in his memory as he watched those fading black and white 16-millimeter films in the comfort of his mother's den.

It was so wonderful to be able to replenish their spirits and bodies with a much-needed trip back home.

Roger's dad even arranged for a new engine to be put into the trusty Chevy; so, things were truly getting a new lease on life, in so many areas.

The new engine allowed The Brothers to safely travel the 60 miles between their father's home in Mansfield and The Olentangy Inn in Columbus without fear of breaking down on the road.

The first show on Monday, December 21st, was a success, even though the crowd was pretty thin.

Mary had arranged for the usual round of media coverage from local newspapers and television stations; so, word was getting out. It just took a little while for people to turn their reading about The Balph Brothers' triumphant return into actually going out to the lounge to hear them perform in person.

The crowd increased the second night when their father brought an entire converted Greyhound Bus full of friends and family from Mansfield to the show.

Of course, their father had to join them onstage in front of his friends. How could he have resisted?

The magic the reunited Balph Trio created in Texas was alive and well on the Ohio stage, basking in the warm affection of their hometown supporters.

Christmas Day, 1964, was divided between meals with their father and his wife, Betty, and their mother and her husband, Bob.

There was more than enough family, and turkey, to go around, with "Steps" even getting her share of the holiday goodies.

David had almost forgotten what the Texas desert smelled like at this point.

He was too busy enjoying as many wonderful home-cooked meals as he could possibly handle.

Christmas night, David met a young lady who would wind up changing his life in every way possible.

Roger and David used to deliver newspapers to a lady named Virginia Gerhart when they were little kids back in Lexington, Ohio.

Virginia came to see The Brothers perform at The Olentangy Inn Christmas night, and she brought her daughter, Trudy, with her.

While David had attended high school with Trudy, he hadn't seen her in over eight years and didn't recognize her as she arrived with her date.

When David discovered, through the time-honored traditional matchmaking network of his mother talking to her mother, that Trudy was not engaged to the date she was with at the club, he made plans to call her up in the very near future to see if she'd consider going out with the younger Balph Brother for dinner, coffee, or anything her heart wanted.

To David's immense delight, Trudy accepted his call, and, more importantly, his offer for the next day.

He had an hour interview on WMAN radio in Mansfield, and was thrilled when childhood friends called the station to share stories and let him know they were going to attend shows in Columbus the following week.

It was nice being back on their home turf where people knew Roger and David as local kids from a good family.

It sure made Mary's job much easier.

The fact that she also had months and months of press clippings and stories from leading media outlets in Arizona, New Mexico, and Texas also helped add credibility to The Walking Musical Balph Brothers' Big Walk story.

It was a feel-good saga of hometown boys facing impossible tasks and thriving in hostile environments.

The Ohio media couldn't get enough of the story.

It seemed like everybody Roger and David had ever met in their entire childhoods heard about The Big Walk and made an effort to call them, drop by to see them, ask them to dinner, or just chat a spell.

Mary was getting a big thrill out of seeing Roger back among friends, telling his stories and showing her off to his buddies.

It was nice to see Roger and David happy and carefree, holding court with their friends, enjoying the admiration and limelight of their hometown.

David drove to Lexington to pick up Trudy for their big date, taking her to another friend's home, Al Hess, in Mansfield to watch The Cleveland Browns vs. The Baltimore Colts football game on television.

Al and his wife Tootsie, Roger and Mary, and David and Trudy shared the evening cheering for The Browns and enjoying each other's company.

The next day, David took Trudy to lunch.

Whether he knew it or not at the time, he was destined to spend many, many, many meals with Trudy in the future.

Monday, December 28th, found The Brothers performing again at The Olentangy Inn in Columbus.

Unfortunately, the club was almost empty. It was obvious the management wasn't advertising the engagement. While the staff wasn't complaining about the lack of paying customers, The Brothers knew it was always better to have packed houses.

They had previously seen how the lack of promotion killed enthusiasm for all things related to The Walking Musical Balph Brothers, and made things go sour in a hurry.

Mary's efforts to get press were always top-notch, but clubs seemed to think that was enough to bring out audiences.

It wasn't.

Roger and David knew it also took advertising to complete the job, a fact that was often overlooked by club managers.

Meanwhile, media attention in The Balph Brothers continued to grow.

There was interest from The Mike Douglas Show in Cleveland and The Ruth Lyons Show in Cincinnati, both of which would provide much needed boosts in exposure.

Press kits, biographies, and records were sent to the producers of those television shows as soon as they were requested.

New Year's Eve at The Olentangy Inn was packed with happy, horn-blowing, champagne-drinking, dancing, noisy fans.

The year of 1965 arrived with a bang, with The Brothers onstage, performing for adoring fans, family, and friends.

Good times were had that night in Columbus, Ohio, even if some of the crowd had to look at photos afterwards to remember it all.

Roger and David could only imagine what 1965 held for them in the months to come.

Chapter 72: Who Says You Can't Go Home?

David and Roger Perform on The Ruth Lyons Show in Ohio

Roger and David could feel the tide turning in their efforts to build their careers.

Ever since their arrival back in Ohio, their home state, everything had been going their way.

They were media darlings, the hometown boys returning triumphantly from an extended road trip through the wild, wild West.

Maybe it was simply a case of the grass being greener on the other side, or more accurately, the desert dirt.

By taking charge of their own destiny, earning respect in Arizona, New Mexico, and Texas, they had proven their value in real world situations that the local media in Ohio seemed to appreciate.

Sometimes you have to leave home to get noticed when you come back.

Opportunities seemed to be opening up for them every single day.

It was a very nice change of pace after so many months of struggles and hardships.

They earned an appearance on one of the most popular shows in the region, The Ruth Lyons Show in Cincinnati on WLWT.

Her show was broadcast on television and radio all over Ohio, reaching several million people during the 14 minutes The Brothers were on the air.

They received phone calls from friends across the Buckeye State, and the response was simply overwhelming.

During a lull in performances between Columbus and Mansfield, Roger and Mary drove to Lansing, Michigan to present their sponsorship program to the marketing executives at Oldsmobile headquarters.

While they didn't come back with contracts, or a new car, they did hold out hope that an offer would be coming their way in the very near future.

If Olds didn't see the value in the affiliation, they would simply approach Ford or Chrysler.

The chance to sponsor a true success story like The Big Walk didn't come around very often, and Roger and Mary were highly confident some modern thinking marketing executive would see the obvious advantages to their proposal.

The Plantation Club, a new nightclub opening in their hometown, Mansfield, had expressed interest in hiring the native sons for the 22nd and 23rd of January.

With this contract in hand, The Brothers were able to generate another round of local articles touting the return of Mansfield's finest, Roger and David Balph.

The Mansfield paper covered their upcoming appearance, while smaller papers in surrounding towns like Ontario, Ashland, and Lexington joined the effort with photos and interviews in their weekly editions.

It would have been next to impossible to not know Roger and David were back in town.

Unlike some of the previous stops along The Big Walk where The Brothers received huge amounts of publicity and nobody cared enough to come to their shows, the home folk of Mansfield, Ohio, and surrounding areas came out in masses to see the local heroes.

Hometown Gig

The first two nights at The Plantation Club were so popular, management had to turn people away at the door. All 253 seats were filled to overflowing with drinking, clapping, dancing, happy customers.

The sound of the cash register was almost as loud as the music itself.

The manager was so happy with the first week's results that he treated The Brothers, Mary, Trudy, their father, and his wife to steak dinners and unlimited drinks on the house.

Then he announced he was extending their engagement for three more weeks.

This extension of good news was duly noted by the local media, resulting in another round of flattering reviews, photos, and interviews.

331

By the following week, David had borrowed a film projector from the manager of The Plantation Club and was complementing their musical performances with film clips from their television interviews on The Big Walk in Arizona, New Mexico, and Texas.

The Ohio audiences were able to see just how extensive the media coverage of The Walking Musical Balph Brothers had been in other parts of the country.

There was no denying that Roger and David were making noise all over the United States of America, and people were noticing them.

Then to have the actual living, breathing hometown celebrity performers share their talents with their neighbors and friends, in person, was simply overwhelming for the local audiences.

Even Frank Sinatra, Jr., would have been jealous of this reception.

By the third week, the local Ampex dealer had brought in larger theater-style speakers to handle the sound levels for the standing-room only crowds. The trustworthy equipment, that had served them so well in the Southwest, was suddenly vastly inadequate for the adoring throngs in Ohio.

The only less-than-enthusiastic response had been the strange silence from the producer of The Mike Douglas Show in Cleveland. While they hadn't received a definite "no," they hadn't been invited to the studio yet, even after their successful appearance and reception on The Ruth Lyons Show in Cincinnati.

What was it about the big time television shows that made them so hard to crack?

How many standing-room audiences did it take to get their attention?

There was also still no news on the promotions deal with Oldsmobile.

Roger didn't understand why there would be any reluctance to spend the estimated $25,000 required by their proposal when it would pay off a hundred times over in genuine grass-roots level exposure with the car-buying public along the route of The Big Walk.

After spending far too much time and money chasing the deal, Oldsmobile officially turned down the offer on February 12th.

The proposal made it through four of the five officials who had to sign off on the deal, and the final link in the chain killed it.

Figuring, if the details were good enough to make it over that many hurdles, The Brothers decided to immediately march forth and talk to the other competitors.

Roger made an appointment with the marketing people at Pontiac Automotive for the very next Monday, and started mapping directions to their headquarters in their namesake Michigan town.

Over the same weekend, they finally learned The Mike Douglas Show was definitely not interested in The Walking Musical Balph Brothers' story.

Like so many times before, the reasons for the rejection were not known.

Maybe the producers were afraid if their reasons were known, it would just show how flimsy and ill-conceived they really were.

There was nothing worse than being denied and not knowing why, or even what they could change or do or alter to improve their chances.

It was a stone wall of silence, and The Brothers would never know the motivation for their rejection.

Just like their dealings with Oldsmobile, all they could do was go on, keep their heads up, perform to the best of their abilities, and keep finding as many opportunities as possible, one step at a time.

Chapter 73: Back in Texas,
Five Months Later

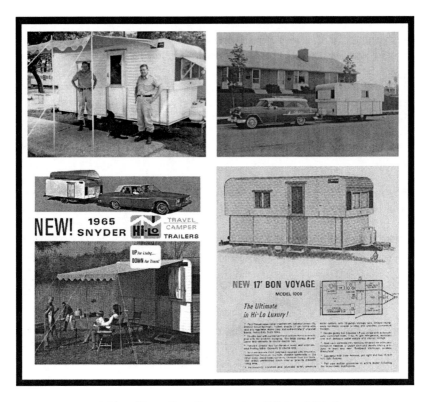

A New Traveling Companion "Hi-ho, Hi-lo"

Tuesday, June 8th, 1965, found The Brothers and Mary back in Fort Worth, Texas, ready to push the cart to Denton.

Their two-week side trip to Ohio had turned into over four months of family reunions, hometown performances, and the usual assortment of broken promises, false leads, and dreams that fell apart.

A few weeks into their joyful reunion with their father, The Brothers and Mary decided to share a cabin by a lake provided by a family acquaintance.

They didn't want to overstay their welcome, seeing as how the initial two-week visit had turned into several months of an extended stay.

By moving out of their father's home, family tensions were reduced, allowing everybody more room to breathe.

On the positive side, they had performed for several high schools in the area, and easily won over a new generation of enthusiastic fans for spirited Dixieland Jazz.

On the negative side, their efforts to secure a promotional deal with a car manufacturer, any car manufacturer, had taken a lot of time and money without producing any tangible results. While there had been some interest from Pontiac and Lincoln, nothing had been finalized.

Using some of the money they managed to earn from their successful extended performances at The Plantation Club in Mansfield, Ohio, they had invested a considerable chunk of cash turning Roger's aging 1955 Chevy into a close version of a new car.

They painted the trusty vehicle, put new leather upholstery on the seats, rebuilt the transmission, replaced the exhaust system, and even installed new carpets on the floors.

Just in case you think the dark cloud of misfortune that sometimes seemed to follow every Balph Brothers' success had disappeared, while a mechanic was working on their muffler, he managed to catch the carpet on fire and burn most of the newly installed interior of the Chevy.

Fortunately, yet another lawsuit was avoided when the repair shop immediately paid to replace the burned and damaged parts, giving the Chevy a new car smell in the process.

One of the best things to happen on the Ohio sidetrip was when they secured use of a $3,000 camper trailer from The High Low Trailer Company of Butler, Ohio.

This deluxe trailer was the kind that cranked up to full size when parked, and then collapsed down for storage when being transported.

It could sleep up to six people and had such modern conveniences as a refrigerator, stove, and even a toilet.

There was no doubt this trailer was a blessing, allowing Mary to have her own portable office, and saving untold money on motels and lodging.

Seeing as how efforts to secure an ongoing arrangement with another motel chain after The Travelodge motels deal fell apart, this was an important consideration.

Efforts to sign promotional sponsorships with Ramada Inn earlier on, and then Holiday Inn on the trip back to Texas, had also come up empty.

At least by having the trailer, they could pull into campgrounds at night, and for a dollar or two fee be able to park the car, erect the camper, and use the hot showers of the facilities.

The ten-year-old Chevy's ability to pull the trailer had been road tested on the scenic return trip from Ohio when they choose to return to Texas by going through Pittsburgh, Pennsylvania, where they had television and radio interviews arranged.

They continued over to Richmond, Virginia, then on to Washington, D.C., where Roger stopped to contact a woman named Skippy Lynn.

Skippy had been in charge of the talent and bookings for the All Army Talent Show, arranging performances all over the nation in 1955 when Roger was a member of the troupe.

Roger told her all about The Big Walk, and hoped perhaps she could put her considerable promotional skills and contacts to use for The Balph Brothers' latest efforts.

Even though a decade had passed since Roger had seen Skippy, her interest in The Walking Musical Balph Brothers' career seemed genuine.

Driving through Virginia, they discovered that towing the trailer, and just as importantly, stopping the trailer, was taking a toll on the Chevy's braking system.

It also put a strain on their recently rebuilt transmission.

They could only wonder if the money they were saving on motel rooms by using the new camper was going to be offset by never-ending repairs on Roger's decade-old Chevy.

A stop in Memphis to talk with people at the headquarters of Holiday Inn hadn't worked to change anybody's mind about giving them a contract. While the proposal had been considered for a few days, the answer on a national level was once again negative.

However, there was talk about having The Brothers perform at an upcoming regional meeting in Arkansas of Holiday Inn managers, and tentative plans were made.

The drive through Arkansas back to Texas had convinced them this route was the one to follow with the cart when they resumed their journey to New York City. Thoughts of going the more southern path through Mississippi, Alabama, and Georgia were dismissed once they had traveled the roads through Tennessee. It was nice being able to actually drive down the same roads by car, previewing the hills and turns for the return trip pushing the cart.

There were already enough surprises on The Big Walk to deal with.

One surprise that greeted The Brothers, when they returned to Fort Worth, met them at the door when they went to pick up the cart.

Five months earlier they had left the cart in the family garage of a girl named Barbara Wilkerson, a nice young lady who David had dated a few times.

David had written and called Barbara over the past five months, keeping her updated about their progress and successes back in Ohio.

In the meantime, Barbara had moved on with her life, and gotten engaged to be married.

By the time The Brothers rolled back into Fort Worth, Barbara's wedding was only a few days off.

While her fiancé was a decent guy and was very understanding, everybody agreed it was high time for The Balph Brothers to retrieve their belongings and get on with their lives.

Roger and David wished Barbara the best of luck with her marriage and the rest of her life, and thanked her profusely for her kindness and patience over the previous months.

Knowing the cart had been safely locked up in her family's garage all that time had provided The Brothers with real security, especially when the planned two weeks in Ohio turned into month after month after month.

No sooner had they checked into a campground outside of Fort Worth than they were back on the road again, heading down the same highway, back to Arkansas.

337

The regional meeting for the Holiday Inn managers took place in Pine Bluff, Arkansas, the upcoming Friday, and Mary arranged for The Brothers to perform at an 8:00 p.m. reception.

Unfortunately, the hotel managers had been enjoying complimentary cocktails since 6:30, and by the time The Brothers hit the stage, half of their audience was plowed under from the effects of the free-flowing booze. The most disappointing aspect of the entire ordeal was the fact that the main decision maker, the one man who could approve the entire promotional sponsorship, had gotten so inebriated that he had been carried back to his hotel room before Roger and David even started their performances.

While Mary had been able to collect a few business cards and make some potential contacts, it sure hadn't turned out like they had hoped.

Mary would try her best to work each lead and see if she could arrange bookings at various Holiday Inns along the way, but it sure wasn't as simple as having a national sponsorship would have been.

It was another case of spending money, time, and energy chasing a deal that may or may not pay off down the road.

The Brothers' court case with The Round Table nightclub contract dispute still hadn't come to trial in the five months they had been gone.

Any idea of a speedy trial had long been given up.

The wheels of Texas justice seemed to turn very slowly when The Brothers were the ones hoping for a moral victory.

Time and time again, the court dates had been postponed and changed.

While many things had happened in the last five months, in many ways things were just the same as they were the day they left Texas.

On Tuesday, June 8th, it was back to pushing the cart, one step at a time.

Push and then push again.

338

Chapter 74: Low Caliber Crowds

DENTON RECORD-CHRONICLE

At The Top Of The Dallas-Fort Worth-Denton Golden Triangle

RVICE—NO. 260   DENTON, TEXAS, FRIDAY AFTERNOON, JUNE 11, 1965

JACK REYNOLDS GREETS TRAVELING BALPH BROTHERS
Dave, Left, And Rog Began Journey On July 18, 1963

Greeted in Denton

Their first gigs back in Texas took place at The Captain Kidd Club in Denton.

Mary secured bookings for Friday and Saturday nights, along with the usual round of newspaper and radio interviews.

The Brothers had been severely disappointed with the radio interview at WKNT. It only lasted three minutes, and was over before The Brothers even opened their mouths. The announcer didn't seem to know anything about The Big Walk and, what's more, didn't seem to care one way or the other.

The front-page story and large photograph in the Denton newspaper somewhat made up for the interview at the radio station and helped to get people out to the club.

After spending the previous four months performing for people in Ohio, who were real fans of Dixieland Jazz and knew what to expect, David and Roger had a tough time adjusting to the rough audiences after returning to Texas.

They were amazed when customers actually got up and tried to dance to such songs as "Tiger Rag."

Didn't they know such songs were show tunes to be listened to and admired?

These people had the nerve to talk all through the shows, holler at the stage, and then get up and try to dance like they were in some country music honky-tonk joint.

David and Roger longed for musically savvy audiences who could appreciate the high caliber of music The Walking Musical Balph Brothers were providing.

It was hard for them to keep from laughing right out loud onstage when they were forced to watch people try to dance to their complicated arrangements.

They had never seen old people jump around and flail so much in their life. It was almost like they were having seizures.

Some of the customers actually threw things at The Brothers while they were onstage, treating them like some lower form of hired help.

Roger and David were extremely glad when their weekend engagements were over.

It would take a while for them to get used to Southern attitudes again after so much time in the sophisticated Buckeye markets.

They had been spoiled by the warm receptions up North.

While David was missing his Ohio audiences in general, he was especially missing one person, in particular.

David had found himself thinking more and more about Trudy Gerhart, the girl he had spent so much time with back in Mansfield.

It had been a few weeks since they had left Ohio for their circular route back to Texas, and David had missed hearing Trudy's voice.

The fact that Barbara Wilkerson, the girl he had been dating in Texas before taking the holiday break to Ohio, had met someone, gotten engaged, and was now married, only made David miss Trudy that much more.

He was painfully aware that people were going on with their lives while The Brothers were stuck on The Big Walk, pushing a cart from town to town to town.

He had mentioned how much he missed Trudy while having dinner with Joe McWillians, the manager of The Captain Kidd Club and his wife at their home, the day after their weekend series of performances at the nightclub.

To his surprise, Mr. McWilliams handed David his phone and told him to call Trudy right then and there.

David was delighted when Trudy answered on the other end in Ohio, and they spent the next ten minutes sharing details of their lives apart.

There was something about Miss Trudy Gerhart that David couldn't get out his mind, even in Texas.

Chapter 75: Marching on
Across Texas

Sherman Democrat

Associated Press Photo Full Leased Wire Report of The (AP) Associated Press and (UPI) United Press International

RAVELING MUSICIANS — The Balph brothers, Rog, 29, left, and Dave, 23, eached Sherman Tuesday on their California-to-New York tour afoot. Pushing cart loaded with musical instruments, they set out two years ago from Los Angeles, playing night club and other engagements along the way. They have a ooking agent, Mary Hinson, who travels ahead by car arranging appearances. hey hope to reach New York next year. (Staff Photo)

A Stop in Sherman

They continued their steady march across Texas, hitting towns like Sherman, Gainesville, South Meade, Bells, Bonham, and Whitesboro.

Mary continued to knock on as many doors as possible, constantly trying to keep The Brothers working and earning money.

Their cash surpluses from the good times in Ohio had evaporated in the Texas heat, eaten up by car repairs, gasoline costs, and the sheer necessities of staying alive.

Mary's gallstones were still flaring up, causing her lots of pain and discomfort. Some days were worse than others, hurting so much she literally couldn't even walk, much less deal with club managers and their silly excuses.

At least they had the trailer at their disposal now, so Mary wasn't forced to sleep in the Chevy.

The Brothers prayed that Mary's health issues didn't become critical. There was no way they would be able to afford time in a hospital.

While they hadn't had much progress in getting booked in area nightclubs, they did have better luck with several American Legions and VFWs. They were able to pick up one and two day contracts to keep a little bit of money flowing into their wallets.

They had a booking at the VFW in Sherman, Texas, on July 3rd, and had expected a good crowd to show up, seeing as how they had been featured on radio, television and newspapers as one of the best entertainment events for the Fourth of July weekend.

The club easily could have held 500 people, so the organizers expected a full house of patriotic, thirsty, music-loving fans to show up for a rousing evening of live Dixieland Jazz.

Everybody was baffled and disappointed when a grand total of three, yes, one, two, three, paying customers were on hand for the 10:00 p.m. show.

By the second show at 11:00 p.m., the crowd had grown to 22 audience members.

It was another case of a nightclub not doing any advertising, depending entirely on local media coverage to fill the seats with spending customers.

As The Brothers had witnessed so many times before on The Big Walk, just because millions of people might see an interview with Roger and David on TV, or read a story on them in the newspaper, it wasn't enough to make them get up out of their easy chairs and actually go out for a night of live music.

David and Roger knew the club had to be taking a beating on the booking, but it really wasn't The Brothers' problem.

They fulfilled the terms of their contract, giving the few people who did bother showing up the best performances possible; therefore, they earned every penny of their promised fees.

They handled their part of the show and could only hope that the other side knew enough to take care of the business part.

Chapter 76: Two Years on the Road
And They Hit Paris... Texas

The Paris News *Good Morning!*

96TH YEAR. NO. 12   PARIS, TEXAS, SUNDAY MORNING, JULY 18, 1965   36 PAGES IN 2 SECTIONS   ESTABLISHED 1869

ON THE ROAD
Hiking Brothers Mark 2nd Year

By DALE JOHNSON
News Staff Writer

Two years ago today, two brothers set out on foot from Los Angeles, Calif., en route to New York City, N.Y., and two years and 1,708 miles later they celebrated their second anniversary on the road in Paris.

Roger and Dave Balph, originally from Mansfield, Ohio, are making this tremendous hike to prove a point.

Both are talented musicians, and have colorful musical backgrounds. They have tried four times, unsuccessfully, to be booked on the Jack Paar Show. Even a Christmas card to him was rejected, so the two brothers conceived the idea of walking across the continent to New York City to see Paar in person, feeling positive, that would allow them an appearance on the show.

His show since then has been taken off the air, but once again he appeared on another show.

"We understand it is to go off the air sometime in the not-too-distant future," the brothers said, "but by the time we get there maybe he will have another show going, and if not, then maybe some other offers will be given to us."

The reason for the long period of time just to reach Paris is that the brothers solicit bookings along the way, and when they get a job, they halt the hike until the contract is fulfilled.

"These shows we give along the way finance our trip across the United States," they said.

An agent, Mary Hinson, goes ahead of the men seeking appearances for them, and pulls a trailer the men use while stopped in a city for a show. She formerly was with Capital Record Co.

Their office and files are in the trailer also, and they said the acquisition of the trailer made the trip much easier.

The trailer was given the men by Snider Trailer Co. of Butler, Ohio.

RALPH BROTHERS WALKING ACROSS CONTINENT—Roger and Dave Balph of Ohio, in an attempt to get an appearance on Jack Paar's television show, are walking from Los Angeles, Calif. to New York City, N.Y. They stopped in Paris Saturday after 1,708 miles have been completed. Playing as they go, for financial reasons, it has taken two years for the brothers to get from Los Angeles to Paris. (Paris News Staff Photo)

Celebrating in Paris

Sunday, July 18th, 1965, marked the second anniversary of leaving Los Angeles and beginning The Big Walk.

The Brothers found themselves the center of attention, literally front-page news in Paris.

Unfortunately, they weren't in the home of the Eiffel Tower, Notre Dame, or The Louvre.

They were the featured story on the Sunday edition of the newspaper in Paris, Texas, a sleepy little town between Honey Grove City and Blossom.

The only things French in this town were the greasy fries at the local burger joint.

Even worse news was the fact that, despite ample newspaper and radio coverage, they hadn't been able to find any work in the area.

The previous day in Honey Grove they thought they had a chance at winning $25 in that town's parade for having the most attention-getting float.

Some policemen had told them about the upcoming festivities and the grand prize when they stopped at a gas station for drinks.

Despite the fact it was raining, and The Brothers were still a good eight miles outside of town, they decided to literally make a run for it, determined to win the parade's prize.

But first they had to push the cart to the town.

They had a real parade waiting for their arrival.

They dog-trotted, almost at a run, for two straight hours, arriving in Honey Grove City to find a police escort waiting to take them to the center of town.

The city's newspaper had a photographer standing by the courthouse to take pictures of the sprinting musicians, who were soaked with rain and sweat by the time they arrived.

Where were all of the other entries for the big parade?

Where was the parade route, and what happened to the typical marching bands and cowboys riding horses down the middle of the street?

Where were all of the floats filled with Boy Scouts, baton twirlers, cheerleaders, and smiling politicians?

Where were the clowns?

Amid all the hoopla about making the run in the pouring thunderstorm, they discovered that, in spite of the assurances of their informative policemen, the town's parade had indeed been called off.

Due to bad weather.

Like any sane people would have done.

Everybody knows you don't parade around in thunderstorms, risking life and limb.

Not even for $25.

In consolation for not having a parade for The Brothers to march in, The Chamber of Commerce gave them free lunches at one of the best restaurants in town, and invited Roger and David to be guests of honor at their annual rodeo held that very evening.

The Brothers were treated like visiting dignitaries at the rodeo grounds, being introduced by the announcer, and receiving a warm welcome from the 1,500 people in the stands.

That night, the very same policemen who had started the entire chain of events earlier in the day by casually mentioning the parade, arranged for Roger and David to spend the night in the city jail.

The big difference this time was they weren't under arrest and locked up in an iron cell.

They were there as guests of Honey Grove City.

They were able to sleep in the air-conditioned front part of the office, sharing the hospitality of the city's finest law enforcers.

The next day's visit in Paris resulted in the front-page story in the town's paper, and while they were big news, they still weren't employed.

Bidding a fair adieu to scenic Paris, they pushed on to Blossom, blooming with hope that they would be able to harvest some fruitful employment in that colorful Texan town.

The only thing budding in Blossom was a drag race on the outskirts of city limits.

The Brothers watched custom rail racecars flying down the drag strip at 170 miles per hour, smoking their tires and filling the air with a deafening roar from the engines.

The race announcer mentioned that The Walking Musical Balph Brothers were in the audience, with their famous cart parked out front, and invited fans to meet Roger and David during breaks between races.

As an added promotional gimmick, the track held a race between a live horse and one of the dragsters.

346

While the horse managed to hold the lead for about all of 25 feet, the 800 horse-powered racecar soon zoomed pass the equine sprinter, leaving it literally in the dust.

The outcome of the challenge didn't seem to be as much of a surprise to anybody other than the horse.

Roger and David were very thankful the promoter didn't try to have The Brothers race their cart against one of the high-performance gas-guzzlers for the amusement of the spectators.

Next stop on The Big Walk was the city of Detroit.

Once again, this wasn't the town you might have thought it was.

They hadn't managed to take a big leap and a jump, and land 900 miles up the road in Michigan.

This wasn't the home of Henry Ford and America's automobile industry.

This wasn't the Motown city made famous by The Supremes, Little Stevie Wonder, or The Temptations.

No.

This was Detroit, Texas.

The most memorable aspect of this little wide spot in the road was an overabundance of wild feral cats that had been abandoned by their owners, and were over-running the campgrounds where The Brothers were trying to get some sleep.

The cats had no fear of humans and were attacking the cart, the tent, and the campfire, looking for scraps of food.

"Steps" was barking at each and every assault, chasing the furry critters into the bushes by the campsite.

Their faithful watchdog chased one of the more stubborn cats right up a nearby tree, and the noise from the barking and hissing made it impossible for The Brothers to get any sleep.

David had had enough.

He picked up his shotgun, and while he seriously wanted to shoot the aggressive feline intruder right between the eyes, he fired off a round into the ground.

The resulting shock from the gunpowder blast scared the cat out of the tree, while also scattering the rest of the feline posse into the darkness.

Unfortunately, "Steps" was also shell-shocked by the blast, and instantly developed a deep fear of the shotgun that lasted the rest of the entire Big Walk.

She had walked over to the tree where the cat had been, then back to the shotgun, where she smelled the barrel, and seemed to make the connection between the pungent smell, the hot metal, and the scattered cats.

Whenever she saw the gleaming barrel of David's 12-guage weapon for the duration of the journey, she would whimper and try to hide from sight.

It was the one lasting souvenir they carried with them from scenic Detroit, Texas.

Pressroom Excitement: Paris New Front Page
Headline Marks Second Year of The Big Walk

Chapter 77: Arkansas Parade and Funeral

*Mrs. Swann, the Kind Cookie Lady of Avery, Texas on Left
and Roger in Texas with David in Arkansas
on Border Line at Post Office in Texarkana*

On Wednesday, July 28th, The Brothers finally made it to the Arkansas line.

They had pushed the cart over 140 miles in the previous ten days, dealing with impossible heat, pouring rainstorms, countless bug bites, and the relentless cycle of oozing blisters and itching rashes.

Along the way they had met the usual assortment of kind people who took The Brothers under their wings.

One sweet lady named Mrs. Swann in Avery, Texas, had stood out on the street, waiting for the cart to pass by so she could give Roger and David a plate of her delicious secret recipe cookies.

They spent about an hour sharing ice cream and homemade treats with her, becoming fast friends in those few short minutes.

For years afterwards, they continued to receive Christmas and birthday cards from this gentle soul, who even became a pen pal with The Brothers' mother back in Ohio.

Outside of Hicks, Texas, they met a nice German lady named Helen Nawroth, who ran an all-night diner in town. Though her accent was very thick, The Brothers were able to decipher that Mrs. Nawroth had been a Holocaust survivor, and had walked 1,200 miles to escape the Nazi in World War II. Most of her family had perished over there, and she told The Brothers she never wanted to go back to Germany the rest of her life. America was her home, and she counted her blessings every day for her life in the United States of America.

She gave Roger and David a big basket of homemade pies and rolls, and told them to call her if they ever ran into trouble and needed her help along The Big Walk.

The Brothers arrived in Texarkana with the usual flurry of newspaper and media coverage.

Mary had worked her usual promotional magic, and had the city's reporters and civic leaders waiting for their arrival.

A police officer escorted them down the town's main road, taking them to the famous post office located right on the border between Texas and Arkansas.

People entered the building in one state and exited in another.

The local television station shot film footage of Roger and David making the two state leap.

The mayor of the Texas half of Texarkana was on hand to welcome The Brothers. The mayor of the Arkansas side was supposed to share the promotional moment, but he wasn't able to attend the photo opportunity.

How could there have been anything more important than meeting The Walking Musical Balph Brothers and being on the evening news with their cart was almost beyond comprehension.

At least representatives of The Chamber of Commerce made the effort, and they were duly recorded glad-handing the visiting celebrities.

While being escorted with roaring sirens, pushing the cart down the right lane of the street, The Brothers met another caravan of escorted vehicles coming the other way.

On one side, the street was lined with spectators watching the arrival of the famous Walking Musical Balph Brothers amid applause and cheers from the spectators.

On the other side of the road, a funeral procession made a somber exit, with dozens of automobiles passing by, each car filled with mourners dressed in black and wiping tears from their eyes.

It was a clash of rituals that caused The Brothers to reflect on the fragile nature of the human condition, the constant ebb and flow of life and death, literally passing each other on the border of Texas and Arkansas.

Appearing on KTAL-TV in Texarkana,
Covering Texas and Arkansas

Chapter 78: Crummy Roads, Biting Skeeters, Big Melons, and Friendly People: Welcome to Arkansas

*"Steps" and The Brothers Admiring the
Pride and Joy of Hope, Arkansas*

August 11th, 1965, found The Brothers in Hope, Arkansas.

The roads were much narrower and rougher than the ones in Texas. The shoulders on the sides of the highways were even worse than they had been in the desert.

The Brothers discovered it took twice as much effort to travel half the distance in the land of razorbacks.

Most of the route was two-lane roads with terrible traffic. The Brothers were constantly having to pull off onto the grass to let backed-up lines of honking, irritated drivers pass by.

The only way they had been able to safely cross the five bridges over the Red River was with the aid of the Fulton County police clearing their pathway.

As bad as the roads were, the mosquitoes were even worse. They were twice as large as their Texan cousins, and when they bit, there was no doubt that they were out for blood, serious blood.

On the good side, the trees were green, the grass was lush, and the terrain was very beautiful.

And the people were friendly.

A guy driving a beer truck gave The Brothers a case of 24 cans of cold malt liquor, which Roger, David, and their benefactor devoured in one evening by the side of the road.

A sharply dressed gentleman, driving a brand new bright yellow Cadillac, paused long enough to hand The Brothers a ten-dollar bill, wishing them the best of luck in New York City.

These kind strangers felt they already knew Roger and David due to their live studio performance for television station KTAL back in Texarkana. They had appeared on a 30-minute show called Texarkana Town Topics, hosted by George Dodson, which was broadcast all over the area, and then even repeated on a sister television station in Shreveport, Louisiana. Untold thousands had invited The Brothers into their homes through their TV sets, making countless strangers feel they personally knew Roger and David Balph and their life stories.

When complete strangers then happened to pass The Brothers pushing the cart along the roadside, they felt like they were bumping into newfound friends and visiting celebrities, not just some unknown drifters floating through town.

It was a constant benefit of Mary's extensive media coverage that continued to pay off with random acts of kindness along The Big Walk.

David had been able to call Trudy Gerhart back in Ohio and talk with her for a full 16 minutes, wishing her a happy birthday and thanking her for the numerous letters she had sent him along the route since leaving Fort Worth.

With so much time on his hands, pushing the cart through the lush Arkansas countryside, David found himself thinking more and more about Trudy.

He was amazed at how close they had become during his extended stay in Ohio. If absence made the heart grow dear, David was certainly experiencing a wide assortment of emotions being away from his younger high-school classmate, the daughter of the man who had sold Roger his Chevy back in 1955, the little neighborhood girl who had grown up to be such an enticing woman.

Instead of being enticed by the endless parade of waitresses, cashiers, store clerks, and assorted tempting females that crossed his path each day on The Big Walk, the younger Balph Brother caught himself wondering what Trudy was doing while he was pushing the cart and then pushing some more.

Being able to hear her sweet voice in the appropriately named town of Hope, Arkansas, David found a new optimism that Trudy Gerhart was going to play a continuing role in his life.

The Brothers also discovered that the biggest things in Hope, Arkansas, were the watermelons, a considerable source of local civic pride.

Roger and David had posed with some of the town's largest specimens, putting a huge 95-pound monster right in the center of the cart.

The resulting photo was front-page news, portraying the visiting celebrities admiring the town's most famous crop.

While Texas was known for everything being bigger than other places, Arkansas seemed to be giving The Lone Star State a run for its money.

They certainly had the biggest cowboy they had seen on the entire trip so far.

The Brothers visited a tourist attraction near Emmitt, Arkansas, called Arkla Village.

It featured a replica of an old western town with fake saloons, pretend general stores, and a miniature train ride for kids.

The real money maker for the park was their buggy factory where they made replica stagecoaches and horse-drawn wagons for Hollywood movies, with some models selling for as much as $8,000 each.

They also had a thriving gas lamp manufacturing plant, providing non-electric lighting for a wide base of international customers.

It was almost as if the touristy western town was just a sideline attraction to bring potential customers in for the other businesses.

The main visual feature of the attraction was a 60-foot tall advertising sign of a cowboy with his hand on his pistol.

"Steps," Roger and David Pose in Front
of the Arkla Village Towering Cowboy

The oversized poster promised more than the amusement park could ever deliver.

It was like the endless roadside billboards for souvenir stands that were bigger than the actual shacks being advertised.

The Brothers pushed the cart in front of the towering artwork and posed for a souvenir portrait.

The photograph lasted much longer than their memory of the amusement park.

A Side Trip in Arkadelphia, Arkansas to Visit a Cotton Plantation.

Chapter 79: Hot Times in Hot Springs

Dave Takes a Solo in Hotel Lounge

After some up and down promises, Mary had secured The Brothers three days of work at The Aristocrat Hotel in scenic Hot Springs, Arkansas.

It started out as an offer for two weeks, and then shrank to three days by the time the contract was signed.

"Steps" Guarding the Cart in Front of Aristocrat Hotel

To make matters even worse, the manager of the hotel demanded The Brothers show up with the cart, so it could be prominently displayed in the hotel's lobby.

If Roger and David hadn't been so financially stretched with less than 20 bucks between them, they would have loved to just tell the demanding hotel manager to take a hike.

Instead, they suddenly had to spend money they didn't have, hauling the cart 100 miles on the back of a trailer so it could appear as a prop for tourists seeking bubbling 143-degree hot water public baths.

They could only hope their first concerts would go well enough that the hotel would extend their contract for additional performances.

They arrived in Hot Springs to find that Mary had arranged for the local high school cheerleaders to ride down the center of town in the cart with David and Roger happily pushing and pushing some more.

They were greeted by the city's Mayor Wolf, had their photos taken by the local newspaper, and did the usual assortment of live radio and television interviews right in front of The Aristocrat Hotel, proudly standing by their famous cart.

Even "Steps" seemed to enjoy the festivities, barking and wagging her tail in response to all the excitement around her.

While waiting for the first evening's performance, Roger had taken time to enjoy the hotel's luxurious swimming pool, and managed to whack his nose on some underwater steps. The collision busted his nose wide open, and caused him considerable embarrassment in the following round of television interviews with Channel 11 from Little Rock. At least his swollen appendage didn't scare any of the listeners on KABS radio.

David took his time off to practice on his trumpet, always having a much tougher time keeping his lips in shape with his horn than Roger did with his woodwind reeds.

Since the hotel was filled to capacity, David found the perfect location to blow his horn to his heart's content without bothering the neighbors: a local cemetery.

Finding a nice secluded corner of the Chapel Wood Memorial Cemetery, David was mindful to be respectful of the deceased, but hoped the resting souls would enjoy his spirited version of "When The Saints Go Marching In."

He was lost in his musical practice when he noticed he had a living admirer hovering among the rows and rows of carved, majestic tombstones.

A gravedigger by the name of Joe Paterson had been working in the cemetery when he heard what he initially thought was Gabriel's trumpet calling to take him home.

He had been digging a grave for a man from Texarkana, who had shot himself earlier in the week.

It turned out Joe had recently seen The Brothers perform in Texarkana, and was already very familiar with David's talents.

David enjoyed sharing his music with the current and future residents of the peaceful resting grounds.

By the time of their first performance at The Aristocrat Hotel, the house was jammed full of eager, thirsty fans.

Unlike so many previous employers, the management of The Aristocrat had purchased a decent amount of radio and newspaper advertisements to compliment Mary's promotional efforts. It paid off with a huge crowd of Dixieland Jazz lovers showing up for the show.

A convention of representatives of The Sara Coventry Jewelry Company was in town, and one of the ladies at the show gave David and Roger an assortment of pearl earrings and necklaces for Trudy and Mary. Another one of the company's top executives, a lady named Nell Welks, gave David a good luck ring with a diamond in the middle of it, insisting that the younger Balph Brother wear the gift all the way to Jack Paar's television studio.

The crowd for the next night's show was so large, they had to move the performance to a larger dining room just to hold the immense crowd.

It just so happened that Sunday, August 22nd, was Roger's 32nd birthday; so, the hotel staff presented the older Balph Brother with a big birthday cake during the Saturday night show, while the entire audience sang "Happy Birthday."

The hotel management was so pleased with the capacity crowds for the first weekend of shows they extended the contract for another week.

As much as The Brothers hated to admit it, renting that trailer to haul the cart and place it in the hotel lobby had been worth the time and expense.

On their day off, they discovered the son of the hotel owner, Mr. Kersh, trained guard dogs how to be more effective and vicious.

One problem they had with "Steps" on the road was the fact she wouldn't growl at people until they actually tried to touch the cart.

Roger and David wanted her to be a little more aggressive, and with Mr. Kersh's training, they were able to accomplish their goal by the end of the week. After five days of putting a menacing broom in her face, "Steps" had turned into quite a growling weapon, baring her fangs whenever anybody seemed to get too close to the cart. As long as she didn't try to chew off the fingers of any innocent cheerleaders or hand-shaking politicians, The Brothers thought the training would come in handy.

Unfortunately, the dog's training didn't include finding a missing trombone mouthpiece.

David's came up missing after one of the performances at The Aristocrat, and he wasn't sure if some wise guy had stolen it or if some misguided fan had seized it as a souvenir of the concert.

Either way, he was in a fix, and none too happy about it. The nerve of some people never failed to amaze the younger Balph Brother.

David spent the next week trying to secure a replacement, otherwise his trombone would have been useless.

The local high school band director had managed to find the same model on a broken trombone buried in the school's storage room, and graciously donated it to the cause in true show-biz generosity.

The show had been a success, with the newly reutilized mouthpiece easily filling in for David's missing one.

At the end of the evening, as Roger was cleaning his saxophone and putting it back in the case, he noticed something clanging around in the bell of his instrument.

It was David's missing trombone mouthpiece!

Had this been somebody's idea of a great big joke?

Were they going to have to train "Steps" to keep a constant eye on even their musical instruments?

What happened to honest people who respected other people's property?

If it wasn't one thing, it was always something else on The Big Walk, but hiding a trombone mouthpiece in a baritone saxophone's bell was just plain mean.

Between their continuing performances at The Aristocrat, they had driven to Little Rock to appear on a television show with Shari Lewis and her famous sidekick, Lamb Chop, a hand puppet loved by millions of fans around the country.

Lewis was appearing at The Vapors Club in Hot Springs, and she had been very impressed with the instrumental talents of The Walking Musical Balph Brothers. After the TV show, she gave The Brothers the phone number of an associate in New York City she thought might be helpful in advancing their careers.

The Brothers were extremely happy to add Shari Lewis to their list of industry contacts.

On the way back to Hot Springs, Roger and David stopped at The Davey Crockett Club in Little Rock, a popular bar that Mary had contacted but hadn't been able to get to sign a contract.

After a few hours of schmoozing and talking with the club manager, Roger and David left the building with a signed contract for three weeks of work.

The ride back to Hot Springs was much more pleasant knowing they were going to a sold-out audience at The Aristocrat with another secure offer for employment signed, sealed, and delivered.

Maybe that good luck ring with the diamond that the jewelry company executive gave David was working after all.

Chapter 80: Rockin' Little Rock and Bad Shrimp in Beebe

Top photo: Governor Faubus Presents The Brothers with Arkansas Traveler Scrolls. Bottom left photo: Davey Crockett Club Marquee, Bottom center photo: Trudy's Little Rock Visit, Bottom right photo: Swingin' in Davey Crockett Club Lounge.

On Saturday, August 28th, The Brothers finished their engagement in Hot Springs by performing with the house band at The Aristocrat Hotel until 4:00 in the morning. Drinks were flowing and people were going out of their way to have a great time.

After the paying customers called it a night, the employees threw a going away party at one of the bartender's apartment for Roger,

Mary, and David, providing food and booze while passing away the hours listening to records and enjoying the Arkansas summer.

It was amazing how close everybody had become in such a short time, going from total strangers to lifelong friends within a matter of weeks.

It was the continuing nature of show business, resulting in intense relationships that flared up like super novas and then cooled off when The Brothers moved to the next stop on The Big Walk.

Their attorney from Abilene, Jack Bryant, was in Hot Springs on vacation with his family, and invited The Brothers to spend one of their last days in town, sharing his rented lakeside cabin.

He told them that Robbie E., the woman who had accused David of attacking her and then caused the younger Balph to be arrested, had died from a heart attack at the age of 33. Unfortunately, she had die before Attorney Bryant had been able to file charges against her for lying on the stand during the trial against David.

On a lighter note, Attorney Bryant also brought The Brothers up to date on the latest gossip concerning which friends had gotten married, had kids, or left town.

When they went back to retrieve the camper trailer from the hotel parking lot, they discovered that some wise guy had turned on the propane gas valves, so all of their cooking fuel had gone up in vapors. They had also turned off the refrigerator, and all the food inside had spoiled, putting out a horrible stink that soaked everything in the camper.

David could only wonder if the same person had been responsible for hiding the mouthpiece of his trombone in Roger's saxophone.

It almost felt like they needed to have a 24-hour security guard watching the cart, the camper, and their instruments onstage.

They arrived in Little Rock with news crews from the local NBC and CBS television affiliates waiting for them to push the cart across the city limits. Reporters from *The Arkansas Gazette* and *The Arkansas Democrat* were also ready to document their police-escorted entry into town.

Mary's promotional skills continued to bring tangible results as they pushed their way into the largest city in Arkansas.

While the crowds at The Davey Crockett Club hadn't been as large as the ones back in Hot Springs, they were just as enthusiastic.

With the cart holding down the usual place of honor in front of The Alamo Plaza Motel, which was connected to the club, The Walking Musical Balph Brothers were the center of attention in town.

Nearly 200 customers demanded four encores before allowing The Brothers to leave the stage.

Even the policemen who provided their escort into the city showed up for the performance, beaming from ear to ear when Roger acknowledged them from the stage.

The only bad news so far had been the worsening condition of Mary's gallstone problem.

Despite her taking medicine and following her doctor's orders, the gallstones continued to flare up, causing her immense, almost crippling pain.

The clock was ticking on her health, and no matter how they tried to wish it away, it kept coming back with a vengeance.

Roger decided to add a comedy routine to the show, a bit he had picked up from a musician named Johnny Stanley back in 1952 when Roger traveled with The Horace Heicht Youth Opportunity Program.

David built Roger a portable podium for the segment, and they were anxious to see how it would go over with the local crowds.

The Brothers received their first letter from an audience member on the entire Big Walk while staying at The Alamo Plaza Motel.

Was it a note praising The Brothers' musical abilities?

Perhaps it was a gushing fan letter raving about their energy and showmanship.

No. It was written by a lady named Mrs. Brainerd, who was threatening to call The Humane Society on Roger and David for leaving "Steps" tied to the cart during a rain shower.

She was outraged that The Brothers treated their faithful guard dog in such a hideous manner, and she wasn't going to stop until every television station, newspaper, and radio broadcaster in Little Rock knew what kind of monsters Roger and David truly were.

David immediately wrote a reply to the lady, explaining that "Steps" absolutely loved being around the cart and that she was much more comfortable outside than if she had been cooped up in a hot motel room. He then explained how much he loved and cared about his loyal canine friend and would never do anything to harm her.

A few days later, Mrs. Brainerd sent a follow-up letter, apologizing for the misunderstanding, and her overreaction to the situation.

David thought it was interesting the woman didn't care a thing about the health and welfare of The Brothers but was ready to have them thrown in jail for their treatment of a dog.

Meanwhile, one of Roger's saxophones had been knocked over by an intoxicated woman wobbling past the stage at Friday night's show.

The Brothers spent an hour in their hotel room working to straighten the two bent keys to get the instrument back in working order.

While they were busy repairing the damaged saxophone, somebody stole one of the toy flutes right off of the stage, taking it home as a souvenir of the evening.

David and Trudy Pose Together in Little Rock

The best thing to happen on Saturday, September 18th, was the arrival of Trudy Gerhart at the Little Rock Airport at 2:59 p.m.

Trudy had arranged to spend the following week with David, and he simply could not have been happier.

Just seeing her smiling face again was enough to make him forget about all the rest of his worries and aggravations.

It gave him such joy to perform for Trudy at that night's three shows, knowing she was watching his every move. There was no doubt in David's mind that Trudy brought out the best in his performances, giving him motivation and inspiration to hit the highest notes and play at his very best.

Mary's gallstones were bothering her so much by Tuesday that she finally gave up and let Roger take her to the hospital.

She had to spend two days in bed while the doctors ran tests on her.

Meanwhile The Brothers had to continue meeting their promotional obligations, including an interview on KRL-TV.

They also had their photos taken with Arkansas Governor Faubus, meeting him at the State Capitol, where they were given scrolls officially making them Arkansas Travelers, a honor first bestowed on President Theodore Roosevelt.

The first thing the honorable governor had said to The Brothers was how much he enjoyed reading about them in the newspapers and seeing their interviews on television.

He also promised Roger and David they wouldn't be unknown by the time they reached New York City and Jack Paar's television studio.

The hospital determined Mary had a lung infection in addition to her gallstone problems, and they instructed her to spend at least five days in bed.

Before David even realized it, Trudy's weeklong visit was coming to an end.

They spent their last night together, having a quiet dinner and talking for hours.

David had Trudy back at the airport in plenty of time for her 11:00 a.m. flight back to Ohio on Saturday, September 25th.

As soon as he got back to The Alamo Plaza Motel, he had to help Roger pack up their equipment and drive to a series of performances in Beebe, Arkansas.

Featured Ad for Beebe, Arkansas Gig

The people who owned the restaurant where The Brothers were performing also owned the local Ford dealership. They wanted Roger and David to help promote the new models for 1966 that were just being revealed to the public.

Bruce Anderson, car dealer and restaurant owner, arranged for The Brothers to have a movie projector so they could show news clips of their previous television interviews during the concerts like they had been able to do at their shows in Ohio.

The newspaper in Beebe devoted a full page to The Brothers' arrival and the multi-media performances. They also featured photos of Roger and David posing beside the brand new Fords, proving exactly the kind of promotional value The Brothers had been trying to sell to Oldsmobile, Pontiac, and Lincoln, without any luck.

When they performed a two-hour concert at the Ford dealership, several cars were sold as a result of The Brothers bringing a large crowd of potential car-buyers to the lot.

The Saturday night show at the restaurant was so crowded they had to turn people away.

Fans from the day's University of Arkansas football game had driven 30 miles from Little Rock to hear The Brothers perform. There were so many customers trying to get into the restaurant, they spilled over into the parking lot, keeping the party going into the early morning hours.

Sunday was spent performing two shows at an Air Force base located between Little Rock and Beebe.

The afternoon show was held at the NCO Club for officers and their families. The evening show featured a more adult crowd and earned The Brothers three encores.

Monday they performed at a 9:00 a.m. assembly show at Beebe College, and were warmly received.

The Brothers were as busy as they had ever been since leaving Los Angeles, playing a steady and profitable chain of performances from Hot Springs to Little Rock to Beebe.

They spent Monday afternoon out on Pier's Ferry Lake, sharing time on a 37-foot luxury yacht owned by a man named Mr. Davidson, who was a friend of Bruce Anderson, the car dealer and restaurant owner back in Beebe.

Mr. Davidson had flown to the lake in his private airplane to join The Brothers.

While they didn't actually catch any fish during their time on the lake, they had a wonderful dinner, courtesy of their influential benefactors.

It was a taste of a comfortable lifestyle The Brothers could certainly have gotten used to.

It just made David and Roger that much more determined to make it to the top of the music industry and buy their own yachts and airplanes.

They would gladly repay Mr. Davidson and Mr. Anderson for their kind hospitality with visits to their own floating mansions, as soon as possible.

Maybe they would arrange for Shari Lewis, Peter Graves, and, yes, Frank Sinatra, Jr., to join them for drinks and steak dinners the same night.

On Thursday, October 7th, The Brothers packed the camper and arranged to head over to West Memphis, Arkansas.

Mr. Anderson treated The Brothers and Mary to shrimp dinners as his parting present for their successful engagement in Beebe.

They arrived at the same trailer camp outside of West Memphis where they had stopped on the drive down from Ohio.

Even though the park was filled, the manager was able to squeeze their trailer into a tiny spot, hooking up water and electricity.

Around 2:00 a.m., David woke up feeling sick to his stomach.

By 7:00 a.m., the entire trio was so sick they didn't know what they were going to do. They were going off at both ends, suffering chills and fevers.

They truly thought they were dying.

Mary and Roger had cramps so bad they could hardly stand up.

David wasn't cramping, but felt as sick as he ever had in his entire life.

While driving to the emergency room of the West Memphis Hospital, the Chevy ran out of gas.

David was the only one strong enough to run across the highway to a nearby gas station.

When they finally arrived at the emergency room, it took 40 minutes for Mary to get a bed and have somebody check her over.

Meanwhile, Roger and David were so sick and weak, they just stared at the walls and waited for relief to come.

Roger and Mary received shots for their cramps, and it was decided that all three of them were suffering from food poisoning, probably from eating bad shrimp back at their going away dinner in Beebe.

They were so upset by the shabby way they had been treated by the emergency room staff, they left the hospital without paying their bill.

Roger and David truly felt they could have died before anybody even checked to see if they were breathing.

They spent the rest of the following day sleeping in the trailer, or at least trying to.

They couldn't eat, move, or do much more than try to take little sips of water.

By 9:30 that night, Mary was about to pass out from pain.

This time, they drove across The Mississippi River into Memphis, Tennessee, taking Mary to The Baptist Hospital.

They received much better treatment in the Memphis facility.

They discovered Mary was severely dehydrated. The advice they had received at the first hospital had actually made them even worse.

By Saturday evening, David was feeling improved enough to do some laundry duties at the trailer camp.

Roger and Mary were recovering but still feeling weak and feverish.

David made a long-distance phone call to their friend Bruce Anderson in Beebe and told him about their losing battle with the bad shrimp. He immediately pulled the questionable item from his restaurant's menu and expressed his apologies for inadvertently causing their sickness.

On Sunday morning, October 10th, Roger and Mary were on the road to recovery, feeling well enough to eat some solid food again.

After being so ill for so many days, Roger, Mary, and David decided to treat themselves to a movie at a Memphis theater, enjoying the musical hit *The Sound of Music.*

It was just what they needed to take their minds off their aches and cramps.

With the worst of their bout with food poisoning behind them, Mary drove The Brothers back to Beebe to arrange for the cart to be taken back to the spot in Little Rock where they had left the route of The Big Walk to perform their series of engagements.

Mary drove back to the trailer camp in West Memphis to work on getting The Brothers lined up with work in Memphis.

The Brothers went back to their endless task of pushing the cart one step at a time, and then pushing some more.

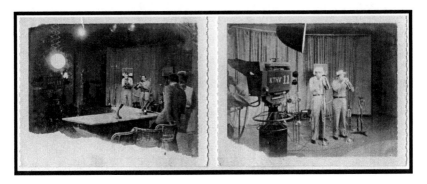

KTHV – Little Rock, Arkansas Television Performance

Chapter 81: Walking to Memphis

David and Roger Share their Adventures with The Carlisle Jaycees

On Wednesday, October 13th, The Brothers were back on the road, walking to Memphis.

Their weeks off of the road had taken a toll on their physical condition.

It always took a while to get back into the routine of pushing the cart, and this time was no exception. The previous month had been very productive, with a steady flow of gigs in Hot Springs, Little Rock, and Beebe. The Brothers had enjoyed the good life of decent meals, complimentary drinks, and relaxing evenings on luxurious yachts.

Other than their life-threatening bout with bad shrimp and the resulting food poisoning, things had been pretty sweet for Roger and David.

But that was over. It was back to the grind of the road, and they were doing well to push 16 miles a day.

Mary was ahead of them in Memphis, working on arranging interviews and getting signed contracts, while hoping that her gallstones didn't force her to stay off her feet.

If Mary didn't keep the promotional machine running, The Big Walk would come to a complete and total stop.

In Roanoke, Arkansas, they met a real estate man named John Latimer who was gracious enough to let The Brothers sleep in the front part of his office in order to keep from being eaten alive by the fierce Arkansas bugs.

The odometer on the cart hit the 1,900-mile mark, and Roger and David were thankful to have use of an air-conditioned space to rest and recover.

In the middle of the night, there was a loud knock on the front door.

A man named Mr. Wolf was angrily pounding away and had a fit when Roger finally opened the entry.

It turned out that this Mr. Wolf owned the building, and when he saw the cart parked out front, he naturally assumed that someone had broken into his property.

Mr. Latimer had called Mr. Wolf's daughter earlier in the evening to tell him about The Brothers, but the message had never made it to the landowner's ears.

With Roger doing his famed fast-talking, he was able to smooth things over in a short while, mostly by going into vast detail about the past two years on The Big Walk.

Once he was sure The Brothers were legitimate guests on his property, Mr. Wolf shifted his attention to the fact that they had only been able to push the cart, what he considered a feeble distance, of 16 miles the previous day.

He went from being a threatening evictor to a pompous know-it-all within the course of a few minutes.

If he hadn't been the owner of the very building where The Brothers were spending the night, Roger would have told him to take a flying leap into the nearest creek.

But, obviously, he didn't.

He humored Mr. Wolf and thanked him for his vigilance.

The next day, after only three miles of pushing, David's ankle started hurting so bad it brought tears to his eyes.

It was all he could do to limp the next nine miles to Carlisle, Arkansas, where the local Jaycees put The Brothers up for the night at The Powers Motel. The kindhearted civic leaders also bought Roger and David meals in return for The Brothers dropping by their weekly meeting that night and talking about The Big Walk.

The road to Hogan, Arkansas, was narrow, hilly, and the worst kind of highway to push the cart on, even if The Brothers had been in good health. With David's ankle swollen to twice its normal size and Roger limping with blisters, it was just that much harder.

They had asked the local Hogan police if they could sleep in the jail, as they had in previous stops along the way, but the cop in this particular town said if they did, he would have to lock them up. David thought he was just kidding around, but evidently he wasn't.

When Roger politely declined to accept the offer, the policeman said maybe he should just go on and arrest them to save the town from being burglarized by unemployed musicians passing through the city limits.

Realizing this guy was not going to become a member of their fan club anytime soon, The Brothers pushed on out of town, finding a spot to sleep at an abandoned gas station.

Camping and Cooking at an Abandoned Gas Station

It was amazing how so many law officers along the route went out of their way to befriend Roger and David, going so far as to provide escorts into towns and even giving them bullets for their guns. Some of the best friends they had made along The Big Walk were policemen.

On the other hand, there were those mean-spirited few who seemed to want to make life as miserable as possible for Roger and David,

373

using their badges and uniforms as justification to bully and abuse The Brothers.

Roger and David were just thankful they had been able to get out of town without rubbing the guy the wrong way.

If they had learned anything during the past 1,900 miles of walking it was the fact that it simply didn't pay to fight the law, especially if they were dealing with pig-headed thugs with small minds and crummy attitudes.

Seven miles down the road from Hogan, they came to another wide spot in the road, De Valles Bluff, where they met the sister of Bill Johnson, the friendly police officer who had escorted them through Little Rock.

Her husband, Don Butler, was the basketball coach at the local high school, and he invited The Brothers to go see one of the most unusual football games they had ever attended.

The senior girls were playing the junior girls in a game of football to raise money for their upcoming prom.

The boys on the real football team were dressed as female cheerleaders and had the bleachers screaming with laughter.

The girls couldn't pass or catch the football, and the boys couldn't cheer to save their lives, but everybody had a great time while raising cash for their annual dance at the end of the year.

The Brothers could never have imagined they would ever be a part of a powder puff football game in a tiny town in Arkansas.

It was another slice of small-town life in America they never could have planned on when they began The Big Walk, so many months earlier in Los Angeles.

On Sunday, October 17th, The Brothers stopped at The Journey's End restaurant and motel, only to discover it was owned by the Mayor of De Valles Bluff, a man named Mr. Church.

The mayor insisted on feeding Roger and David on the house, and then arranged for a police escort across a dangerous mile and a half long bridge on the outskirts of town.

Once again, The Brothers were overwhelmed by the continuing generosity of so many total strangers.

In Brinkley, Arkansas, Bob Holland from KBRI-AM radio station met the cart on the road, and arranged for an interview the next day, while recommending they consider spending the night at The Fuller Motel in town.

Using Mr. Holland's name as a reference, David was able to turn the promise of mentioning the motel on the radio into a free night's stay in the best room of the entire motel.

Mary would have been proud of the younger Balph Brother's promotional skills.

The radio interview the next day was friendly and professional. David kept his promise of giving The Fuller Motel large amounts of praise, which pleased the owner to no end.

After basking in the media spotlight of Brinkley, signing autographs, and posing for pictures, The Brothers pushed on to the next town down the road.

Less than a mile outside of Brinkley, and still within range of the radio station's signal where they had just been interviewed, a black 1957 Ford station wagon drove by with the driver tossing a carton of ice cream at the cart.

Fortunately, he missed The Brothers, but he did manage to hit the steering wheel, throwing melted, gooey ice cream all over the cart and the contents.

The car was so dirty that Roger couldn't even read the license plate on the back of their attacker's vehicle.

It took Roger and David a good 30 minutes to clean the messy goop off. Then, they resumed pushing and pushing some more.

It never failed to amaze them how extreme things could be on the road.

One minute they were posing for newspaper photographers, doing radio interviews, and performing on live television shows.

The next minute they were dodging food bombs tossed at them by passing motorists.

David was pretty sure even Shari Lewis, much less Frank Sinatra, Jr., never had to deal with such extremes.

375

Chapter 82: Still Walking to Memphis

David Picks Up Mail at Goodwin, Arkansas Post Office in 1965

On October 19th, The Brothers were still walking to Memphis.

They spent the night in an old American Legion building that was about to be condemned in Wheatley, Arkansas, population: 409.

The next stop was Goodwin, with an even smaller population of 312 citizens.

Seven miles down the road, they passed through Palestine, home to another 407 proud Americans.

They tried to spend the night at The Tower Motel, but the people running the place were so drunk they couldn't even talk to Roger and David. Yes, drunk.

This was a first for The Brothers.

While they had certainly seen their share of inebriated fans, drivers, and occasionally a waitress or bartender, this was the first time they had been unable to check into a motel because the managers were fall-down drunk, oscillating between snoring and cackling in a booze-induced stupor.

Seeing as how the restaurant beside the motel was also boarded up, The Brothers figured the place was on its last legs.

They decided to push on down the road.

Forrest City looked like New York City compared to the tiny burgs they had been passing through.

It actually had a traffic light.

They received coverage from the local newspaper and were interviewed by a reporter from radio station KXJK.

Forrest City also marked the first time a rubberneck driver had caused an accident while gawking at The Brothers pushing their cart.

A new Pontiac slammed into the rear of a Chrysler when both cars slowed down to check out Roger and David making their way down the road.

Fortunately it was only a fender and bumper bender, and nobody had to go to the hospital, but the owners of the two cars in the accident weren't very happy about The Brothers' arrival in their town.

While Roger and David continued pushing the cart down the highway, the two crumpled piles of metal waited for a local police officer to come along and fill out the proper forms.

The Brothers pushed to the next motel and checked in for the night.

After taking relaxing baths, and having a few beers at the end of a long day of cart pushing, there was a knock at the door to their room.

Mr. and Mrs. McLaughlin were at their threshold, saying they were fans and wanted to meet the famous Walking Musical Balph Brothers.

They were liars.

This deceitful couple standing at their door owned the car that had just slammed into the other car on the highway.

Mr. McLaughlin demanded to know how many other accidents The Brothers had caused along their so-called "Big Walk," how many innocent people had been maimed, or even killed, since Roger and David started their foolishness.

David listened to the arrogant man rant and rave until he couldn't take it any longer.

He told him there wouldn't have been any accident if Mr. McLaughlin had been watching where he was going.

Nobody made him turn his head completely around to gawk at the cart while continuing to propel his automobile down the highway.

Mr. McLaughlin retorted that he hadn't even seen the cart at first. He said he had been distracted by all of the children following the cart.

David asked the man how in the world The Brothers could be held responsible for what anonymous children did or didn't do.

The fact was Mr. McLaughlin was the man with his foot on the gas pedal who had slammed his car into another person's vehicle, and he simply didn't want to take responsibility for his reckless actions.

While The Brothers were trying to get the McLaughlins out of their motel room, a bellboy delivered a letter from Mayor Roger Deadrick, welcoming them to Forrest City and wishing them the best of luck.

The timing of that letter couldn't have been better.

Seeing that The Brothers had the official welcome of the town's mayor seemed to take the wind out of Mr. McLaughlin's argument.

David was amazed the man had tried to blame the entire mishap on The Brothers, and was very relieved when they finally left their motel room, mumbling and cursing as they departed.

In David's opinion, instead of stalking The Brothers down in their motel room, Mr. McLaughlin should have been thankful he hadn't run over any of the town's children or hurt the occupants of the car he slammed into.

The best news of the night came when they talked with Mary and discovered she had secured two weeks of work in Memphis at The El Cid Lounge.

Knowing they had a paying gig waiting for them across the border in Tennessee certainly helped put some pep in their steps the next day as they pushed through Madison and Hicks Station.

They also discovered the reporter from radio station KXJK had filed his story on The Big Walk with The Associated Press wire service. His feature had been sent to over 17,000 radio, television, and newspaper outlets, from Los Angeles to New York City.

The Brothers could only hope with that much national publicity, Jack Paar and his producers would finally take notice and realize how much Roger and David could help his ratings.

On October 24th, they pushed the final distance to Memphis, admiring miles and miles of busy cotton plantations, manned by armies of pickers and grinners, living in plantation-owned houses, shopping at plantation-owned stores, and earning 50¢ an hour for backbreaking labor in the fertile fields.

David looked across the river, admiring the glowing Memphis skyline, wondering what adventures their time in Tennessee would bring them.

Would they find success in a city known world-wide for The Blues, barbeque ribs, and Elvis?

Would The Volunteer State, home of that famous Southern hospitality, welcome The Walking Musical Balph Brothers with open arms and generous wallets?

Only time would tell.

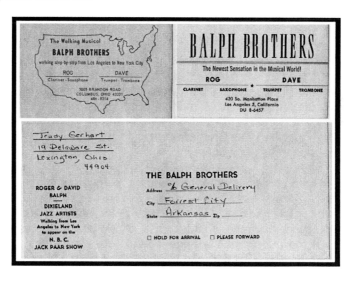

Business Cards Created by their Mother, Envelope Created by their Father. Note: Envelope Sent by Trudy

Chapter 83: Bridging the Gap

Making Friends with Memphis Police,
Prior to Crossing The Mississippi

On Thursday, October 28th, The Brothers officially crossed the bridge from the West to the East, but as so often was the case on The Big Walk, it wasn't without difficulties.

It almost took an act of Congress to arrange for the cart to get across the mighty Mississippi River dividing Arkansas from Tennessee. There was a big, wide, muddy river, and a single, huge, steel span providing entry.

Mary worked her usual promotional magic, arranging for Officer Bob Wilson of the Arkansas State Police to escort Roger and David to the center of the bridge, where they were met by Officers J. K. Collins and H. P. Standridge of the Memphis Police force.

Typically, right when The Brothers started to cross the bridge from the Arkansas side, they got a flat tire.

Was it an omen or just another challenge to be overcome?

With two of Tennessee's finest law enforcers, various media representatives, and one of the mayor of Memphis' top assistants waiting on the middle of the huge steel bridge connecting the two states, The Brothers were forced to do an emergency tire change on the spot.

The law officer on the Arkansas side literally acted like a human jack, saving critical time by holding the cart aloft while the tire was removed and repaired.

In record time, they had the cart rolling once again.

It was amazing how fast repairs could be made when teams of photographers, reporters, and government officials were waiting midstream.

"Take it slow boys, you need all the promotion you can get,"
Quote Taken from Police Escort into Memphis

Even though the Mayor of Memphis wasn't able to attend the crossing, he did provide keys to the city for Roger, David, and even "Steps." While The Brothers were suitably impressed, "Steps" seemed a little disappointed to discover that the ceremonial metal gift wasn't edible.

A tour of the city was arranged by the mayor.

Everywhere they went, The Brothers were welcomed like visiting celebrities. They were treated to a VIP lunch at the exclusive 100 Club, and given behind-the-scenes, guided tours of the airport, the courthouse, the new football stadium, and the city's sports arenas.

The two leading entertainment reporters from the two Memphis daily newspapers provided extensive coverage in multiple stories over the following weeks.

One week, Bill Burke from the *Press-Scimitar* would showcase The Brothers, and then the next week, John Knott of *The Commercial Appeal* provided coverage. This gave each reporter a chance to have exclusives for their readers, while providing continuing coverage for The Big Walk.

Tootin' the Toy Flutes at El Cid Lounge

Their first series of performances at El Cid Lounge were the usual assortment of packed houses and empty rooms. It was feast or famine, with club owner, Carl Kramer, being mildly happy when the lounge was filled with paying, thirsty customers, but more vocally upset when the club was empty.

David couldn't understand why the man would focus entirely on the negative aspects, bitching and moaning every single moment, while begrudgingly tolerating the profitable shows.

They certainly had a love-hate relationship with the man while performing at his club and staying at his house, as required in the terms of their contract.

While he seemed to ignore the times when The Brothers would perform double and triple encores, going way over their required hour sets, he was quick to enforce the time rules when the club was empty and Roger and David were performing for the napkins at the empty tables.

It appeared he went out of his way to look for things to be upset about.

One bone of contention was the fact The Brothers had made a copy of the key to the club without asking for Mr. Kramer's permission.

It started when The Brothers needed to get into the club early one morning to retrieve their instruments for a 9:00 a.m. television show called *Town and Country* on WBHQ-TV, Channel 13. The interview lasted for ten minutes, and The Brothers were able to mention El Cid Lounge four times.

While taking the keys to the club back to Mr. Kramer, they decided to make a copy, with the idea of saving everybody some hassle.

Mr. Kramer had demanded that The Brothers keep doing as many interviews as possible, and that required early morning trips to the club. In Roger and David's minds, having a spare key to get into El Cid was a very logical solution to a real problem. They could come and go from the club as they pleased, and retrieve their instruments without bothering anybody.

Unfortunately, they didn't mention this fact to Mr. Kramer for a few days, and by the time he found out about the duplicate key, he was already on a rampage for a wide assortment of perceived issues with The Brothers.

He tried to charge them $16 for clogging up a toilet in his house. He also said that two shotguns were missing from his home. Then he claimed that somebody stole $62 from the club's cash register.

Meanwhile, the club was bringing in over $1,000 a night when the house was full.

Many of the customers were fans of The Brothers who drove from Arkansas to show their support. Dottie Harrison from the Forest City Chamber of Commerce made the 120 mile round trip to cheer Roger and David on in the big city. Several people from as far away as Little Rock made a point of saying hello to The Brothers onstage, proving their grass-roots appeal.

They also discovered that several high level executives with Pepsi Cola had been to their shows, and were seriously considering sponsoring The Big Walk with advertising and promotional support on a national level.

Bill Burke from the *Press-Scimitar* continued to endorse The Brothers, generously giving them lots of ink in his entertainment column, while plugging El Cid.

His support went beyond that of just reporting on The Brothers' performances.

He also became a good friend, going out of his way to introduce Roger and David to members of the Memphis business, political, and social communities.

Mr. Burke introduced The Brothers to Mr. Bill Lowe, a wealthy and generous Memphis businessman who owned a chain of laundry stores.

That led to The Brothers attending a swimming pool party at Mr. Lowe's mansion, where they met a true show-biz legend, best-selling vocalist and entertainment personality Pat Boone.

Mr. Lowe had challenged the Tennessee native to beat him swimming across his pool, with the loser giving $1,000 to the other's favorite charity.

What made this particular challenge even more interesting was the fact that Mr. Lowe was crippled from the waist down.

It was a wonderful gesture of generosity, with Mr. Boone's charity assured of receiving a nice donation.

The Brothers had been able to personally shake hands with Pat Boone, which gave Roger the opportunity to remind the celebrity that they had met before in 1954, appearing on the same show at The Memorial Coliseum in Columbus, Ohio.

Pat Boone's sole comment was to say that performance was back at the very beginning of his career.

It wasn't the big bonding moment reaction Roger had hoped for.

At least Mr. Boone was friendly.

The Brothers had to leave the party early in order to get back for their evening performance at El Cid Lounge, so they didn't get to work the crowd for any additional contacts. However, they were pleased Reporter Burke had invited them to mingle with so many important Memphis movers and shakers.

They also were able to perform at one of the most exclusive clubs in Memphis, the famous Hunt and Polo Club, so exclusive, they limited membership to 135 hand-chosen millionaires.

The Brothers performed for only one evening's engagement, meeting some very nice people, a few more friendly than others..

David couldn't help but wonder if the friendlier ones were the self-made businessmen, who personally earned their fortunes, while the others had inherited their wealth from their bloodlines. It was almost like there were two distinct classes in the club, with an invisible line dividing the members with new money from the old money crowd.

It certainly made The Brothers appreciate their less wealthy friends and supporters.

John Knott of *The Commercial Appeal* finally made it out to see The Brothers perform live and in person, after weeks of promises, right before their stay at El Cid Lounge came to an end.

While Mr. Knott appeared to be in his mid-40s, his attractive date was much younger.

As soon as The Brothers realized the influential reporter was in the house, they called Mary to come down and schmooze with him, realizing how vital it was to develop a personal relationship with Mr. Knott.

Mary had been under the weather, still suffering with her gallstones and the added issue of an aching tooth, but gamely made it to the club specifically so she could meet and greet the powerful reporter.

She arrived just as the last notes of the final encore were fading.

She had no sooner introduced herself to Mr. Knott than a very drunk customer rushed over to where they were talking, pushing Mary out of the way while grabbing the reporter's arm.

Mr. Knott was obviously in no mood to deal with drunken hecklers, so he took his young date by the arm and immediately left the club.

Mary was upset, and The Brothers were speechless.

The fact the drunken heckler then came up and thrust a ten-dollar bill into David's hand didn't keep the younger Balph Brother from wanting to ring the guy's neck.

Fortunately, Mr. Knott didn't blame The Brothers for the alcoholic-induced assault, and he continued to write glowing reviews of their performances.

There was no denying how much power the man had in Memphis. Whenever he wrote about Roger and David, wherever they were performing the next time would be filled with readers who trusted his judgment. The man sure knew how to put bodies in chairs and sway public opinion. Maybe that was why he was such a hit with women.

By any measure, the shows at El Cid were profitable and entertaining, bringing a wide assortment of customers to the club who never would have considered going through the door otherwise.

The proof of their success, despite all the accusations and negative comments, was that Mr. Kramer kept extending their contract, many times waiting until the last minute possible. It seemed like he really enjoyed playing petty power games with The Brothers.

When they finally left to go to work at Sir Robert's Lounge, they discovered Mr. Kramer had been lying to other club owners around town, telling them that he was only paying The Brothers $200 a week, $100 less than the actual amount. He also left out the fact he was providing room and board in their contract.

It was all an effort to keep The Brothers from finding work anywhere else in town. If the other club owners thought Mary was trying to overcharge them, compared to what good ole Carl Kramer was paying at El Cid, they would never sign any contracts for The Walking Musical Balph Brothers.

Fortunately, the owner of Sir Robert's, an ex-con named Bob Lloyd was no friend of Mr. Kramer.

He happily signed a contract with The Brothers, and immediately shared a few of his real world tips with them, including the fact that if they were ever arrested, they should always try to get sent to federal prisons instead of state ones. He said the federal facilities were much nicer, and that the state-run lockups were rat holes.

Roger and David had no doubts Mr. Lloyd knew what he was talking about.

Even though Sir Robert's was a much smaller club than El Cid, The Brothers liked the feel of the place. The customers weren't stuffy, and seemed to be already drunk before they even entered the room. While hecklers sometimes gave them problems, the entire atmosphere of the joint was much less tense than the constant hassles they faced with Mr. Kramer.

They also liked that Mr. Lloyd's office was hidden from sight, with a secret entry requiring a knock on a certain part of the hallway paneling to open. The fact that it also had a two-way mirror looking out over the club's bar made The Brothers laugh. Mr. Lloyd could be safely squirreled away in his hidden office, shielded from drunks, thugs, and would-be attackers, and yet watch everything going on in his club at anytime without anybody knowing he was even there.

The Brothers didn't even stop to consider why Mr. Lloyd wanted to be so invisible.

While performing at Sir Robert's, The Brothers also arranged for a weeklong engagement a month away at the end of December at a club called The Vault.

Roger had put the deal together with the lady who booked talent for the place, evidently winning her over with his charms and smooth-talking good nature.

The Brothers discovered they always had better luck with female club owners and contract signers when Roger did the negotiations.

There always seemed to be some issues when Mary tried to represent them with women executives. They weren't sure if it was simple jealousy or just a clash of cultures; however, for whatever reason, Roger was able to sign contracts with women, while Mary worked her persuasive wonders with the male counterparts.

Whatever worked to get signed contracts was fine with the trio. They were more than willing to play whatever games came their way when it meant putting money in their pockets.

With the addition of The Vault contract, Memphis was turning out to be one of the best, if not the best, cities for The Brothers.

They were getting more continuing media coverage than ever before, and working nearly every night of the week in a steady stream of paying gigs.

They didn't even mind when one of the Memphis radio reporters made a point of asking them what they were going to do now that Jack Paar's show had been cancelled.

The reporter acted like it was some big secret that The Brothers were keeping from the public.

Just like most of the nation, The Brothers knew that Jack Paar had gone off of the air on June 25th, a good six months earlier, but this wasn't the first time that Mr. Paar had taken a break in broadcasting.

He had previously left his hugely popular daily nighttime talk show when he had a dispute with one of the network's censors, only to return a few months later without missing a beat.

The Brothers had no way of knowing, at that time, that it would be another decade before Jack Paar would return to the airwaves. By the time they arrived in Memphis, the fact Mr. Paar was off the air didn't mean a thing to their destinations or their goal.

They had known Jack Paar didn't want them on his television show from the very first day of The Big Walk. They had received a phone call, way back then, from one of Paar's producers, telling them not to make the trip, emphatically stating that there was absolutely no chance of Roger and David ever appearing on his television show.

It didn't stop them in Los Angeles, and it sure wasn't going to stop them years later in Memphis.

The Brothers had always assumed that it didn't really matter which television show had them on as guests once they reached New York City. They sincerely believed that just making it the thousands of miles to The Big Apple would result in enough national attention to kick-start their careers.

After over two years of pushing the cart and then pushing some more, the fact that Jack Paar had gone off the air didn't matter one single bit.

The idea was still the same.

What were Roger and David going to do?

They couldn't just quit.

Where could they go?

They didn't have a home in Los Angeles anymore. Their mother had remarried and moved back to Ohio, starting a new life with her new husband.

They couldn't move back home and stay with their dad. He also had remarried and had a life of his own to live and enjoy with his new bride.

The Brothers had no choice but to keep doing what they had been doing for so many months.

They still wanted to have careers in the music industry.

They still wanted to entertain audiences and make people happy.

They still wanted to tell their story to the world, and continue pushing the cart and then pushing some more.

The fact that Jack Paar had gone off the air for maybe a few months, maybe a few years, or maybe forever, didn't really change anything.

It was just another gap they would have to bridge.

One step at a time.

Carl Kramer and Holiday Inn Manager, Jim McMany, Welcome David and Roger to Memphis at the Edge of the Big Bridge

Chapter 84: Roger and Mary
Make It Legal

Photos following Roger and Mary's Wedding Ceremony

With a day off between performances, Roger and Mary decided to take their enduring romance to the next level and make things legal in the eyes of God and the State of Tennessee.

On November 25th, 1965, they drove to The First Methodist Church in nearby Covington and were married by a Reverend Consol. David was the best man. He presented the minister with a toy flute and a copy of The Brothers' 45-single from Auburn Rubber Company.

Roger and Mary had been wanting to tie the knot for months and months, but there never was enough time to make arrangements.

They finally ran out of excuses in The Volunteer State.

The people at the marriage license bureau gave Mary a complimentary box of Cheer laundry detergent, and wished the newlyweds the best of luck.

They asked the performing minister to keep news of the marriage a secret until The Brothers reached New York City.

They didn't want anybody to know their booking agent and promotions director, Mary, was married to one of The Walking Musical Balph Brothers.

The belief was it would only make Mary's job that much harder if club managers knew she was trying to get work for her husband, seeing as how flirting and teasing the various male decision-makers was an integral part of the process.

The Brothers also truly believed they attracted more single women to their performances when those same women believed Roger and David were single and available for dates, real and fantasized.

So instead of openly celebrating what should have been one of their most joyous moments in Roger and Mary's entire lives, the trio was forced to remain secretive for the sake of their careers.

Photo left: David Celebrates his 26th Birthday at El Cid,
Photo right: KREC-TV Interview with Kitty Kelly

At least David had been able to openly enjoy his 26th birthday, first by talking to Trudy, back in Ohio, for 15 minutes on the phone, and then by sharing a celebration cake shaped like a map of the United States that had been sent to the nightclub by David's mother and Trudy.

David had invited everybody in the club that night to share his birthday sweets, and he enjoyed watching the fans' faces when they studied the icing map and realized just how many miles The Brothers had already covered on The Big Walk.

They had a home-cooked spaghetti dinner with some of their most enthusiastic fans in Memphis, Lewis and Nell Lingua, who had gone out of their way to make Roger, David, and Mary feel welcomed and appreciated during their time in town.

The Brothers even arranged to get an air-conditioner for Roger's aging Chevy by trading out a performance at a house party for Mr. Jim Fulghum, who was a distributor for a leading line of automotive climate control devices.

Since leaving El Cid and the free housing provided by Carl Kramer, The Brothers had found their own rental apartment at Holiday Towers, enjoying the luxury of being able to have a place to call their own for at least a month. The apartment featured two bedrooms, two baths, two sets of closets, and a kitchen. Maid service and telephones were also included in the fee.

Even "Steps" seemed to appreciate having a spot in the living room to call her own.

It didn't even bother The Brothers too much when their second-hand dining room table collapsed on them right in the middle of one of Mary's first home-cooked meals, sending the entire dinner flying all over the floor.

"Steps" enjoyed feasting on her best meal of the entire trip, while David repaired the flimsy furniture and made it sturdy enough for any and all future dining experiences.

With a safe place to call home, The Brothers invested in some new clothes, finding some wonderful bargains at a store that was going out of business. They bought six brand-new dress coats for $10 each, in red, blue, and gold colors. The coats originally sold for $40 dollars each, and The Brothers truly felt like they were stealing the items.

When the store clerk tossed in an additional pair of shirts and ties, and only charged them $74.00, Roger and David knew it was truly a blessing from above.

With a fairly decent stream of money coming in from their steady string of performances, Roger and David decided to invest $122.00 in purchasing a professional 1,000-watt spotlight for their stage show. There was never any doubt they needed decent lighting for their performances. While some of the lounges and nightclubs had the proper equipment to illuminate the stage, most of the places where they performed only had the most basic lights at best, and sometimes nothing at all.

While The Brothers had always been able to provide professional sound equipment to make their music be heard above the noise of the nightclubs, it was always a gamble when it came to the spotlight situation.

By purchasing their own theatrical light, Roger and David would be able to guarantee their moments in the spotlight in the most literal sense.

Unfortunately, they still weren't able to control the sound and music at their various television interviews.

While this had been an ongoing problem as far back as Arizona, with technicians playing the wrong tape, the wrong song, or any number of issues, the problem kept coming up over and over.

It always seemed as though the television crews put all of their focus on the visuals, and simply ignored the audio part of the program.

At an interview with Kitty Kelly on the morning show on KREC-TV, Channel 3, the quality of the musical taping had been so bad that The Brothers begged her to not run the tape the next day.

They were certain it would cause more harm than good, driving customers away.

Fortunately, Kitty agreed, and she allowed The Brothers to come back the next day and perform along with their master tape of their recordings from the Auburn Rubber Company 45-single.

The next day, The Brothers arrived at 6:30 a.m. at the television studios in the legendary Peabody Hotel, famous for their performing ducks that swim in the hotel's lobby and then parade back to the elevator for their exit to their living quarters.

The Brothers could only wish the television studio's technician was as competent as the hotel's ducks. While threading up their only copy of the master tape, the technician hit the wrong button and immediately snapped the fragile tape into pieces.

To make matters worse, the technician didn't even apologize for his mistake. This forced The Brothers to have to use an actual vinyl record for their background music.

While all of this was happening, a woman who played the organ live on the show, along with a drummer and a bass player, came over and started harassing Roger and David about union rules. She demanded to see their union cards and wanted to know how they could get away with playing music to prerecorded tapes.

Meanwhile, The Brothers were minutes away from performing on the show and doing their interview with Kitty Kelly.

The irritated female union musician kept getting up in Roger and David's faces, growing louder and louder with each passing second.

When it became evident that nobody was going to clear this woman out of their pathway, The Brothers reached their breaking point.

They told Kitty they simply couldn't perform under such conditions, citing the problems with the tape and the harassment from the show's organ player.

They walked off the set. Left the studio. It was the first time in their professional careers they had ever had to bail out on a television show, and at that point they couldn't have cared less.

They had endured all they could take, and the fact that they left the television show with 12 empty minutes to fill was an unfortunate, but unavoidable, situation.

Later that afternoon, while The Brothers were trying to catch up on the sleep they had lost by wasting their morning at the television studio, Kitty Kelly called their apartment, apologizing for the horrible events at the morning's taping, with assurances the organ player had been taken care of, and efforts were being made to reschedule The Brothers' appearance.

On Friday, December 17th, Kitty Kelly made good on her promise, and this time the interview came off without any problems. The mouthy union card-carrying organ player didn't say a word to The Brothers, choosing instead to act like they didn't even exist.

On Monday, December 20th, a man from the musicians union came by Sir Robert's, demanding to speak to The Brothers moments before they were supposed to begin their show. The club was packed to the rafters with happy, paying, drinking, holiday fans, and Roger politely told the union representative they would be glad to talk with him after their first set.

The man didn't like this news, one little bit, storming out of the club in a huff.

While The Brothers knew this would probably bring them more trouble in the future, they didn't think it was fair to make a roomful of paying customers wait for entertainment while some impatient union official tried to collect work dues money just when The Brothers' show was about to begin.

In theory, the union is supposed to make sure conditions are decent for musicians, and represent the rights of the entertainers, protecting them from cheating nightclub managers and dishonest talent bookers.

In reality, it didn't always work out that way.

On top of their hassles with the union, The Brothers were also having problems with a local laundry, who had messed up several of The Brothers' tuxedo shirts, and had the irritating habit of sending over other people's clothing, losing The Brothers' items.

After dealing with pretty much every employee in the store, David had made his way up to the company president, trying to get issues with one particular shirt resolved.

The head honcho assured the younger Balph Brother the problem would be solved in time for that night's performance, and as promised, had a supposedly cleaned shirt delivered to The Brothers' apartment an hour before the show.

Unbelievably the shirt in the package wasn't David's. Even worse, it was the wrong size and had spots all over it. David wound up wearing a dirty shirt of his own to the concert.

The next morning, David was at the laundry as soon as it opened, desperately trying to recover his treasured lost $8.00 tuxedo shirt.

The cashier said they didn't have his shirt, didn't know anything about his shirt, wouldn't be able to find his shirt, and, at this point, doubted the supposedly missing shirt even existed in the first place.

David was positively livid with rage. He was bouncing off the counter, pounding his fist, and getting nowhere.

The cashier called him a son-of-a-bitch, and told him to haul his sorry butt out her store, or she would call the cops.

It went downhill from there. At some point you'd think the issue would have been resolved or tempers would have calmed down.

Wrong. David left the store screaming he would be back the next day, and the next, and the next, demanding his shirt and refusing to leave until they gave it to him.

It was safe to say the staff of that laundry would be added to the list of people who would never, ever become fan club members of The Walking Musical Balph Brothers.

David was pretty sure Pat Boone never had any problems like these to deal with.

Chapter 85: Christmas Eve in Memphis and One Step from Elvis

Performing at Sir Robert's

On Christmas Eve, 1965, legendary record producer and founder of Sun Records, Sam Phillips, the man who discovered Elvis Presley, came to see The Brothers perform at Sir Robert's.

Sam was one of the most influential men in the entire record business, having been personally responsible for developing the careers of Johnny Cash, Jerry Lee Lewis, Carl Perkins, and Roy Orbison, not to mention The King of Rock and Roll, Elvis.

He was also the owner of WHER-AM radio station in Memphis, which featured an all-female staff and had been one of the stations in town to support The Brothers with an interview.

While people like Frank Sinatra, Jr., and Pat Boone had considerable power in show business, Sam Phillips was a star-maker of the first magnitude.

He had a proven history of repeatedly taking talented unknowns and turning them into household names.

Since their first day in town, The Brothers had been working to get Mr. Phillips down to see one of their performances.

After they had appeared live for five weeks at El Cid and 12 days at Sir Robert's, Sam Phillips finally made it out to hear The Walking Musical Balph Brothers perform at 3:00 on Christmas morning.

Unfortunately, by the time the legendary producer arrived, The Brothers had finished their shows, and Mr. Phillips was possibly a little inebriated.

Sam was more in search of Christmas cheer than talking seriously about the music business, but at least he was in the same room as Roger and David.

This was potentially a life-changing moment for The Brothers, the one single event that would make every sacrifice, hassle, and struggle over the last two years on The Big Walk worthwhile.

Meeting a man of Sam Phillip's caliber was exactly the kind of career-making experience that could instantly catapult Roger and David to the very top of the entertainment world.

It was a moment that could have been an answer to several lifetimes of prayers.

It wasn't to be.

The Brothers soon realized, after a few minutes of attempted discussion with Mr. Phillips, that it was a complete waste of time.

Their perfect moment was only perfect in theory.

Reality proved to be much less fulfilling.

They had found their ruby slippers, killed the witches, and at the very last moment, looked behind the wizard's curtain and came away completely disillusioned.

It was obvious Sam was too distracted with spirits, Yuletide and otherwise, to contemplate advancing the careers of The Walking Musical Balph Brothers.

Roger seriously doubted the man would even remember meeting them in the light of day.

Their potentially life-changing Christmas present from the man who discovered Elvis turned out to be a bag of coal.

Like so many previous close encounters with potential greatness, this was another time when destiny's fickle finger wasn't pointing The Brothers' way.

Talk was cheap, especially on Christmas day, at 3:30 in the morning, at Sir Robert's in Memphis, Tennessee.

The Brothers went back to their apartment, had some bowls of Yuletide soup, and finally hit the sack at 4:30 a.m.

While the sun would soon be coming up, The Brothers' potential future with Sun Records was very, very dim.

Merry Christmas, 1965, everyone, and to all, a good night.

Roger and Mary – Christmas at Holiday Towers

Chapter 86: Cashing in at The Vault

New Year's Eve, 1965 at The Vault

The last week of 1965 was spent at the third club to host The Brothers in Memphis, a venue known as The Vault. The club was located in the downstairs of an old bank building, which previously was the steel-clad safety holding area for untold millions of dollars and assets for the former financial institution, hence the totally appropriate name of the club.

The bar area was literally inside the security stronghold behind massive metal doors, rumored to have cost in excess of $100,000 when the bank was built.

The lounge area of the club occupied former bank offices, and was unlike any performance hall The Brothers had performed in along The Big Walk.

The reinforced walls provided the perfect environment for live music, featuring fantastic acoustics for the customers' listening pleasure.

Jim Presler, the club owner, seemed like a competent businessman who took pride in his establishment.

Their first show had a decently sized crowd in attendance, considering publicity hadn't really sunk in yet. Their second show only had an audience of two paying customers, and those fans were holdovers from El Cid.

One of those dedicated fans was a lady named Virginia Nichols, a motel phone operator who had been at nearly every show Roger and David gave at El Cid for over a month.

She had spent three dollars a night in taxi fare to attend the shows and was one of The Brothers most ardent supporters.

It had been nice to see her smiling face in the almost empty Vault.

An hour-long interview the next day on WRAC radio had been one of the best of the entire trip.

Roger and David had been guests on a wild show called *The Zero Hour*, hosted by John Powell and Fred Cook.

The program enjoyed a huge following in the Memphis area and was several levels above most of the other rinky-dink interviews The Brothers had endured in smaller towns along the way.

Roger and David had given a live concert on their toy flutes, and their hosts joked and laughed the entire hour, even making references to hypnotized charmed cobras coming out of the wastebaskets when hearing the sounds from the plastic flutes.

The interview gave The Brothers a chance to show their personalities, share their music, and present their story in an entertaining way that made the 60 minutes on the air fly by with ease.

On Wednesday, December 29th, Mary discovered she needed a $375 root. Added to her continuing gallstone pain, her health issues were turning into a considerable problem that just didn't seem to be going away.

On New Year's Eve, The Vault was jumping with people drinking, partying, and closing out 1965 with a toot and a snoot full of good cheer.

The Brothers put on three shows that night, instead of the usual two, and the place was buzzing with high energy and good vibrations.

At midnight, David was on the house phone, bringing in the New Year with Trudy back in Ohio.

Roger did the countdown to 1966 onstage and put on dance tapes so the entire audience could shake in the New Year with style.

While David was in the phone booth, making promises to Trudy that 1966 would be their year together, he was fighting off the amorous advances of four women in the nightclub who were trying to kiss the younger Balph Brother under some hand-held sprigs of mistletoe.

While David battled the good-natured attention from his affectionate fans, he was more interested in talking to his true love in Ohio.

He could only hope Trudy wasn't able to hear the celebrating women pawing over his protesting body, trying to assault his horn-blowing, smooth-talking lips.

The owner of The Vault gave The Brothers a nice New Year's present when he extended their contract right there on the spot.

The first day of 1966 was spent watching The Sugar, Rose, Cotton, and Orange Bowl football games on television.

The Brothers spent the second day of 1966 watching The Green Bay Packers beat The Cleveland Browns in the National Football League's championship game.

The next two weeks continued the series of performances at The Vault.

Kitty Kelly from WREC-TV made it to one of the shows to show her ongoing support for The Brothers.

The Brothers' investment in their professional spotlight continued to pay off with quality lighting that certainly illuminated their performances.

Unfortunately, when they arrived for their show on Monday, January 17th, they discovered their spotlight had been knocked over, breaking the bulb and banging up the casing.

It would have been nice if somebody had bothered to call The Brothers to inform them about the accident, instead of just letting them discover the problem minutes before their scheduled showtime. The Brothers were forced to perform with the normal houselights used so diners could see their meals in front of them.

It was almost like playing in the dark.

To say the least, The Brothers were disappointed, for their fans as much as themselves.

The next day it took David over three hours to disassemble the entire light, knock out the dents, bend the brackets back in place, and replace the bulb, which cost $11.50.

Of course, nobody at the club knew anything about anything. No one came forward accepting responsibility for the accident. Once again, no one did the right thing, simply leaving The Brothers to truly pick up the pieces.

Jeannie Boto of the all-female radio station owned by legendary record producer Sam Phillips, WHER-AM, did another interview with The Brothers, helping to fill seats at The Vault.

The Brothers continued to hold out hope that perhaps Mr. Phillips would come back to the club and actually hear their live performances during a show, instead of arriving after Roger and David left the stage.

David could only wonder if this tendency to show up after performers had left the building had anything to do with Sam Phillip's most famous discovery, Elvis Presley.

Was that why The King of Rock and Roll always announced that he had left the building, perhaps as an inside joke for his first record producer?

On Friday, January 25th, Memphis was hit by one of the heaviest snowstorms in years. The Brothers played to a completely empty room. Unlike most Northern cities that were accustomed to winter snow, Memphis didn't even put salt on the roads; so, the entire town just shut down when bad weather hit.

Being Ohio natives, David and Roger were accustomed to yearly blizzards, hardly giving anything less than a foot of snow a second thought; so, they had arrived for the show ready to blow.

At least the waitresses and bartenders seemed to enjoy the performances, even if there weren't any customers leaving tips.

On February 1st, the weather was still bad. The fallen snow had turned to ice, and the roads were impossible to navigate.

Marty Judge from the largest newspaper in Memphis, *The Commercial Appeal*, came down to conduct a parting interview with

The Brothers about their leaving town after several months of steady performances.

Marty was so excited with The Brothers' music, he came back the following night with his wife and shot photos of Roger and David in their full stage outfits.

That same day, Frank Clement, the Governor of Tennessee had visited The Vault, even though he hadn't been able to stay for The Brothers' show.

Like so many previous times along The Big Walk, it was another missed opportunity that could have produced big results for Roger and David.

They could only hope that maybe their paths would cross with Governor Clement later in Nashville, the capitol city and home of country music.

The only excitement in the audience came when one woman hauled off and slugged another lady in the face. One of the females broke out in tears, and the other one ran out of The Vault.

Naturally, this all happened right in front of the reporter from the town's largest newspaper.

Typical Balph Brothers' timing.

On Saturday, February 5th, Roger and David closed out their string of performances at The Vault and said goodbye to their Memphis fans.

A visiting group of officials from Pakistan were in the audience and stayed until the last note of the third encore, proving that music truly is the international language.

A friend named Ed Cox even joined The Brothers for their final performance of "When The Saints Go Marching In," complementing Roger with his enthusiastic alto saxophone accompaniment.

The Brothers took extra efforts to thank the good people of Memphis for their kind support over the previous months, giving special attention to Joe Dobbins, who played piano at The Vault and always went out of his way to tell David how much he enjoyed his high notes on the trumpet.

Once again, The Brothers were leaving the security of good friends and receptive audiences to march forth to unknown towns and uncertain receptions.

While closing their affairs in Memphis, Marty Judge's feature story in *The Commercial Appeal* came out on Thursday, February 10th.

The Brothers were pleased to receive continued publicity, but a little disappointed the story had once again portrayed them as down-and-out, struggling musicians walking down the road, looking for money.

While that angle certainly made for interesting reading, David felt like the article ignored the fact that The Walking Musical Balph Brothers were professionals who cared about their appearances, their performances, and their careers.

Even if they weren't wealthy, they were successful performers with a proven track record.

They most certainly didn't see themselves as a bunch of losers, trying to scam audiences across the country.

Chapter 87: Great People and Mean Folks

It rained so hard while The Brothers were preparing to leave Memphis, it took them three days longer to get out of town than they had planned.

After almost four months in The Bluff City, Roger and David had a hard time getting back into the routine of pushing the cart and then pushing some more.

They only made it eight miles down the highway on Wednesday, February 16th, and they were technically still within the Memphis city limits at the end of the first day back on The Big Walk..

They left the cart at the city's Fire Station Number 13 at 460 East Parkway, having coffee with the firemen at the invitation of Station Captain Carson.

They also met Officer Moore, of the Memphis Police Department, who was on the city's canine corps. He offered to give The Brothers a demonstration at the training academy, showcasing the attack skills of the city's four-legged law enforcers.

David was amazed at how much larger the canine officers were compared to "Steps," their own faithful attack dog. Those highly trained animals looked like ferocious lions in contrast to The Balphs' happy-go-lucky, tail-wagging companion.

Mary had gone ahead to Jackson, Tennessee, to arrange the usual assortment of promotions and, hopefully, job opportunities.

The Brothers were able to push the cart down parts of the recently developed Interstate 40, one of the most modern public four-lane divided freeways in the nation at the time.

The asphalt lanes were smooth as silk compared to the roads they'd been forced to push the cart over in Arkansas.

Unfortunately, The Brothers weren't able to actually use the silken highway. They were required to use the uneven gravel berm by the side of the pavement, which was hard to push on.

They also couldn't seek protection from the rain storms by hovering under the concrete bridge overpass supports since Tennessee State Troopers considered such practices to be illegal.

While they had always been able to sleep under bridges in Texas and Arkansas, law officers in The Volunteer State were not impressed, or swayed.

This forced The Brothers to have to push the cart off of the interstate at exit ramps and find a place to store the cart on private property at the end of each day.

This process usually involved having Roger walk down the exit road, looking for suitable places to request permission to stash the cart overnight, while David kept guard over the cart.

That is how The Brothers met various landowners like Mr. and Mrs. David Lawrence, two kind people who graciously allowed them free access to their farm for as long as they needed it.

The Lawrences were friendly people who freely offered their support to Roger and David without a moment's hesitation.

This is also how they ran into people who weren't so accommodating, to say the least.

They approached one Tennessee farmer with plenty of land to spare, and he flat out refused to even consider allowing The Brothers to store their cart on his property.

Roger had tried to reason with the man, truthfully saying they only needed a tiny spot of land to stake the cart to for the night.

Initially, he simply didn't care. The more Roger tried to persuade him, the angrier he became. He wasn't impressed by the signs on the cart and couldn't care less about the newspaper clippings.

He didn't know or want to know any more about The Walking Musical Balph Brothers.

All he cared about was getting The Brothers off of his porch and out of his face.

When he saw "Steps" waiting out by the cart, wagging her tail, he even threatened to send his mangy pack of barnyard canines out to attack The Balphs' faithful companion.

Realizing they were getting deeper and deeper into a futile situation, The Brothers thanked the man for his time and walked away.

While they were pushing the cart down the road, the by now fully enraged farmer walked out into the middle of the road, repeating his threat to let his dogs loose to attack the departing travelers.

David yelled back he would bet ten dollars of his hard-earned money that "Steps" would hold her own in any fight with the man's flea-bitten mongrels, and walked on down the highway.

The farmer yelled something decidedly unpleasant, spit on the road, and walked back into his house.

At least shotguns hadn't been used, and nobody got killed, though it easily could have escalated into something much more serious within moments.

A few miles down the road, The Brothers came upon a closed Texaco gas station and parked the cart for the night, thankful for a place to rest.

At 8:00 a.m., they were confronted by a truck honking its horn inches away from where they slept on their cots.

The man in the truck wanted to get out and talk to The Brothers, but he was obviously afraid that "Steps" would attack him.

David ambled over to the vehicle to see if he could be of assistance, and he came face-to-face with the very angry manager of the Texaco gas station where they had just spent the night.

Once again, The Brothers politely tried to explain their story.

Just like the previous angry landowner up the road, this esteemed local businessman didn't care one bit about anything related to The Balph Brothers.

Roger could only wonder if the ill-tempered two men were blood-kin.

The Brothers quickly packed up their camping gear, and went to the station's restroom to shave and clean up for their departure.

The station manager was not the least bit sympathetic to their personal hygiene needs, and he demanded that Roger and David get out of his restroom. He told them to leave his property and push their cart where the sun didn't shine, which was physically impossible in the sense that the irate man intended.

Roger was able to finish shaving, but David was forced to leave his morning ritual unfinished.

The man had been so rude and demeaning that David didn't even feel bad about leaving the restroom in a complete mess.

The Brothers could only assume the man didn't read newspapers, listen to the radio, or watch television. Otherwise, he wouldn't have treated The Walking Musical Balph Brothers so shabbily.

As David struggled to push the cart down the road, memories of their recent good life back in Memphis came rushing back.

In his mind, he was back onstage at The Vault, performing for yet another standing room only crowd of screaming fans and adoring women throwing him kisses.

In reality, he was struggling to keep from twisting his ankle on the uneven country roadside, hoping he hadn't left anything important, like his wallet, back in the gas station's restroom.

He didn't even bother wondering about what Pat Boone would have done.

Chapter 88: Prison Ink

While pushing the cart down the side road off the interstate, a truck passed The Brothers, then stopped.

Two men got out of the vehicle and walked towards them.

The gentlemen were Captain Cory of The Shelby County Penal Farm, and Joe Varreli, an inmate at the facility.

Joe worked for the daily prison newspaper, and the reason they were riding up and down the road was specifically to find The Walking Musical Balph Brothers to arrange for an interview.

While Joe was serving his five-year sentence for robbery and assault with intent to kill, he also had developed a reputation for his reporting skills.

Arrangements were made for The Brothers to visit the correctional facility the next day.

The penal farm was temporary home to 750 inmates, and the prison newspaper, *The Lantern*, was a major source of pride among the population.

In addition to being avidly read by the local inmates, the paper was sent out to over 60 other prisons around the country, with copies of each issue also going to government officials including U.S. Senators, Congressmen, and even Frank Clement, The Governor of Tennessee.

The Brothers were happy to discover that a story in the paper, for what they originally thought of as a very captive audience, was actually going to be seen by a national readership, including some very influential people.

Roger and David were given the VIP tour of the facility, meeting many of the inmates.

David realized that, if things had turned out just a little differently back in Texas when he was accused of attacking that woman at her apartment, he could easily have been an inmate at a similar facility himself.

The Brothers were pleased to learn the prisoners had access to radios and televisions, but surprised they weren't allowed to have any playing cards, in order to discourage gambling.

The prison had an incentive rewards program in place where inmates were able to reduce their sentences if they stayed out of trouble. They also received credit for productive work, including such jobs as helping with the prison newspaper.

It gave The Brothers encouragement that Mr. Varreli's interview with them would also help reduce the man's time behind bars.

The Brothers noted most of the people they met in the facility seemed happy and positive. Seeing as how secure the penal farm was with barbed wire fences, guard towers, canine attack officers, and armed patrols, they figured anybody thinking about escape had to be crazy.

The best course of action appeared to be to work with the system, stay out of trouble, and do everything possible to reduce the sentences.

David knew first-hand how futile it was to try to fight the law.

One stop on their tour of the facility was a visit to the area of solitary confinement, otherwise known as "the hole." It was just as dark and dank as they had expected. An occupant of the infamous holding area lived on bread and water two out of three days; and if his behavior was satisfactory, he would receive a decent meal on the third day. Every ten days in the hole would result in being allowed out for one day to take a shower.

It was certainly not a plush, luxury country club for white-collar criminals, by any means.

Though The Brothers only spent three hours at the facility, the memory of the inmates and the hole stayed with them for decades to come.

Just leaving the enclosed gates to the penal farm brought a deep feeling of relief to Roger and David, with each brother counting his blessings.

Chapter 89: Tennessee Hayride

On Saturday, February 26, 1966, The Brothers were offered a *Tennessee Hayride* right in the middle of winter.

A gentleman named Al Davis passed the cart on the highway and immediately stopped with an entertaining offer.

Mr. Davis owned WBAT-FM, a radio station in nearby Brownsville, and he wanted The Brothers to take a *Tennessee Hayride* with him, or at least that is what The Brothers thought he was offering.

The idea of riding on an open hay wagon down a bumpy road in the rural boonies of West Tennessee during a winter ice storm didn't seem all that appealing to Roger and David at the time.

It was 32 degrees, and the pellets of ice had been hitting The Brothers' faces for several miles, stinging their skin and irritating their eyes.

It was a pretty miserable day to be walking, much less riding in a horse-drawn wagon, going nowhere fast.

The more they talked with the gentleman about The Big Walk, the more insistent he was that they join him on The Tennessee hayride.

The Brothers weren't sure if Mr. Davis was crazy, slightly buzzed, or just suffering brain freeze from the sleet and ice.

Then they discovered that he wasn't even talking about taking them on the hayride until 8:00 in the evening.

That made the offer even less attractive in The Brothers' minds.

Just as Roger and David were about to reject the man's curious offer, Mr. Davis pulled out one of his business cards, solving the mystery.

Turns out the *Tennessee Hayride* was a long-running, country-and-western music show, featuring live entertainers performing every Saturday night at a former roller skating rink near Brownsville. The show was broadcast on Mr. Davis' radio station and was very popular with the listening public.

It was amazing how much sense things made when The Brothers knew what people were actually talking about, instead of just letting their minds wonder and fill in the gaps with their own logic.

The Brothers spent the rest of the day pushing the cart down the road, and were picked up at 7:15 that evening by Bob Scarboro, one of the staff members of Al Davis' radio station.

They arrived at the converted roller rink to find an auditorium with 400 old movie seats. A different band played every 30 minutes, and the entire proceedings were broadcast from 8:00 until 11:00 p.m.

The Brothers had never experienced a performance like the *Tennessee Hayride*.

Some of the bands were top-notch performers with excellent vocals and professional musicianship. Then, more often than not, the next group up onstage was totally amateurish, tone-deaf, and totally lacking in any showmanship.

David was amazed that some of the bands even turned their backs to the audience and carried on conversations with each other right in the middle of their songs.

He had never seen such a slack level of performance standards in his entire life.

The fact that every single note of the evening was being broadcast live on the radio made the lack of professional behavior even more puzzling to the younger Balph.

Not that any of this seemed to matter to the paying customers listening in the movie seats.

The audience consisted of 350 hardy souls who braved the February sleet and ice to pay one dollar each to listen to the various bands in Brownsville that night.

Regardless of the level of talent onstage, each group received enthusiastic applause from the audience.

David noticed there was very little talking in the audience between sets by the various groups.

Everybody seemed to be totally focused on the proceedings onstage, except for perhaps the actual musicians themselves.

Al Davis, the radio station owner, arrived later at the show, having been across town at the local basketball tournament broadcasting the game.

It was obvious Mr. Davis and his radio station were vital parts of the Brownsville community, providing valuable services ranging from local news coverage to athletic events to live musical concerts.

The Brothers left the *Tennessee Hayride* with a deeper appreciation of the talents and energy found in some of the most unlikely places along The Big Walk.

Who could have ever guessed that little Brownsville, Tennessee, was such a hotbed of live musical performances?

Especially on a frigid Saturday night in the middle of winter?

In a converted roller rink with mismatched movie theater seats?

With over 350 paying customers supporting each and every note with rapturous applause?

The more The Brothers thought they knew about show business, the less they understood the meaning of any of it.

Meanwhile, they were back to sleeping by the side of the road, next to their handmade cart they had pushed 2,000 miles across the country for months and months and months, trying to shield themselves from sleet and ice and desperately hoping that their toes wouldn't freeze and fall off during the night.

Chapter 90: Swinging Times In Jackson

Arriving in Jackson

The Brothers' big push down Main Street in Jackson, Tennessee, had been delayed a day due to nonstop thunderstorms.

Television station WDIX carried stories about their impending arrival on the 6:00 and 10:00 p.m. newscasts for Monday, February 28th, but the big parade with cheerleaders filling the cart was postponed until the weather cleared up. There was nothing worse than soggy pom-poms.

The city's newspaper, *The Jackson Sun*, took photos of The Brothers, even if there wasn't any sun shining through the clouds.

Mary had arranged for the cart to be displayed in the showroom window of the Wilson Ford dealership, and part of the promotional considerations included use of a 1966 Mustang while in town.

The Brothers were riding in style.

David enjoyed driving to the town's two radio stations, WTJS and WJAX, in the sporty vehicle, basking in the publicity spotlight that had seemed too far away just a few days earlier while pushing the cart through sleet and ice storms.

They discovered a great local restaurant in town called Joe's Café, and were able to enjoy full meals, including desserts for 80¢ each.

They were so pleased with the dining establishment that they conducted a live radio interview from the restaurant's booth.

The big event in town was a benefit concert Mary arranged with the local Jaycees to raise money for the local Babe Ruth youth baseball league.

Starting on Friday, March 4th, The Brothers spent the next week promoting the event at every possible meeting, venue, and media outlet in town.

David certainly made good use of the courtesy Mustang, driving all over Jackson to spread the word about the arrival and upcoming concert of The Walking Musical Balph Brothers.

They even bought new matching sweater outfits at Sears for their appearance on the local teen dance show on WDIX, making every effort to fit right in with their youthful audience.

They were supposed to play two songs live on the show, talk about The Big Walk, and then show a film clip of their previous television interviews from Arizona, Texas, and Arkansas.

As it turned out, the show was actually run by the teenagers themselves, and production values were very relaxed, to say the least.

Like so many previous times on The Big Walk, the cameramen missed their cues and showed David and Roger holding their instruments in their hands when they were supposed to be playing notes. The music started much too early, and despite specific instructions to keep the camera on Roger when David was switching from playing his trumpet to the trombone, the hapless cameraman did the exact opposite and actually followed David putting his trumpet down and picking up the other instrument.

One of the cameramen decided to just walk away from his equipment in the middle of the song, and another one turned the controls over to a local teenage girl without giving her any instruction.

Roger and David could only wonder if the crew was purposely trying to make The Brothers look bad on live television.

Later in the week, The Brothers heard several comments from some of the Jaycees saying how silly it made Roger and David look on the broadcast, almost as if the entire performance had been a joke.

Their one paying gig at the local Moose Lodge had been very successful. They had a large crowd on hand and even met a genuine music star and Jackson resident, Carl Perkins.

Carl was the man who wrote the classic song, "Blue Suede Shoes," a million-seller for Elvis Presley, and was one of the original discoveries of Sam Phillips and Sun Records back in Memphis.

Carl went out of his way to introduce himself to The Brothers, telling them how much he enjoyed their performances and admired their musicianship.

Unlike so many other so-called "celebrities" that The Brothers had met over the years, Carl seemed very friendly and down-to-earth.

He casually informed them he had been busy writing a few songs for some of his musical friends, a little group from England known as The Beatles.

The following week, Roger and David continued promoting the upcoming benefit concert for the Jaycees, who had provided the use of a second automobile for The Brothers to get around town in.

The addition of the 1962 four-door Oldsmobile gave The Brothers a degree of transportation options they hadn't experienced at any other time during The Big Walk.

They made appearances at every elementary, junior high, and high school in the area, talking about The Big Walk, their music, and the big Saturday night performance.

The Jaycees arranged for a big parade to be held through the center of town Saturday, featuring cheerleaders, baseball teams, police cars, fire trucks, and, of course, The Brothers pushing their legendary cart.

David and Roger thought maybe even their new friend, Carl Perkins might show up in his famous blue suede shoes.

Tickets were going to be given to school kids to sell as fund-raisers for the Saturday night concert, while The Brothers continued to speak to every civic club in town.

They were doing everything within their power to make sure the auditorium was filled to overflowing the night of the concert.

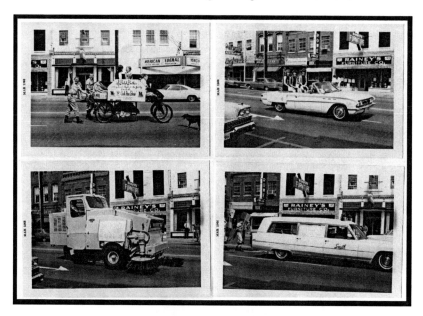

The Jaycees Parade

Sometime during the week, the decision was made to move the concert from Saturday to the following Friday, in order to give the community more time to prepare for the big event.

Saturday's parade was a noisy success with most of the town's cheerleaders, majorettes, youth baseball players, and band members proudly marching down the middle of town.

They even brought out the city's street cleaning machine to close out the parade while carrying a banner saying, "Let's Make a Clean Sweep for The Babe Ruth League."

Unfortunately, Carl Perkins didn't show up, with or without his blue suede shoes.

Suddenly finding themselves with an extra week on their hands before the big benefit show, The Brothers spent Sunday drumming up support at The First Methodist Church, sharing their story with the 200 worshippers in the audience.

Reverend James Moore humorously informed his congregation The Brothers were visiting their community from Mansfield, Ohio, by way of Los Angeles, Arizona, New Mexico, Texas, Arkansas, and Memphis. Right from the church's pulpit, he told his followers that Jackson was lucky to have The Walking Musical Balph Brothers amongst them, saying the big city of Memphis simply wouldn't let them leave for almost four months due to popular demand.

Roger and David admired Reverend Moore's highly effective promotional skills and, of course, his flattering words of praise.

Amen.

On Monday, March 14th, The Brothers were up and optimistically telling their story at the 6:45 morning meeting of The Optimist Club of Jackson.

They had previously given a civilized report to the city's Civitan Club and were looking forward to roaring off to their scheduled meeting with, yes, The Lions Club. It goes without saying they also kicked it with The Kiwanis Club members. They even rotated their agenda to spend time with The Rotary Club.

Mary, Roger and David Receiving the Key
to the City from Mayor George Smith

They had publicity photos taken with Mayor George Smith, having come to know his twin sons, Jerry and Jack, through their involvement with The Jaycees.

The twins ran one of the town's leading funeral homes, and they had gone out of their way to befriend The Brothers since their arrival,

418

inviting them to their homes for dinners and introducing them to members of the community.

The Jaycees arranged for a huge 30 foot by 20 foot map of the United States to serve as a backdrop for their Friday night show at the junior high school auditorium, giving the stage a look that was unique among all of their appearances along The Big Walk.

This way, the audience could enjoy the live music while following the immense route Roger and David had traveled, pushing the cart 2,000 miles in order to appear onstage before them in Jackson, Tennessee.

A local veterinarian named Dr. Leech even gave "Steps" a free bath and her shots, in honor of the benefit show.

The Brothers arrived at the big show on Friday evening, expecting to see lines of cars waiting around the school's auditorium.

Having worked to promote the Babe Ruth youth baseball benefit concert harder and more thoroughly than any other event during the years they had been on The Big Walk, Roger and David were bitterly disappointed to see that only about 150 people made it to the show.

They discovered one of the main officials of The Jaycees had lied about getting posters and tickets out to the general public.

While The Brothers had been turning over every possible promotional stone in town, they thought the posters and tickets had been distributed and made available to every business and office in the area.

To make matters worse, The Brothers had repeatedly questioned this one Jaycee, asking if he was doing his job and getting the materials out to the public.

They had noticed this particular person seemed to be much less enthusiastic about the idea of the benefit in the first place, compared to his fellow club members.

After being repeatedly assured the job was being taken care of, The Brothers had reluctantly left the man alone to do his work, only to find that he had lied and not delivered on his word.

By the time the truth was discovered, it was too late to do anything about it.

The Jaycees took a huge beating on the fund-raiser, and more importantly, were embarrassed in the eyes of the community.

Roger and David also discovered the man who had neglected his duties and then lied about it was planning on running for president of the club the following year. They could only wonder if he had some hidden agenda to make the event fail.

Despite the small attendance, the show was a success from an entertainment perspective.

The audience enjoyed the songs and gave each number loud rounds of applause.

At the end of the show, Roger thanked everybody for making the effort to attend the concert, and then casually mentioned there had been a goof-up with the tickets and the posters, resulting in the small turnout for the benefit.

While he didn't mention the neglectful Jaycee by name, there was little doubt among the club members as to who Roger was talking about.

Evidently the bitter truth stung, because as soon as Roger walked off stage, the unnamed man came over to the elder Balph and tried to start a fight.

It took the combined efforts of several other Jaycees to keep fists from swinging in both directions.

Club officials sent their enraged member out of the school's auditorium, with demands to calm down and cool off.

The Brothers joined the Smith twins at Jerry's home after the concert and enjoyed talking and having breakfast with the funeral home operators until 3:00 a.m.

Jerry generously gave David an assortment of pistols he had in his gun collection. Some of the guns were in working order, others weren't, but David was thrilled to have the chance to work on them and add them to his arsenal.

On Sunday, March 20th, Julian Townsend, president of the local Moose Lodge, took Roger and David up for a ride in his new airplane. They flew all the way to Nashville and back, covering the 240 miles in a few hours. They were able to see the exact path they would soon be pushing the cart down, heading to Music City. The only difference

420

between the two trips was the plane flight took minutes, whereas it would take at least 16 days for The Brothers to walk the distance.

Before leaving Jackson, The Brothers spent some time with Jerry and Jack Smith at their family's funeral home business.

Roger and David had grown quite close to the Smiths over the past few weeks and were hopeful their friendship would continue even after they left town for bigger opportunities down the road in Nashville.

The Brothers were at the funeral home when a recent heart attack victim was brought in to be prepared for his funeral services.

The elder Balph Brother kept thinking how the man before him had been alive less than two hours earlier, making plans for his daily life, going about his job as a carpenter. He had a family, dreams, ambitions, hopes, and, then, without any warning, he was killed by a heart attack.

Dead.

Life over.

All that remained was a shell of a man who had to be prepared for public viewing by his grieving family and friends in the Smith Brothers' Funeral Home the next day.

Roger couldn't help but wonder what the future held for himself, his new bride, and his younger brother.

Did The Big Walk even make any sense anymore?

They were slightly more than halfway to New York City, and three years into their journey.

What did they have to show for it?

Every fleeting moment of triumph along The Big Walk had been followed by stinging defeats and missed opportunities.

The time was rapidly approaching when Roger and David would have to make some hard decisions about their careers, their goals, and The Big Walk.

Being aware of the poor deceased carpenter only made Roger that much more uncertain as to the wisdom of their continuing efforts.

Did Roger really want his life to end on the middle of some unnamed road in the middle of nowhere, pushing a cart down the street with his younger brother, going nowhere fast?

It was so easy to get caught up in the day-to-day rituals of trying to keep The Big Walk going, struggling to keep some money in their pockets, their minds alert, and their bodies healthy enough to walk another day that it was highly possible they had missed the entire point of the journey.

If Roger had a fatal heart attack himself the next day while pushing the cart and then pushing it some more, would his last thought be that it had been worth it?

David Hamming it up with Jackson Police
while Preparing to Leave for Nashville

Chapter 91: Lots of Promise

Friends and Fans, Left photo: Jack Smith Family
Right photo: Jerry Smith Family

On March 31st, 1966, The Brothers had pushed the cart about halfway from Jackson to Nashville, making the trip back to Jackson by car most of the nights to spend time with Jerry and Jack Smith and their families.

Even though they had left town almost two weeks earlier, they had worked to maintain their friendship with the funeral home owners that had been so kind to them.

The Smiths were close to the same age as The Balphs and seemed to have very similar outlooks about life and the world around them. They also liked music, guns, and good company.

Mary had become fast friends with Ruth Ann and Betty, the better halves of the Smith brothers, and the three women enjoyed cooking meals and entertaining the mingled families together.

The Smith children even played a game based on The Big Walk where two of them would push a toy wagon around the backyard while their sister rode her bicycle down the street, playing the role of Mary doing her promotional runs.

That night, The Brothers performed at the Jackson Country Club for a crowd of 260 movers and shakers of the community.

Mary came back from Nashville with news of a two-week contract to perform at Boots Randolph's Carousel Club in Nashville's famous Printers' Alley.

Boots was one of the world's best-known saxophone players, having had an international hit called "Yakety Sax" in 1963.

He had recorded with such musical greats as Roy Orbison and Elvis Presley, and he was certainly one of the most influential musicians in all of Nashville.

Roger was especially excited to know they would soon be sharing the stage with one of the best players in the business.

It was beginning to look like all of his moments of doubt back at the funeral home might have been without cause. Each day drove them that much closer to success, and days like this one only brought that point home to the older Balph Brother.

Another promising development had come when Jerry Smith introduced The Brothers to one of his friends from the area.

Lee Price was a multi-millionaire who had helped produce shows on Broadway in New York City and was always looking for new projects.

He took an interest in The Brothers, was fascinated by the details of The Big Walk, and expressed enthusiasm about bankrolling an album of Roger and David's music.

Jerry Smith assured The Brothers that Mr. Price was the real thing, a serious businessman with the means and the resources to make things happen, once he decided to get involved.

Jerry casually added that Mr. Price had already personally paid for 342 students to attend college, and the number continued to grow every year.

Things were looking so promising that David was about to burst with outright joy. He had an urgent need to talk with Trudy and share the good news.

Once again, the Smith brothers came to the rescue, taking David to the country club office and placing the long-distance call back to Trudy. David spent the next 15 minutes telling her all about the potentially wonderful things that were going on around him.

The next day found The Brothers back out in the middle of nowhere, pushing the cart towards Nashville.

The section of Interstate 40 between Jackson and Music City was still under construction. The road was covered with thick coats of oil, which made it even harder to push the cart down the highway.

They were walking down a segment of the highway that wasn't technically open to the public; so, they hadn't had to deal with as much traffic as usual.

They were even willing to risk sleeping under the forbidden bridges, betting the Tennessee State Troopers, who normally gave them so much trouble, were busy chasing speeders down other roads in the area.

They seemed to make better progress pushing the cart at night; so, they got in the habit of sleeping in the daylight hours and marching towards Music City under the stars.

On Good Friday night, April 8th, 1966, they were pushing the cart and then pushing some more when they encountered a wobbly possum blocking their pathway.

The scary-looking night creature exhibited no fear of The Brothers, the cart, or even "Steps," showing its sharp teeth with a foamy drool coming out of its mouth.

They had been warned about possible encounters with rabid skunks and possums in the area, with the veterinarian in Jackson going out of his way to tell The Brothers to keep "Steps" out of any fights with questionable wild animals.

The closer the animal came towards the cart, the more "Steps" wanted to jump on the intruder and tear it to shreds. It was all Roger could do to keep their faithful guard dog from pouncing on the toothy attacker.

Things were getting serious, and potentially lethal. The diseased animal continued to approach the cart. Seeing very few options left to them, David pulled out his loaded 38 pistol and solved the problem.

They had come too far with too much effort to have to deal with rabies and potential death in the rural countryside of Tennessee.

It would have been a shame to throw away so much promise, with a drooling rabid animal bite, in the middle of the highway, in the middle of the night.

Chapter 92: Music City, U.S.A.

Arriving in Music City

On April 13th, 1966, The Brothers were escorted to the city limits of Nashville, Tennessee, by an initially reluctant State Trooper Mitchell.

The law enforcer originally stopped The Brothers to hassle them about being on the interstate with their cart.

Roger immediately told Officer Mitchell they had been cleared by Governor Frank Clement to use the public freeway.

Of course, they hadn't been cleared by the Governor, anybody on his staff, or a local dog catcher, for that matter.

The Brothers were just trying to get this hard-working public servant off their backs long enough to actually make it into Nashville.

Officer Mitchell called Mary at The Hermitage Hotel and asked for details of their so-called "road use approval."

After almost three years on the road, Mary certainly knew how to play the political game at this point, having used her wits every single day to keep The Big Walk moving.

She calmly asked Officer Mitchell if she really needed to bother the governor's office to clear up what was obviously a lack of communication on the officer's part.

Within five minutes, Mary had placed enough calls to the right people to warrant instructions from Officer Mitchell's superiors in Nashville, ordering him to politely escort The Walking Musical Balph Brothers into Music City, U.S.A.

By the time they arrived at the city limits, Officer Mitchell's attitude had changed from open hostility to downright friendliness. He even promised to visit Printers Alley to see them perform at Boots Randolph's Carousel Club.

On Stage at The Carousel

The Brothers came to Music City with a two-week contract waiting for them at one of the best nightclubs in town.

Located in a historic downtown entertainment area known as Printers Alley, the three-block stretch of clubs featured a wide assortment of honky-tonks, strip joints, and nightclubs.

Since Nashville didn't allow the purchase of liquor by the drink at that time, the clubs were known as mixer bars, where customers brought their own bottles of booze with them, often in brown paper bags, and paid the establishments for ice, glasses, and sodas.

While saxophonist Boots Randolph had his name on the club, it was actually owned by Jay and Marguerite Henry, a couple who had been married and divorced three times during their turbulent personal and business relationship.

Mary had considered it quite an accomplishment to get The Brothers a two-week signed contract at such an established club, seeing as how Nashville was literally filled to overflowing with talented musicians and bands. There was so much competition for the few performance venues in town that musicians were almost willing to play for free, just to get some exposure.

She also discovered that Music City's media outlets were less than impressed by the fact that yet another pair of struggling musicians had arrived at the city limits.

Every single day brought countless hundreds of equally talented performers to Nashville via buses, airplanes, bicycles, mules, and broken-down jalopies. The fact that Roger and David were pushing a cart was not enough to make the city stop and take notice. By all measures, Nashville proved to be a tough town for The Walking Musical Balph Brothers.

Red O 'Donnell's Welcoming Announcement

Like so many previous stops along the way, the first week at The Carousel Club went well. They had decent-sized crowds, considering the owners hadn't done any advertising about the arrival of The Balphs.

Tourists normally flocked to Printers Alley as a destination point, so there was always a steady flow of new customers discovering the area. A large percentage of those people would naturally stop by The Carousel Club for a chance to see a performer of the stature of Boots Randolph in such an intimate surrounding.

The Brothers were happy to alternate sets with the acclaimed recording artist and his top-notch band of live musicians.

Boots was friendly and supportive of The Brothers, especially for the first two weeks.

The only problem centered around the use of recorded tapes in such a strong music union town like Nashville. Even after assurances from union officials that the use of the backing tapes was fine as long as other live musicians were employed by the nightclub, it remained an item of contention that continued to grow like a fungus.

Boots was of the opinion that the use of tapes restricted the show's spontaneity and kept The Brothers from responding to requests for songs from the audience. Little attention was given to the fact their performances were a show, not a dance.

He also told Roger and David that he felt like their own musical talents were strong enough to make the use of canned musical recordings needless.

Seeing as how Boots always performed with an energetic live band and was also on the board of directors of the Nashville Musicians Union, it was easy to see how the use of tapes in a club with his name on the front could cause him some concern.

As usual, The Walking Musical Balph Brothers had some issues with these objections. They took their case to the local union, which once again assured them they could use the prerecorded backup tapes as much as they liked, as long as they also used live musicians in the club.

At the end of their initial two-week contract, The Brothers were thrilled to receive a four-month extension, guaranteeing them steady employment until the start of September. Or so they thought.

With the security of such a long-term contract in hand, The Brothers felt confident enough to rent a small apartment in Nashville and put down stakes for a while.

The housing complex didn't allow pets or carts in the parking lot, so they made arrangements to leave the cart, and, yes, "Steps," under the protective eyes of The Belle Meade Police Department, where both spent the next several months resting and recovering from the strains of The Big Walk.

"Steps" became such a favorite of the local police force that they even taught her to smoke cigarettes, or at least she appeared to, holding a lit cigarette in her teeth, much to the amusement of visitors to the station.

Mary's health continued to deteriorate. Often, she was completely unable to get out of bed for days at a time.

The Brothers knew Mary had been in constant pain for months, seldom complaining while trying to keep jobs coming their way; but, it was obvious things were getting worse and worse.

Having the four-month contract with The Carousel Club took a big load of stress off of everybody. Part of that stress had been caused by yet another lawsuit The Brothers were going through from their very first day in Music City.

While Mary had been staying at one of Nashville's finest hotels, The Hermitage, during the week leading up to The Brothers' arrival, there had been an accident with the camper trailer in the hotel's parking garage.

A parking attendant had unbelievably moved the car with the camper trailer top still extended, resulting in smashing the top of the camper on the concrete support beams of the parking facility.

It had knocked a six-inch by four-inch gash in the top of the trailer and had whacked the entire mechanism out of alignment.

The Brothers obviously expected the Hotel to pay for the damages but were amazed to discover The Hermitage didn't even own the parking garage.

By the time they tracked down the true owner of the building, contacted various lawyers in town, and tried to get a settlement, the parking garage management claimed the accident was Mary's fault, and refused to offer a penny for repairs.

To add insult to injury, the owners of the parking garage charged The Brothers storage fees for each day they left the car and trailer under their roof. To make sure they got paid, they went so far as to take the ignition coil out of Roger's 1955 Chevy and blocked it in the parking space using a company vehicle.

The longer it took to settle the disagreement, the more it cost The Brothers in parking fees.

Every lawyer they contacted told them to just pay the fees, get their car out of the parking lot, and then worry about lawsuits later.

Meanwhile, The Brothers continued to get the runaround concerning their almost forgotten lawsuit back in Texas with the club that didn't pay them for their contract. Other than paying yet another lawyer money they didn't have, there hadn't been any settlement or revenue coming their way. Since that lawsuit had been filed, the club in question had gone out of business, and efforts to get money out of the former owners had been a complete waste of time.

All of the continued stress wore on Mary's mental condition and physically caused her pain and cramps.

She felt like she was carrying the weight of the world on her shoulders, and her body was simply giving out on her, minute by minute.

Having the security of their four-month contract with Boots Randolph's Club gave the trio time to save up some cash, rebuild their strength, and plan for the next phase of The Big Walk. And, then, it didn't.

Almost as soon as the contract extension had been signed, things took a turn for the worse with the club owners.

There were daily arguments with Jay and Marguerite Henry over the tapes, the length of the shows, even whether or not The Brothers were polite to Marguerite.

The Brothers tried to calm things down by hiring a three-piece band of living, breathing backup musicians to take the place of the offending tapes.

Unfortunately, the caliber of musicians they were able to afford on the money they were being paid by The Carousel was lacking.

In a town filled with talented performers, The Brothers were only able to attract a limited number of available musicians.

They especially had a problem with their piano player when informing him of the next song coming up. He would literally change the song being played and go into the next tune in the middle of the show. The Brothers learned later he had severe problems from war injuries.

Compared to the mechanical precision of their professional backing tapes, The Brothers felt every performance with the live musicians was akin to playing Russian roulette.

One night they weren't even able to start their second set of the night on time because they couldn't find their piano player. After much effort, they finally located the missing keyboard man outside in The Alley, helping the garbage men load the evening's trash while wearing his stage show tuxedo.

When The Brothers expressed their concerns about the questionable quality of their live performers, Boots Randolph laughingly told them that such problems were one of the downsides of using human beings.

Meanwhile, The Brothers continued to do their best to entertain the nightly audiences at The Carousel Club.

One night a visitor from New York City stood up in the middle of the show, demanding to hear a song called "Twilight Time," which The Brothers knew and often performed. Roger told the man they would be glad to play the song after their first set.

The man walked up to the stage and tossed a $20 bill at Roger's feet. Roger repeated his promise to honor the gentleman's request at the first break. The man threw another $20 bill onstage, then another.

With $60 in cold hard cash now staring The Brothers in the face, Roger turned off the tape recorder and played the requested song with as much gusto as he could muster. As soon as the song was over, the man placed another $20 in the hands of The Brothers.

In talking with their generous benefactor at the next break, they discovered the man had just won $60,000 at the horseraces and had flown to Music City to celebrate his good fortune at The Carousel Club with Boots Randolph, one of his favorite musicians.

The drawing power of Boots also brought celebrities such as Chet Atkins and Eddy Arnold out to the club, along with untold numbers of celebrities who remained anonymous on the sidelines, enjoying the shows.

The Brothers could only imagine how many famous people had seen them perform at the club.

There had also been yet another knock-down fight onstage with another customer from the audience. This time the encounter was with an actor named Randy Boone, who had made a name for himself appearing in various television Westerns.

Mr. Boone had been in the area filming a movie and was listening to The Brothers perform when The Brothers accidentally insulted his attractive wife.

His wife had been hollering up at the stage during songs, interrupting the show so much that Roger finally tried to nip it in the bud by inviting the sexy female up onstage to sing along with The Brothers.

Roger had effectively used this method several times in the past to calm hecklers down, and he hoped it would work again this time.

As soon as the shapely woman got up onstage, she kicked her shoes off, saying she wanted to be more comfortable. That spontaneous action prompted the band to immediately start playing David Rose's famous song, "The Stripper," and it went downhill from there.

At this point, a very inebriated Randy Boone jumped up onstage to join the festivities.

As can be expected, things got out of hand on the tiny stage area, and, before either of them realized it, Roger and the acclaimed actor were falling off the stage, crashing into tables, and rolling around on the floor.

Meanwhile, the club's 6-foot, 8-inch-tall bouncer did nothing, as usual.

Seeing a riot developing beneath his very eyes, David picked up the box they used to hold their backing tapes and whacked the actor over the top of his head as hard as possible.

The actor hardly even took notice, rising to his feet.

Finally, a friend of David's named Eddie Edenfield took charge of matters and escorted the troublemakers out of the club. Eddie was a deputy sheriff with the county and had been on hand to watch The Brothers perform, having no idea that his security services would be called upon.

Leaving the club, the actor's wife, who had started the entire chain reaction in the first place, walked up to the stage and apologized for all of the trouble.

There was talk about lawsuits and pressing charges, but cooler heads prevailed when everybody sobered up the next day.

David was at such a low point mentally and emotionally he actually momentarily thought a nice, juicy lawsuit might be just what The Brothers needed to get some vital publicity in Music City.

Nothing else seemed to work.

The erratic behavior of club owners continued to plague The Brothers. They were just as likely to not be paid at the designated times as when they were. This irritating habit was made worse by the fact that The Brothers weren't able to pay their live musicians when their own checks were late. The fact that Jay Henry had been too drunk to sign his name didn't instill much confidence in his employees.

The continuing abuse of alcohol and who knows what else led to public fights in the club with Jay taking swings at Marguerite, knock-down screaming matches at the bar, and all sorts of tension and pathetic behavior. The walls of the club's upstairs dressing room had holes where Jay had taken potshots in drunken fits of rage.

Things came to a complete boil one night when a very inebriated Jay approached David. He stuck a loaded pistol into David's stomach, with his alcoholic-addled finger nervously twitching on the trigger.

If not for some fast-talking on the part of David while he gently removed the cocked firearm from Jay's hand, the younger Balph could easily have been shot dead right there on the spot, another victim of senseless violence in Nashville's Printers Alley.

Despite the fact that Marguerite checked Jay into a hospital the next day, the problems didn't end.

With over two months remaining on their contract, The Brothers arrived for work one night to find workers taking their names off the marquee lights.

Marguerite Henry decided she didn't want The Walking Musical Balph Brothers performing in her club anymore, and she wasn't going to let a little piece of paper keep her from doing what she wanted to do in her own establishment.

As always, The Brothers took the matter to the union, trying to use every means possible to resolve their problems.

Marguerite came up with a list of complaints and reasons for terminating the contract. She finally settled the dispute by offering The Brothers $200 to go away.

But not before charging them $80 for what she claimed was an outstanding bar tab.

While Roger and David knew there was no way possible for them to have consumed that many drinks, at this point they were so totally fed up with everything they accepted the offer and never looked back.

It had taken a while, but The Brothers were slowly learning that, whenever they got involved with lawsuits, it seldom worked out to their advantage.

Fortunately, Mary had seen the handwriting on the wall and figured the Henrys would try to end the four-month contract ahead of schedule.

Arrangements had been made to hire a local publicity agent to help spread the word around town about The Brothers. For the agreed amount of $125 per week, the agent promised to make Roger and David household names in Music City.

Like so many things in Nashville, it fell through.

Less than two days after agreeing to represent The Brothers, the local man with all of the solid media connections had a change of heart and begged off of the assignment, claiming he didn't have time to do the job.

The Brothers could only wonder if they were being blackballed by the powers that be in Music City, U.S.A.

It sure seemed like they had more luck getting jobs out of town than in the city of music, Nashville, Tennessee.

They contacted a talent booker in town who managed to get them a shared booking with one of her female singers at a club in Alabama.

If Nashville didn't want to hear The Walking Musical Balph Brothers perform anymore, they would simply have to find places that would give them a chance.

Chapter 93: Going in Circles In Birmingham

WBRC-TV Interview with Pat Gray

The Fourth of July, 1966, found The Brothers performing at The Canebreak Club in scenic Birmingham, Alabama.

There was a big bloody deal of excitement earlier in the afternoon after The Brothers finished their rehearsal with the club's excellent house band.

When David walked out to retrieve their stage coats for the evening's show, he caught a man breaking into their car.

He was astonished to see a one-armed man, with only a stub for his remaining limb, break out a window of Roger's 1955 Chevy and try to steal The Balphs' colorful performance jackets.

David chased the thief halfway down the block, wrestled him to the ground, and then forced him to walk back to the scene of the crime.

The crook's remaining stub of an arm had been cut by broken glass from the Chevy, and he was bleeding profusely all over David and himself.

David sent Roger to call the police. While waiting for their arrival, the bleeding criminal tried to run away one more time.

David was forced to spray the man in the face with his security tear gas pen, but the burglar was so drunk or high that the irritating chemicals didn't even bother him.

The younger Balph was forced to punch the man in the stomach, turn him around, and keep his head against the side of the car.

The police took the offender away, while David was left bloody and dazed.

The next day, David appeared in court and watched as the car's attacker was found guilty, fined $100 and ordered to serve ten days in jail.

The city got the money, and Roger and David were left with bloody stage coats and a broken car window.

The shows at The Canebreak Club had been successful, but very unusual.

The stage was located in the center of the club and actually rotated around and around while the band performed in the center.

While it didn't spin fast enough to make the musicians dizzy, it did take a while to get used to the constant movement.

It also made it hard to maintain any connection with the audience.

They would start out playing the song for one group of people; and, just as that segment seemed to be getting into the music, the stage would rotate The Brothers to face another set of fans, repeating the process over and over.

The fact the musicians literally had their backs to their audiences half of the entire show didn't help matters.

It was an idea that probably made more sense as a dream than in the real world of live performances.

Relationships with their new booking agent also took a turn for the worse. The Brothers discovered the lady hadn't secured them any additional jobs after the Birmingham contract was to end.

After being so enthusiastic about their act when they were in Nashville, she suddenly seemed to have big problems with the use of the prerecorded backing tapes being used at The Canebreak Club.

They also discovered the talent booker seemed much more interested in the career of the attractive female singer she had forced The Brothers to share the bill with in Birmingham than she was in promoting Roger and David.

An inside connection at The Canebreak Club told them the female performer had been forced on the club managers in order to get the services of The Balph Brothers. The insider with all of the information also asked Roger and David if they realized their female booking agent was known for her lesbian relationships with some of her clients.

While The Brothers considered themselves as tolerant as anybody else, they certainly didn't like the idea of having their hard-earned reputations being used to book questionable talent for the hidden agendas of their one-time booking agent.

The insider went on to say The Canebreak Club wanted to invite The Brothers back for another series of performances later in the month, but only without the extra baggage of the female performer on the ticket.

Mary had much better luck arranging television and newspaper coverage in Birmingham during one week than she did in three months in Nashville.

She arranged interviews with WBRC television, where Pat Gray did two programs' worth of segments.

They also appeared on a local children's television show that was broadcast at 3:00 in the afternoon.

A reporter from United Press International spent two hours interviewing The Brothers for a story that went out over the UPI wire service, commemorating the third year of The Big Walk.

Newspapers, magazines, radio stations, and television outlets all over the nation were made aware of The Walking Musical Balph Brothers and their continuing efforts.

Thursday, July 14th, 1966, found The Brothers performing for a decent crowd of fans at The Canebreak Club. While David and Roger were known for their hot musical talents, things were truly amiss during the second set of the night.

Somebody accidentally turned off the air conditioning; and before anybody realized the problem, the temperature inside the club had reached 105 degrees.

Customers were leaving in carloads, while David and Roger were drenched with sweat, literally filling their shoes with moisture.

The club owners closed down for the night, losing untold hundreds of dollars in the process.

The next night a lady from a local downtown department store came up after the show and offered to take some professional portraits of The Brothers on Saturday, free of charge at the store's third floor studios.

The Brothers arrived on time for their 3:00 appointment, enjoying the chance to replace their dated promotional poses with some new quality images.

They spent an hour and a half posing and smiling every way the photographer requested.

Their snappy female fan promised to mail the finished portraits back to The Brothers in Nashville within a week. Does it really surprise anybody to learn that the photos never arrived?

Roger and David never heard another word from the woman and could only wonder if it had been some elaborate scheme to get some exclusive photographs of The Walking Musical Balph Brothers for her very private collection.

Chapter 94: Pop Shots in Nashville

Thursday, July 19th, found The Brothers back in Nashville, beginning the third year of The Big Walk.

Even though they were well over halfway to New York City, the remaining miles seemed insurmountable.

While there had been nibbles of interest from clubs around the country, supposedly including Al Hirt's club in New Orleans, the contracts never seemed to arrive.

They would get a call in the morning that such-and-such club in Whateverland wanted to hire The Brothers for $1,000 a week for the next four weeks. Then, by the afternoon, the deal had completely fallen apart, if it ever even existed in the first place.

Mary's health continued to decline.

She had spent several days in a Nashville hospital to discover she had some disease in her intestines that was eating away at her body, causing intense pain.

She had even gone back to see her favorite doctor in Arkansas, who confirmed that her health was seriously at risk if she continued her present lifestyle.

The doctor wanted her to go to bed and stay there for at least six months, without any excuses.

Instead of following her doctor's advice, on July 25th, Mary took it upon herself to travel to Louisville, Kentucky, to try to find work for The Brothers before everybody starved.

While waiting for news from The Bluegrass State, David was going stir-crazy with worries and doubts about the future.

Midnight found him on the outskirts of Nashville by the construction site of The Percy Priest Dam, a huge hydro-electrical project being built by The U.S. Army Corps of Engineers, known for their massive public works projects and their famed castle coat-of-arms.

Even at this late hour, tractors and trucks were busy moving massive loads of earth.

David didn't think playing his trumpet would even be noticed in the noisy workplace.

He was busy practicing his riffs when he was startled by a noise that sounded like a tractor backfiring.

To his amazement, he saw a bullet strike a tree a few feet beside him.

Somebody was shooting at him in the middle of the night!

He looked down towards the area where the dam was being constructed and saw a car filled with two guys leaving the riverbank.

He jumped in his car, threw his trumpet in its case, grabbed his pistol out from under the car seat, and roared out after his attackers.

Passing the area where the other car had been parked, he saw a row of broken soda bottles in pieces in the gravel.

Had the target shooters accidentally sent a bullet in his direction while breaking glass?

Seeing as how the bottles were facing an entirely different direction than where David had been practicing his trumpet solos, he could only assume they had intentionally set their sights on him.

Having recently survived the time when Jay Henry stuck a loaded pistol in his stomach, David was in no mood to let total strangers get away with taking potshots at him in the middle of trumpet practice.

He chased the car down the two-lane road leading away from the construction site, going at a much higher speed than anybody would have considered safe.

He followed the other car to a dead-end road and watched them drive out into a field.

Evidently, their late-night antics down the highway had attracted the attention of a passing police car.

David was standing beside his car when the officers drove up, giving him time to explain the situation from his point of view.

Fortunately for the younger Balph Brother, some of the construction workers at the dam had witnessed the whole ordeal and had contacted the law enforcers.

A second patrol car joined the efforts and finally brought the other car under control.

Two teenage boys were in the car with a 22 rifle and admitted to shooting soda bottles by the riverbank back at the construction site.

They told the police they certainly hadn't intentionally fired any shots at David; they were simply running away from him because they thought he was chasing them for shooting the glass containers.

They swore on a stack of Bibles that they never fired a single shot at the younger Balph; and, much to David's disgust, the police officers took them at their word.

David wanted them arrested, hauled to the slammer, and forced to pay serious jail time.

Instead, the law officers tried to put the fear of God into the teens by forcing them to consider what could have been the tragic results of their late-night foolishness.

By this time it was obvious the kids were simply guilty of being out much too late with a rifle, and having lousy aim.

The cops let the teenage shooters leave with a stern warning, and David drove back to his apartment to try and get some sleep.

It certainly hadn't been a very relaxing evening of practicing his trumpet.

Chapter 95: Dark Horse
Troubles in Kentucky

While waiting for news of work in Kentucky, David took time to go back by bus to Ohio to visit Trudy, after months of being apart.

August 13th found the younger Balph Brother back in his mother's home, visiting family and friends.

Seeing his beloved Trudy was almost enough to make David forget about his worries back in Nashville.

They even drove to Cedar Point amusement park to attend an Al Hirt concert, paying an enterprising ticket taker an extra $12 to sneak a ticketless Trudy through the turnstiles.

Both shows were among the best either David or Trudy had ever seen, and the younger Balph Brother was thrilled to have the brief chance to talk with Mr. Hirt as he walked out of the concert arena.

David mentioned The Balph Brothers to the legendary trumpeter. When that didn't get much of a response, he name-dropped Boots Randolph and even the name of Mr. Hirt's manager, Jerry Purcell, while shaking his hand.

Mr. Hirt was polite but was obviously not in the mood to have a business discussion by the side of the stage after performing two energetic shows.

It was 5:00 in the morning when Trudy and David arrived back in Mansfield. They had been up all night, and the date had clicked over to August 14th, 1966. Enjoying each other's company and definitely not wanting to stop having a wonderful time, they decided to have breakfast at a local all-night restaurant. They later drove around looking at various homes and buildings, including where they went to school.

At 10:00 a.m., it was time for David to drive Trudy to The Presbyterian Church in Lexington, where she played the organ during Sunday services.

This gave David the opportunity to go visit Frank Griebling, an old family friend who was retired from the post office and was crippled from the waist down.

Mr. Griebling spent most of his retirement time in his workshop, building the most amazing clocks out of odds and ends.

David had known the man since he was four years old, and it was great being able to spend time with his family friend after so many years.

Mr. Griebling gave David a standing offer to stay at his house anytime he needed a place to sleep.

Trudy arranged to take the following week off from the Tappan Company for vacation. She was able to spend more time with David than they had ever imagined would be possible.

While David's family had taken Trudy to heart as one of their own, her family had shown concerns when it came to The Big Walk.

Some family members felt there was no future in pushing a cart across the country. David was glad Mr. Griebling had offered to let him stay at his home while visiting Trudy.

He certainly didn't want to cause more problems for Trudy with her own family.

The last night at Mr. Griebling's house, David was awakened at 1:30 in the morning by two bats flying around his bedroom. While he wasn't bitten by the nocturnal creatures, it did remind him of the drooling, possibly rabid possum they had encountered on the road outside of Nashville.

He didn't even have any regrets about killing the furry fanged flyers with an old dustpan.

The next morning, September 1st, Trudy drove David to the bus station, where they said their tearful goodbyes.

It was a long and uneventful 11-hour ride back to Music City.

David couldn't help but feel he was leaving the best part of his life back in Ohio.

Trudy was on his mind all the way back to Nashville.

On Labor Day, September 5th, 1966, The Brothers were in Louisville, Kentucky, performing their first show at The Dark Horse Tavern, which happened to be located inside a bowling alley.

Roger couldn't help but consider the irony of The Brothers performing in such a facility, since his last job in Los Angeles three years earlier, before The Big Walk even began, was performing with a pop band at, yes, a bowling alley.

He couldn't help but feel he had traveled so far to come full circle, and what did he have to show for it?

Dark Horse Tavern Promotion

Was he beating a dead horse at, yes, The Dark Horse Tavern?

At least the pay was better in The Bluegrass State.

The Brothers were getting $600 a week, but they had many more expenses than they faced back in Nashville. They had to pay room and board, a commission to their booking agent, union fees, and the usual list of costs. By the time everything was paid out, there was very little left for Roger and David.

They soon discovered their new booking agent had neglected to specify how many shows The Brothers were supposed to perform each night.

They normally did three shows per evening, but the manager of The Dark Horse started out wanting four shows. Later, he increased it to five shows a night.

The manager seemed to take great joy in exerting his power over his contracted laborers.

Roger and David appeared on WAVE-TV on September 8th, performing three songs.

They even took live calls from viewers, including one lady who wanted to know why The Brothers weren't trying to get on Johnny Carson's talk show.

She was of the opinion that being on *The Tonight Show* would be a much better showcase for their talents. While The Brothers agreed with her comments, getting on the couch with Johnny was much easier said than done.

On Friday night, September 9th, David was overjoyed to see Trudy's smiling face staring back at him from the audience. She had driven down from Ohio to see the band perform and was very pleased at how entertaining the show was. It had been over a year since the last time she saw The Brothers perform together, and her eyes sparkled every time David took a solo in the spotlight. There was no doubt that he was already a superstar in her heart.

As usual, the initial success of the early shows faded as the week wore on.

The manager of the club was upset that the place wasn't filled to overflowing each and every performance.

He wanted to cancel their contract and send The Brothers packing back to Nashville.

When The Brothers refused to let the man out of the contract, he took it very personally.

He claimed The Walking Musical Balph Brothers misrepresented their act and were bad for his business. He said he wasn't paying good money to listen to tapes.

The Brothers had unknowingly met yet another hothead determined to run things his way.

The Dark Horse Tavern was his turf, and he ruled it with an iron fist.

The gloves were off.

Roger tried to reason with the businessman, but it soon became a shouting match between two highly opinionated personalities.

Neither side was interested in compromising, and the owner's temper flared to the point of outrage.

The man said he was going to charge The Brothers $25 for every drink they had in his club.

He then refused to give receipts for anything they had paid for.

Even after talking to The Brothers' booking agent on the phone, the man still refused to compromise.

He wanted Roger and David out of his club. Period.

He offered The Brothers $100 just to leave.

Their contract called for them to be paid $600 for a second week of work.

The man said if they didn't accept his settlement, he would make them play the second week in the men's restrooms.

He wasn't kidding.

While Roger and David had often considered some of the places they had played in over their career to be toilets, this was a first.

Was this what their career had come down to after years and years of struggles, effort, sacrifices, and untold hardships?

The next day they accepted the settlement offer of $100 and left town, never looking back.

When they realized they had performed 29 shows at The Dark Horse for the grand total of $700, it was a very sobering moment.

After paying their travel expenses, commissions, and hotel bill, they wound up making less than ten dollars per show.

It was a long, depressing drive back to Music City, U.S.A.

Chapter 96: The Big Walk Ends

On September 15th, 1966, it was over.

Done. They had pushed the cart 2,250 miles.

The Big Walk was officially over, stuck in Nashville, Tennessee, never to be resumed.

Mary's health finally gave out.

Mary's doctor told her that if she didn't stop working immediately, she would die.

Plain and simple.

No ifs, ands, or buts about it.

Her body had lost the battle with the road.

Her doctor demanded she go to bed and stay there for at least six months.

He was positive she would either have a nervous breakdown or die if she continued down the path they had been on for the previous three years of The Big Walk.

There was no wiggle room to fudge the outcome.

It wasn't a suggestion, or a hint, or good advice.

It was an order.

They discovered that Mary was suffering from a cyst the size of an egg. Her intestines were also being attacked by disease, weakening her body, and sapping her energy. Compounded with her mental anxiety and the nonstop stress of The Big Walk, things had finally reached the breaking point.

Her resistance was shot.

While The Brothers held out hope that sometime, somehow, someway down the road they might be able to resume The Big Walk and triumphantly march into New York City, it wasn't to be.

On the positive side, Roger and David appreciated how much they learned and matured from all of their experiences during their three years on The Big Walk.

The millions of people who saw them on television and in the newspapers, plus the thousands they met and performed for along the way, changed their lives in so many ways.

They learned that staying out of lawsuits and jail was paramount.

They also developed a greater understanding of another side of life that few people will ever experience. Even though dreams do happen, the results aren't always what might be expected. Their real world experiences not found in books were priceless.

They learned how much can be accomplished with the right attitude, *find a way* determination, faith and deep desire. They also learned just how much guts they really had.

Though they didn't make it to New York City, they did push a thousand pound cart 2,250 miles through extremely difficult circumstances on every front.

They found a way to survive every situation they ran into, while providing entertainment for countless fans across the country.

The Big Walk provided them with a feeling of accomplishment that could never be forgotten.

And they survived. They didn't die in the desert.

Roger and David spent the next 40 years building lives for themselves in Nashville, Tennessee.

David married his one true love, Trudy Gerhart, on April 27th, 1967, at St. Phillip's Episcopal Church in Donelson, Tennessee, a suburb of Nashville.

They remain devoted to each other to this day.

David with the Original Cart and his Trusty Trumpet in 2008

David developed a successful 17-year career in the insurance business, discovering that he could, at least for the time being, make far more money selling policies than he ever had in the music business. However, he always kept an eye out for opportunities that might develop in music, his first love.

In 1980, an opportunity came about with the Tennessee Army National Guard. Both Brothers, having had past military service, joined the 129th Tennessee Army National Guard Band as part-time soldiers, performing at concerts and military functions. They became featured soloists with this 57-member military band.

Soon they became known as The Musical Minutemen and were assigned to the recruiting division. Together they performed patriotic recruiting shows for various high schools in Tennessee. This eventually led to an assignment entertaining the troops in Germany.

Roger and David, after having served their required time, retired from the 129th Army Band in 1998 and 1999, respectively.

In 1989, a great opportunity opened for David, which turned into a ten-year engagement with the world-famous Opryland amusement park. He performed in the house orchestra on the famous General Jackson Showboat and in the amusement park as leader of their acclaimed Dixieland Jazz band, entertaining visitors from all over the world.

David has also recorded several CD albums, which can be found on his Website, along with additional photos and information about The Big Walk, at www.DavidBalph.com.

Trudy found her place in the banking business, working and finally retiring from Third National Bank with an outstanding 36-year service record.

Still Smiling: Roger at VA Hospital in 2008

Roger put his considerable skills of persuasion to work in the retail automotive sales industry, where he consistently won awards and broke existing sales records. He stopped performing in 1998, retiring completely.

As these words are being written, David continues to perform with area orchestras, combos, and society bands, keeping his lips in shape for the next gig that comes his way.

Mary's health improved over the years, but her relationship with Roger didn't survive. They were divorced in 1969. She moved away from Nashville and lost contact with The Balph Brothers.

Trudy and David, living in a small apartment after their marriage, were unable to keep "Steps." They found her a wonderful home with some good Nashvillian friends, who made her a part of their family. Trudy and David visited "Steps" often and were so pleased they were able to find such a great home for her. "Steps" ended her nasty habit of smoking cigarettes and lived out her remaining days being a normal dog.

Most of what remains of The Big Walk is memories and aging scrapbooks filled with fading photos and crumbling newspaper clippings.

The cart survives, as recent photos prove.

Every once in a while, David goes out to his storage barn to see if air is still in the tires. He sometimes drags the ancient cart out into his backyard and spends a few hours polishing and dusting it, remembering the thousands of miles spent pushing the cart down the road, one step at a time.

Without fail, he recalls the last time they moved the cart from The Belle Meade Police Department into town.

They were busy pushing and then pushing some more when a little boy came up beside them, bursting with curiosity.

The boy was beside himself with questions, finally unable to hold his tongue one second longer.

He yelled at Roger and asked the elder Walking Musical Balph Brother a simple question. "What are you selling, mister?"

Roger stopped pushing, wiped his brow, smiled, and confidently answered the child. "Personality, kid…personality."

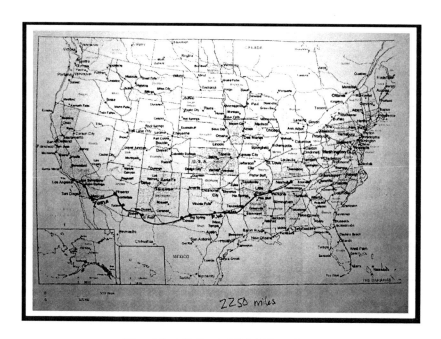

The Big Walk: 2,250 Miles from
Los Angeles, California to Nashville, Tennessee

Authors' Closing Thoughts

My co-author, Thom King, showed great interest in our story the first day we met. The more he learned about The Big Walk, the more he felt this was a story that needed to be told.

Working with a 700 page transcription from my road diaries, Thom was able to take my nightly reports of the days' activities, and capture the events, and as importantly, the emotions of The Big Walk.

Over the past year, Thom and I have worked to recreate the once-in-a-lifetime experience of pushing a thousand pound cart 2,250 miles for three years in the 1960s.

During the writing of this book, we have become good friends, while admiring each other's talents and abilities.

I sincerely thank you, Thom, for your outstanding efforts.

- David Balph

Working with David Balph and his lovely wife, Trudy, over the last year has been a true writing experience. Bringing the events of The Big Walk to life has been a constant challenge. Giving voices to forty year old events was a creative exercise that made each chapter unique and memorable.

Turning the yellowed pages of David's road diaries into chapters brought long forgotten places and faces back to life. I could feel the heat, see the desert, experience the aches of each and every step as Roger and David followed the dusty highways and their dreams.

Each photo, every press clipping, all of the fading letters saved by David for forty years brought back vivid accounts of a time long gone, and an America never to be revisited.

Thanks to Roger and David for allowing me to be a part of their story, one step at a time.

- Thom W. King

*David and Roger Display their Musical Arsenal in 1964
on Stage at The Vault in Memphis, Tennessee*

Printed in the United States
135420LV00003B/3/P

9 780972 045568